# DESIGNING
# DIGITAL FILTERS

## PRENTICE-HALL INFORMATION AND SYSTEM SCIENCES SERIES

Thomas Kailath, *Editor*

# DESIGNING DIGITAL FILTERS

**CHARLES S. WILLIAMS**

*Stanford University*

Prentice/Hall International, Inc.

*Library of Congress Cataloging in Publication Data*

WILLIAMS, CHARLES S. (CHARLES STERLING).
  Designing digital filters.

  Includes index.
  Bibliography: p.
  1. Electric filters, Digital—Design and
construction.  I.  Title.
TK7872.F5W56  1986      621.3815'324      85-6453
ISBN  0-13-201831-4

Editorial/production supervision: *Mary Carnis*
Manufacturing buyer: *Rhett Conklin*

Printed in the United States of America

10  9  8  7  6  5  4  3  2  1

ISBN  0-13-201831-4

Prentice-Hall International (UK) Limited, *London*
Prentice-Hall of Australia Pty. Limited, *Sydney*
Prentice-Hall Canada Inc., *Toronto*
Prentice-Hall Hispanoamericana, S.A., *Mexico*
Prentice-Hall of India Private Limited, *New Delhi*
Prentice-Hall of Japan, Inc., *Tokyo*
Prentice-Hall of Southeast Asia Pte. Ltd., *Singapore*
Editora Prentice-Hall do Brasil, Ltda., *Rio de Janeiro*
Whitehall Books Limited, *Wellington, New Zealand*
Prentice-Hall, Inc., *Englewood Cliffs, New Jersey*

*To Toni:*

*For your support*
*and contributions*

# Contents

## 3    DESIGN OF NONRECURSIVE FILTERS        75

## 4    WINDOWING        97

## 5    RECURSIVE FILTERS AND THE $z$-TRANSFORM        127

## APPENDICES                                                       319

## INDEX                                                              345

# Preface

This book is an introductory treatment of the design of simple digital filters. Because the treatment requires a background only in calculus and trigonometry (no analog filtering or other electrical engineering), it can be used in a first course in digital filters for students in engineering, computer science, or the physical sciences. The book is self-contained and attempts to provide motivation for each new concept, so it is also appropriate for individual study.

I came very close to titling this book YADFB – Yet Another Digital Filtering Book. There are so many good books on the market that I wondered if another was either necessary or wanted. But, as my class notes evolved into this book, I became convinced that the approach and some of the ideas were indeed new and it was worth my time and Prentice-Hall's money to publish. The book was developed over a five-year span as the text for an undergraduate electrical engineering course at Stanford University.

This book is built on the following ideas:

- Digital filters are far easier than analog filters, so there is no reason to make the obvious obtuse by "building" digital filters on an analog filter foundation.

- An introductory treatment of digital filters requires only calculus and trigonometry. Also, an introduction should be as self-contained as possible.

- An introductory treatment should be rigorous, yet easy to understand. I've done this by narrowing the scope of material and making extensive use of relatively simple mathematics.

- Most beginning digital filter designers readily understand the material, but have trouble with the applications. Therefore, motivation and examples are as important as development and explanations.
- Most people want to design as quickly as possible and not spend too much time on tool developments without much motivation. I've organized the book so that the reader can use the tools to design as quickly as possible.
- Most people enjoy learning from stories rather than dry textbook stuff. Therefore, I've used a storytelling approach to develop the material. Topics build on topics in a direct and natural way.

The book works well as a text for an introductory course in digital filtering. My primary audience has been juniors and seniors in electrical engineering, but I've also found that seniors or graduate students in computer science, the physical sciences, or economics can grasp the material just as easily.

Learning how to design digital filters requires practice, which is available through the end-of-chapter questions. The concepts presented in each chapter are reinforced with 13 to 30 exercises, varying significantly in difficulty. Some are simple drills in the mathematics or manipulative skills required for the chapter. Others stretch the material and ask the reader to apply the concepts in different situations. The rest of the exercises provide design opportunities. Solutions to the exercises are presented in a complete and easily used manual, prepared by Florin Gheorghiu. Instructors who are using this book as a text may request a copy of the solutions manual from Prentice-Hall. Because of the computational complexity of meaningful digital filter design, some of the problems require computer programs to help with the calculations. However, the programs are very short and can be run on almost any personal computer. Furthermore, I've provided BASIC listing of the programs in the solution manual.

As previously noted, one of the major goals of this work is to provide a rigorous treatment of digital filters without demanding a raft of prerequisites. The reader must have a good understanding of differential and integral calculus; one year of college-level study should be enough. The reader should also have had some exposure to complex variables (remember the square root of -1?), and enough trigonometry to understand the roles of sines and cosines. It is not necessary nor desirable for the reader to have any background in analog filter design. I use analog mapping techniques to design digital filters in Chapter 6 (unfortunately, there is no better way to design this class of digital filters in an introductory treatment), but an uninitiated reader should be able to get all of the necessary information from the chapter and Appendix C.

The book is organized in four major sections of two chapters each. The first section provides introduction and motivation. The next section develops the design techniques for nonrecursive filters. The following section presents the design techniques for the recursive filters. The final section introduces the topic of digital signal processing. I debated whether to include the final chapters in the book and

decided to do so because the material is so important and useful. The organization is driven by the desire to develop the material as a story and the need to get
the reader designing as soon as possible. For example, rather than developing the
z-transform at the beginning of the book, I postponed it until Chapter 5. In this
way, the development of tools is motivated by challenging the reader to use the tool
quickly. This approach tends to spread topics throughout the book, but I feel that
this is a small price to pay for the benefits of getting the reader to design early. The
book is full of examples. Some of them show how a recently developed technique
can be applied and others serve as motivation. In either case, the examples are a
very important part of this book.

Chapter 1 provides an introduction and motivation to digital filters, and it
shows how digital filters manipulate input signals to produce output signals. It
first explains the importance of filtering in general. It then presents analog and
digital signals and shows how to sample an analog signal to produce a digital one.
This treatment explains quantization (although we won't deal with it) and the
consequences of sampling an analog signal too slowly (aliasing). We then turn our
attention to the operation of digital filters: how do they manipulate the input data
to produce an output? The operation of a filter is further illustrated as the concepts
of impulse, step, and ramp responses are introduced. A great deal of attention is
given to the impulse response, as we find that it is a compact way of representing a
digital filter's input-output relationship. Finally, the chapter develops the abstract
properties of digital filters (linear and time-invariant) and shows the impact of these
properties. The chapter concludes with the properties of combinations of digital
filters.

Chapter 2 develops the frequency response. I chose to approach the frequency
response rather formally and show that it is a special case of an eigenvalue. This
approach introduces the reader to the very powerful concepts of eigenfunctions and
eigenvalues, and it begs many of the transform issues that plague other approaches.
We compute the frequency responses for the general digital filters and show how
to display the complex response. Finally, we look at some general properties of the
frequency response and how those might be useful. The last section illustrates the
importance of the frequency response by using it to compare digital integrators and
differentiators.

Chapter 3 develops the Fourier design technique for nonrecursive filters (recursive filters are handled in Chapters 5 and 6). We begin by defining and motivating
the concept of a squared design error. We minimize the design error and thereby
produce a technique for designing nonrecursive filters: the Fourier method. A good
portion of this chapter is devoted to examples and discussions on how to manipulate the Fourier design equation. Unfortunately, the design technique generally
produces infinite-length filters, which are impractical. The last section shows the
consequences of truncating these infinite-length filters.

Chapter 3 shows how to design nonrecursive digital filters, but many of the
filters designed this way are impractical — they cannot be built. Chapter 4 shows

how the use of windows can turn these impractical filters into useful filters with a minimum of degradation of their frequency response. This chapter starts by developing the effect of truncating on the filter's frequency response. It then introduces windows, which are used to gracefully truncate a filter. The chapter next presents four windows (uniform, von Hann, Hamming, and Kaiser) and shows the utility of each. After Chapters 3 and 4, the reader is able to design general nonrecursive digital filters.

Chapter 5 begins the design of recursive digital filters, which is completed in Chapter 6. It begins by introducing the z-transform and showing its utility in the analysis of recursive digital filters. We show that a recursive filter can be conveniently represented in terms of its poles and zeroes. The final section of the chapter explores a problem that is unique to recursive filters: instability. We use decomposition techniques to show how the stability of a filter is affected by its poles.

Chapter 6 uses the tools developed in Chapter 5 to design recursive digital filters. We use analog mapping techniques exclusively, so Chapter 6 begins with an introduction to analog filters. This is not meant as a course in analog filter design. Rather, it provides enough background that the reader can appreciate analog filters when they are used as a way to design digital filters. The remainder of the chapter develops and discusses two techniques for designing recursive digital filters. The first is the impulse invariant technique and the second is the bilinear transformation. These techniques are studied and compared. We find that a particular design might best be served by one technique and another design might call for the other method. Chapter 6 completes the discussion of digital filter design. At this juncture the reader will be able to design recursive and nonrecursive digital filters.

Chapter 7 is an introduction to digital signal processing using polynomial curve fitting. I've personally used many of these techniques in my own work and find them both useful and broadly applicable. An engineer or scientist will find many places to use these polynomial tools. The chapter begins by showing how polynomials can be used to bridge the gulf between digital and analog data. The discussion then turns to techniques for modeling digital data with a polynomial by curve fitting. The next two sections illustrates a number of applications of this technique: estimating missing data, interpolation, extrapolation, differentiation, and integration. The last section develops and uses least-squares techniques to fit a polynomial to digital data and shows the utility of such a fit.

Chapter 8 presents the most widely used digital signal processing technique: the discrete Fourier transform (DFT) and its efficient implementation, the fast Fourier transform (FFT). Both of these techniques are developed as a computerized way of calculating a nonrecursive filter's impulse response from its frequency response or vice versa. After the DFT is developed, we look at some of the properties of the algorithm. We then apply DFTs to general signals, and find that this is more useful than just computing frequency and impulse responses. The next section looks at some applications of the DFT and shows why the DFT is so widely used to process digital signals. We find that the DFT has characteristics that are similar to the nonrecursive filters in Chapter 4. So, we apply Chapter 4's techniques to the DFT and find that the windows can greatly improve the DFT results. The final section develops a faster realization of the DFT by reorganizing the algorithm. This is called the FFT.

The book concludes with four appendices. Appendix A presents some useful mathematical formulas for those readers who can never find the old math books. Appendix B is an introduction to complex variables. I found that most students were exposed to complex numbers, but many were a little rusty. This appendix concentrates on the manipulation rather than the theory. Appendix C is a longer introduction to analog filters. Again, even readers who have had analog filter design need some refreshing in Chapter 6. The last appendix is a list of references. It is not an all-inclusive list. Rather, it shows those books and articles that might interest a new digital filter designer.

I suspect that most readers will be using this book as a text in an undergraduate course. My experience shows that the first six chapters fit very nicely into a one quarter, 30-lecture-hour course. I've been able to cover all of the material at a reasonable pace. If you are facing a semester course, it is possible to include Chapter 7 or 8 (I doubt that you can do justice to both) or stick to the first six chapters and add some supplemental material. I've found that a significant portion of the student's effort is in the homework, so it is relatively easy to adjust the work load by increasing or decreasing the amount of the out-of-class work.

It is possible to teach this material without using computers, but I highly recommend using them for many of the homework assignments. The reason for this is twofold. First, meaningful designs demand a great deal of computation. It could be done by hand, but it would demand so much effort that the class would focus on the "accounting" and not on the design issues. Second, most engineers and scientists must use computers to practice their craft. The digital filtering material is an ideal vehicle for exposing the students to the computer as a tool. Fortunately, the programs and the computational demands are modest, so the computer tools can be developed quickly on personal computers.

This book is the result of the efforts and sometimes perseverance of many people. I especially wish to thank the 400 or so Stanford students who have participated in the evolution of the course notes and finally the book. The students gave me a most cooperative forum to test what works and what doesn't. I also received many suggestions on better ways of presenting the more difficult topics. I thank my Teaching Assistants, who not only helped with the course but in many cases actively worked on the book. Phil DesJardin was especially active in reviewing the manuscript, and he contributed Appendix B on complex variables. Florin Gheorghiu assisted me for two years in the course and wrote the solutions manual.

I also wish to thank the many folks at Prentice-Hall, some of whom I know and others I don't. I especially wish to thank Bernard Goodwin for his belief in the project. I also wish to thank Mary Carnis and Colleen Brosnan for their editorial assistance, patience, and good humor. Finally I thank my wife, Toni, for all of her support and help during this project. She not only gave me the understanding and time for this work, but she taught me most of what I know about writing. I prepared this book using the TEX typesetting system. Much thanks goes to the TEX user community at Stanford and to Professor Donald Knuth and David Fuchs.

For those who are still with me this far into the Preface, I've had a great deal of fun writing this book. I hope that all of you will find some joy in using it.

*Stanford, California*                                                   Chuck Williams
*May 1985*

# DESIGNING
# DIGITAL FILTERS

# Introduction
# and Motivation

Digital filters are neither new nor difficult. People have been "building" digital filters since they began counting and adding. Unlike their analog counterparts, digital filters are based on the simple operations of multiplication and addition. Therefore, anyone who can perform these elementary operations can understand digital filters.

Some people have introduced digital filtering as a new area in electrical engineering — this is not so. Rather, the computing technology has only recently become capable enough to make digital filters an economic alternative to analog filters. Currently, the primary application of digital filters is for use in those sophisticated systems that demand the capabilities of the filters and can afford their cost. However, as the computer and integrated-circuit technology advances, these filters are finding their way into a wider circle of applications. Digital filters are now used in many electronic measurement systems, and they are even turning up in home appliances.

Digital filters are becoming increasingly popular because:

- They can be implemented with software running on a general purpose computer. Therefore, they are relatively easy to "build" and test.
- They are based solely on the arithmetic operations of addition and multiplication. Therefore, they are extremely stable — they do not change with time or temperature.
- They are easier to modify than their analog counterparts.
- They are easier to understand.

This does not mean that the digital filter is the answer to all filtering problems. Analog filters will continue to dominate the filtering world. However, the digital filter will become more prevalent and will provide the scientist or engineer with capabilities that were only dreams a few years ago.

## 1.1   WHAT IS A FILTER?

In the most general terms, a filter is a *black box* with a set of inputs and a set of outputs. The box contains some form of processing that generates the outputs from the inputs. This general filter is depicted in Figure 1.1.

**Figure 1.1** A general filter.

To justify the expense of the filter, the filter's output(s) must be, in some way, more useful or interesting than the filter's input(s). There are two general motivations for filtering. One is to improve the quality of the inputs; the other is to process or extract information from the inputs. These two needs are illustrated with a couple of examples.

The first example comes from medicine (a growing application for digital filtering). The electrocardiogram (EKG) is an important tool in the diagnosis and treatment of heart disease. The EKG is simply the electrical potential generated by the heart as it beats. From this electrical signature, the physician can infer many conditions that are associated with heart disease. As you might remember from an introductory biology class, all muscles, not just the heart, generate electrical potentials. Therefore, the EKG is the aggregate of the electrical potential of the heart and the surrounding muscles. This muscle "noise" is useless and simply interferes with the diagnosis.

It would help the physician and, one hopes, the patient, if we could filter the EKG to remove, or at least attenuate, the muscle noise component. The output of the filter has much less muscle noise than its input, so the physician can make a more accurate diagnosis by observing the filter's output than she could have made from the unfiltered EKG. In this way, the filtering process has improved the quality of the data. This application of filtering is illustrated in Figure 1.2.

The second example shows how filters are used to extract data from the inputs. Suppose that we wished to build an automatic weatherman. The filter would predict tomorrow's weather, temperature, winds, and rainfall from measurements of past temperature, winds, rainfall, and barometric pressure. In this application we assume

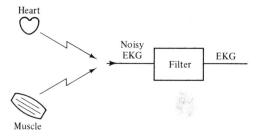

**Figure 1.2** Filtering to remove noise.

that all measurements (inputs) are accurate, so there is no reason to filter for improved measurement quality. The filter's sole purpose is to extract information from the data. This application is shown in Figure 1.3. Note that the inputs are today's weather, yesterday's weather, the day before yesterday's, and so on. Therefore, the number of inputs for this filter is four times the number of past days processed (if we are processing only last week's weather, the filter has 28 inputs).

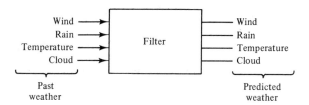

**Figure 1.3** Filtering to extract data.

The processing for the weatherman filter would be quite complicated (even though some TV weathermen don't look as though they know when to come out of the rain). A simple processing is to predict tomorrow's weather as a carbon copy of today's — this is what most of us do. The filter would simply copy the four inputs that represent today's weather to the outputs.

$$
\begin{aligned}
\text{temperature(tomorrow)} &= \text{temperature(today)} \\
\text{winds(tomorrow)} &= \text{winds(today)} \\
\text{rainfall(tomorrow)} &= \text{rainfall(today)} \\
\text{pressure(tomorrow)} &= \text{pressure(today)}
\end{aligned}
$$

A more sophisticated and more accurate weatherman filter must also look for trends in the data (a day-to-day warming trend) or interrelations among data (it is warm and the barometer is dropping). The design of the processing in a filter can be quite complicated and depends very much on the application.

**Example:** A Cash Register as a Filter

A cash register is probably the best known example of a filter. It satisfies all our notions of a filter: it accepts inputs (the price of each item) and produces an output (the total cost, plus tax).

We can describe the operation of a cash register only after defining some notation. The first step is to assign a number to each item purchased; let's use the integers from 1 to $N$. So the first item taken from your shopping basket is item 1, the second item (a can of tuna) is item 2, and so on, until the last item — $N$ — is taken. The next step is to develop some notation for the price of each item. Let's denote the price of the $k$th item as $x_k$. For example, that can of tuna cost $x_2$ cents. Finally, we must assign the output of the cash register a symbol. Let's use $y_k$ to denote the total after the $k$th item has been entered. Now we can descibe the operation of this filter, the cash register.

The basic form of a cash register just adds the prices of all the items to produce a total. So the cash register's output is related to its inputs through the following equation.

$$y_k = x_k + x_{k-1} + x_{k-2} + \ldots + x_0 \tag{1.1}$$

The grand total, the amount you have to pay, is the cash register's output after the last item has been "rung up." Since we have $N$ items, the grand total is $y_N$.

We can express the operation in another, more compact form by noting that $y_k$ is the running total. So to get a new running total, we simply add the price of the new item to the old running total. In this way, the cash register is descibed as below; $y_k$ is the new total, $y_{k-1}$ is the previous total, and $x_k$ is the price of the new item.

$$y_k = y_{k-1} + x_k \tag{1.2}$$

Make sure that you understand why these representations are equivalent. The easiest way to prove this is to express $y_{k-1}$ in terms of the prices of the items.

$$y_{k-1} = x_{k-1} + x_{k-2} + \ldots + x_0 \tag{1.3}$$

Apply this result to equation (1.2) and find that the new total agrees with the description of equation (1.1).

$$\begin{aligned} y_k &= (x_{k-1} + x_{k-2} + \ldots + x_0) + x_k \\ &= x_k + x_{k-1} + x_{k-2} + \ldots + x_0 \end{aligned} \tag{1.4}$$

These two descriptions of the cash register, equations (1.1) and (1.2), are examples of digital filters. The first description is called a *nonrecursive digital filter* and the second is called a *recursive digital filter*. We will see much more of these two forms later.

However, our cash register description is too simplistic because we forgot about sales tax. Sales tax is a charge added to the total to support government activity. Well, how do we go about describing that? The easiest approach is to represent sales tax as a scaling of the prices before they are totaled. Therefore, a 10% sales tax adds $0.10 to a $1 item. We can deal with a 10% sales tax by multiplying the cost of each item by 1.1. Doing so produces the following descriptions of a cash register with a 10% tax.

$$y_k = 1.1x_k + 1.1x_{k-1} + 1.1x_{k-2} + \ldots + 1.1x_0 \qquad (1.5)$$

We can also add sales tax to the recursive representation as shown below.

$$y_k = y_{k-1} + 1.1x_k \qquad (1.6)$$

Convince yourself that equations (1.5) and (1.6) describe the same cash register. Also, is the following description a good one for a 10% sales tax? If there were two cash registers, one operating by equation (1.6) and one by equation (1.7), which one would you choose? [Hint: the government would favor equation (1.7).]

$$y_k = 1.1y_{k-1} + x_k \qquad (1.7)$$

## 1.2  DIGITAL VERSUS ANALOG FILTERS

Analog and digital filters differ by the nature of the input and the output signals. An analog filter processes analog inputs and generates analog outputs. A digital filter processes and generates digital data. These differences in the input and output data dictate different processing techniques. Analog filters are based on the mathematical operator of differentiation, and digital filters require no more than addition, multiplication, and delay operators.

You are probably wondering about the differences between analog and digital data. For the purpose of most of this discussion, the differences are solely in the data's independent variable. Most data are represented by a dependent and an independent variable. The dependent variable is the data and the independent variable represents the ordering of the data. For example, if we are measuring temperature versus time, the dependent variable is temperature and the independent variable is time. If the data are student height versus student ID number, the dependent variable is height and the independent variable is the student ID number.

Analog data are characterized by a continuous independent variable and digital data have a discrete independent variable. Time is continuous, so our example of temperature versus time is an example of analog data. However, the student ID numbers are integers and are, therefore, not continuous variables — they are discrete. Hence height versus ID number is an example of digital data.

Sometimes the differences between analog and digital data can become blurred. Suppose that we alter our temperature versus time example, taking only hourly temperature measurements. In this case, temperature versus time is still analog, but our data, temperature versus hours, are digital. This is because the independent variable is now discrete: 1 o'clock, 2 o'clock, .... It is always possible to convert analog data to digital data. We do so by restricting our attention to discrete values of the independent variable. In the preceding case we restricted time to on-the-hour. We could have just as easily restricted it to the half hours, or on-the-second, and we would have generated a new set of digital data.

In summary, digital data are characterized by a discrete independent variable. Some data are naturally digital, and all data can be converted to digital by restricting the independent variable. Digital filters operate on digital inputs and generate digital outputs.

Digital data are enumerated by indices. These either follow the data in parentheses or follow the data as subscripts. Because the independent variable is discrete, it is generally possible to use integer indices. For example, the temperature in the room at 1 o'clock is denoted $t(1)$ or $t_1$. The temperature at 2 o'clock is $t(2)$ or $t_2$.

An integer index is always more convenient than a natural index. Suppose that we are generating some digital data by measuring the temperature every 15 minutes, and suppose we start the measurements at 1:10. A natural representation of the data would appear as follows:

$$x(1:10), x(1:25), x(1:40), x(1:55), x(2:10), \ldots$$

This is cumbersome. So why not use integer indices and leave the starting time, and the time between observations, understood. Therefore, the data can be represented as

$$x(0), x(1), x(2), x(3), x(4), x(5), \ldots$$

starting time = 1:10
time between data = 15 minutes

This second representation is much more convenient and is generally used — the time between data and the starting time are left understood.

The indices of discrete data provide an ordering of the data. We interpret larger indices as following smaller indices. For example, $x_{k-1}$ precedes $x_k$, and $x_{k+1}$ follows $x_k$. This interpretation is natural when the indices are associated with time. It can become arbitrary when the indices represent quantities such as student ID number. In either case, the indices dictate the ordering of the data.

Digital data are represented as an ordered sequence of numbers. The sequence can be finite and start and end at arbitrary indices:

$$x_3, x_4, x_5, \ldots, x_{10348}$$

The sequence can start at some arbitrary time and go on forever:

$$x_{11}, x_{12}, x_{13}, \ldots$$

The most general data sequence is started at minus infinity and goes on and on:

$$\ldots, x_{-1}, x_0, x_1, \ldots$$

In summary, the digital data are represented by an ordered sequence. The sequence is usually indexed by integers, because they are easy to work with. A member of a data sequence is denoted $x$(index) or $x_{\text{index}}$. These indices can range over a finite interval or take on an infinite range of values. Most people use the letter $k$ for the general index and start the index at $0$ — $x_0$ is the first element of a data sequence.

**Example:** Computing the 24-Hour Average Temperature

Suppose that you have been assigned to monitor the energy consumption in a building. You have on-the-hour measurements of the temperature in the building, and you wish to process, *filter*, them to compute the average temperature over the last 24 hours. Let us denote the temperature measurements $t_k$. Suppose that the first measurement taken is $t_0$. Therefore, the input data to the filter comprise the sequence

$$t_0, t_1, t_2, \ldots, t_M$$

We have $M + 1$ measurements. Denote the 24-hour average as $y_k$. This is the output of the filter. Now for the challenging part: What is the processing to generate the 24-hour average from the measurements? The average is simply the sum of the last 24 temperatures, divided by 24. Therefore, the input and output are related through

$$y(k) = \frac{1}{24} \left[ x(k) + x(k-1) + \ldots + x(k-23) \right] \qquad (1.8)$$

This equation defines the processing of a digital filter.

Although the first element of the input sequence is $x(0)$, the output sequence is undefined until $y(23)$. This is because the computation of $y$ for indices less than 23 involves undefined inputs — those before $x(0)$. We have successfully designed our first digital filter. We will later find that this filter is called a *24-point smoother*, and it is a special case of a broad family of filters.

**Example:** Two-Point Smoother

Compute the output, $y_0, y_1, y_2, \ldots$, of a two-point smoother with the following inputs.

$$x(0) = 1 \qquad x(1) = 3 \qquad x(2) = 7 \qquad x(3) = 2$$

All others inputs are 0.

The general form of the two-point smoother is

$$y_k = \frac{1}{2} \left( x_k + x_{k-1} \right) \qquad (1.9)$$

Therefore, the zeroth output of this filter is just the average of $x_0$ and $x_{-1}$.

$$y_0 = \frac{1}{2}(x_0 + x_{-1}) = \frac{1}{2}(1+0) = \frac{1}{2}$$

The output of this filter for the first index is

$$y_1 = \frac{1}{2}(x_1 + x_0) = \frac{1}{2}(3+1) = 2$$

The second output of this filter is

$$y_2 = \frac{1}{2}(x_2 + x_1) = \frac{1}{2}(7+3) = 5$$

In this arduous way we can compute the output of this digital filter for any index and any set of data. In general, the digital filtering process requires the operator to identify which data to use to compute the particular output and then arithmetically manipulate the data to compute the output. More on this process later.

**Example:** EKG Processing

Consider the problem in which the EKG is corrupted by muscle noise. We wish to process the measurements so as to reduce the muscle noise without affecting the heart's signal.

The corrupted EKG is recorded as an analog signal, say $x(t)$. We must convert it to a digital signal before we can apply it to a digital filter. We convert $x(t)$ to a digital signal $x_k$ by evaluating $x(t)$ every $\frac{1}{1000}$ second – $x_k = x(k \cdot \frac{1}{1000})$. So the corrupted EKG signal, $x_k$, is applied to the input of a digital filter.

We have assumed that the signal is a composite of the heart's contribution, say $h_k$, and the muscle noise, $m_k$. Therefore, our problem is to build a filter that processes $h_k + m_k$ and produces an output $h_k$.

I have only one intuitive filter for this problem, but it requires two inputs. Suppose that we are measuring the muscle noise, $m_k$, as well as the corrupted EKG, $x_k$. We could then build an intuitive filter that has two inputs, $x_k$ and $m_k$. This filter would simply subtract the muscle noise from the corrupted EKG and generate an output, which is the pure EKG. This filter is defined as follows:

$$y(k) = x(k) - m(k) \tag{1.10}$$

This simple filter is the basis for a *noise canceling* filter. But it will not satisfy our application, because we do not have the muscle noise input.

For the time being, the next two filters should be treated as if they were pulled out of thin air. The remainder of this book develops the tools to design such filters. The first filter looks a little like the 24-point smoother, which we saw before. In this case the last seven input data are multiplied by constants and then added to get the output. This filter is defined below.

$$y_k = \frac{1}{21}\left(-2x_k + 3x_{k-1} + 6x_{k-2} + 7x_{k-3} + 6x_{k-4} + 3x_{k-5} - 2x_{k-6}\right) \quad (1.11)$$

For reasons probably unknown by you, this filter attenuates the muscle noise without greatly affecting the EKG signal. An input and resulting output are shown in Figure 1.4. Note that the output is a better-quality EKG than the input. The physician should be delighted, or at least impressed.

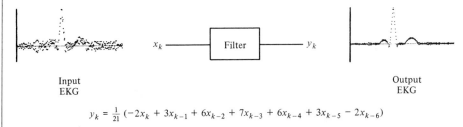

$$y_k = \tfrac{1}{21}\left(-2x_k + 3x_{k-1} + 6x_{k-2} + 7x_{k-3} + 6x_{k-4} + 3x_{k-5} - 2x_{k-6}\right)$$

**Figure 1.4**  Use of a six-point digital filter to attenuate muscle noise in an EKG.

The second filter is based on another design technique that you will learn later. In this case the output at index $k$ is a function of the past outputs as well as the input. This filter is defined below.

$$y_k = 0.14x_{k-2} + 1.77y_{k-1} - 1.19y_{k-2} + 0.28y_{k-3}$$

The utility of this filter is illustrated in Figure 1.5. Notice that it has significantly reduced the muscle noise. Again, a feather in your cap.

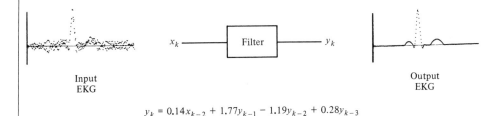

$$y_k = 0.14x_{k-2} + 1.77y_{k-1} - 1.19y_{k-2} + 0.28y_{k-3}$$

**Figure 1.5**  Use of a four-point recursive digital filter to attenuate the muscle noise.

By now you should have a fair idea of what you can do with digital filters. We have seen that filtering can improve data or extract information from data. The digital filters process digital data. These data are represented by a sequence of numbers that are indexed by integers. The examples illustrate the reality of digital filters. Very simple filters can be designed from intuition, but more involved applications demand skills that this work will develop.

## 1.3   SAMPLING: CONVERTING ANALOG TO DIGITAL SIGNALS

Many of the signals that are processed with digital filters have their origins as analog signals. These signals must be converted to digital signals before they are processed with a digital filter. In the examples of the temperature and the EKG, the analog signals were converted to a digital sequence before being passed through the digital filters. The process of converting an analog to a digital signal is an important part of most digital filtering systems, and it must be understood before discussing the actual digital filtering process.

Converting an analog signal, say $x(t)$, to a digital sequence, $x_k$, is illustrated in Figure 1.6. The analog-to-digital converter (**ADC**) is presented with $x(t)$ and produces the digital output $x_k$.

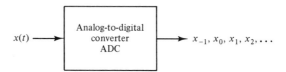

**Figure 1.6** Converting an analog signal to a digital signal.

An analog-to-digital converter actually samples the analog signal in two ways. It takes samples of the signal along the independent variable (usually time) as well as sampling the signal's amplitude. The independent variable must be sampled because the sampling process must convert the continuous independent variable of the analog signal to the discrete indices of the digital signal. The amplitude must be sampled because most digital filters are implemented on digital computers, which cannot represent numbers to an arbitrary precision. Before the digital signal can be presented to the computer the ADC must convert the potentially infinite-precision values to finite-precision values. This process is known as *quantization*.

Because of quantization it is impossible to represent the analog signal's values precisely in the computer. The ADC uses a number that the computer can represent and that is closest to the true value of the data. The difference between the actual data and the values that are presented to the computer is called the *quantization error*, and causes uncertainty in the computer's representation of the data. Generally, the accuracy of the computer and the ADC is selected so that the quantization error is smaller than the inherent noise in the analog signal. This allows the designer to treat the quantization error as noise and simply ignore the quantization effects. When this is not possible (generally because of the cost of higher-precision ADCs and computers), quantization error can become a problem and can significantly degrade the performance of the digital filter. For this introductory treatment we will assume that we can afford all of the necessary precision, so we will ignore quantization.

**Example:** Quantization

Suppose that we have an ADC with a precision of 1 part in 256. This ADC represents the amplitude of the input with 1 of 256 possible values. Furthermore, assume that the ADC can accommodate input signals with amplitudes between $-1.0$ and $1.0$ V (volts).

This ADC effectively divides the input interval from $-1$ to $1$ V into 256 equally spaced regions. Each region is only $\frac{2}{256}$ V wide, or 7.81 mV (millivolts). An input voltage of $-3.91$ to $3.91$ mV is assigned a value of 0, while an input between 3.92 and 11.2 mV is repesented by 7.81 mV. In this way this ADC quantizes the data to within 3.91 mV of their true value — the maximum quantization error is 3.91 mV.

Quantization is presented graphically by plotting the value of the output of the ADC as a function of the amplitude of the ADC's input, as shown in Figure 1.7.

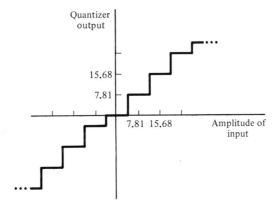

**Figure 1.7** Graphical presentation of quantization – the ADC's output versus its input.

Ideally, this relationship should be a straight line, but it is actually a staircase because of the quantization. The height of each step in the staircase represents the accuracy of the quantizer — for this example each step is 7.81 mV high.

The ADC samples the analog signal along its independent variable by evaluating the analog signal at periodic values of its independent variable and then assigning the quantized values to successive elements of the digital sequence. Generally, the analog signal is sampled at a fixed rate, so the samples are equally spaced along the independent variable. We will denote this spacing $T$, the sampling period. The $k$th element of the digital sequence is the analog signal quantized at $kT + t_0$.

$$x_k = Q\{x(kT + t_0)\} \tag{1.12}$$

The operator, $Q\{\ \ \}$, represents the quantization process, and $t_0$ is the value of the independent variable when the zeroth element was sampled. In the example of digital filtering of room temperature, $T$ is 15 minutes and $t_0$ is $1:10$.

The sampling process is illustrated in Figure 1.8. The horizontal lines denote the data values that can be represented by the digital computer (quantization), and the vertical lines represent the values of the independent variable where samples are taken. The $k$th element of the digital sequence is determined by the intersection of the horizontal line and the $k$th vertical line that is closest to the value of the analog data at time $kT + t_0$. The resulting digital sequence does not accurately represent the analog signal because it has imprecise values of the amplitude of the analog signal. More important, it presents the analog signal at only certain values of its independent variable. We have assumed that the ADC has sufficient accuracy so that we can ignore the effects of quantization. However, we cannot so casually treat the effects of sampling along the independent variable — that requires some further thought.

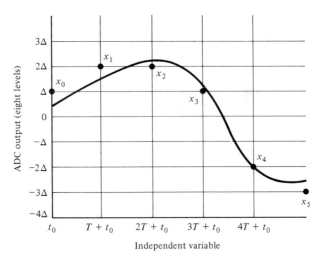

**Figure 1.8** Sampling process – quantization and sampling along the independent variable.

## Sampling Rate

How does a designer go about picking the sampling period, $T$ — or equivalently, the sampling rate of $1/T$ — of a digital system? The naive approach is to sample the analog signal as rapidly as possible, because more closely spaced samples will preserve more of the analog signal. However, this is a very costly solution because fast ADCs and the computers to keep up with them are very expensive. It is possible to derive a rule of thumb for sampling that is analogous to the rule proposed for quantization. In other words, we can determine a minimum sampling rate for a given signal. In the case of quantization we found that the accuracy was dictated by the amount of noise on the signal. For sampling, we are going to find out that the sampling rate is governed by the rate of fluctuation of the signal.

The minimum sampling rate is dictated by the signal being sampled. To see this, consider two extremes: a signal that does not change with its independent variable (a constant) and a signal that changes very quickly (a step function). These two signals are sketched in Figure 1.9.

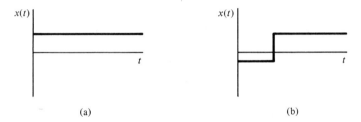

**Figure 1.9** Extremes of analog signals: (a) constant signal;
(b) instantaneously changing signal.

Because the constant signal is fully described by only one value, we can perfectly (ignoring quantization) represent it with a single sample — it can tolerate a very slow sampling rate. On the other hand, a signal with a discontinuity in it cannot be perfectly represented with a digital signal. No matter how closely the samples are spaced there is an ambiguity of $T$ where the jump actually took place. The ambiguity is reduced by increasing the sampling rate, but it cannot be eliminated.

On the basis of these two examples, it appears likely that analog signals that change slowly can be accurately represented with digital signals derived from slow sampling rates. Rapidly varying signals appear to demand fast sampling. These observations are supported by looking at functions that contain precise measures of the notions of "slowly and rapidly varying" — cosines and sines.

Suppose that we sample a cosine signal (this development could just have easily been made with a sine) of frequency $\omega$.

$$x(t) = \cos \omega t \tag{1.13}$$

We chose the cosine function because the variable $\omega$ is a convenient measure of how rapidly this function varies with its independent variable. When $\omega = 0$ this is a constant function. A large value of $\omega$ means that the cosine is a rapidly varying function.

By sampling this cosine every $T$ units we generate the following digital signal.

$$x_k = \cos kT\omega \tag{1.14}$$

The product of $T\omega$ determines how rapidly this digital signal varies with the index, $k$. $T\omega$ is called the *normalized frequency*, and is expressed in radians per sample. We are tempted to extend the results of the analog world and say that large values of $T\omega$ mean that the digital signal varies rapidly with $k$, but that is not the case. Because the index takes only integer values, there is a more complicated relationship between the normalized frequency and the variations of $x_k$. For example, if $T\omega = 0.1$, the cosine changes 0.1 rad/sample. As shown in Figure 1.10, this signal has about 63 samples/period. If $T\omega$ is increased (an increase of the analog signal's frequency, $\omega$, or the sampling period, $T$) to 6.2 rad/sample, the digital signal actually varies more slowly with $k$ — it looks like a cosine with a normalized frequency of only 0.08319 rad/sample (Figure 1.10b). As depicted in Figure 1.10c, the signal becomes a constant when the normalized frequency is increased to $2\pi$ (6.28319). Because the digital signal uses an integer independent variable, the notions of frequency and variations must be altered. We do so by the following development.

Reconsider the digital cosine signal but express the normalized frequency, $T\omega$, as the sum of two terms. The first of these terms is denoted $\omega'$ and is restricted to a magnitude less than $\pi$. The second term is an integer times $2\pi$ and is denoted $\Omega$.

$$\omega T = \omega' + \Omega \quad \text{where} \quad |\omega'| < \pi \quad \text{and} \quad \Omega = \text{integer} \times 2\pi \tag{1.15}$$

This decomposition is shown in Figure 1.11.

The digital cosine signal can be rewritten in terms of $\omega'$ and $\Omega$.

$$x_k = \cos\left[k(\omega' + \Omega)\right] \tag{1.16}$$

or

$$x_k = \cos(k\omega' + k\Omega)$$

Because $\Omega$ is an integer times $2\pi$ and $k$ is an integer, the product $k\Omega$ is also an integer times $2\pi$. So the $k\Omega$ portion of the cosine's argument does not affect the cosine's value; we can therefore ignore it.

$$x_k = \cos k\omega' \tag{1.17}$$

The digital cosine signal depends only on the portion of the normalized frequency that is less than $\pi$; it is independent of the $\Omega$ component. This means that sampling an analog cosine signal can generate an ambiguity, because it is possible

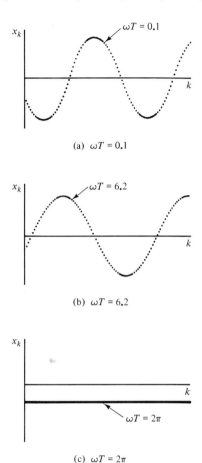

(a)  $\omega T = 0.1$

(b)  $\omega T = 6.2$

(c)  $\omega T = 2\pi$

**Figure 1.10**  Sampling a cosine waveform: (a) $\omega T = 0.1$;
(b) $\omega T = 6.2$; (c) $\omega T = 2\pi$

for two analog signals of different frequencies to generate identical digital signals. For example, analog signals of frequencies $\omega$ and $\omega + 2\pi/T$ will yield the same digital signals. This process is called *aliasing*, because through the sampling process cosines of different frequencies can assume the same "digital identity"; one can assume the alias of another.

It is impossible to determine precisely the true frequency of a digital cosine signal because the factor of $\Omega$ is hidden. Therefore, we are forced to assume a value of $\Omega$ if we are to make any sense of normalized frequency. For most applications it is most reasonable to assume an $\Omega$ of 0. That is, the normalized frequency, $\omega T$, is restricted to the interval $-\pi$ to $\pi$.

It is certainly possible to sample a high-frequency analog signal (large $\omega$) at

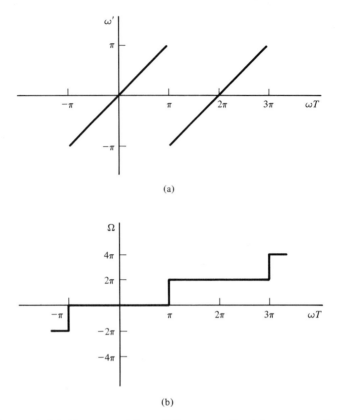

**Figure 1.11** Decomposition of the normalized frequency: (a) $\omega'$, fractional part; (b) $\Omega$, the integer part.

a low sampling rate (large $T$) and thereby produce a normalized frequency greater than $\pi$. In such cases the assumption of $\Omega = 0$ is wrong, so the digital signal will be misinterpreted as being produced by the sampling of a lower-frequency analog cosine function. The high-frequency cosine is aliased to a lower-frequency cosine by the sampling process. To prevent such aliasing the sampling period must be small enough to accommodate the variations in the analog signal. More precisely, the sampling period must be small enough so that $\Omega = 0$.

$$|\omega T| < \pi \qquad (1.18)$$

or

$$T < \frac{\pi}{|\omega|}$$

In other words, the cosine wave must be sampled at least twice a period. If it is not, the digital sequence will be interpreted as coming from a lower frequency analog signal. Consider some examples.

**Example:** Selecting the Maximum Sampling Period

Suppose that we wish to sample a sine function that can vary as rapidly as 1000 rad/in (see, the independent variable can be something other than time). What is the maximum separation necessary between samples (in inches) so that this signal will not be aliased by sampling?

We use the inequality of equation (1.18) to solve for $T$.

$$T < \frac{\pi}{1000} \tag{1.19}$$

or

$$T < 0.00314 \qquad \text{in.}$$

Therefore, we can sample as slowly as one sample every 0.00314 in., or, in other words, take as few as 319 samples/in. In practice, most designers select sampling rates that are at least 20% faster than the minimum. Therefore, this signal should be sampled at about 400 samples/in.

**Example:** Determine the Highest-Frequency Signal

Suppose you are confronted with a system that takes a sample every tenth of a second. Find the highest-frequency sinusoidal function that can be sampled, yet not aliased.

We solve this by supplying the inequality of equation (1.18) with $T = 0.1$ and computing the upper bound for $\omega$.

$$|\omega| < \frac{\pi}{T} \tag{1.20}$$

or

$$|\omega| < 10\pi \qquad \text{rad/sec}$$

Signals with frequencies higher than $10\pi$ will be aliased by this system. In practice, many designers would be more restrictive than this theoretical limit and would use $8\pi$ as a maximum frequency.

We used the cosine and sine functions for this development because frequency is a convenient way of measuring how fast a signal changes with its independent variable. However, the aliasing results can be extended to arbitrary signals. We can do this because many signals can be represented as a weighted sum of cosines and sines. By expressing signals this way, it is possible to talk of the frequency components in a square wave or even an EKG. Any components with frequencies greater than $\pi/T$ will be aliased by the sampling process. So an analog signal containing high frequency components will be inaccurately represented by a digital sequence, because the high frequency components are aliased by the sampling. The sampling rule for arbitrary signals is that the sampling rate must be large enough to accommodate the highest-frequency component in the signal.

Aliasing is the scourge of the digital designer. No matter how careful you are, some aliasing is bound to occur when analog signals are converted to digital sequences. This is because all analog signals have some very high frequency components, so no matter how fast the signal is sampled, some of it will be aliased. The designer must ensure that the aliased components have such small amplitudes that the aliasing can be effectively ignored. This is generally done by passing the analog data through an analog filter that attenuates the high-frequency components before the signal is sampled. These are called *anti-aliasing* filters (somewhat of a misnomer because they do not prevent aliasing; they just reduce its consequences).

## 1.4   DEFINITION OF DIGITAL FILTERS

The previous discussion of filtering may have been useful for general motivation, but this definition of a filter is far too broad. The input-to-output processing could involve anything from simple mathematical relationships (as in the examples) all the way through magic. This wide flexibility makes it impossible to develop the design tools for filters. How would you go about designing magical relationships between the input and output? Because magic is seldom in our "toolbox", we must severely restrict the kind of processing that can go on inside a digital filter. Does this mean that you can't build more general digital filters? Absolutely not. Just, if you violate these restrictions, the future design rules may not work, and you are on your own — you specify the magic.

Because this is an introduction to digital filters, we are going to ignore the multi-input, multioutput filters. From now on, all the filters are going to have one input and a single output. This restriction is more from convenience than necessity. Many of the ideas developed in this work are directly applicable to multi-input and multioutput systems.

We will restrict all digital filters to either of two forms: nonrecursive or recursive. A *nonrecursive filter* generates its output by simply weighting the inputs by constants and then summing the weighted inputs. The constants are called *coefficients* and these constants determine the filter. A design of a filter is tantamount to computing (or maybe just picking) the values for these coefficients. The nonrecursive filter is defined below.

$$y_k = c_m x_{k-m} + c_{m-1} x_{k-m+1} + \ldots + c_0 x_k + \ldots + c_{-m+1} x_{k+m-1} + c_{-m} x_{k+m} \quad (1.21)$$

This filter computes the "current" output, $y_k$, from the current input, $x_k$, and the $m$ inputs that preceded $x_k$, $x_{k-1} \ldots x_{k-m}$, and the $m$ inputs that follow $x_k$, $x_{k+1} \ldots x_{k+m}$. The output is a weighted sum of the current input and its $2m$ "neighbors". Note that the inputs do not contribute equally to the output. The contribution of each data element is governed by the coefficient with which it is multiplied. If the coefficient is large, the particular data element can dramatically affect the output. If the coefficient is small the data element has a proportionally small effect on the filter's output. For example, if the zeroth coefficient, $c_0$, is zero, the input, $x_k$, has no effect on $y_k$. However, $x_k$ may affect the future outputs, $y_{k+1}, y_{k+2}, \ldots$.

The notation used for the definition is quite cumbersome. We will compact it by using the sigma symbol for summation. Sigma is simply a compact way of expressing the sum.

$$\sum_{i=-m}^{m} a_i = a_{-m} + a_{-m+1} + \ldots a_{m-1} + a_m \tag{1.22}$$

Therefore, our definition of a nonrecursive digital filter becomes the following compact expression.

$$y_k = \sum_{i=-m}^{m} c_i x_{k-i} \tag{1.23}$$

The operation of this filter is diagrammed in Figure 1.12. The input data, $x_{k-m} \ldots x_{k+m}$, are multiplied by the coefficients, $c_{-m} \ldots c_m$, and the products are passed to a large adder to generate the output, $y_k$. The next output, $y_{k+1}$, is generated the same way, but in this case the data are moved one position to the left before the multiplication. Therefore, $c_0$ multiplies $x_{k+1}$ rather than $x_k$. In general, the $m$th coefficient multiplies $x_{k+1-m}$ to generate the $y_{k+1}$ output.

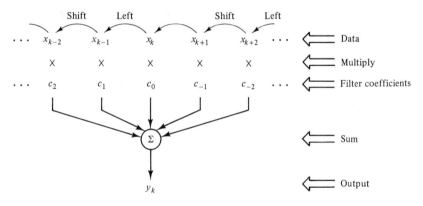

**Figure 1.12** Nonrecursive digital filter.

If you have trouble visualizing this shift, just substitute $k = j + 1$ into the definition of the nonrecursive filter. This substitution shows how the output $y_{j+1}$ is computed.

$$y_{j+1} = \sum_{i=-m}^{m} c_i x_{j+1-i} \tag{1.24}$$

But the choice of index is completely arbitrary. So can substitute $k$ back in for $j$ — this is simply a formal way of advancing $k$.

$$y_{k+1} = \sum_{i=-m}^{m} c_i x_{k+1-i} \tag{1.25}$$

The data sequence $x_{k+1-i}$ is just the data in equation (1.25) advanced by one index.

The filter's outputs for all possible indices are computed by multiplying the proper input data by the filter coefficients and then adding together all the products. Although this operation requires little beyond multiplication, addition, and some bookkeeping, it is easy to make mistakes. The most error-prone portion of the operation is the bookkeeping. Make sure that you are using the correct input data for the multiplications and that you have properly paired up the coefficients and the data. Many people try to run the filter backwards. That is, they attempt to multiply $c_i$ by $x_{k+i}$ rather than by $x_{k-i}$.

**Example:** Nonrecursive Digital Filter Operation

Consider the three-coefficient digital filter with the following coefficients:

$$c_{-1} = -1 \qquad c_1 = 1 \qquad c_2 = 2$$

The input-output relationship for this particular filter is obtained by substituting the values of the coefficients into the general definition of the nonrecursive filter.

$$y_k = -1x_{k+1} + 1x_{k-1} + 2x_{k-2} \qquad (1.26)$$

Therefore, given any particular input sequence, $x_k$, it is fairly straightforward to compute the output of this filter. First, you pick a $k$ for which you wish to compute the output, and then substitute the three values of the input needed for that particular $k$. For example, if we are interested in the value of $y$ for index 0, we would simply plug in $k = 0$ and obtain

$$y_0 = -1x_1 + 1x_{-1} + 2x_{-2} \qquad (1.27)$$

The output for the index 1 is simply the equation evaluated for $k = 1$,

$$y_1 = -1x_2 + 1x_0 + 2x_{-1} \qquad (1.28)$$

and so on. In this way we can laboriously implement this digital filter for any given input sequence. These filters are usually implemented on computers, which just love to perform these repetitive tasks.

The second form of digital filter is recursive. In this case, the output is not only a function of the inputs, but it also depends on the past outputs. The recursive digital filter is defined below.

$$y_k = \sum_{i=-m}^{m} c_i x_{k-i} + \sum_{j=1}^{n} d_j y_{k-j} \qquad (1.29)$$

The first sum is our old friend the nonrecursive filter. The second sum is called the *recursive* portion of the filter. This second sum shows how the output is related to past outputs. The recursive coefficients are denoted $d_j$, and are used to weight the past outputs, $y_{k-j}$. When all the recursive coefficients are zero, this becomes a nonrecursive filter. Therefore, the nonrecursive filter is really a special case of the recursive filter.

The operation of the recursive filter is illustrated in Figure 1.13. The left side of the figure is the nonrecursive portion of the figure. The right side is the recursive part. The output of this filter is the sum of the left and right sides. Notice that the right side gets its "input" from the output of the filter.

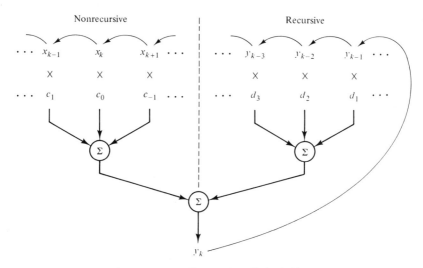

**Figure 1.13** Recursive digital filter.

This filter is implemented in a similar manner as the nonrecursive filter — pick a particular index, $k$, and compute the output for that index. However, the operation of the recursive filter is complicated by the fact that the output at time $k$ depends on previous outputs as well as the inputs. Therefore, these filters must be operated sequentially — the output for index $k$ must be computed before the output for index $k+1$. The problem is: Where do you start computing the outputs?

You should convince yourself that the filter must have some assumed, initial output(s) before you start computing the subsequent outputs. If not, you do not know where to start your computation. These initial outputs are called *initial conditions*. Generally, the filter is assumed to be at "rest" before the input data start affecting the output. That is, the inputs and outputs are assumed to be zero for very negative indices. If we assume that the filter is at rest, we begin computing the outputs when the first nonzero input enters the nonrecursive portion of the filter. After that, we must compute the outputs sequentially, because they will be used in successive outputs of the filter.

**Example:** Recursive Filter

Consider the recursive filter in the EKG example. In that case, the coefficients are

$$c_2 = 0.14 \quad d_1 = 1.77 \quad d_2 = -1.19 \quad d_3 = 0.28$$

Let's assume that the filter is initially at rest and that the input data are zero for negative indices, $x_k = 0 \quad k < 0$, and linearly increase with positive indices, $x_k = k + 1$ for $k \geq 0$.

Where do we start computing the output? We know that the output is zero until the first nonzero input affects the filter. The first possible nonzero input is $x_0$. When does $x_0$ affect the filter? It is not necessarily $k = 0$, because it depends on the coefficients of the nonrecursive portion of the filter. In this case, because $c_2$ is the first nonzero coefficient, $x_0$ will affect the output at index $k = 2$; two steps after $k = 0$. Therefore, the first nonzero output for this filter is $y_2$.

The computation of the outputs of this filter is illustrated in Figure 1.14. Each computation involves four distinct steps:

1. Write the filter equation for this particular index.
2. Substitute the proper values of the inputs into the equation.
3. Substitute the proper values of the past outputs into the equation.
4. Compute the output by performing the multiplications and then adding the products.

We arbitrarily start the computation at $k = 0$ and express $y_0$ in terms of the input at $k = -2$ and the outputs at $k = -1, -2$, and $-3$. All the past outputs are zero, because we assumed that the filter was initially at rest and the input has not yet influenced the output. Furthermore, the input is still zero, so $y_0$ is 0. The output for $k = 1$ is still zero, because the input has not had a chance to affect the output. The long-awaited input data start influencing the output at $k = 2$, so the output of the filter is $c_2$ times $x_0$ or $0.14 \times 1$. the computation for $k = 3$ and 4 involves new inputs and past outputs, but is conceptually no more difficult than the previous calculations.

These are the only two forms that we will consider. There are others (e.g. lattice forms), but they are beyond the scope of an introductory treatment. Most digital filters are recursive or nonrecursive. You should spend some time making sure that you understand the operation of these filters. As mentioned before, the bookkeeping is more involved than the multiplication and addition. Some people find it convenient to build tables to aid them in keeping track of the inputs and outputs of these filters. These filters can be as extensive as Figure 1.14 or as condensed as that shown in Figure 1.15. The form of the table is generally dictated by the personal preferences of the user. Now you know why computers, rather than people, implement digital filters.

$k = 0$

$$y_0 = 0.14x_{-2} + 1.77y_{-1} - 1.19y_{-2} + 0.28y_{-3} = 0$$

$\quad\quad\quad\quad\| \quad\quad\quad\quad \| \quad\quad\quad \| \quad\quad\quad \|$

$\quad\quad\quad\quad 0 \quad\quad\quad\quad 0 \quad\quad\quad 0 \quad\quad\quad 0$

$\underbrace{\qquad\qquad\qquad\qquad\qquad}$

Filter at rest

$k = 1$

$$y_1 = 0.14x_{-1} + 1.77y_0 - 1.19y_{-1} + 0.28y_{-2} = 0$$

$\quad\quad\quad\quad\| \quad\quad\quad\quad \| \quad\quad\quad \| \quad\quad\quad \|$

$\quad\quad\quad\quad 0 \quad\quad\quad\quad 0 \quad\quad\quad 0 \quad\quad\quad 0$

$\underbrace{\quad\quad}\quad\underbrace{\qquad\qquad\qquad}$

Previous          Filter at rest

calculation

$k = 2$

$$y_2 = 0.14x_0 + 1.77y_1 - 1.19y_0 + 0.28y_{-1} = 0.14$$

$\quad\quad\quad\quad\| \quad\quad\quad \| \quad\quad \| \quad\quad \|$

$\quad\quad\quad\quad 1 \quad\quad\quad 0 \quad\quad 0 \quad\quad 0$

$\underbrace{\qquad\qquad}\quad\underbrace{\qquad}$

Previous          Filter

calculation       at rest

$k = 3$

$$y_3 = 0.14x_1 + 1.77y_2 - 1.19y_1 + 0.28y_0 = 0.5278$$

$\quad\quad\quad\quad\| \quad\quad\quad \| \quad\quad \| \quad\quad \|$

$\quad\quad\quad\quad 2 \quad\quad 0.14 \quad 0 \quad\quad 0$

$\underbrace{\qquad\qquad\qquad\qquad\qquad}$

Previous

calculation

$k = 4$

$$y_4 = 0.14x_2 + 1.77y_3 - 1.19y_2 + 0.28y_1 = 1.1876$$

$\quad\quad\quad\quad\| \quad\quad\quad \| \quad\quad\quad \| \quad\quad \|$

$\quad\quad\quad\quad 3 \quad 0.5278 \quad 0.14 \quad 0$

$\underbrace{\qquad\qquad\qquad\qquad}$

Previous

calculation

**Figure 1.14** Computing the output of a simple recursive digital filter.

## 1.5  INTERESTING RESPONSES

It is possible to compute a particular filter's output for any given input. But some inputs are more interesting than others. This section introduces three special inputs and defines the filter's output as a *response* to these inputs.

The first and far most interesting input is the impulse. The digital impulse (unlike its analog counterpart) is a very simple input — it is a 1 at index 0 and 0 otherwise. The impulse is defined as follows:

$$i_k = \begin{cases} 1 & \text{if } k = 0 \\ 0 & \text{otherwise} \end{cases} \tag{1.30}$$

The filter's impulse response is simply its output when its input is an impulse. In other words, the impulse response is the filter's response to an impulse.

The digital step is 1 for positive indices (including zero) and 0 for negative

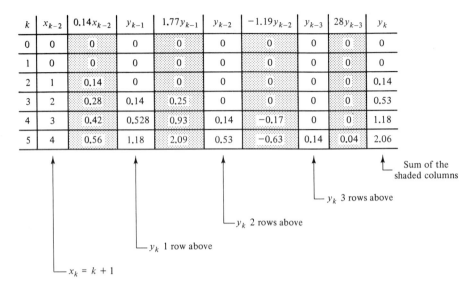

| $k$ | $x_{k-2}$ | $0.14x_{k-2}$ | $y_{k-1}$ | $1.77y_{k-1}$ | $y_{k-2}$ | $-1.19y_{k-2}$ | $y_{k-3}$ | $28y_{k-3}$ | $y_k$ |
|---|---|---|---|---|---|---|---|---|---|
| 0 | 0 | 0 | 0 | 0 | 0 | 0 | 0 | 0 | 0 |
| 1 | 0 | 0 | 0 | 0 | 0 | 0 | 0 | 0 | 0 |
| 2 | 1 | 0.14 | 0 | 0 | 0 | 0 | 0 | 0 | 0.14 |
| 3 | 2 | 0.28 | 0.14 | 0.25 | 0 | 0 | 0 | 0 | 0.53 |
| 4 | 3 | 0.42 | 0.528 | 0.93 | 0.14 | −0.17 | 0 | 0 | 1.18 |
| 5 | 4 | 0.56 | 1.18 | 2.09 | 0.53 | −0.63 | 0.14 | 0.04 | 2.06 |

Sum of the shaded columns

$y_k$ 3 rows above

$y_k$ 2 rows above

$y_k$ 1 row above

$x_k = k + 1$

**Figure 1.15** Table to aid in the calculation of a filter.

indices. It is defined as follows:

$$s_k = \begin{cases} 1 & k \geq 0 \\ 0 & \text{otherwise} \end{cases} \qquad (1.31)$$

When a step is presented to a filter as an input, the output is called the filter's *step response*.

**Example:** An Impulse-to-Step Filter

Design a digital filter that converts an impulse to a step — when its input is an impulse, its output is a step.

This filter is designed by common sense (very few chances to do this type of design). We want a filter that essentially latches its input. The filter's output is initially zero and when the impulse comes along, the output rises to 1 and stays at 1 forever. This is a filter with an infinite memory.

We should convince ourselves that a nonrecursive filter just will not do the job, because its output will go to zero after the impulse has passed through the filter. Therefore, we consider only recursive filters for this application. We want a filter whose output is zero until the impulse arrives at $k = 0$, and after that the output stays constant — the output at $k$ equals the output at $k - 1$. We have just described the following filter.

$$y_k = x_k + y_{k-1} \qquad (1.32)$$

Convince yourself that this filter does the trick.

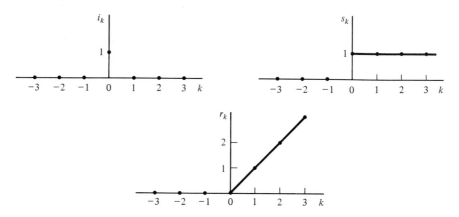

**Figure 1.16** Impulse, step, and ramp functions.

The last input of interest is the digital ramp. This is a linearly increasing sequence for positive indices and is zero for negative indices.

$$r_k = \begin{cases} k & \text{if } k \geq 0 \\ 0 & \text{otherwise} \end{cases} \tag{1.33}$$

You guessed it — the filter's output when presented with a ramp is called the *ramp response*.

**Example:** A Step-to-Ramp Digital Filter

Design a digital filter that generates a ramp when its input is a step.

This is just a variation of the preceding example. The input is a constant after $k = 0$, and the output should increase at a constant rate after $k = 0$. Therefore, we want a filter that computes the output at $k$ as the sum of the output at $k - 1$ and the input. This looks a good deal like the filter in the preceding example, so let's try it.

$$y_k = x_k + y_{k-1} \tag{1.34}$$

This filter produces a ramp, but the ramp starts at $k = 0$ ($y_0 = 1$) and the definition of a ramp function states that it starts at $k = 1$. Therefore, we must delay the filter's output by one index, by delaying the input's effect on the output. This is done by changing the index on the input to $k - 1$.

The desired filter has the following equation:

$$y_k = x_{k-1} + y_{k-1} \tag{1.35}$$

Convince yourself that this filter does the job.

These inputs are sketched in Figure 1.16. We consider these three responses because some designs are specified in terms of the impulse, step, or ramp responses. Furthermore, computation of these responses gives us a better understanding of the operation of a digital filter.

**Example:** Impulse Response of a General Nonrecursive Filter

The impulse response is simply the output of the filter when an impulse is applied as input. This response is important enough to deserve its own symbol — call the impulse response $h_k$. The general form of a nonrecursive filter is taken from our definition.

$$h(k) = y(k) = \sum_{i=-m}^{m} c(i)x(k-i) \qquad x_k = \text{impulse} \qquad (1.36)$$

The input is an impulse, which means that

$$x_k = i_k = \begin{cases} 1 & \text{if } k = 0 \\ 0 & \text{otherwise} \end{cases} \qquad (1.37)$$

or

$$x_{k-i} = \begin{cases} 1 & \text{if } i = k \\ 0 & \text{otherwise} \end{cases} \qquad (1.38)$$

Therefore, each product of the sum is zero except the product where $k = i$. The impulse response of the nonrecursive filter consists of the coefficients of the filter.

$$h(k) = c(k) \qquad (1.39)$$

This relationship between the impulse response and the coefficients of a nonrecursive digital filter makes the impulse response a natural way of describing these filters. Suppose that you were given a nonrecursive filter in a "black box" and you wished to measure its coefficients. You could do so by putting an impulse into its input and observing its impulse response.

The length of the nonzero portion of the impulse response is dictated by the number of coefficients in the filter. Since these filters have at most $2m + 1$ nonzero coefficients, the impulse response can be no longer than $2m + 1$. For this reason, nonrecursive filters are sometimes called *finite impulse response* (FIR) *filters*.

**Example:** Impulse Response of a General Recursive Filter

The recursive filter's impulse response is more involved. The general form of the recursive filter is repeated below.

$$h(k) = y(k) = \sum_{i=-m}^{m} c(i)x(k-i) + \sum_{j=1}^{n} d(j)y(k-j) \qquad x(k) = \text{impulse} \quad (1.40)$$

We use the same line of reasoning as above — note that only the $k = i$ term contributes to the nonrecursive sum.

$$h(k) = c(k) + \sum_{j=1}^{n} d(j)h(k-j) \qquad (1.41)$$

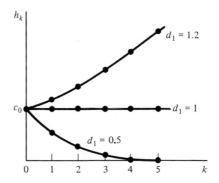

**Figure 1.17** Examples of impulse responses of a simple recursive filter.

Unfortunately, there is no simple interpretation for this result. The impulse response of a recursive filter is more complicated and not nearly as nicely related to the coefficients of the filter. We will return to the recursive impulse response later.

Note that the impulse response of a recursive filter can remain nonzero for even large indices. The recursive portion continues to generate an output long after the $c(k)$s are zero. Therefore, the recursive filters have infinite impulse responses. They are sometimes referred to as *infinite impulse response* (IIR) *filters*.

**Example:** Impulse Response of a Simple Recursive Filter

Consider a simple recursive filter with only two nonzero coefficients: $c(0)$ and $d(1)$. Its impulse response is just a special case of equation (1.41).

$$y_k = c_0 x_k + d_1 y_{k-1} \qquad (1.42)$$

When an impulse is presented to this filter, the input affects the output only at $k = 0$, because the input is zero for all other indices. If we assume that the filter is at rest, $y_k$ is zero for all negative indices, and $y_0$ is just $c_0$.

$$y_0 = c_0 1 + d_1 0 = c_0 \qquad (1.43)$$

Because the input is an impulse and $c_0$ is the only nonzero coefficient, the input does not directly affect the output for $k \neq 0$. Therefore, the output for positive indices is simply the last output scaled by $d_1$.

$$y_k = c_0 0 + d_1 y_{k-1} = d_1 y_{k-1} \qquad \text{for} \quad k \neq 0 \qquad (1.44)$$

The impulse response of this filter is sketched in Figure 1.17. Note that the nonrecursive coefficient merely controls the amplitude of the response at $k = 0$. The recursive coefficient determines the shape of the response. If $d_1$ is negative, the response alternates sign. If $d_1$ is between 0 and 1 the response exponentially decays to zero. If $d_1$ is greater than 1, the response grows.

**Impulse Response and the Input-Output Relationship**

The impulse response is much more important than the other responses that were introduced. This is because the inputs and the outputs are related through the filter's impulse response.

Consider a nonrecursive filter. The input and output are related through the filter's coefficients.

$$y_k = \sum_{i=-m}^{m} c_i x_{k-i} \tag{1.45}$$

However, for a nonrecursive filter, the impulse response, say $h_k$, is equal to the coefficients. Therefore, the input and output are related through the impulse response.

$$y_k = \sum_{i=-m}^{m} h_i x_{k-i} \tag{1.46}$$

This relationship is called *convolution*. The output of a nonrecursive digital filter is just the convolution of the input and the filter's impulse response.

Let's turn our attention to the recursive form of the digital filter and attempt to compute the relationship between the filter's impulse response and its input and output. The word "attempt" is important here, because we are going to have trouble relating a nonrecursive filter's input and output through its impulse response. This is because we do not yet have the correct tools. But let's go ahead anyway to gain more experience with the nonrecursive filter and to develop a better appreciation of the more advanced tools we will be getting.

Assume that we have a nonrecursive digital filter as follows:

$$y_k = \sum_{j=-m}^{m} c_j x_{k-j} + \sum_{j=1}^{n} d_j y_{k-j} \tag{1.47}$$

The first problem is to find a place to start. If we do not put some restrictions on the filter, we will not know where to begin computing the output. Let's assume that the filter is initially "at rest" — that is, $y_{-\infty} = 0$. This assumption forces the filter to produce a zero output until the input signal comes along. For the sake of simplicity, let's assume that the input is zero before $k = 0$, $x_k = 0$ for $k < 0$. Therefore, the first possible nonzero output for this filter occurs when $x_0$ encounters $c_{-m}$, and this happens at $k = -m$.

$$y_{-m} = c_{-m} x_0 \tag{1.48}$$

Previous to $k = -m$, this filter was at rest.

The filter's next output depends on $y_{-m}$ and $x_0$ and $x_1$ and is computed by applying equation (1.48) to equation (1.47).

$$y_{-m+1} = d_0 \left( c_{-m} x_0 \right) + c_{-m} x_1 + c_{-m+1} x_0 \tag{1.49}$$

Notice how the feedback coefficients, $d_i$s, are starting to appear in the expression. This looks complicated but manageable. So let's look at the next output.

$$y_{-m+2} = d_0 \left( d_0 c_{-m} x_0 + c_{-m} x_1 + c_{-m+1} x_0 \right) + d_1 \left( c_{-m} x_0 \right)$$
$$+ c_{-m} x_2 + c_{-m+1} x_1 + c_{-m+2} x_0 \tag{1.50}$$

The trouble with recursive filters is that their output expressions continue to get more and more complicated. The feedback coefficients keep bringing more and more of the past outputs into the computation of the current output. We could continue this development and hope that a pattern would develop, but that will not happen. The feedback coefficients will continue to complicate the expression, thus preventing us from developing a convolution relationship between the filter's input and output. Does this mean that such a relationship does not exist? No, it simply means that we do not have the tools to develop it. Those tools are the subject of the following section.

We have shown that the inputs and outputs of a nonrecursive filter are related through a convolution of the filter's impulse response. Unfortunately, we are unable to show the same for a recursive filter. But convolution is such a powerful tool that we are going to devolop more sophisticated methods of dealing with digital filters in order to show the convolution result for the recursive filters. Make sure that you understand convolution and how it relates the inputs and outputs of a nonrecursive filter. You are going to see a great deal of it later.

**Example:** Convolution

Compute the output of nonrecursive digital filter that has an impulse response and input defined as follows:

$$h_k = \begin{cases} 1 & \text{for } k = -1, 0, 1 \\ 2 & \text{for } k = 2, 3 \\ 0 & \text{otherwise} \end{cases} \tag{1.51}$$

$$x_k = \begin{cases} 2 & \text{for } k = 0, 1, 2 \\ 0 & \text{otherwise} \end{cases} \tag{1.52}$$

The most straightforward solution is to apply the impulse response and the input directly to equation (1.46). For example,

$$y_k = \sum_{l=-\infty}^{\infty} h_l x_{k-l}$$
$$= \sum_{l=-1}^{3} h_l x_{k-l} \tag{1.53}$$

We were able to reduce the region of summation because $h_l$ is nonzero for only five  indices. The convolution is completed by picking $k$s and evaluating equation 1.53.

$$y_0 = \sum_{l=-1}^{3} h_l x_{0-l}$$

$$= 2 \cdot 1 + 2 \cdot 1 + 2 \cdot 0 + 0.2 + 0 \cdot 2 = 4$$

$$y_1 = \sum_{l=-1}^{3} h_l x_{1-l}$$

$$= 2 \cdot 1 + 2 \cdot 1 + 2 \cdot 1 + 0 \cdot 2 + 0 \cdot 2 = 6$$

$$y_2 = \sum_{l=-1}^{3} h_l x_{2-l} \qquad (1.54)$$

$$= 0 \cdot 1 + 2 \cdot 1 + 2 \cdot 1 + 2 \cdot 2 + 0 \cdot 2 = 8$$

$$y_3 = \sum_{l=-1}^{3} h_l x_{3-l}$$

$$= 0 \cdot 1 + 0 \cdot 1 + 2 \cdot 1 + 2 \cdot 2 + 2 \cdot 2 = 10$$

$$\vdots$$

Notice that the impulse response's contribution to the sums above is constant and the signal appears to shift throught the impulse response at different indices of $y$ are evaluated. This is a general property of convolution and leads some people to a graphical interpretation of the operation. This graphical representation is illustrated in Figure 1.18. The impulse response, $h_l$, and the shifted and flipped input signal, $x_{k-l}$, and plotted. As $k$ changes the shifted input moves with respect to the stationary impulse response. The result of the convolution for any time, $k$, is computed by shifting the input $k$ time units and multiplying the elements of the impulse reponse by the aligned elements of the shifted signal and summing all the products. If this graphical representation of convolution helps your understanding, use it. If it seems to confuse the issues, rely on the algebraic form of convolution and forget the graphical interpretation.

In summary, the impulse, step, and ramp responses are useful tools for measuring some special cases of the input–output relationship of a filter. Occasionally, a design specification is given in terms of one of these responses, and the design is performed directly from these specifications. The impulse response of a nonrecursive filter is directly related to its coefficients. The response of a recursive filter is more complicated because the impulse affects the filter's output through the past outputs as well as the nonrecursive coefficients. The impulse response also relates the filter's inputs and outputs through the convolution operator.

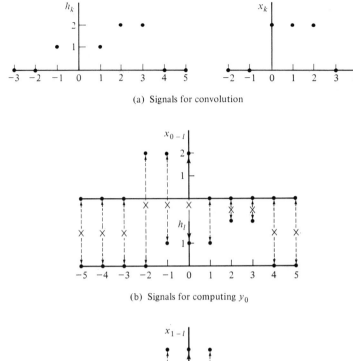

(a)  Signals for convolution

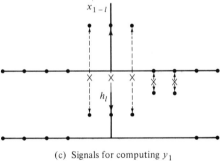

(b)  Signals for computing $y_0$

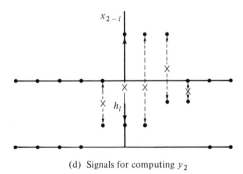

(c)  Signals for computing $y_1$

(d)  Signals for computing $y_2$

**Figure 1.18**  Graphical representation of convolution.

## 1.6   PROPERTIES OF DIGITAL FILTERS

We restricted the form of the digital filter but not because we are short on imagination or those were the only forms possible. Rather, we chose the recursive and nonrecursive forms because they exhibited some properties that will allow us to build design and analysis tools for digital filters. This section presents some of the properties that will be useful in future developments.

We will consider only the recursive form, because the nonrecursive form is a special case. What we decide for the recursive form will also hold for the nonrecursive, so we have lost nothing.

### Superposition

The property of superposition specifies how the filter behaves with inputs that are sums of data sequences. It is not that sums of sequences are interesting in themselves. Rather, superposition is used as a tool that will simplify the design and analysis.

Suppose that we have a filter that produces an output sequence of $y_k$ when we apply the input sequence, $x_k$. Also suppose that the same filter produces an output of $v_k$ when we apply the input of $u_k$. What does the filter produce when we apply the sum, $x_k + u_k$, to the input? If you guessed $y_k + v_k$, you are correct. Let's see why.

We supposed that $x_k$ produced $y_k$ and $u_k$ produced $v_k$. Therefore, the outputs can be expresses in terms of the filter coefficients and the inputs.

$$y_k = \sum_{i=-m}^{m} c_i x_{k-i} + \sum_{i=1}^{n} d_i y_{k-i} \tag{1.55}$$

and

$$v_k = \sum_{i=-m}^{m} c_i u_{k-i} + \sum_{i=1}^{n} d_i v_{k-i} \tag{1.56}$$

Let's add the two equations.

$$y_k + v_k = \sum_{i=-m}^{m} c_i \left( x_{k-i} + u_{k-i} \right) + \sum_{i=1}^{n} d_i \left( y_{k-i} + v_{k-i} \right) \tag{1.57}$$

Therefore, $y_k + v_k$ is the output of the filter when $x_k + u_k$ is applied as the input. The output of this filter is just the sum of the outputs that are associated with the individual inputs.

This property is called *superposition*. It says that if the sum of two sequences is presented to the input of the filter, the resulting output is simply the sum of the outputs that are produced if the inputs were applied one at a time. Superposition is defined formally below.

**Definition:** Superposition.

A filter exhibits the property of superposition if and only if the input of $x + u$ generates an output of $y + v$, where $y$ is the output generated by $x$, alone, and $v$ is the output generated by $u$. This must hold for all $x$ and $u$ inputs.

The definition is illustrated in figure 1.19.

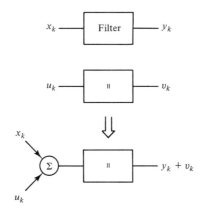

**Figure 1.19** Superposition.

The preceding discussion showed that our digital filters exhibit the property of superposition. It is quite easy to specify simple filters that do not obey superposition. Let's look at one.

**Example:** A Filter without Superposition

Consider the "squaring" filter defined below. Note that this filter does not satisfy our definition of a recursive filter — be suspicious.

$$y_k = (x_k)^2 \tag{1.58}$$

Does this filter exhibit the superposition property? We start the investigation by applying the general input $x_k$ and $u_k$ to generate $y_k$ and $v_k$.

$$y_k = (x_k)^2 \tag{1.59}$$

and

$$v_k = (u_k)^2 \tag{1.60}$$

Now apply the sum of the inputs to the filter and see if the resulting output is $y_k + v_k$.

$$? = (x_k + u_k)^2 \tag{1.61}$$

or

$$? = (x_k)^2 + 2x_k u_k + (u_k)^2 \tag{1.62}$$

The two squared quantities are the outputs, $y_k$ and $v_k$. But the cross term, $2x_k u_k$, prevents this filter from satisfying the requirements for superposition — the square of the sum does not equal the sum of the squares.

$$? = y_k + v_k + 2x_k u_k \neq y_k + v_k \tag{1.63}$$

The "squaring" filter does not exhibit the property of superposition.

## Homogeneity

The property of homogeneity specifies how the filter behaves when the input is scaled by a constant. Again, homogeneity is a means to an end, not an end in itself.

Suppose that we have a filter that produces an output $y_k$ when its input is $x_k$. What happens when we apply a scaled version, $ax_k$, to the filter? If the scaling constant, $a$, is an integer, we can use the superposition property of digital filters to show that the output is simply scaled by the same value, $a$. When the scaling factor is noninteger, we must investigate.

Suppose that an $x_k$ input produces the output $y_k$. Furthermore, suppose that $ax_k$ ($x_k$ multiplied by the constant $a$) produces the output $z_k$. The following development shows that $z_k$ really is $ay_k$, the original output scaled by $a$.

$$y_k = \sum_{i=-m}^{m} c_i x_{k-i} + \sum_{i=1}^{n} d_i y_{k-i} \tag{1.64}$$

and

$$z_k = \sum_{i=-m}^{m} c_i a x_{k-i} + \sum_{i=1}^{n} d_i z_{k-i} \tag{1.65}$$

Now, divide the entire second equation by the constant $a$ (we assume that $a \neq 0$).

$$\frac{z_k}{a} = \sum_{i=-m}^{m} c_i x_{k-i} + \sum_{i=1}^{n} d_i \frac{z_{k-i}}{a} \tag{1.66}$$

This equation is identical to equation 1.64 with $z_k/a$ taking the place of $y_k$. Therefore, $z_k/a = y_k$ or $ay_k = z_k$ — scaling the input of a digital filter simply scales the output by the same amount.

## Definition: Homogeneity.

A filter exhibits the property of homogeneity if and only if the input of $ax_k$ generates an output $ay_k$, where $y_k$ is the output generated by $x_k$. This must hold for all $x_k$ and all constants, $a$.

This definition is illustrated in Figure 1.20.

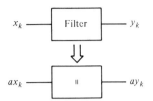

**Figure 1.20** Homogeneity.

**Shift Invariance**

   The last property that we will consider is *shift invariance*. This specifies how the filter responds to index shifts of the inputs.

   Suppose we have a filter that produces an output of $y_k$ when presented with an input of $x_k$. What is the filter's output when a shifted version of $x_k$, say $x_{k+l}$, is applied as the input? If you guessed that the filter generates a shifted version of the original output, you are right again.

   We begin the discussion as before. Assume that the original input, $x_k$, produces an output, $y_k$. Furthermore, assume that the filter produces an output of $z_k$ when we shift the original input by $l$ indices — the input is now $x_{k+l}$. We will now show the relationship between $y_k$ and $z_k$.

   From the definition of the recursive digital filter, we see that the outputs are related to the inputs and the filter's coefficient.

$$y_k = \sum_{i=-m}^{m} c_i x_{k-i} + \sum_{i=1}^{n} d_i y_{k-i} \tag{1.67}$$

and

$$z_j = \sum_{i=-m}^{m} c_i x_{j+l-i} + \sum_{i=1}^{n} d_i z_{j-i} \tag{1.68}$$

   Note that the index in the second equation is $j$ instead of $k$. This should not be an issue, because the "name" of the index is completely arbitrary. If it is arbitrary, we can substitute it at will. Let's replace $j + l$ with $k$ in the second equation — substitute $k = j + l$, or equivalently $j = k - l$. The second equation becomes

$$z_{k-l} = \sum_{i=-m}^{m} c_i x_{k-i} + \sum_{i=1}^{n} d_i z_{k-l-i} \tag{1.69}$$

This equation is exactly the first equation with $z_{k-l}$ replacing $y_k$. Therefore,

$$z_{k-l} = y_k \tag{1.70}$$

or

$$z_k = y_{k+l} \tag{1.71}$$

Shifting the input by $l$ indices causes the output to be shifted the same amount. This property is called *shift invariance*, and is defined formally below.

**Definition:** Shift Invariance.

A filter exhibits the property of shift invariance if and only if the input of $x_{k+l}$ generates the output of $y_{k+l}$, where $y_k$ is the output generated by $x_k$. This must hold for all inputs and integer $l$.

This definition is illustrated in Figure 1.21.

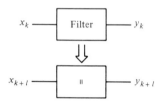

**Figure 1.21** Shift-invariance.

## Linear Time-Invariant Filters

A filter that exhibits the properties of superposition, homogeneity, and shift invariance is called a *linear time-invariant filter*. The recursive filter has all those properties, so it is linear.

It is important to keep these characteristics in perspective. We are restricting our investigation to linear digital filters, making it easier to develop design and analysis tools. There is a wide range of very useful nonlinear digital filters, but we will ignore these in this introductory treatment.

## Impulse Response Revisited

In an earlier treatment, we showed that the input-output relationship for a nonrecursive filter is the convolution of the input and the filter's inpulse response. Unfortunately, we could not develop the input-output relationship for a recursive filter. Now that linear systems are defined, we can revisit the problem and present a better development.

We know that if we apply an impulse, say $i_k$, to the filter, the filter will produce its impulse response, $h_k$. If we present a shifted impulse to the filter, say $i_{k+l}$, the filter will produce a shifted impulse response, $h_{k+l}$. If we presented a shifted and scaled impulse to the filter, $ai_{k+l}$, the filter's output is the impulse response that is shifted and scaled, $ah_{k+l}$. These observations are just straightforward applications of the properties of linear time-invariant filters.

Suppose that we represent the input to a filter as a sum of shifted impulses.

Each impulse is weighted by a value of the input.

$$x_k = \sum_{j=-\infty}^{\infty} x_j i_{k-j} \qquad (1.72)$$

This decomposition of the input is illustrated in Figure 1.22. We are essentially isolating each term of the input sequence.

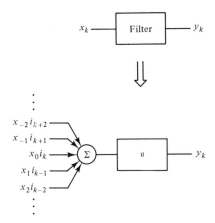

**Figure 1.22**  Derivation of convolution result.

Because of superpositon and homogeneity, the output of the filter is just the sum of the filter's output to each one of the inputs. But we know that each scaled and shifted impulse generates a scaled and shifted impulse response. Therefore, the filter's output is the sum of all these impulse responses.

$$y_k = \sum_{j=-\infty}^{\infty} x_j h_{k-j} \qquad (1.73)$$

This equation is an alternative form of the convolution. We produce the other form by substituting $l = k - j$.

$$y_k = \sum_{l=-\infty}^{\infty} h_l x_{k-l} \qquad (1.74)$$

Therefore, the input and output are related through the convolution of the impulse response. This is a much more intuitive development than our previous method. The notions of linear systems provided us with the tools that were necessary for this development.

## 1.7   COMBINATIONS OF DIGITAL FILTERS

This section explores the combination of digital filters. We consider combinations of filters for three reasons:

1. Some systems are composed of combinations of digital filters.
2. Some design schemes break the filter into a combination of filters. Each of these individual filters is easier to design than the original filter.
3. Manipulating combinations of filters gives you more practice with the filter definitions and the concepts of impulse response and linearity.

This section deals solely with the cascade and the parallel combination of filters. Other arrangements are possible, but they will not be considered, because we will not need them in the future.

The cascade of two filters is shown in Figure 1.23. The output of one filter serves as the input to the other. The cascade form has one input (far left) and one output (far right). Therefore, the cascade of two filters can be represented as a new, equivalent filter, shown by the dotted lines in figure 1.23.

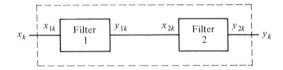

**Figure 1.23**  Cascade combination of two filters.

The parallel form is shown in Figure 1.24. Both filters share a common input, so this form also has only one input. The output of the parallel filters is just the sum of the individual filters' outputs. Hence this form has a single output. Again, a larger, equivalent filter could be drawn around the parallel combination.

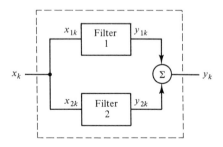

**Figure 1.24**  Parallel combination of filters.

What is the relationship between the impulse responses of these equivalent filters and those of the smaller filters? In other words, if you parallel two filters, what is the impulse response of the equivalent filter?

Let's begin with the parallel form, because it is simpler. Unfortunately, we will have to modify the standard notation if we wish to work the problem easily. We must specify the inputs, outputs, and impulse responses for the individual filters and the equivalent filter. A pair of subscripts will denote the particular filter and the sequence index. The first subscript denotes which filter we are dealing with, and the second subscript is the sequence index. Therefore, $x_{1k}$ is the input to filter 1, $x_{2k}$ is the input to filter 2, and $x_k$ is the input to the equivalent filter. Similar notation holds for the filters' outputs, the coefficients, and impulse responses.

The output of the equivalent parallel filter is simply the sum of the outputs of the individual filters.

$$y_k = y_{1k} + y_{2k} \tag{1.75}$$

The individual filters share the same input.

$$x_{1k} = x_{2k} = x_k \tag{1.76}$$

Therefore, the output of the equivalent filter can be expressed in terms of the input to the filter and the coefficients of the individual filters.

$$y_k = \sum_{i=-m}^{m} (c_{1i} + c_{2i})\, x_{k-i} + \sum_{i=1}^{n} \left( d_{1i} y_{1(k-i)} + d_{2i} y_{2(k-i)} \right) \tag{1.77}$$

The first sum of this equation looks promising; the equivalent filter has nonrecursive coefficients that are the sum of the coefficients of the individual filters. But the recursive term is much more complicated, because there is no straightforward way of relating the weighted sum of the individual outputs to the overall output. If both filters have identical recursive coefficients ($d_{1i} = d_{2i}$), the coefficients of the equivalent filter are simply the sum of the coefficients of the individuals. Otherwise, we cannot say much about the recursive coefficients.

Let's try another approach. Rather than dealing with the coefficients, find the relationship between the impulse responses. Denote the impulse response of the first filter $h_{1k}$ and the impulse response of the second filter $h_{2k}$. The impulse response of the equivalent filter is $h_k$. How are these related?

First note that the impulse response is the filter's output when its input is an impulse (remember?). Therefore,

$$h_k = y_k \qquad \text{when} \quad x_k = \text{impulse} \tag{1.78}$$

But the output is just the sum of the individual outputs.

$$h_k = y_{1k} + y_{2k} \qquad \text{when} \quad x_k = \text{impulse} \tag{1.79}$$

Remember that the filters share the same input, so $y_{1k}$ and $y_{2k}$ are just the impulse responses of filter 1 and 2. Hence we have shown that the impulse response of the equivalent parallel filter is the sum of the impulse responses of the individual filters.

$$h_k = h_{1k} + h_{2k} \tag{1.80}$$

Note that we took two approaches to this problem. The first one was direct but provided few usable results. We could conclude only that the nonrecursive coefficients of the parallel form add. The second approach was more abstract – and more productive. We ignored the filter definitions and proceeded with the notion of impulse response, so were able to relate the impulse responses for all filters. A similar development could be used to compute the step and ramp responses of the parallel form. This approach could also be used to compute the various responses of three or more filters in parallel. You have probably already guessed the result.

Let's follow a similar line of reasoning and compute the equivalent impulse response for the cascade form. In this case, the input to the first filter is $x_k$, and the input to the second filter is the output of the first. The output of the equivalent cascade form is the output of the second filter.

$$x_{1k} = x_k \qquad x_{2k} = y_{1k} \qquad y_k = y_{2k} \tag{1.81}$$

Suppose that we apply an impulse to the first filter.

$$x_k = \text{impulse} \tag{1.82}$$

The output of the first filter is just the first filter's impulse response, $h_{1k}$. Therefore, the output of the equivalent cascade form is the second filter's response to the first filter's impulse response. We know, or should know, that this is a convolution of the two impulse responses.

$$h_k = \sum_{l=-\infty}^{\infty} h_{1l} h_{2(k-l)} \tag{1.83}$$

Hence the impulse response of the equivalent cascade filter is the convolution of the impulse responses of the individual filters.

These lines of reasoning can be extended to many filters in cascade by grouping the filters into pairs, computing the equivalent impulse responses for the pairs, then grouping the pairs into pairs, and so on. Very complicated arrangements of filters can be handled by repeatedly applying the parallel and cascade results to the filters. This is illustrated in Figure 1.25.

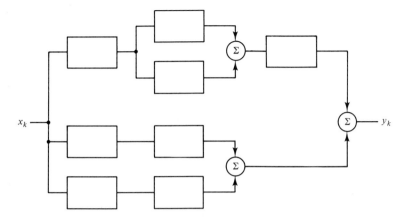

**Figure 1.25** Arbitrary arrangement of filters showing
cascade and parallel forms.

## 1.8  SUMMARY

In this chapter you have been introduced to the world of digital filtering. We
have found that a digital filter accepts a digital input sequence and produces a
digital output. We have restricted our attention to the recursive and nonrecursive
forms of digital filters. In both cases the filters are completely specified by their
coefficients. The impulse response plays a very important role in characterizing the
digital filter, because the output of any filter can be expressed as the convolution
of the input and the filter's impulse response.

## EXERCISES

1-1. Evaluate the following sums.

(a) $\sum_{j=-1}^{4}(j)^2$

(b) $\sum_{k=-1}^{3}(j)^2$

(c) $\sum_{j=-1}^{3} c_j x_{-1}$      where $c_k = k - 3$ and $x_l = l$

1-2. Find the maximum sampling period, $T_{max}$, that will prevent aliasing of
the following analog signals.

(a) $\sin 100t$

(b) $\cos 0.1\pi t$

1-3. Are the following analog signals aliased when sampled at 100 samples/sec $(T = 0.01)$?

  (a) $\sin 10\pi t$

  (b) $\cos 320t$

  (c) $\cos 400t$

1-4. Compute the digital frequencies, $\omega'$ (radians per sample), for the following analog signals when sampled. Assume a sampling rate of 10 samples/sec.

  (a) $\sin 0.4t$

  (b) $\cos 0.6t$

  (c) $\cos 0.8t$

1-5. Compute the analog aliased frequencies, $\omega'/T$, for Exercise 1-4.

1-6. Suppose that we had defined $\omega'$ differently by restricting it from 0 to $2\pi$ instead of $-\pi$ to $\pi$. Rederive equation (1.18) (the condition for no aliasing) under the new definition.

1-7. Find the impulse responses of the following filters.

  (a) $y_k = 3x_{k-2}$

  (b) $y_k = 4x_{k-1} + 3x_{k+1} + 2x_{k+2}$

  (c) $y_k = 3x_{k-1}^2$ (It is not linear, but it has an impulse response.)

1-8. Find the first 10 nonzero terms of the impulse responses of the following recursive filters.

  (a) $y_k = x_k + 3y_{k-1}$

  (b) $y_k = 2x_{k-2} + 3y_{k-1}$

  (c) $y_k = 2x_{k-2} + x_k + 3y_{k-1}$

  (d) $y_k = x_k + 0.5y_{k-1} + y_{k-2}$

1-9. Compare the impulse responses of parts (a) and (b) of Exercise 1-8. What two properties of linear time-invariant filters are illustrated?

1-10. Compare the impulse responses of parts (a) and (b) of Exercise 1-8 with the response of part (c). How are they related, and what properties of linear, time-invariant filters are illustrated?

1-11. Find the ramp responses of the following filters.

  (a) $y_k = 3x_{k-2}$

(b) $y_k = 4x_{k-1} + 2x_{k+2}$

1-12. Find the first 10 nonzero terms of the ramp responses of the following filters.

(a) $y_k = x_k + 3y_{k-1}$

(b) $y_k = 2x_{k-2} + x_k + 3y_{k-1} + y_{k-2}$

1-13. Design a digital filter that converts a ramp to a step function (an input of a ramp generates an output of a step).

1-14. Design a digital filter that converts a ramp to an impulse function.

1-15. Are the following digital filters linear, time invariant? If not, why not?

(a) $y_k = \sqrt{2}x_k + x_k + y_{k-4}$

(b) $y_k = 0x_k + 3y_{k-2}$

(c) $y_k = x_{k-3} + 2y_k$

(d) $y_{k+2} = x_{k-1} + y_{k+1}$

(e) $y_k = 0.5x_k + 0.5x_{k-1} + 1$

(f) $y_k = kx_k + x_{k-1}$

(g) $y_k = \sin(\pi i)x_k + 3y_{k-1}$

(h) $y_k = x_k^2$

(i) $y_k = x_k + 1 - y_{k-1} - 1$

1-16. Compute the impulse response of the cascade of the following two filters.

$y_{1k} = x_{1k} + x_{1(k-1)}$

$y_{2k} = 2x_{2(k+1)} + x_{2k} - 2x_{2(k-1)}$      Watch the notation.

1-17. Compute the first 10 nonzero terms of the impulse response of the cascade of the following filters.

$y_{1k} = x_{1k} + 0.5y_{1(k-1)}$

$y_{2k} = x_{2(k-1)} + y_{2(k-1)}$      Watch the notation.

1-18. Design digital filters with the following impulse responses.

(a) $\ldots, h_0 = 0, h_1 = 1, h_2 = 2, h_3 = 0, \ldots$

(b) $\ldots, h_1 = 0, h_2 = 2, h_3 = 1, h_4 = \frac{1}{2}, h_5 = \frac{1}{4}, \ldots$

(c) $\ldots, h_{-2} = 0, h_{-1} = 2, h_0 = 3, h_1 = 3, h_2 = 3, \ldots$

(d) $\ldots, h_{-1} = 0, h_0 = 1, h_1 = 1, h_2 = \frac{1}{4}, h_3 = \frac{1}{4}, h_4 = \frac{1}{16}, h_5 = \frac{1}{16}, h_6 = \frac{1}{64}, h_7 = \frac{1}{64}, \ldots$

1-19. Design digital filters with impulse responses that are twice the amplitude of the impulse responses of the following filters.

    (a) $y_k = x_{k-1} + x_{k+1}$

    (b) $y_k = 2x_{k-2} + 0.9y_{k-1}$

    (c) $y_k = 2x_{k-1} + x_0 + 1.1y_{k-1}$

    What do you conclude?

1-20. Perform the convolution of the following digital sequences. Assume that all nonspecified terms are zero.

    (a) $x_0 = 1, x_1 = 2, x_2 = 3$      with      $z_1 = 2, z_2 = 1$

    (b) $x_{-1} = 2, x_0 = 1$      with      $z_k = \frac{1}{2}^k$ for $k \geq 0$

1-21. Consider the following digital sequences.

$$x_k = \begin{cases} \neq 0 & \text{if } a \leq k \leq b \\ 0 & \text{otherwise} \end{cases}$$

$$z_k = \begin{cases} \neq 0 & \text{if } c \leq k \leq d \\ 0 & \text{otherwise} \end{cases}$$

    (a) What is the greatest number of nonzero terms in the convolution of $x_k$ and $z_k$?

    (b) What is the fewest number of nonzero terms in the convolution?

    (c) What is the smallest index of a nonzero term of the convolution?

    (d) What is the largest index of a nonzero term of the convolution?

1-22. Recursive digital filters are also called infinite impulse response (IIR) filters. This is because the impulse responses can have an infinite number of nonzero terms. Compute the impulse response of the following IIR filter:

$$y_k = x_k - \frac{8}{27}x_{k-3} + \frac{2}{3}y_{k-1}$$

    Is it true that all IIR filters have infinitely long impulse responses?

# Frequency Response

At this point we understand the operation of digital filters, but we do not really have the tools to design them. We will become frustrated quickly if we attempt to design filters on the basis of coefficients or impulse response. There is a better way — characterizing and designing filters on the basis of the frequency response.

This chapter develops the concept of the frequency response of a digital filter. The frequency response is an abstraction of the operation of a digital filter. This is an elegant, if somewhat removed concept. However, once you master the frequency response you have a powerful tool for describing and designing digital filters.

## 2.1  MAGIC FUNCTIONS: EIGENFUNCTIONS

Our development begins with the search for a special set of functions. We are looking for functions that are relatively unaffected when passed through any filter, that is, inputs that are minimally altered by digital filters. It is fruitless to search for a function totally unaffected by passing though a filter. Such function does exist — the all-zero function, $x_k = 0$ — but it is neither interesting nor particularly useful. So let's look for a set of functions that are least affected by any digital filter. We will look for functions that are scaled by a constant only when they are passed though a filter. Such a function is called an *eigenfunction* and the scaling constant is called an *eigenvalue*.

**Definition:** Eigenfunctions and Eigenvalues.

The digital function, $e_k$, is an eigenfunction of a digital filter if and only if the output resulting from the application of $e_k$ to the input is simply $e_k$ multiplied by a constant. The constant is called the eigenvalue, $\lambda$, and it is a function of the particular eigenfunction and the filter. Because the input and output are related through the convolution of the impulse response, $h_k$, an eigenfunction must satisfy

$$\lambda e_k = \sum_{i=-\infty}^{\infty} h_i e_{k-i} \tag{2.0}$$

This definition is illustrated in Figure 2.1.

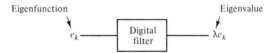

**Figure 2.1** Eigenfunctions and eigenvalues

There is no general technique for deriving the eigenfunction, nor even a method for showing that eigenfunctions exist. So we are going to search for the eigenfunction by proposing candidates and then trying them. If started from scratch, this type of search is both frustrating and fruitless. Fortunately, others have derived eigenfunctions and our search will be based on their results.

Why not try the impulse function as our first candidate? The impulse was an important, fundamental function in Chapter 1, but it is not an eigenfunction for a general digital filter. When an impulse is applied to the input of a filter, by definition, the output of the filter is the filter's impulse response. Few filters have an impulse response that is an impulse multiplied by a constant. Therefore, the impulse is not an eigenfunction for digital filters.

Using similar arguments, we can also dismiss the step and the ramp functions. Both of these functions are significantly altered when passed through a digital filter.

Let's turn to periodic functions, which are minimally affected when subjected to delays through digital filters. The first candidate is a cosine function of frequency $\omega$. The output of the filter is simply the convolution of the impulse response and $\cos \omega k$.

$$y_k = \sum_{i=-\infty}^{\infty} h_i \cos[\omega(k - i)] \tag{2.1}$$

The expression involves a cosine of the sum of angles. Looking into our past or a convenient book of tables, we find that the sum of angles can be alternately represented as products of sines and cosines.

$$\cos[\omega(k - i)] = \cos \omega k \cos \omega i - \sin \omega k \sin \omega i \tag{2.2}$$

Therefore, the output of the filter is the sum of a cosine and a sine wave, both at frequency $\omega$.

$$y_k = \sum_{i=-\infty}^{\infty} h_i \cos \omega k \cos \omega i + \sum_{i=-\infty}^{\infty} h_i \sin \omega k \sin \omega i$$

$$= \cos \omega k \left[ \sum_{i=-\infty}^{\infty} h_i \cos \omega i \right] + \sin(\omega k) \left[ \sum_{i=-\infty}^{\infty} h_i \sin \omega i \right]$$

(2.3)

The cosine function comes awfully close to satisfying the definition of an eigenfunction. The first term of the output is simply the input, $\cos \omega k$, multiplied by the summation. The value of the summation is determined by the filter's impulse response and the frequency of the input, and does not vary with time. Therefore, the cosine looks like an eigenfunction if we ignore the second term. Unfortunately, the second term is a sine wave with frequency $\omega$ and amplitude that is determined by the frequency and the impulse response of the filter. Because of this sine term, the cosine is not an eigenfunction.

We can repeat the development with a sine wave instead of a cosine and come to a similar conclusion. The sine wave is also almost an eigenfunction, because the output involves a sine and a cosine term.

The sines and cosines miss being eigenfunctions because a sine-wave input can generate cosine components in the output, and a cosine input can cause sine components in the output. This suggests that we look for a function that is a mixture of sines and cosines. Such a function satisfies the definition of an eigenfunction even when the output contains both sines and cosines. However, we cannot build this composite function by simply adding a cosine and a sine, because simple addition results in a sine or cosine with a phase shift.

$$a \cos \omega k + b \sin \omega k = c \cos(\omega k + \phi)$$

(2.4)

Therefore, we must combine the cosine and the sine terms in a manner that prevents them from collapsing into a single term with a phase shift. This suggests a complex function of the cosine and sine — the complex exponential.

If you feel rusty with complex numbers you should visit the first few sections of Appendix B, which introduces imaginary and complex numbers and explains some of the common complex operations. You should spend some effort in understanding these beasts because they play an important role in digital filter analysis.

The next candidate for the eigenvalue is a complex combination of a sine and cosine — the cosine is the real part of this complex function and the sine is the imaginary.

$$\cos \omega k + j \sin \omega k$$

(2.5)

where

$$j = \sqrt{-1}$$

(2.6)

Some of you may have used $i$ as the square root of $-1$. We use $j$ here because digital filtering comes from electrical engineering and they reserve the symbol $i$ for current.

This complex function can be expressed as a complex exponential by exploiting Euler's identity.

$$e^{j\omega k} = \cos \omega k + j \sin \omega k \tag{2.7}$$

Because the complex notation is more compact, we will generally prefer it to the sine-cosine form.

We have spent a good deal of effort introducing this complex exponential function, and it is all worthwhile because this is the long-awaited eigenfunction. We verify it by applying this function to a filter. The output is simply the convolution.

$$y_k = \sum_{i=-\infty}^{\infty} h_i e^{j[\omega(k-i)]} \tag{2.8}$$

But

$$e^{j[\omega(k-i)]} = e^{j\omega k} e^{-j\omega i} \tag{2.9}$$

Therefore,

$$y_k = \sum_{i=-\infty}^{\infty} h_i e^{j\omega k} e^{-j\omega i} \tag{2.10}$$

Note that the $e^{j\omega k}$ term is independent of the index of summation, $i$. Therefore, this term can be factored out of the summation.

$$y_k = e^{j\omega k} \left[ \sum_{i=-\infty}^{\infty} h_i e^{-j\omega i} \right] \tag{2.11}$$

The output is just the input multiplied by the term in brackets. This multiplication term is a function of the filter's impulse response and the frequency of the input, $\omega$, and is independent of $k$. So the complex exponential is an eigenfunction of all digital filters. The corresponding eigenvalue is the quantity in the brackets. The eigenvalue plays such an important role in the analysis and design of digital filters that it is given a special name, the frequency response, and it is denoted by $\mathcal{H}(\omega)$. Therefore, the frequency response is a weighted sum of the filter's impulse response.

$$\mathcal{H}(\omega) = \sum_{i=-\infty}^{\infty} h_i e^{-j\omega i} \tag{2.12}$$

The frequency response is a complex function with an independent variable of $\omega$. The character of the function is completely determined by the impulse response of the digital filter — different impulse responses result in different frequency responses.

## 2.2   FREQUENCY RESPONSE OF DIGITAL FILTERS

The frequency response can also be related to the coefficients of the digital filter. First, consider a nonrecursive filter with an input of $e^{j\omega k}$.

$$y_k = \sum_{i=-m}^{m} c_i e^{j[\omega(k-i)]} \tag{2.13}$$

Again, the exponential is factored into a term that depends on $k$ and another that depends on $i$.

$$y_k = e^{j\omega k} \sum_{i=-m}^{m} c_i e^{-j\omega i} \tag{2.14}$$

We recognize $e^{j\omega k}$ as the eigenfunction and the summation as the eigenvalue, now called the filter's frequency response.

$$\mathcal{H}(\omega) = \sum_{i=-m}^{m} c_i e^{-j\omega i} \tag{2.15}$$

This equation is just equation (2.12) for the special case of nonrecursive filters, because for these filters $h_i = c_i$.

The derivation of the frequency response of the recursive filter is more complicated. The problem is that the recursive filter has output terms on both sides of the equation — we cannot simply apply an input and then factor the output.

Start the derivation by applying $e^{j\omega k}$ to the input of a recursive filter.

$$y_k = \sum_{i=-m}^{m} c_i e^{j[\omega(k-i)]} + \sum_{i=1}^{n} d_i y_{k-i} \tag{2.16}$$

The trick is to express the output solely in terms of the input and the frequency response. We have previously shown that the output is just input, $e^{j\omega k}$, scaled by the frequency response. Therefore,

$$y_k = \mathcal{H}(\omega) e^{j\omega k} \tag{2.17}$$

This result holds for all $k$. So

$$y_{k-i} = \mathcal{H}(\omega) e^{j[\omega(k-i)]}$$

The trick is consummated by expressing the output in terms of the input and frequency response.

$$\mathcal{H}(\omega) e^{j\omega k} = \sum_{i=-m}^{m} c_i e^{j[\omega(k-i)]} + \sum_{i=1}^{n} d_i \mathcal{H}(\omega) e^{j[\omega(k-i)]} \tag{2.18}$$

We finish the derivation with a few strokes of algebra. Multiply both sides of the equation by $e^{-j\omega k}$ and collect the $\mathcal{H}$ terms on the left side.

$$\mathcal{H}(\omega)\left[1 - \sum_{i=1}^{n} d_i e^{-j\omega i}\right] = \sum_{i=-m}^{m} c_i e^{-j\omega i} \tag{2.19}$$

Divide both sides by the bracketed term.

$$\mathcal{H}(\omega) = \frac{\sum_{i=-m}^{m} c_i e^{-j\omega i}}{1 - \sum_{i=1}^{n} d_i e^{-j\omega i}} \tag{2.20}$$

The frequency response of a recursive digital filter is determined by the weighted sums of the recursive and nonrecursive coefficients. As before, the nonrecursive coefficients appear in the numerator and the recursive coefficients in the denominator. Note that this result is consistent with the frequency response derived for the nonrecursive filter. When all the recursive coefficients are zero, the denominator is 1.

The previous form is compact and easy to manipulate. However, for computational purposes, it is best to express the frequency response in terms of sines and cosines:

$$\mathcal{H}(\omega) = \frac{\sum_{i=-m}^{m} c_i \cos \omega i - j \sum_{i=-m}^{m} c_i \sin \omega i}{1 - \sum_{i=1}^{n} d_i \cos \omega i + j \sum_{i=1}^{n} d_i \sin \omega i} \tag{2.21}$$

In general, the frequency response is a complex function of $\omega$ — it has a real and an imaginary component. How do we go about representing such a function? The most straightforward approach is to represent it as two functions of $\omega$, one for the real part and one for the imaginary component. Unfortunately, this representation is not especially useful, since designers are seldom interested in the real or imaginary components of $\mathcal{H}(\omega)$ themselves. Rather, they want a representation that readily shows what effect the filter has on $e^{j\omega k}$ terms. A magnitude-phase representation of $\mathcal{H}$ turns out to be much more useful.

A complex number can be expressed in terms of its real and imaginary parts,

$$x = \text{Re}\{x\} + j\text{Im}\{x\} \tag{2.22}$$

or in terms of its magnitude and phase,

$$x = |x| e^{j\phi} \tag{2.23}$$

The magnitude of the complex number is the square root of the sum of the squares of the real and imaginary component.

$$|x| = \sqrt{\text{Re}\{x\}^2 + \text{Im}\{x\}^2} \tag{2.24}$$

The angle of the complex number is the angle defined by the real and the complex parts.

$$\phi = \tan^{-1}\left[\frac{\mathrm{Im}\,\{x\}}{\mathrm{Re}\,\{x\}}\right] \tag{2.25}$$

There is a one-to-one correspondence between the magnitude-phase representation and the real-imaginary representation — one is equivalent to the other.

**Example:**  Compute the frequency response of the following nonrecursive digital filter.

$$y_k = 0.04x_k - 0.05x_{k-2} + 0.06x_{k-4} - 0.11x_{k-6} + 0.32x_{k-8}$$
$$- 0.5x_{k-9} + 0.32x_{k-10} - .11x_{k-12} + .06x_{k-14} - .05x_{k-16} + .04x_{k-18} \tag{2.26}$$

We begin the computation by applying these coefficients to equation (2.15). Since these coefficients are real, we can easily break the frequency response into its real and imaginary components. The real part of the frequency response is the "cosine" (remember Euler?) part of equation (2.15) and is shown below.

$$\mathrm{Re}\{\mathcal{H}(\omega)\} = 0.04\cos 0\omega - 0.05\cos 2\omega + 0.06\cos 4\omega - 0.11\cos 6\omega$$
$$+ 0.32\cos 8\omega - 0.5\cos 9\omega + 0.32\cos 10\omega - 0.11\cos 12\omega \tag{2.27}$$
$$+ 0.06\cos 14\omega - 0.05\cos 16\omega + 0.04\cos 18\omega$$

The imaginary component of the frequency response is simply the "sine" part of equation (2.15) (remember that this holds only for nonrecursive filters with real coefficients).

$$\mathrm{Im}\{\mathcal{H}(\omega)\} = -0.04\sin 0\omega + 0.05\sin 2\omega - 0.06\sin 4\omega + 0.11\sin 6\omega$$
$$- 0.32\sin 8\omega + 0.5\sin 9\omega - 0.32\sin 10\omega + 0.11\sin 12\omega \tag{2.28}$$
$$- 0.06\sin 14\omega + 0.05\sin 16\omega - 0.04\sin 18\omega$$

These expressions for the real and imaginary components of the frequency response are meaningless. So it is better to present the frequency response in terms of its magnitude and phase. The magnitude is found by applying equations (2.27) and (2.28) to equation (2.24).

$$|\mathcal{H}(\omega)| = \sqrt{\mathrm{Re}\{\mathcal{H}(\omega)\}^2 + \mathrm{Im}\{\mathcal{H}(\omega)\}^2} \tag{2.29}$$

The phase of this filter at frequency $\omega$ is computed by applying the real and imaginary components to equation (2.25).

$$\phi(\omega) = \tan^{-1}\frac{\mathrm{Im}\{\mathcal{H}(\omega)\}}{\mathrm{Re}\{\mathcal{H}(\omega)\}} \tag{2.30}$$

Unfortunately, these expressions for the magnitude and phase do not have a nice, closed-form solution. So we must resort to computer evaluation of the equations and present the magnitude and phase as plots. Figure 2.2 shows the magnitude and phase of this filter's frequency response for $-\pi < \omega \leq \pi$. This filter has a large magnitude for frequencies close to $-\pi$ and $\pi$ and a very small magnitude between $-\pi/2$ and $\pi/2$. In other words, this filter has a large eigenvalue for high frequency exponentials and small eigenvalues for lower-frequency complex exponentials. For this reason, this filter is called a *high-pass filter* — it passes high frequency exponentials by scaling them with a large eigenvalue. Figure 2.2b shows the phase of the frequency response changing from $-\pi$ to $\pi$ with the frequency of the input. The phase plot shows how the angle of the complex eigenvalue changes with input frequency.

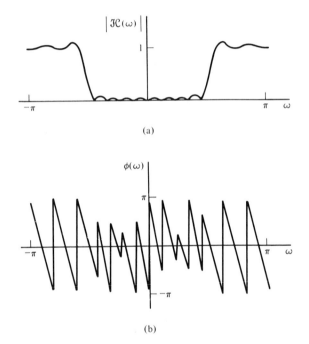

(a)

(b)

**Figure 2.2** Frequency response of a highpass filter: (a) magnitude of the frequency response; (b) phase of the frequency response.

Generally, we will express the frequency response by its magnitude and phase.

$$\mathcal{H}(\omega) = |\mathcal{H}(\omega)| e^{j\phi(\omega)} \tag{2.31}$$

So if we apply an $e^{j\omega k}$ to the input of the filter, the output is the input scaled by

$|\mathcal{H}(\omega)|$ and phase-shifted (is that a verb?) by $\phi(\omega)$.

$$
\begin{aligned}
y_k &= \mathcal{H}(\omega)e^{j\omega k} \\
&= |\mathcal{H}(\omega)|\, e^{j[\omega k + \phi(\omega)]}
\end{aligned}
\tag{2.32}
$$

Note that the scaling and phase shift are functions of the input frequency, $\omega$, and the coefficients of the filter, through $\mathcal{H}(\omega)$. Therefore, the magnitude and phase representation of the frequency response gives the designer a good deal of information about the filter — much more than a real-imaginary representation provides.

**Example:**   Use the frequency response to compute the output of equation (2.26) when $\cos\omega k$ is applied as an input.

We could resort to the techniques of Chapter 1 and apply $\cos\omega k$ directly to the filter. But the example suggests that we use concepts developed from the frequency response work. The frequency response tells us how the filter responds to complex exponentials, and fortunately $\cos\omega k$ can be written as the sum of two exponentials.

$$
\cos(\omega k) = \frac{1}{2}\left(e^{j\omega k} + e^{-j\omega k}\right)
\tag{2.33}
$$

So rather than applying the cosine to the filter, we will compute the filter's output by applying the sum of the exponentials [the right-hand side of equation (2.33)].

Applying $e^{j\omega k}$ to the filter produces an output of $\mathcal{H}(\omega)e^{j\omega k}$ or, in magnitude and phase notation, $|\mathcal{H}(\omega)|\, e^{j\omega k + \phi(\omega)}$. Therefore, when $\cos\omega k$ is applied to the filter the filter's output is the composite of the outputs associated with the two exponentials.

$$
y_k = \frac{1}{2}\left[|\mathcal{H}(\omega)|\, e^{j\omega k + \phi(\omega)} + |\mathcal{H}(\omega)|\, e^{-j\omega k + \phi(-\omega)}\right]
\tag{2.34}
$$

Equation (2.34) is a complicated representation of the filter's output and really does not provide much meaning. But it can be greatly simplified by using some of the properties of the filter's frequency response. A close inspection of Figure 2.2 shows that the magnitude of this filter's frequency response is an even function, $|\mathcal{H}(\omega)| = |\mathcal{H}(-\omega)|$, and the phase is an odd function, $\phi(\omega) = -\phi(\omega)$. The application of these observations significantly reduces equation (2.34).

$$
\begin{aligned}
y_k &= |\mathcal{H}(\omega)|\,\frac{1}{2}\left[e^{j[\omega k + \phi(\omega)]} + e^{-j[\omega k + \phi(\omega)]}\right] \\
&= |\mathcal{H}(\omega)|\cos[\omega k + \phi(\omega)]
\end{aligned}
\tag{2.35}
$$

Equation (2.35) shows that the output of this filter is its input scaled by $|\mathcal{H}(\omega)|$ and shifted in phase by $\phi(\omega)$. So we can use plots like those contained in figure 2.2 to get a feeling for what a particular filter will do with cosines. For example, Figure 2.3 repeats the magnitude response of the high-pass filter and shows the the inputs and outputs for four frequency cosines. Figure 2.3b shows that a cosine of $0.72\pi$ rad/sec is attenuated by about 0.96 (the low "wiggle" of the filter's passband). Figure 2.3c shows that a slightly lower frequency cosine ( $0.61\pi$ rad/sec) has a slightly higher gain of about 1.1, which corresponds to the "hump" in the filter's frequency response at $0.61\pi$. Figure 2.3d shows that the output is very small when a $0.43\pi$ rad/sec cosine is applied to this filter. This frequency is associated with the first "zero" in the filter's frequency response. However, decreasing the frequency slightly to $0.39\pi$ increases the filter's gain to about 0.1.

Therefore, the frequency response tells us a great deal about the filter's response to cosines. We can easily extend this example to sinusoids by expressing the sine as a sum of two exponentials. The real power of the frequency response comes from the fact that most signals can be expressed as a sum of exponentials. Hence the frequency response can provide insight into the effect of a filter on arbitrary signals.

The next question is how to actually compute the magnitude and phase of the frequency response of a general digital filter. If we restrict our attention to nonrecursive filters, we can directly use the definitions of the magnitude and phase. Compute the real and imaginary part of the filter for each frequency and transform them into the magnitude and phase. The recursive filters pose a more difficult problem (they always do), because the frequency response is a ratio. We cannot directly apply the definitions of magnitude and phase to a ratio of complex functions. Rather, the denominator and numerators must be individually converted to the magnitude-phase representation, and the frequency response is the ratio of the magnitudes with a phase of the difference of the phases. Suppose that we express the numerator as a magnitude, say $\mathcal{N}(\omega)$ with a phase of $e^{j\nu(\omega)}$, and similarly express the denominator in magnitude and phase, $\mathcal{D}(\omega)e^{j\delta(\omega)}$. Then the frequency response is the ratio of these.

$$\mathcal{H}(\omega) = \frac{\mathcal{N}(\omega)e^{j\nu(\omega)}}{\mathcal{D}(\omega)e^{j\delta(\omega)}} \tag{2.36}$$

Such a division is just the ratio of the magnitudes with a phase of the difference of the phases.

$$\mathcal{H}(\omega) = \frac{\mathcal{N}(\omega)}{\mathcal{D}(\omega)}e^{j[\nu(\omega)-\delta(\omega)]} \tag{2.37}$$

or

$$|\mathcal{H}(\omega)| = \frac{\mathcal{N}(\omega)}{\mathcal{D}(\omega)} \tag{2.38}$$

and

$$\phi(\omega) = \nu(\omega) - \delta(\omega) \tag{2.39}$$

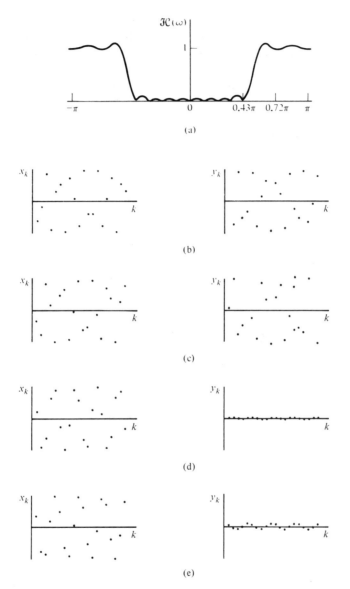

**Figure 2.3** Relationship between the frequency response and filter gain:
(a) magnitude of the frequency response;
(b) input and output for $\omega = 0.72\pi$;
(c) input and output for $\omega = 0.61\pi$;
(d) input and output for $\omega = 0.43\pi$;
(e) input and output for $\omega = 0.39\pi$.

Therefore, you can compute the magnitude-phase representation of the frequency response by finding the real and imaginary components of the denominator and numerator, then expressing the denominator and numerator in terms of magnitude and phase, and finally dividing the magnitudes and subtracting the phases. It is a great deal of work, but is conceptually straightforward. Note that the nonrecursive filters have a denominator with a unity magnitude and zero phase. Hence the frequency response of a nonrecursive filter is computed by just expressing the numerator as magnitude and phase.

**Example:** Compute the frequency response of a simple filter.

Consider the simple, recursive digital filter

$$y_k = 2x_k + 3x_{k-1} + 0.5y_{k-1} \tag{2.40}$$

Find its frequency response, $\mathcal{H}(\omega)$.

We begin the computation by substituting the specific values of the coefficients ($c_0 = 2, c_1 = 3, d_1 = 0.5$) into the general form of the frequency response.

$$\mathcal{H}(\omega) = \frac{2e^{-j\omega 0} + 3e^{-j\omega 1}}{1 - 0.5e^{-j\omega 1}} \tag{2.41}$$

It is a ratio, so we must compute the magnitude and phase for both the denominator and the numerator.

We first compute the magnitudes.

$$\mathcal{N}(\omega) = \sqrt{(2\cos\omega 0 + 3\cos\omega 1)^2 + (2\sin\omega 0 + 3\sin\omega 1)^2}$$
$$= \sqrt{(2 + 3\cos\omega)^2 + (3\sin\omega)^2} \tag{2.42}$$

and

$$\mathcal{D}(\omega) = \sqrt{(1 - 0.5\cos(\omega))^2 + (0.5\sin(\omega))^2} \tag{2.43}$$

The phases are the arctangents of the ratios of the imaginary and real parts.

$$\nu(\omega) = \tan^{-1}\left(\frac{3\sin\omega}{2 + 3\cos\omega}\right) \tag{2.44}$$

and

$$\delta(\omega) = \tan^{-1}\left(\frac{0.5\sin\omega}{1 - 0.5\cos\omega}\right) \tag{2.45}$$

All that is left to do is to divide the magnitudes and subtract the phases.

$$|\mathcal{H}(\omega)| = \sqrt{\frac{(2 + 3\cos\omega)^2 + (3\sin\omega)^2}{(1 - 0.5\cos\omega)^2 + (0.5\sin\omega)^2}} \tag{2.46}$$

and

$$\phi(\omega) = \tan^{-1}\left(\frac{3\sin\omega}{2 + 3\cos\omega}\right) - \tan^{-1}\left(\frac{0.5\sin\omega}{1 - 0.5\cos\omega}\right) \tag{2.47}$$

These functions are plotted in Figure 2.4.

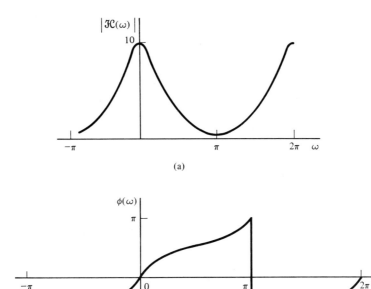

(a)

(b)

**Figure 2.4** Frequency response of $y_k = 2x_k + 3x_{k-1} + \frac{1}{2}y_{k-1}$:
(a) magnitude; (b) phase.

In the examples you have seen so far, the frequency responses are plotted on a linear scale. Occasionally a designer needs more resolution than a linear scale affords. In these instances it is preferable to plot a nonlinear function of the magnitude of the response. This function is selected so that the especially interesting values of the frequency response are plotted at a high resolution, and less important amplitudes are displayed with correspondingly lower resolution. Most of the time, designers are more concerned with the values of the frequency response around zero than they are with larger amplitudes. Because of this, most designers like to plot the *log* of the magnitude of the frequency response rather than the magnitude itself.

It is standard practice to display the magnitude of the frequency response in *decibels*, tenths of bels, which are defined as follows:

$$\mathcal{H}(\omega)_{dB} = 20 \log_{10} (|\mathcal{H}(\omega)|) \tag{2.48}$$

or

$$\mathcal{H}(\omega)_{dB} = 10 \log_{10} \left( |\mathcal{H}(\omega)|^2 \right) \tag{2.49}$$

The factors of 10 or 20 in the definitions are merely scale factors, which are included for convenience. It is the log function that gives the decibel its utility, as supported in the sketch in Figure 2.5 — $\mathcal{H}(\omega)_{dB}$ versus $\mathcal{H}(\omega)$. This curve changes slowly for large magnitudes, but becomes steeper as $|\mathcal{H}(\omega)|$ becomes closer to zero. A small change around $|\mathcal{H}(\omega)| = 0.1$ will have 10 times the effect of the same change around $|\mathcal{H}(\omega)| = 1$. Therefore, by plotting the frequency response in decibels, we differentially distribute the resolution — high resolution for small magnitudes and lower resolution for higher magnitudes.

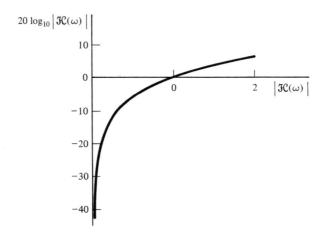

**Figure 2.5** Nonlinear decibel function.

Consider the frequency responses that are shown in Figure 2.6. Figure 2.6a shows the response of a 21-point ($m = 10$) nonrecursive digital filter. The linear plot shows some rippling between $\pi/2$ and $\pi$, but there is not enough resolution to see much detail. The rippling is far more apparent in Figure 2.4b, which is a plot of the same frequency response but in decibels. Figure 2.6b shows the lower-amplitude features of the response in far greater detail than does its linear counterpart. Generally, a decibel plot of the frequency response gives the designer a far better picture of the filter.

## 2.3   PROPERTIES OF THE FREQUENCY RESPONSE

The frequency response of the preceding example looks periodic. Is this a coincidence or is this a general property of frequency responses? Surprisingly, the frequency response is a periodic function of $\omega$, with a period of $2\pi$.

We will show the periodicity by adding $2\pi$ to the argument of the frequency response and then show that the result is still the frequency response. When we

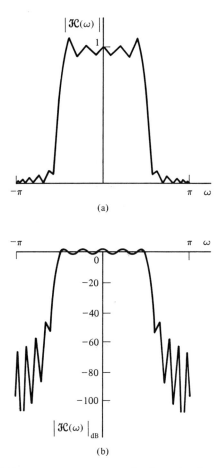

(a)

(b)

**Figure 2.6** Frequency response of a 21-point low pass filter:
(a) linear plot; (b) decibel plot.

add $2\pi$ to the response, we get a frequency-shifted frequency response.

$$\mathcal{H}(\omega + 2\pi) = \frac{\sum_{i=-m}^{m} c_i e^{-j(\omega i + 2\pi i)}}{1 - \sum_{i=1}^{n} d_i e^{-j(\omega i + 2\pi i)}} \tag{2.50}$$

We can factor the exponentials as we have done before.

$$e^{-j(\omega i + 2\pi i)} = e^{-j\omega i} e^{-j 2\pi i} \tag{2.51}$$

Because $i$ is an integer,

$$e^{-j 2\pi i} = 1 \tag{2.52}$$

Therefore,

$$e^{-j(\omega i + 2\pi i)} = e^{-j\omega i} \tag{2.53}$$

If we were to substitute this result back into the expression for $\mathcal{H}(\omega + 2\pi)$, we would obtain the regular (*i.e.*, unshifted) frequency response. So we conclude that a $2\pi$ shift of the argument has no effect on the frequency response.

$$\mathcal{H}(\omega + 2\pi) = \mathcal{H}(\omega) \tag{2.54}$$

The frequency response is periodic, both phase and magnitude, with a period of $2\pi$. It is necessary to compute the frequency response only over a $2\pi$ interval — we are just wasting our time if we compute more than one period of the response. It is conventional to use the frequency interval of $-\pi$ to $\pi$. We will follow that convention throughout this work.

If the filter has real coefficients (*i.e.*, the $c_i$s and $d_i$s are real), the frequency response for positive frequencies is related to the response for negative frequencies. For this study we will employ the frequency response definition that is based on the filter's impulse response.

$$\mathcal{H}(\omega) = \sum_{i=-\infty}^{\infty} h_i e^{-j\omega i} \tag{2.55}$$

Let's break it up into the real and imaginary components.

$$\mathrm{Re}\,\{\mathcal{H}(\omega)\} = \sum_{i=-\infty}^{\infty} h_i \cos \omega i \tag{2.56}$$

and

$$\mathrm{Im}\,\{\mathcal{H}(\omega)\} = -\sum_{i=-\infty}^{\infty} h_i \sin \omega i \tag{2.57}$$

Notice that the real part depends on cosine terms and the imaginary part is expressed totally in terms of sines. Because the cosine is an even function [$\cos \omega = \cos(-\omega)$], the real part of the frequency response is an even function. The imaginary component is an odd function, because the sine is an odd function. Therefore,

$$\mathrm{Re}\,\{\mathcal{H}(\omega)\} = \mathrm{Re}\,\{\mathcal{H}(-\omega)\} \tag{2.58}$$

and

$$\mathrm{Im}\,\{\mathcal{H}(\omega)\} = -\mathrm{Im}\,\{\mathcal{H}(-\omega)\} \tag{2.59}$$

Remember that this result applies only to filters with real impulse responses. Filters with complex coefficients do not generate such a nice result.

We can also apply these odd and even results to the magnitude and phase representation of the frequency response of a real filter. The magnitude of the frequency response is a function of the square of the real and imaginary components. Therefore, the magnitude is an even function.

$$|\mathcal{H}(\omega)| = |\mathcal{H}(-\omega)| \qquad (2.60)$$

The inverse tangent is an odd function and the imaginary part of the response is also odd, so the phase is an odd function of $\omega$.

$$\phi(\omega) = -\phi(-\omega) \qquad (2.61)$$

Again, this holds only for filters with real impulse responses.

By exploiting these results, we can cut our work in half when computing frequency responses. We need only compute the response for positive frequency, because we now know the relationship between positive and negative frequencies. Most designers compute the frequency response from 0 to $\pi$ when dealing with real filters.

**Example:** Compute the frequency response of chapter 1's filter.

In Chapter 1 we saw that a nonrecursive digital filter could be used to improve an electrocardiogram (EKG). Now that we understand frequency response, we can see why the filter worked. The filter is repeated below.

$$y_k = \frac{1}{21}\left(-2x_k + 3x_{k-1} + 6x_{k-2} + 7x_{k-3} + 6x_{k-4} + 3x_{k-5} - 2x_{k-6}\right) \quad (2.62)$$

The first step is to compute the frequency response of the filter. Since it is a nonrecursive filter we are concerned only with the numerator.

$$\mathcal{H}(\omega) = \frac{-2e^{-j\omega 0} + 3e^{-j\omega 1} + 6e^{-j\omega 2} + 7e^{-j\omega 3} + 6e^{-j\omega 4} + 3e^{-j\omega 5} - 2e^{-j\omega 6}}{21}$$
$$(2.63)$$

The next step is to break it into its real and imaginary components (cosines and sines).

$$\mathrm{Re}\{\mathcal{H}(\omega)\} = \frac{1}{21}\left[-2 + 3\cos\omega + 6\cos 2\omega + 7\cos 3\omega + 6\cos 4\omega \right.$$
$$\left. + 3\cos 5\omega - 2\cos 6\omega\right] \qquad (2.64)$$

and

$$\mathrm{Im}\{\mathcal{H}(\omega)\} = \frac{1}{21}\left[2\sin 0 - 3\sin\omega - 6\sin 2\omega - 7\sin 3\omega - 6\sin 4\omega \right.$$
$$\left. - 3\sin 5\omega + 2\sin 6\omega\right] \qquad (2.65)$$

The magnitude and phase of this frequency response is computed by a straightforward application of equations (2.24) and (2.25).

$$|\mathcal{H}(\omega)| = \sqrt{\mathrm{Re}^2\{\mathcal{H}(\omega)\} + \mathrm{Im}^2\{\mathcal{H}(\omega)\}} \tag{2.66}$$

and

$$\phi(\omega) = \tan^{-1}\left(\frac{\mathrm{Im}\{\mathcal{H}(\omega)\}}{\mathrm{Re}\{\mathcal{H}(\omega)\}}\right) \tag{2.67}$$

The magnitude of the frequency response is plotted in Figure 2.7. Notice that this filter multiplies low-frequency signals ( $\omega \approx 0$ ) by a unity magnitude, and multiplies the higher-frequency signals by smaller magnitudes. In filter lingo, we say that the filter passes the low-frequency signals and attenuates the higher-frequency signals. As such, this filter discriminates against higher frequency signals.

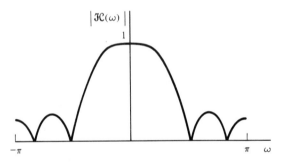

Figure 2.7 Frequency response of Chapter 1's nonrecursive filter.

In the EKG example, the EKG is a relatively low frequency signal, and the corrupting muscle noise is a high-frequency signal. When we apply the sum of the EKG and the muscle noise to the input of the filter, the filter multiplies the EKG component of the signal by about unity, and attenuates the higher frequency muscle noise. Therefore, the filter improved the EKG signal by discriminating against the muscle noise on the basis of frequency. Try to explain the operation of the filter without using the concept of frequency response — you will find it difficult-to-impossible.

**Example:** Compute the frequency response of chapter 1's recursive filter.

Chapter 1 presented a recursive filter for the EKG example. Let's compute its frequency response and compare it to the response of the nonrecursive

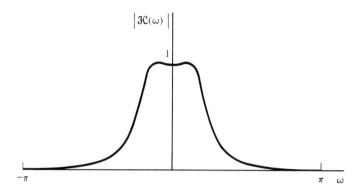

**Figure 2.8** Magnitude of the frequency response of Chapter 1's recursive filter.

filter. The filter has one nonrecursive coefficient and three recursive terms.

$$y_k = 0.14x_{k-2} + 1.77y_{k-1} - 1.19y_{k-2} + 0.28y_{k-3} \qquad (2.68)$$

Because this is a recursive filter, the frequency response involves a numerator and a denominator.

$$\mathcal{H}(\omega) = \frac{0.14e^{-j\omega 2}}{1 - 1.77e^{-j\omega 1} + 1.19e^{-j\omega 2} - 0.28e^{-j\omega 3}} \qquad (2.69)$$

The magnitude of the frequency response is simply the ratio of the magnitude of the numerator over the denominator.

$$|\mathcal{H}(\omega)| = 0.14\sqrt{\frac{(\cos 2\omega)^2 + (\sin 2\omega)^2}{\text{Re}^2 + \text{Im}^2}} \qquad (2.70)$$

where in this case

$$\text{Re} = 1 - 1.77\cos\omega + 1.19\cos 2\omega - 0.28\cos 3\omega$$
$$\text{Im} = -1.77\sin\omega + 1.19\sin 2\omega - 0.28\sin 3\omega$$

The numerator is just cosine squared plus sine squared; that is 1. So the shape of this frequency response is completely determined by the denominator. The magnitude of the response is plotted in Figure 2.8. Notice that this filter multiplies low-frequency signals by a gain of about unity, and attenuates high-frequency signals. The concept of frequency response is used to explain the operation of recursive as well as nonrecursive filters. The response graphically shows how the filter will affect the various frequency components of its input.

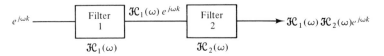

**Figure 2.9** Cascade combination of two filters.

## 2.4  PARALLEL AND CASCADE FILTERS

As mentioned in Chapter 1, a designer is often faced with filters in parallel or cascade combinations. This section computes the equivalent frequency response of filters in cascade or parallel. Surprisingly, we are going to find it much easier to compute the frequency responses of combinations of filters than to find the impulse responses.

The derivation of the frequency response of two filters in cascade is supported by Figure 2.9. Suppose that filter 1 has a frequency response of $\mathcal{H}_1(\omega)$ and filter 2 has $\mathcal{H}_2(\omega)$. We compute the frequency response of the combination of these two filters by applying an $e^{j\omega k}$ to the input of filter 1 and then compute the output of filter 2. Filter 1 has the input of the combination and filter 2 has the output.

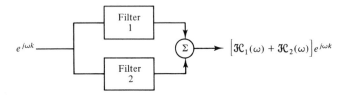

**Figure 2.10** Parallel combinition of two filters.

When $e^{j\omega k}$ is applied to filter 1, this filter produces an output of $\mathcal{H}_1(\omega)e^{j\omega k}$; a straightforward application of the definition of frequency response. If we apply $e^{j\omega k}$ to the input of filter 2, it will generate an output of $\mathcal{H}_2(\omega)e^{j\omega k}$. By judicious application of the homogeneity principle, if we apply $\mathcal{H}_1(\omega)e^{j\omega k}$ to filter 2, it will produce an output of $\mathcal{H}_2(\omega)\mathcal{H}_1(\omega)e^{j\omega k}$. Therefore, an input of $e^{j\omega k}$ to the cascade of the filters results in an output of $\mathcal{H}_1(\omega)\mathcal{H}_2(\omega)e^{j\omega k}$. The frequency response of the cascade is simply the product of the individual responses.

$$\mathcal{H}_{\text{cascade}}(\omega) = \mathcal{H}_1(\omega)\mathcal{H}_2(\omega) \tag{2.71}$$

The computation of the frequency response of the parallel combination is approached in a similar fashion. As illustrated in Figure 2.10, we apply an input of $e^{j\omega k}$ to the inputs of both filters and thereby produce an output of $\mathcal{H}_1(\omega)e^{j\omega k} + \mathcal{H}_2(\omega)e^{j\omega k}$. Therefore, the frequency response of the parallel combination is the sum of the individual responses.

$$\mathcal{H}_{\text{parallel}}(\omega) = \mathcal{H}_1(\omega) + \mathcal{H}_2(\omega) \tag{2.72}$$

Cascade and parallel arrangements of filters are quite common in many larger digital filtering systems. In many cases the filters are arranged to perform a specific function and the system is a collection of such functions. In other cases, the filters are combined to improve the performance of a particular filter. An example of using combinations of filters to improve the performance is "squaring" filters.

Cascading a filter with itself is an old analog design trick to generate a squared filter which has a better frequency response than the original filter. It is called "squared" because the frequency response of a filter cascaded with itself is the square of the filter's frequency response.

$$\begin{aligned} \mathcal{H}_{\text{cascade}}(\omega) &= \mathcal{H}(\omega)\mathcal{H}(\omega) \\ &= \mathcal{H}^2(\omega) \end{aligned} \tag{2.73}$$

Let's try to improve the frequency response of the 19-point high-pass filter by squaring it.

Figure 2.11a shows the frequency response of the high-pass filter. Notice that it has ripples in the stopband and passband — ideally the passband is 1 and the stopband is zero. This filter also requires about $0.1\pi$ rad/sec to transition between the stopband and the passband; an ideal filter does this instantaneously.

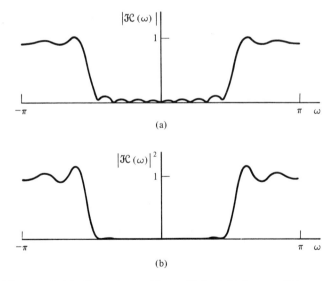

**Figure 2.11** Squaring a 19-coefficient high-pass filter:
(a) frequency response of the original filter;
(b) frequency response of the squared filter.

Figure 2.11b shows the frequency response of the cascade of this filter with itself, $\mathcal{H}^2(\omega)$. Notice that the stopband has been significantly improved, and the transition between the stopband and the passband is about two-thirds that of the original filter. But the bad news is that the ripples in the passband are about twice as large as the ripples in the original filter. So the stopband and the transition region are improved by squaring this filter, but the passband is plagued by larger ripples. If your application can tolerate large ripples in the passband, squaring the filter is an appropriate way of improving the filter. However, most applications are quite sensitive to passband ripples, and in these cases squaring should be avoided.

The effects of squaring can best be understood with the help of Figure 2.12; this is a plot of $|\mathcal{H}(\omega)|^2$ as a function of $|\mathcal{H}(\omega)|$. Notice that $\omega$ is parametric in this plot, so it does not explicitly exist. We use this plot to get the magnitude of the squared filter at a particular frequency from the magnitude of the original filter at that frequency. For example, if the original filter has a frequency response of 0.5 at a certain frequency, the squared filter has a frequency response of 0.25 at that frequency.

The stopband of the original highpass filter has magnitudes between 0 and 0.1, so the stopband is represented by the region of the horizontal axis near the origin. Therefore, the stopband of the squared filter has magnitudes between $0^2 = 0$ and $0.1^2 = 0.01$ along the vertical axis. This means that the rippling in the stopband of the squared filter is restricted to 0.01 — an order-of-magnitude reduction of the original filter's stopband ripples. The passband of the original filter has magnitudes between 0.96 and 1.09, which is the region of the horizontal axis near $|\mathcal{H}(\omega)| = 1$. This means that the passband of the squared filter lies between $0.96^2 = 0.92$ and $1.09^2 = 1.18$, so the ripples in the passband of the squared filter are about twice as high as those in the original filter.

These observations can be extended to arbitrary filters by noting that the amplification or attenuation of ripples is determined by the slope of the curve in Figure 2.12. If the slope is near zero ($|\mathcal{H}(\omega)| \approx 0$), the ripples are greatly attenuated because small changes in the original filter's frequency response produce almost no change in the squared filter's response. If the slope is near 2 ($|\mathcal{H}(\omega)| \approx 1$), the ripples of the squared filter are about twice as large as those of the original filter. In this example, the stopband ripples are near $|\mathcal{H}(\omega)| = 0$, so the stopband ripples are attenuated. The passband ripples are around $|\mathcal{H}(\omega)| = 1$, so the ripples are approximately doubled by squaring the filter.

The moral is, if you are going to square a filter with ripples, make sure that the gains of the filter do not lie in the regions that amplify ripples. In this case, we can reduce the passband gain of the original filter (effectively move the passband to the left along the horizontal axis of Figure 2.12) so that it experiences a lower slope portion of the curve when it is squared. For example, the slope is one at $|\mathcal{H}(\omega)| = \frac{1}{2}$, so reducing the passband gain of the original filter to $\frac{1}{2}$ would result in a squared filter with about the same passband rippling as the original filter.

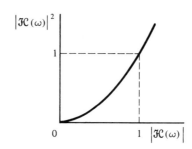

**Figure 2.12** Gain of the squared filter versus gain of the original filter.

## 2.5  APPLICATIONS: INTEGRATORS AND DIFFERENTIATORS

This section illustrates the utility of the frequency response by using it to compare various digital filter approximations to integrators and differentiators. We begin by computing the frequency response of a perfect integrator and differentiator, and then contrast these perfect responses to those of popular digital approximations.

**Integrators**

A perfect integrator is an analog filter. Its output, $y(t)$, is the integral of its input, $x(t)$.

$$y(t) = \int_{-\infty}^{t} x(\tau) \, d\tau \tag{2.74}$$

The frequency response of an analog filter is obtained by applying an input of $e^{j\omega t}$ and then expressing the resulting output as $\mathcal{H}_{\text{analog}}(\omega)e^{j\omega t}$, where $\mathcal{H}_{\text{analog}}(\omega)$ is the analog frequency response. If we follow this tack and apply $e^{j\omega t}$ to the integrator, we will get an output of $\frac{1}{j\omega}e^{j\omega t}$. So the frequency response of a perfect integrator is

$$\mathcal{H}_{\text{integrator}}(\omega) = \frac{1}{j\omega} \tag{2.75}$$

We will consider three digital integrators and compare them to the ideal integrator by comparing the frequency responses. The digital integrators are defined as follows:

Running sum:

$$y_k = x_k + y_{k-1} \tag{2.76a}$$

and

$$\mathcal{H}_{\text{rs}}(\omega) = \frac{1}{1 - e^{-j\omega}} \tag{2.76b}$$

Trapezoid rule:

$$y_k = 0.5x_k + 0.5x_{k-1} + y_{k-1} \qquad (2.77a)$$

and

$$\mathcal{H}_{\text{trap}}(\omega) = \frac{0.5 + 0.5e^{-j\omega}}{1 - e^{-j\omega}} \qquad (2.77b)$$

Simpson's rule:

$$y_k = 0.333x_k + 1.333x_{k-1} + 0.333x_{k-2} + y_{k-2} \qquad (2.78a)$$

and

$$\mathcal{H}_{\text{simp}} = \frac{0.333 + 1.333e^{-j\omega} + 0.333e^{-j2\omega}}{1 - e^{-j2\omega}} \qquad (2.78b)$$

The magnitudes of these frequency responses are plotted in Figure 2.13 together with the response of the perfect integrator, which is represented by crosses every 0.2 rad. All three approximations are good for low frequencies, say $|\omega| < \pi/3$, but they behave very differently at higher frequencies. For the higher frequencies the running sum has a higher gain than the perfect integrator (Figure 2.13a). The trapezoid (Figure 2.13b) has a much lower gain at high frequencies. Simpson's rule (Figure 2.13c) is a much closer approximation to the perfect integrator for frequencies less than $\pi/2$; after that it increases very quickly and blows up at $\omega = \pi$.

Figure 2.13 provides a compact overview of the three digital integrators and gives most of the information necessary to select one integrator over another. For example, if the input signal is restricted to low frequencies, the integrators will all yield good results. One is as good as the others. However, if the input is a somewhat higher frequency but still below $0.8\pi$, Simpson's integrator will perform more closely to the ideal integrator, the other two will generate significant errors. If you are expecting a high-frequency input, avoid the Simpson integrator because of its infinite gain at $\pi$ — the running sum or trapezoid integrators should be used instead.

**Differentiators**

A differentiator produces an output that is the differential of its input.

$$y(t) = \frac{dx(t)}{dt} \qquad (2.79)$$

We compute the frequency response by applying an $e^{j\omega t}$ and then factoring the output as we have done before.

$$\mathcal{H}_{\text{diff}}(\omega) = j\omega \qquad (2.80)$$

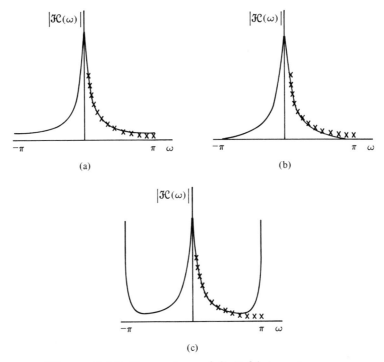

**Figure 2.13** Comparison of digital integrators:
(a) running sum; (b) trapezoid rule;
(c) Simpson's rule.

We will consider two digital approximations to the differentiator as follows:

Difference:

$$y_k = x_k - x_{k-1} \tag{2.81a}$$

and

$$\mathcal{H}_{\text{diff}}(\omega) = 1 - e^{-j\omega} \tag{2.81b}$$

Central difference:

$$y_k = 0.5x_k - 0.5x_{k-2} \tag{2.82a}$$

and

$$\mathcal{H}_{\text{cdiff}}(\omega) = 0.5 - 0.5e^{-j2\omega} \tag{2.82b}$$

The magnitudes of these frequency responses, together with the response of the perfect differentiator, are shown in Figure 2.14. Note again that the digital approximations are quite close for low frequencies, but they deviate as the frequency gets larger. The difference differentiator (Figure 2.14a) has a monotonically increasing gain between $\omega = 0$ and $\pi$, just like the ideal differentiator. The central difference differentiator (Figure 2.14b) reaches its maximum gain at $\pi/2$ then decreases for higher frequencies. The difference differentiator is a better match to the perfect differentiator, but the central difference differentiator is very useful when you wish to attenuate high-frequency differentials.

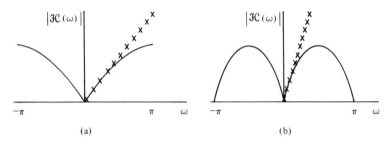

**Figure 2.14**  Comparision of digital differentiators:
(a) difference; (b) central difference.

## 2.6  SUMMARY

This chapter has introduced and derived the most useful characterization of a digital filter — the frequency response. Although the frequency response was derived from a rather limited set of inputs, $e^{j\omega t}$, it provides a tremendous insight into the utility of the filter. Only through the frequency response can we explain the selective amplification or attenuation of input signals.

### EXERCISES

2-1. Evaluate the following sums.

(a) $\sum_{i=-2}^{2} i e^{j\omega i}$

(b) $\sum_{i=-2}^{2} |i| e^{j\omega i}$

(c) $\sum_{i=-m}^{m} c_i e^{j\omega i}$       where       $c_i = c_{-i}$

(d) $\sum_{i=-m}^{m} c_i e^{j\omega i}$       where       $c_i = -c_{-i}$

(e) $\sum_{i=-m}^{m} c_i e^{-j\omega i}$       where       $c_i = -c_{-i}$

2-2. Plot the magnitude and phase of the following functions. Use a range of $-\pi < \omega < \pi$.

(a) $e^{j\omega i}$

(b) $\cos \omega$

(c) $j \sin 2\omega$

(d) $e^{j\omega} + 2e^{2j\omega}$

2-3. We found that $e^{j\omega k}$ is an eigenfunction of a general digital filter.

(a) Is $ae^{j(b\omega k + c)}$ an eigenfunction of a general digital filter? Support your answer.

(b) If it is, what is the associated eigenvalue?

2-4. Consider the digital signal $z^k$, where $z$ is a complex constant.

(a) Is this signal an eigenfunction of a general digital filter?

(b) If so, what is its eigenvalue?

2-5. Consider the following, three-coefficient, nonrecursive digital filter.

$$y_k = 0.25x_{k-1} + 0.5x_k + 0.25x_{k+1}$$

(a) Compute the general expression for $y_k$ when

$$x_k = 3 + 2\cos\left(\frac{\pi}{4}k\right) + \cos\left(\frac{\pi}{3}k\right)$$

(b) Which of the three frequency components in part (a) are passed through the filter unaffected (unity gain)?

c) Which of the three frequency components are blocked out (zero gain)?

2-6. We found that $\cos \omega k$ was not an eigenfunction for a general digital filter.

(a) What are the minimal restrictions on the coefficients of a nonrecursive filter so that $\cos \omega k$ is an eigenfunction?

(b) What is the associated eigenvalue?

2-7. What are the minimal restrictions on the coefficients of a nonrecursive filter so that $\sin \omega k$ is an eigenfunction?

2-8. Consider a nonrecursive antisymmetric filter; $c_i = -c_{-i}$.

(a) Compute its frequency response (express your answer in sines or cosines).

(b) Compute $\mathcal{H}(0)$.

2-9. Compute $\mathcal{H}(0)$ for a nonrecursive filter. What is the significance of $\mathcal{H}(0)$?

2-10. Consider the following nonrecursive filter:

$$y_k = -3x_{k-2} + 12x_{k-1} + 17x_k + 12x_{k+1} - 3x_{k+2}$$

(a) Compute its frequency response. Hint: express your answer in cosines.

(b) Evaluate the frequency response at

$$\omega = 0$$

$$\omega = \frac{\pi}{2}$$

$$\omega = \frac{3\pi}{4}$$

$$\omega = \pi$$

$$\omega = 2\pi$$

(c) Plot the frequency response for $-2\pi < \omega < 2\pi$.

2-11. Suppose that we turn a noncausal filter into a causal filter by shifting the indices. That is, we run

$$y_k = \sum_{i=-m}^{m} c_i x_{k-m-i}$$

instead of

$$y_k = \sum_{i=-m}^{m} c_i x_{k-i}$$

(a) What does this do to the magnitude of the frequency response?

(b) What does it do to the phase?

2-12. Suppose that you run a digital filter backwards. That is,

$$y_k = \sum_{i=-m}^{m} c_i x_{k+i}$$

rather than

$$y_k = \sum_{i=-m}^{m} c_i x_{k-i}$$

(a) What does this do to the magnitude of the frequency response?

(b) What does it do to the phase?

2-13. Consider the simple delay filter

$$y_k = x_{k-n}$$

(a) Compute the frequency response.

(b) Plot the magnitude of the frequency response for $-3\pi < \omega < 3\pi$.

(c) Plot the phase for $-\pi < \omega < \pi$.

(d) For what values of $n$ is $\sin \omega k$ an eigenfunction?

2-14. Consider the following filter.

$$y_k = \sum_{i=-m}^{m} c_i x_{k-2i}$$

This filter uses every other input.

(a) Compute its frequency response.

(b) What is the period of this frequency response?

2-15. Consider the EKG filter of Chapter 1,

$$y_k = x_{k-2} + 1.77 y_{k-1} - 1.19 y_{k-2} + 0.28 y_{k-3}$$

and a shifted version of that filter,

$$y_k = x_k + 1.77 y_{k-1} - 1.19 y_{k-2} + 0.28 y_{k-3}$$

(a) How is the magnitude of the frequency response of the shifted filter related to the magnitude of the frequency response of the original filter?

(b) How are the phases related?

2-16. You are given a filter with coefficients $c_i$ and $d_i$, with a frequency response of $\mathcal{H}(\omega)$. Design a filter that has a frequency response of $2\mathcal{H}(\omega)$. Express your answer in terms of the $c_i$s and $d_i$s of the original filter.

2-17. Consider a nonrecursive filter with imaginary coefficients.

(a) Is the impulse response real, imaginary, or complex?

(b) Compute the real part of the frequency response. Is it an even or odd function?

(c) Compute the imaginary part of the frequency response. Is it even or odd?

(d) Compute the magnitude of the frequency response. Is it even or odd?

2-18. Consider a digital filter with complex coefficients.

$$y_k = (1 + 2j)x_k + (j)x_{k-1}$$

(a) Compute the real part of its frequency response.

(b) Compute the imaginary part.

(c) Compute the magnitude. Is it an even or odd function of $\omega$?

2-19. Find the frequency response of the cascade of 4 filters, $\mathcal{H}_1(\omega)$, $\mathcal{H}_2(\omega)$, $\mathcal{H}_3(\omega)$, and $\mathcal{H}_4(\omega)$.

2-20. Consider the $\frac{3}{8}$ rule of integration.

$$y_{k+3} = y_k + \frac{1}{8}(x_{k+3} + 3x_{k+2} + 3x_{k+1} + x_k)$$

(a) Plot the magnitude of its frequency response.

(b) Compare it to the three integrators of Section 2.6.

2-21. Suppose that you are integrating a low-frequency signal that is corrupted with high-frequency noise. Which of the three integrators of Figure 2.13 would you use? justify your answer.

# Design
# of
# Nonrecursive Filters

We have found that the frequency response is a very effective way of characterizing a digital filter. In chapter 2 we showed how to compute the frequency response of a given filter — that process is called analysis. In this chapter we turn the problem around and address the process of synthesis, or design. That is, how do we compute the coefficients of a filter so that the filter's frequency response best matches a given, desired response?

In this chapter we develop a design methodology for calculating the impulse response of a filter from a desired frequency response. Once we have the filter's impulse response, it is easy to find the coefficients of a nonrecursive filter with that impulse response; remember, $c_i = h_i$. Unfortunately, there are no simple techniques for finding the coefficients of a recursive filter for a particular impulse response. Therefore, these techniques are not applicable to recursive filters. Recursive filter design will require a completely different tack and will be discussed in Chapters 5 and 6.

## 3.1   DESIGN CRITERIA

Suppose that your are given a frequency response (your boss sketches it on the back of a napkin) and are told to compute the coefficients of a digital filter that will match this response. In other words, you are told to *design* a digital filter with a specific frequency response. The "input" to the design process is a desired frequency response, say $\mathcal{D}(\omega)$, and the output is a set of filter coefficients, $c_i$ and $d_i$. How do you go about computing the coefficients?

$$\mathfrak{D}(\omega) \longrightarrow \boxed{\begin{array}{c}\text{Design}\\\text{process}\end{array}} \longrightarrow (c_i,\ d_i) \to \mathfrak{H}(\omega)$$

**Figure 3.1** The design process; compute coefficients
from a given frequency response.

Ideally the design process (Figure 3.1) will generate a filter with a frequency response, say $\mathfrak{H}(\omega)$, that is an exact match to the desired response. However, an exact match is not always possible, so the design technique should generate the best set of coefficients, a filter that comes closest to the desired frequency response.

The problem now is to define such words as "best" and "closest", but any definition will be subjective, and therefore unreliable. So we must propose a mathematical measure of "best," a design criterion. One of the simplest measures is the difference between the desired response and the filter's response, called the design error, $\mathcal{E}(\omega)$.

$$\mathcal{E}(\omega) = \mathcal{D}(\omega) - \mathcal{H}(\omega) \qquad (3.1)$$

The design error is a complex (real and imaginary components) function of the frequency, $\omega$. Most designers treat the components of the design error equally, and are not concerned with real and imaginary components individually. Therefore, we will consider the magnitude squared of the error function rather than the error function itself.

$$|\mathcal{E}(\omega)|^2 = \text{Re}\left\{\mathcal{E}(\omega)\right\}^2 + \text{Im}\left\{\mathcal{E}(\omega)\right\}^2 \qquad (3.2)$$

This is more compactly written as the product of $\mathcal{E}(\omega)$ and its complex conjugate, $\mathcal{E}(\omega)^*$.

$$|\mathcal{E}(\omega)|^2 = \mathcal{E}(\omega)\mathcal{E}(\omega)^* \qquad (3.3)$$

The magnitude squared of the design error is preferred over the design error because it is a real function, is easier to work with, and it reflects an equal contribution from the real and the imaginary components of the design error. We use the magnitude squared rather than the magnitude, because it is easier to manipulate (we will need that later) and it differentially amplifies errors. Larger errors affect the magnitude squared more than smaller errors do. In this way the design is more sensitive to larger errors than to small errors, a feature that most designers appreciate.

These concepts are illustrated in Figure 3.2. These examples assume a purely real frequency response (why complicate the example?). Figure 3.2a shows the desired frequency response, $\mathcal{D}(\omega)$, and the response of a designed filter, $\mathcal{H}(\omega)$. Figure 3.2b shows the design error, $\mathcal{E}(\omega)$, and Figure 3.2c is the squared error. Notice that squaring the error makes it more sensitive to larger design errors.

Most designers are equally concerned with the design error over all frequencies. Therefore, rather than deal with the squared error as a function of frequency, let's look at the total design error over all frequencies. This suggests the integral of the

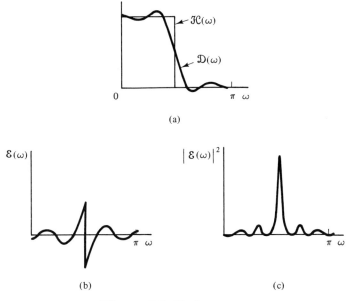

(a)

(b)                                                    (c)

**Figure 3.2**  Design error.

squared error. The choice of the frequency region for the integration is easy because the frequency responses and, hence, the squared error are periodic in $2\pi$. Therefore, a reasonable design criterion for digital filters is the integral squared error of the frequency response.

$$\mathcal{E} = \int_{-\pi}^{\pi} |\mathcal{E}(\omega)|^2 \, d\omega \tag{3.4}$$

This measures the total error between $\mathcal{D}(\omega)$ and $\mathcal{H}(\omega)$. When the responses are equal, the integral squared error is zero. As the frequency responses become more dissimilar, the error grows.

Figure 3.3 provides some examples of $\mathcal{D}(\omega)$ and $\mathcal{H}(\omega)$ and the resulting errors. Most people find that the error agrees with their notions of closeness — the closer the responses, the smaller the error.

## 3.2  MINIMIZING THE DESIGN CRITERION

This section develops a design technique for computing the filter's impulse response that minimizes the design criterion. Unfortunately, this development works only for nonrecursive filters, so we must postpone recursive filter design techniques to later chapters.

We first note that the integral squared error is a function of the desired frequency response and the response of the filter that we are designing. The desired response is given, so nothing can be done with it to minimize the error. We can effect the response of the design filter through the terms of the impulse response we

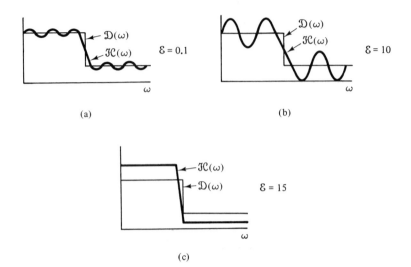

(a)                                                    (b)

(c)

**Figure 3.3** Design errors

select; as a matter of fact, that is the process of design. Therefore, we should develop a design methodology that will compute an impulse response that minimizes the design criterion.

This is a classical minimization problem — we wish to minimize a function with respect to each term of the impulse response. Such a minimization suggests differentiation of the criterion with respect to the impulse response and then setting the derivatives to zero.

$$\frac{d\,[\mathcal{E}]}{dh_i} = 0 \tag{3.5}$$

In general, we must also check the second derivative to make sure that this impulse response generates a minimum and not a maximum, and also make sure that this is the global minimum. However, this specific application is much easier, because the criterion is a quadratic function of the impulse response; there is only one minimum and the maximums are at positive and negative infinity. Therefore, the impulse response that sets all the derivatives to zero is guaranteed to minimize the design criterion.

We begin the calculation of the derivative by expressing the design criterion in terms of the frequency responses.

$$\frac{d\mathcal{E}}{dh_i} = \int_{-\pi}^{\pi} \frac{d}{dh_i} \left\{ [\mathcal{D}(\omega) - \mathcal{H}(\omega)] \, [\mathcal{D}(\omega) - \mathcal{H}(\omega)]^* \right\} d\omega = 0 \tag{3.6}$$

We now invoke the chain rule of differentiation.

$$\frac{d\mathcal{E}}{dh_i} = \int_{-\pi}^{\pi} \frac{d}{dh_i} \left\{ [\mathcal{D}(\omega) - \mathcal{H}(\omega)] \right\} [\mathcal{D}(\omega) - \mathcal{H}(\omega)]^* \, d\omega$$
$$+ \int_{-\pi}^{\pi} [\mathcal{D}(\omega) - \mathcal{H}(\omega)] \frac{d}{dh_i} \left\{ [\mathcal{D}(\omega) - \mathcal{H}(\omega)]^* \right\} \, d\omega \tag{3.7}$$

The derivative is the sum of two integrals: zero when both integrals are zero or when the integrals are nonzero but cancel one another. However, the integrals are complex conjugates of one another, so the derivative is zero only when both integrals are zero. Therefore, we must look for an impulse response that sets both integrals to zero. The job is made easier because setting one integral to zero will automatically zero the other (remember, they are complex conjugates). So we will arbitrarily pick the second integral and find the impulse response that sets it to zero.

$$\int_{-\pi}^{\pi} [\mathcal{D}(\omega) - \mathcal{H}(\omega)] \underline{\frac{d}{dh_i} \left\{ [\mathcal{D}(\omega) - \mathcal{H}(\omega)]^* \right\}} \, d\omega = 0 \tag{3.8}$$

The underlined term is the derivative of the design error with respect to the $i$th term of the impulse response. We will compute it by expressing the conjugate of the frequency response of the design filter in terms of the filter's impulse response.

$$\mathcal{H}(\omega)^* = \sum_{k=-\infty}^{\infty} h_k^* e^{+j\omega k} \tag{3.9}$$

So

$$\frac{d}{dh_i} \left\{ [\mathcal{D}(\omega) - \mathcal{H}(\omega)]^* \right\} = \frac{d}{dc_i} \left\{ \mathcal{D}(\omega)^* \right\} - \frac{d}{dc_i} \left\{ \sum_{k=-\infty}^{\infty} h_k^* e^{+j\omega k} \right\} \tag{3.10}$$

The first term of the right-hand side is zero, because the desired frequency response is given and does not depend on the impulse response of the designed filter. The second term is the variation of the designed filter's frequency response as the $i$th term of the impulse response is varied. Since all the terms of the impulse response are independent of one another, only the $i$th term of the sum remains — all of the others are zero. Therefore,

$$\frac{d}{dh_i} \left\{ [\mathcal{D}(\omega) - \mathcal{H}(\omega)]^* \right\} = e^{+j\omega i} \tag{3.11}$$

Let's return to the integral that we were setting to zero and substitute this result.

$$\int_{-\pi}^{\pi} [\mathcal{D}(\omega) - \mathcal{H}(\omega)] e^{j\omega i} \, d\omega = 0 \tag{3.12}$$

This requires that the integral involving $\mathcal{D}(\omega)$ must equal the integral involving $\mathcal{H}(\omega)$.

$$\int_{-\pi}^{\pi} \mathcal{H}(\omega)e^{j\omega i} \, d\omega = \int_{-\pi}^{\pi} \mathcal{D}(\omega)e^{j\omega i} \, d\omega \tag{3.13}$$

This is just about as far as we can go with the right-hand side, but one final manipulation remains in the left-hand side. If we express $\mathcal{H}(\omega)$ in terms of the filter's impulse response, the left-hand side involves integrals of products of exponentials.

$$\int_{-\pi}^{\pi} \mathcal{H}(\omega)e^{j\omega i} \, d\omega = \int_{-\pi}^{\pi} \left[ \sum_{k=-\infty}^{\infty} h_k e^{-j\omega k} \right] e^{j\omega i} \, d\omega$$
$$= \sum_{k=-\infty}^{\infty} h_k \int_{-\pi}^{\pi} e^{-j\omega(k-i)} \, d\omega \tag{3.14}$$

We can rewrite these integrals in terms of sines and cosines (remember Euler?).

$$\int_{-\pi}^{\pi} e^{-j\omega(k-i)} \, d\omega = \int_{-\pi}^{\pi} \cos\left[\omega(k-i)\right] \, d\omega - j\int_{-\pi}^{\pi} \sin\left[\omega(k-i)\right] \, d\omega \tag{3.15}$$

When $k \neq i$, the integrals are sines or cosines that are integrated over an integral number of periods. These terms are always zero. When $k = i$, the cosine term is one and the sine term is zero. The integral of $\cos 0$ from $-\pi$ to $\pi$ is just $2\pi$. Therefore,

$$\int_{-\pi}^{\pi} e^{-j\omega(k-i)} d\omega = \begin{cases} 2\pi & \text{if } k = i \\ 0 & \text{if } k \neq i \end{cases} \tag{3.16}$$

Therefore, we get the somewhat surprising result that

$$\int_{-\pi}^{\pi} \mathcal{H}(\omega)e^{+j\omega i} \, d\omega = 2\pi h_i \tag{3.17}$$

If we substitute this into equation (3.13), we get the long-sought-after design equation.

$$h_i = \frac{1}{2\pi} \int_{-\pi}^{\pi} \mathcal{D}(\omega)e^{j\omega i} \, d\omega \tag{3.18}$$

The $i$th term of the "best" impulse response is computed by multiplying the desired frequency response by $e^{j\omega i}$ and integrating over a $2\pi$ interval. This impulse response will generate a lower integral squared error than any other. Notice that each term of the impulse response is independently computed; that is, the value of one term is independent of all others.

Our result is identical to the equation for computing the Fourier coefficients of the Fourier expansion of $\mathcal{D}(\omega)$, so we will call this method the *Fourier design*.

## 3.3  FOURIER DESIGN METHOD

Suppose that you are given a desired frequency response and are told to design a digital filter that minimizes the integral squared error between the frequency responses. The filter's impulse is computed from the desired frequency response, $D(\omega)$, by

$$h_i = \frac{1}{2\pi} \int_{-\pi}^{\pi} D(\omega)e^{j\omega i}\ d\omega \tag{3.19}$$

A nonrecursive filter is designed by choosing coefficients, $c_i$, to match the impulse response.

$$c_i = \frac{1}{2\pi} \int_{-\pi}^{\pi} D(\omega)e^{j\omega i}\ d\omega \qquad i = -m\ldots m \tag{3.20}$$

Unfortunately, there is no direct technique for computing the coefficients of a recursive filter with a given impulse response. So the Fourier design method is useful for only nonrecursive filters.

The Fourier design technique is the most widely used method for designing nonrecursive digital filters. It will work for all desired responses, and the manipulations are easily automated.

**Example:** A Simple Verification of the Fourier Design Technique

Suppose that we are given the desired frequency response in the following form:

$$D(\omega) = \sum_{k=-\infty}^{\infty} a_k e^{-j\omega k} \tag{3.21}$$

We would hope that our design technique will result in filter impulse response $h_i = a_i$. Let's try it, by substituting this $D(\omega)$ into the Fourier method.

$$h_i = \frac{1}{2\pi} \int_{-\pi}^{\pi} \left[ \sum_{k=-m}^{m} a_k e^{-j\omega k} \right] e^{j\omega i}\ d\omega \tag{3.22}$$

We interchange the sum and integral and combine the two exponentials.

$$h_i = \frac{1}{2\pi} \sum_{k=-m}^{m} a_k \int_{-\pi}^{\pi} e^{-j\omega(k-i)}\ d\omega \tag{3.23}$$

We have seen this integral before. It is zero when $k \neq i$ and is $2\pi$ when $k = i$. Therefore, the Fourier design technique checks.

$$h_i = \frac{1}{2\pi} a_i 2\pi$$
$$= a_i \tag{3.24}$$

In this case the Fourier design technique computes a filter with a perfect match to the desired frequency response. We achieved a perfect match only because $D(\omega)$ was in a special form — a weighted sum of exponentials.

Don't let this example fool you into thinking that the computation of the Fourier method is always that easy. The desired frequency response was in a fortunate form. In general, we will not be this lucky and the computation of the coefficients will be much more involved. Let's look at another simple example.

**Example:** Designing a Low-Pass Filter

The desired response for this design example is given in Figure 3.4. This filter scales all frequencies between $-\pi/2$ and $\pi/2$ by unity, and multiplies all higher-frequency signals by zero. In the parlance of filtering, this filter stops all high frequencies and passes all low frequencies. It is called a *low-pass filter*. The demarcation frequency between high and low is called the *cutoff frequency*. Figure 3.4 shows the frequency response of a low pass filter with a cutoff of $\pi/2$ radians.

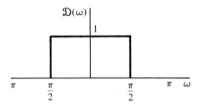

**Figure 3.4** Desired response of a low-pass filter.

We will use the Fourier design method to compute the impulse response of a nonrecursive filter that comes closest to the ideal low-pass filter response. We start with the general form of the Fourier equation.

$$h_i = \frac{1}{2\pi} \int_{-\pi}^{\pi} D(\omega) e^{j\omega i} \, d\omega \tag{3.25}$$

In this specific case $D(\omega)$ is one for $\omega$s between $-\pi/2$ and $\pi/2$, and is zero in the other intervals between $-\pi$ and $\pi$ [I wanted to say that it was zero otherwise, but that is not correct because $D(\omega)$ is periodic]. Therefore, we can account for this $D(\omega)$ by simply reducing the region of integration.

$$h_i = \frac{1}{2\pi} \int_{-\frac{\pi}{2}}^{\frac{\pi}{2}} 1 e^{j\omega i} \, d\omega \tag{3.26}$$

We have two options here. One is to integrate the exponential directly and the other is to express the integrals in terms of sines and cosines. This example will use the exponential notation, but you may wish to try the sine/cosine form. You will get the same result. The indefinite integral of the exponential was dragged out of an old and dusty calculus book or Appendix A.

$$\int e^{j\omega i} d\omega = \frac{1}{ji} e^{j\omega i} \tag{3.27}$$

Therefore, the filter's impulse response is simply the exponentials evaluated at $-\pi/2$ and $\pi/2$.

$$
\begin{aligned}
h_i &= \frac{1}{2\pi} \, \frac{1}{ji} e^{j\omega i} \Big|_{\frac{-\pi}{2}}^{\frac{\pi}{2}} \\
&= \frac{1}{2\pi} \frac{1}{ji} \left[ e^{\frac{i\pi i}{2}} - e^{\frac{-j\pi i}{2}} \right]
\end{aligned}
\tag{3.28}
$$

The real parts of the sum of the exponents cancel one another, and the imaginary (sine) components add. Therefore, the impulse response is a function of sines.

$$
\begin{aligned}
h_i &= \frac{1}{2\pi i} \frac{1}{j} (2j) \sin(\frac{\pi}{2} i) \\
&= \frac{1}{\pi i} \sin(\frac{\pi}{2} i)
\end{aligned}
\tag{3.29}
$$

We have successfully computed the impulse response for a digital, low-pass filter. Note that the impulse response decreases like $1/i$ as the indices get larger. In general, the small-indexed terms are larger than the large-indexed terms. Notice that indices that are even numbers cause the argument of the sine to be an integer multiple of $\pi$; the even-indexed terms of the impulse response are zero. Computing the zeroth coefficient is tricky because both the denominator and numerator are zero for $i = 0$. We must resort to l'Hospital's rule.

$$h_0 = \frac{\frac{\pi}{2}\cos(\frac{\pi}{2}i)}{\pi} \qquad i = 0 \tag{3.30}$$

Therefore, the zeroth term of the impulse response is $1/2$. Alternatively, we could have computed the zeroth term by reevaluating the integral [equation (3.26)] for the special case of $i = 0$.

$$
\begin{aligned}
h_0 &= \frac{1}{2\pi} \int_{-\frac{\pi}{2}}^{\frac{\pi}{2}} 1 e^{j\omega 0} \\
&= \frac{1}{2\pi} \pi \\
&= \frac{1}{2}
\end{aligned}
\tag{3.31}
$$

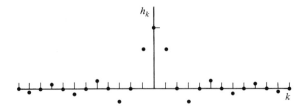

**Figure 3.5** Impulse response of the low-pass filter

**Table 3.1** Low-pass Filter Impulse Response

| $|i|$ | $h_i$ |
|-------|-------|
| 0 | 0.5 |
| 1 | 0.32 |
| 2 | 0 |
| 3 | −0.11 |
| 4 | 0 |
| 5 | 0.06 |
| 6 | 0 |
| 7 | −0.05 |
| 8 | 0 |
| 9 | 0.04 |

The impulse response of this low-pass filter is plotted in Figure 3.5 and the first few terms are listed in Table 3.1. Notice that the impulse response is symmetric, $h_i = h_{-i}$, and the magnitude of the terms rapidly decrease as $|i|$ becomes large. Also note that even terms, $h_2, h_4, \ldots$, are zero.

Because there is no easy way of going from an impulse response to the coefficients of a recursive filter, we are forced to implement this impulse response with a nonrecursive filter. The nonrecursive implementation forces us to truncate the impulse response because we cannot realize an infinite-length impulse response with a nonrecursive filter. Figure 3.6 shows the frequency responses obtained with 7 ($m = 3$), 11 ($m = 5$), and 19 ($m = 9$) coefficients. The longer filters generate a more faithful frequency response, because they realize more of the designed impulse response. This is a typical trade-off — longer filters require more computations to run, but they can have frequency responses that are closer to the desired response. We do not consider the nine-coefficient filter ($m = 4$) because it has the same impulse response and frequency response as the seven-coefficient filter (remember that $h_{-4} = h_4 = 0$). Similarly, it makes little sense to consider $13, 17, 21, \ldots$ coefficient implementation of this particular impulse response.

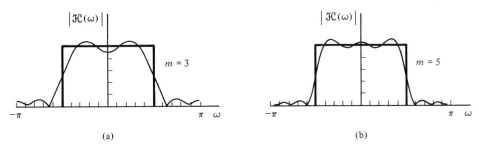

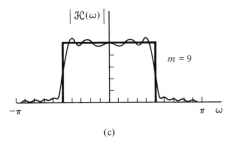

**Figure 3.6** Frequency responses of different-length low-pass filters:
(a) seven-coefficient realization;
(b) 11-coefficient realization
(c) 19-coefficient realization

## 3.4  NOTES ON COMPUTATION

Do not be fooled by the compactness of the Fourier design equation. Computing the coefficients for a particular desired response can be quite involved, but it should not be conceptually difficult. Rather, the computation is fraught with pitfalls in calculus, trigonometry, and worse yet, plain old algebra.

The design technique can be broadly categorized into a four-step process:

1. Plug the particular $D(\omega)$ into the general Fourier design equation. This may require breaking the integral into subintervals.
2. Perform the indefinite integration. This is usually the most difficult part of the design.
3. Apply the limits of integration to the indefinite integrals.
4. Compute the coefficients by substituting the indices into the general form. This is the most error-prone part of the design.

When the manipulations become especially arduous, neophyte designers are tempted by shortcuts. Unfortunately, some of these time savers are near misses, and the design is in error. Be very careful when exploiting the odd and even characteristics of the sine and cosine functions. Occasionally, a sine is treated as an even function and a cosine is treated as an odd. Such creative design techniques generate some surprising filters — very seldom do they yield useful ones. Remember, the sine is odd and the cosine is even.

$$\sin \omega i = -\sin(-\omega i) \tag{3.32}$$

$$\cos \omega i = \cos(-\omega i) \tag{3.33}$$

Some designers inadvertently interchange the limits of integration without negating the integral. Remember

$$\int_a^b [\quad\quad] \, d\omega = -\int_b^a [\quad\quad] \, d\omega \tag{3.34}$$

Also be careful when evaluating trigonometric functions. Sure, $\cos(\frac{\pi}{2})$ is zero, but $\cos(\frac{\pi}{2}i)$ is not necessarily zero; it is nonzero half the time.

In many applications the filters are designed to behave one way in a certain frequency region and behave differently in others. For example, a filter may pass signals in one interval and stop them in another. When the desired response is plugged into the Fourier design equation, it is often necessary to break the integral into subintervals of integration. One integral could account for the frequency interval where the filter passes signals, and the other integral for the stop region. These ideas are illustrated in Figure 3.7.

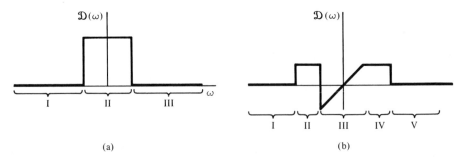

**Figure 3.7** Breaking up the regions of integration.

Figure 3.7a is a low-pass filter, which is represented by three regions: the negative stop interval (I), the passband (II), and the positive stopband (III). Figure 3.7b suggests a more complicated frequency response, which is represented by five regions. In computing these integrals, you would probably pair the integrals of regions I and V and the integrals in II and IV, and exploit the oddness of the function in regions III, the evenness in regions II and IV, and the oddness and evenness in regions I and V.

Many designers prefer to expand the exponentials into sines and cosines at the start of the design, and by doing this they integrate sines and cosines rather than exponentials. You should find it easier to leave the Euler expansion to the very end of your design. The exponentials are generally easier to integrate, and you are dealing with half the number of terms.

If you wish to design in terms of sines and cosines, the Fourier design equation can be expanded to your liking. The impulse response has a contribution from a cosine and sine integral.

$$h_i = \frac{1}{2\pi} \int_{-\pi}^{\pi} D(\omega) \cos \omega i \, d\omega + j \frac{1}{2\pi} \int_{-\pi}^{\pi} D(\omega) \sin \omega i \, d\omega \tag{3.35}$$

Because the cosine is an even function and the sine is odd, these two integrals contribute differently to the impulse response. When $D(\omega)$ is an even function of $\omega$, the sine integral is zero and the cosine integral can be performed only over the positive frequencies.

$$h_i = \frac{1}{\pi} \int_0^{\pi} D(\omega) \cos \omega i \, d\omega \qquad \text{when} \quad D(\omega) \quad \text{is even} \tag{3.36}$$

When $D(\omega)$ is odd, the roles are reversed, and the impulse response depends only on the sine integral.

$$h_i = \frac{j}{\pi} \int_0^{\pi} D(\omega) \sin \omega i \, d\omega \qquad \text{when} \qquad D(\omega) = -D(-\omega) \tag{3.37}$$

Note that these observations have nothing to do with a $2\pi$ interval. The sine or cosine terms will drop from any balanced interval of integration. It is necessary only that all positive regions have an exact negative counterpart — for every interval of $(b,a)$ there is also an interval of $(-a,-b)$. In the previous examples the regions where $(0, \pi)$ and $(-\pi, 0)$.

These odd and even results can be applied to frequency responses that are neither totally odd nor even. In this case, the frequency response is broken into an odd and an even component. The odd component contributes to the coefficient through the sine integral, and the even component contributes through the cosine integral. First, express the response in terms of its odd and even components.

$$D(\omega) = D_{\text{odd}}(\omega) + D_{\text{even}}(\omega) \tag{3.38}$$

where

$$D_{\text{odd}} = \frac{1}{2}[D(\omega) - D(-\omega)] \tag{3.39}$$

$$D_{\text{even}} = \frac{1}{2}[D(\omega) + D(-\omega)] \tag{3.40}$$

Then

$$h_i = \frac{1}{\pi} \int_0^{\pi} \mathcal{D}_{\text{even}}(\omega) \cos \omega i \; d\omega + \frac{j}{\pi} \int_0^{\pi} \mathcal{D}_{\text{odd}}(\omega) \sin \omega i \; d\omega \qquad (3.41)$$

If you choose to design in the sine-cosine form, these odd and even results can be used directly to expedite your design. Even if you use the exponential form, these results are very useful as quick checks on your work. For example, a real and even $\mathcal{D}(\omega)$ results in purely real coefficients. If you compute complex coefficients for such a desired response, you know right off the bat that you have made a mistake.

**Example:**  Design a Nonrecursive Digital Differentiator

      Our assignment is to design a digital filter that approximates a differentiator. The frequency response of a differentiator is sketched in Figure 3.8; that is our desired response.

      Fortunately, the example calls for a nonrecursive differentiator. If it had asked for a recursive filter we would have been out of luck, because we cannot go from an impulse response to the coefficients of a recursive filter. Since the impulse response of a nonrecursive filter equals its coefficients, $h_i = c_i$, we can directly design the nonrecursive filter by using equation (3.20).

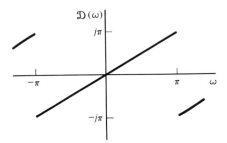

**Figure 3.8**  Desired frequency response for a differentiator.

We note that the desired response is an odd, imaginary function. So we know immediately that the filter coefficients are real and are generated by the sine integral.

$$c_i = \frac{j}{\pi} \int_0^{\pi} [j\omega] \sin \omega i \; d\omega$$

$$= -\frac{1}{\pi} \int_0^{\pi} \omega \sin \omega i \; d\omega \qquad (3.42)$$

Unless you are lucky enough to find this particular integral in some table, you must resort to integration by parts. If you do so, you end up with the following mess.

$$c_i = -\frac{1}{\pi} \left[ \frac{\omega(-\cos \omega i)}{i} \right] \bigg|_0^{\pi} + \frac{1}{i} \int_0^{\pi} \cos \omega i \; d\omega \qquad (3.43)$$

We can evaluate the expression for all coefficients except $c_0$, and we will treat that coefficient as a special case by going back to the original integral. When $i = 0$, we are integrating $\sin(\omega 0)$ — that is 0. Therefore, $c_0$ is zero. Compute the other coefficients by installing the limits of integration into equation (3.43) for $c_i$.

$$c_i = \frac{\cos \pi i}{i} \qquad i \neq 0 \tag{3.44}$$

The coefficients of the nonrecursive differentiator are shown in Figure 3.9. The impulse response is an odd function, $h_i = -h_{-i}$, and the nonzero coefficients decrease as $1/i$ and have alternating signs. The frequency responses of different-length implementations of this filter are shown in Figure 3.10. Again, note that the longer filters have a closer match with the desired response.

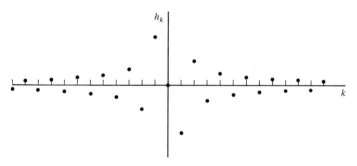

**Figure 3.9** Impulse response of a differentiator.

## 3.5  LENGTH OF THE FILTER

The Fourier design technique computes an impulse response which is possibly infinite length, but we are forced to implement such impulse responses with finite impulse response filters. Therefore, we are forced to compute the impulse response then determine how many terms we are able to afford. All the examples suggest that the filter's frequency responses become closer to the desired response as more terms of the impulse response are used (as the filter is made longer). This is true for all digital filters. We will show this by expressing the design criterion as a function the coefficients that are actually used in the filter.

The minimum design criterion is achieved when all of the impulse response is realized by the filter. This might require a filter with an infinite number of coefficients, but let's not worry about the practicalities for the moment. Denote this minimum design criterion by $\mathcal{E}_{\text{all}}$.

$$\mathcal{E}_{\text{all}} = \int_{-\pi}^{\pi} \left| \mathcal{D}(\omega) - \sum_{\text{all}} h_i e^{-j\omega i} \right|^2 d\omega \tag{3.45}$$

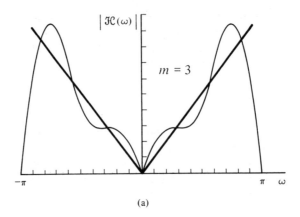

(a)

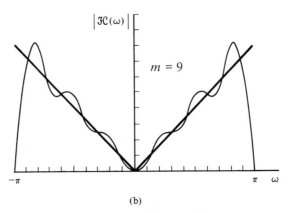

(b)

**Figure 3.10** Differentiators of different lengths.
(a) seven-coefficient differentiator;
(b) 19-coefficient differentiator.

We next expand the magnitude squared in terms of its four components.

$$\mathcal{E}_{\text{all}} = \int_{-\pi}^{\pi} |\mathcal{D}(\omega)|^2 \; d\omega - \int_{-\pi}^{\pi} \mathcal{D}(\omega) \sum_{\text{all}} h_i^* e^{j\omega i} \; d\omega - \int_{-\pi}^{\pi} \mathcal{D}(\omega)^* \sum_{\text{all}} h_i e^{-j\omega i} \; d\omega$$

$$+ \int_{-\pi}^{\pi} \sum_{\text{all}} h_i e^{-j\omega i} \sum_{\text{all}} h_k^* e^{j\omega k} \; d\omega$$

$$(3.46)$$

By rearranging the second term, we see that its integral is just the $i$th term of the impulse response.

$$\int_{-\pi}^{\pi} \mathcal{D}(\omega) \sum_{\text{all}} h_i^* e^{j\omega i} \, d\omega = \sum_{\text{all}} h_i^* \int_{-\pi}^{\pi} \mathcal{D}(\omega) e^{j\omega i} \, d\omega$$
$$= 2\pi \sum_{\text{all}} |h_i|^2 \tag{3.47}$$

The third term also reduces to the sum of the squares of the impulse response.

$$\int_{-\pi}^{\pi} \sum_{\text{all}} h_i \mathcal{D}^*(\omega) e^{-j\omega i} \, d\omega = 2\pi \sum_{\text{all}} |h_i|^2 \tag{3.48}$$

The last term is the magnitude squared of the designed filter's frequency response. Because the integral of the exponents is almost always zero, the last term is also the sum of the squared impulse response.

$$\int_{-\pi}^{\pi} \sum_{\text{all}} h_i e^{-j\omega i} \sum_{\text{all}} h_k^* e^{j\omega k} \, d\omega = \sum_{\text{all}} h_i \sum_{\text{all}} h_k^* \int_{-\pi}^{\pi} e^{j\omega(i-k)} \, d\omega$$
$$= \sum_{\text{all}} c_i (2\pi h_i^*)$$
$$= 2\pi \sum_{\text{all}} |h_i|^2 \tag{3.49}$$

If we combine the results above into equation (3.46), we find that the minimum error is the difference between the integral of the square of the desired response and the sum of the squares of the impulse response.

$$\mathcal{E}_{\text{all}} = \int_{-\pi}^{\pi} |\mathcal{D}(\omega)|^2 \, d\omega - 2\pi \sum_{\text{all}} |h_i|^2 \tag{3.50}$$

Although we will not need it for our work, it is interesting to know that the minimum design criterion is zero for almost any desired response. In other words, if we are allowed to use an infinitely-long filter, we can exactly match almost any desired frequency response.

If we repeat the computation of the design criterion, but this time assume that we are using only some of the impulse response, we find that the development is virtually unchanged. The resulting criterion is the difference between the integral of the square of the desired response and the sum of the square of the portion of the impulse response that is actually used by the filter.

$$\mathcal{E}_{\text{some}} = \int_{-\pi}^{\pi} |\mathcal{D}(\omega)|^2 \, d\omega - 2\pi \sum_{\text{used}} |h_i|^2 \tag{3.51}$$

The question now is how these two design criteria are related: What happens to the design criterion when we use only some of the impulse response? The answer is right in front of us. Divide the impulse response into two groups: those terms that are used and those that are not used.

$$\sum_{\text{all}} |h_i|^2 = \sum_{\text{used}} |h_i|^2 + \sum_{\text{not used}} |h_i|^2 \tag{3.52}$$

Applying this grouping of the impulse response to the previous computation of the criteria shows us that the criterion is increased by the square of the portion of the impulse response that is not used.

$$\mathcal{E}_{\text{some}} = \mathcal{E}_{\text{all}} + 2\pi \sum_{\text{not used}} |h_i|^2 \tag{3.53}$$

Therefore, if we use all the nonzero terms of the impulse response, we will get a filter with a minimum design criterion. However, practical restrictions on the filter length will generally force us to ignore (truncate) some of the impulse response. In that case, the criterion will be increased by the sum of the squares of the impulse response terms that we do not use. As we shorten the filter (use fewer coefficients and shorten its impulse response), the criterion generally increases. This result supports our observations of the examples.

**Example:** Compute the design error, $\mathcal{E}_{\text{some}}$, as a function of filter length for the high-pass filter and differentiator designed in this chapter.

We begin by modifying equation (3.51).

$$\mathcal{E} = \int_{-\pi}^{\pi} |D(\omega)|^2 \, d\omega - 2\pi \sum_{i=-m}^{m} |h_i|^2 \tag{3.54}$$

This is the design error when $2m + 1$ terms of the impulse response are implemented by the filter. In the case of the lowpass filter, equation (3.54) takes the following form:

$$\mathcal{E} = \pi - 2\pi \sum_{i=-m}^{m} \left[ \frac{1}{\pi i} \sin\left(\frac{\pi}{2}i\right) \right]^2 \tag{3.55}$$

The plot of this error as a function of filter length is shown in Figure 3.11a. The design error is rapidly reduced by just a three-coefficient filter. Lengthening the filter causes modest reduction of the design error. Notice that the design error is not changed as $m$ is increase by one from an odd value. This is because the even terms of this filter's impulse response are zero and therefore do not reduce the design error.

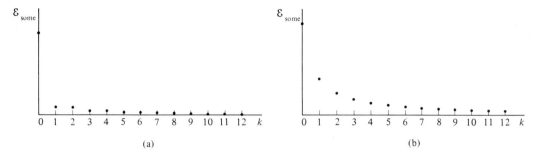

**Figure 3.11** Design error as a function of $m$, half the filter length

The calculation of the error for the differentiator follows the same lines. Plug the expression for the differentiator's coefficients into equation (3.54).

$$\mathcal{E} = \frac{2}{3}\pi^3 - 2\pi \sum_{i=-m}^{m} \left(\frac{\cos \pi i}{i}\right)^2 \tag{3.56}$$

The design error as a function of the filter's length is shown in Figure 3.11b. Notice that the error decreases more slowly in this example. This is because the impulse response of the differentiator does not fall off as fast as the response of the low-pass filter. Therefore, the design of the differentiator is more sensitive to the filter length than the design of the low-pass filter.

## 3.6  SUMMARY

We now have a very general method for designing nonrecursive digital filters. It will work for any desired response: real, imaginary, complex, odd, even, or what have you. The design is based on the Fourier expansion and requires the computation of the Fourier integral. The technique computes coefficients independently of the length of the filter, and we pick the length after we compute the coefficients. We have both observed and shown that the filter's frequency response becomes closer to the desired response as we include more and more coefficients by making the filter longer.

## EXERCISES

3-1. Will the use of the following design criteria result in the the Fourier design technique? Justify your answer.

(a) $\int_0^{2\pi} |\mathcal{H}(\omega) - \mathcal{D}(\omega)|^2 \, d\omega$

(b) $\int_{-2\pi}^{2\pi} |\mathcal{H}(\omega) - \mathcal{D}(\omega)|^2 \, d\omega$

(c) $\int_{-\pi}^{\pi} |\mathcal{H}(\omega) - D(\omega)| \ d\omega$

(d) $\int_{-\pi}^{\pi} |\mathcal{H}(\omega) - D(\omega)|^4 \ d\omega$

3-2. Evaluate the following expressions.

(a) $\int_{\pi}^{\pi} \sum_{i=-m}^{m} c_i \sin[(k-i)s] \ ds$

(b) $\int_{-\pi}^{\pi} \sum_{i=-m}^{m} c_i \cos[(i-k)s] \ ds$

(c) $\int_{-\pi}^{0} e^{-j\omega k} e^{j\omega i} \ d\omega$

(d) $\int_{0}^{2\pi} e^{j\omega k} e^{j\omega i} \ d\omega$

3-3. Design (find the simplest expression for the $c_i$'s) nonrecursive digital filters for the following desired responses.

(a) $D(\omega) = \sum_{k=-3}^{3} \frac{1}{k} e^{j\omega k}$

(b) $D(\omega) = \sum_{k=-m}^{m} \left| \frac{1}{k} \right| e^{j2\omega k}$

(c) $D(\omega) = \sum_{k=-4}^{4} k \cos \omega k$

3-4. Suppose that we use the following erroneous Fourier design equations. How are the coefficients and the frequency responses of the resulting filters related to those of the correctly designed filters?

(a) $c_i = \int_{-\pi}^{\pi} D(\omega) e^{j\omega i} \ d\omega$

(b) $c_i = \frac{1}{2\pi} \int_{0}^{\pi} D(\omega) e^{j\omega i} \ d\omega$

(c) $c_i = \frac{1}{2\pi} \int_{-\pi}^{\pi} D(\omega) e^{-j\omega i} \ d\omega$

3-5. Break the following functions into the odd and even parts.

(a) $1 + j \cos \omega$

(b) $e^{j\omega k} \sin 0.1\pi$

(c) $e^{j\omega k} \cos k\omega$

(d) $1 + t + t^2 + t^3$

(e) $1 + \sin \omega$

(f) $2\omega e^{j\omega k}$

3-6. Design a 13-coefficient nonrecursive high-pass filter with the following frequency response.

(a) Compute the general equation for the $c_i$'s.

(b) List the values of the 13 coefficients, $c_{-6} \ldots c_6$.

(c) Plot the magnitude of the frequency response of a 13-coefficient realization.

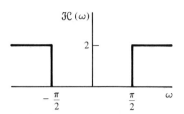

(d) Plot the magnitude of the frequency response for an infinite number of coefficients. Think this problem out before plotting (or is it plodding?).

3-7. Design a nonrecursive clipping differentiator.

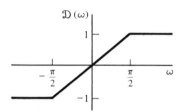

(a) Compute a general equation for the coefficients.

(b) Plot the magnitude of the frequency response for 7 and 19 coefficient realizations.

(c) Compare your results to the frequency responses in Figure 3.9.

3-8. Consider a real and odd desired response $\mathcal{D}(\omega) = -\mathcal{D}(-\omega)$.

(a) Show that the coefficients that are generated through the Fourier design method are odd, $c_i = -c_{-i}$.

(b) Show that the filter has a dc gain of zero, $\mathcal{H}(0) = 0$, for any symmetric implementation ($i = -m$ to $m$).

3-9. Suppose you have a signal that is corrupted with a 60 Hz sinusoidal noise (from the 120 V house current?). You wish to remove this 60 Hz noise by passing the signal plus noise through a digital filter. You have a digital filter that will sample the signal plus noise 240 times/sec and implement a nonrecursive filter.

(a) Sketch a symmetric frequency response for a digital filter that will stop (gain of zero) all signals between 50 and 70 Hz and passes those signals between 0 and 50Hz and those from 70 to 120 Hz. Label your sketch in digital frequency (radians per sample).

(b) Design a nonrecursive digital filter with the characteristics computed in part (a).

(c) Plot the magnitude of the frequency response of this *notch* filter for 11 and 17 symmetrically placed coefficients.

(d) What are the gains of the 11- and 17-point filters at 60 Hz. Which filter would you use?

3-10. Many applications require digital filters with frequency responses that change rapidly with frequency. For example, the frequency response of a low-pass filter should instantaneously change from the stopband to the passband. However, we know that finite-length nonrecursive filters are plagued by slowing varying frequency responses.

(a) Compute the slope, $\frac{d\mathcal{H}(\omega)}{d\omega}$, for the frequency response of a $(2m + 1)$-coefficient nonrecursive filter.

(b) Compute the maximum slope of an antisymmetric nonrecursive filter.

(c) At what frequency does the maximum slope occur for an antisymmetric nonrecursive filter?

3-11. Most applications demand causal filters. However, many of our designs generate filters with symmetric impulse responses — noncausal filters. Fortunately, there is a simple method of changing a noncausal filter to a causal one.

(a) Design a seven-point causal low-pass filter, $c_0, c_1, \ldots, c_6$. The magnitude of this filter's passband must be 1 for $-\pi/2 < \omega < \pi/2$ and 0 for other frequencies between $-\pi$ and $\pi$.

(b) Plot the magnitude of this filter's frequency response and compare with the responses in Figure 3.6.

3-12. Consider the design error for the differentiator designed in Section 3.4.

(a) Compute the design error when only seven points are used.

(b) Compute the design error when 19 coefficients are used.

(c) How does the design error decrease as more and more coefficients are used? For example, compare the reduction in error as the filter is increased from seven to nine coefficients with the reduction as it is increased from 19 to 21 coefficients. What does this tell you about very long filters?

# Windowing

The Fourier design technique is not the be all and end all of nonrecursive digital filter design. Sure, the Fourier method computes the best possible filter, but only in the integral squared error sense. Many applications are sensitive to other features of the frequency response, and the designer must be willing to increase the integral squared error to improve these other features.

The examples in Chapter 3 showed us that finite length filters that are designed through the Fourier method have two obvious deficiencies.

1. The frequency response has significant oscillations around transitions in the desired response. These are called *ripples*. The period of the ripples appear to decrease as the filter is made longer.
2. The frequency response does not follow quick transitions in the desired response. The desired response of a low-pass filter changes abruptly from 1 to 0 (passband to stopband), but the finite-length Fourier filter changes slowly. This region of gradual change is called the filter's *transition region*. The examples suggest that the width of the transition region shrinks as the filter is made longer.

These observations should not come as a big surprise. The frequency response of a finite-length digital filter is the weighted sum of sines and cosines.

$$\mathcal{H}(\omega) = \sum_{i=-m}^{m} c_i \left( \cos \omega i - j \sin \omega i \right) \tag{4.1}$$

The sines and cosines are smooth, oscillatory functions, so a sum of them cannot match an instaneous transition in the desired frequency response — hence the transition regions. The rate that $\mathcal{H}(\omega)$ can change with $\omega$ is restricted by $m\omega$. Longer filters have larger $m$s and can change more rapidly with $\omega$. The oscillations in the frequency response are understandable because $\mathcal{H}(\omega)$ is composed of a finite set of oscillatory functions.

Most applications are sensitive to the amplitude and the period of the ripples as well as the width of the transition region. This chapter develops a design technique that allows us to control the rippling and the transition width. It would be nice if we could reduce both, but as life has it, we are going to encounter a trade-off between the ripples and the transition width. For a fixed-length filter, efforts to lower the amplitude of the ripples will increase the transition width, and vice versa.

We could approach this problem in two ways. After the success of Chapter 3, we could be tempted to develop a completely new design technique from first principles. Start by defining a design criterion that is sensitive to ripples, transition regions, the length of the filter, or what have you. Then develop a new design procedure by minimizing your design criterion with respect to the filter's coefficients. If successful, the technique will be broadly accepted and named after you.

Unfortunately, we are going to cower from fame and fortune and take a more productive approach. Let's reconsider the Fourier design technique and identify the sources of the ripples and transition regions. Once identified, we can propose a modification to the Fourier method, which will reduce the rippling and/or transitions. This investigation will lead to the concept of *windowing*.

## 4.1   WINDOWS

Figure 4.1 shows a desired frequency response (Figure 4.1a) and three realizations of it. Figure 4.1b shows the frequency response of an infinite-length filter (no, I didn't really build it). The infinite-length filter exactly matches the desired response, no rippling, and no transition region. Figures 4.1c and d show finite realizations of the same filter. As expected, the rippling and the transition regions are more noticable, as fewer coefficients are used. Therefore, in this example the rippling and transitions do not originate in the Fourier computation, but are the result of the truncation of a potentially infinite-length filter. If we are to understand the sources of rippling and transitions, we must concentrate on the truncation part of the Fourier design.

The truncation part of the design is really a likely candidate for trouble, because it was added to the design process as an afterthought. The first phase of the Fourier design was well developed from first principles. The truncation part was introduced as a practical necessity because we could not implement infinite-length digital filters. The problem now is to express the action of truncation in a mathematical way, and then see how truncation affects the frequency response. We will express truncation as the process of windowing.

Suppose that the Fourier computation generated an infinite impulse response, $h_i$. We will truncate this impulse response by multiplying each term of the impulse

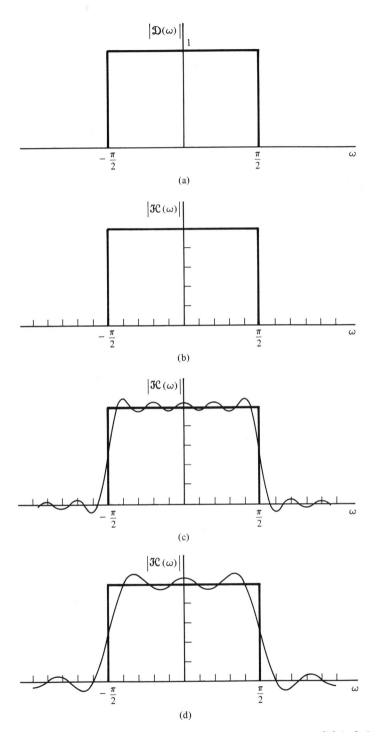

**Figure 4.1** Truncation of a low-pass filter: (a) desired response; (b) infinite number of coefficients; (d) 21 coefficients; (e) 11 coefficients

**99**

response by a corresponding window coefficient $w_i$. The window coefficients are 1 for those terms that we wish to keep and are 0 for those we wish to truncate.

$$w_i = \begin{cases} 1 & \text{if } |i| \leq m \\ 0 & \text{if } |i| > m \end{cases} \tag{4.2}$$

This set of coefficients is called the $(2m+1)$-point uniform window. The truncated filter has coefficients $c_i$, which are the products of the Fourier coefficients and the window coefficients.

$$c_i = w_i h_i \tag{4.3}$$

This is a finite-length filter ($2m + 1$ coefficients). We have successfully expressed truncation as a simple matematical operation — a coefficient-by-coefficient multi-plication of the Fourier coefficients and the uniform window.

Now that we have expressed truncation in terms of windowing, we can look at the effect of truncation (windowing) on the frequency response. The impulse response, $h_i$, computed by the Fourier design technique is associated with the desired frequency response.

$$\mathcal{D}(\omega) = \sum_{i=-\infty}^{\infty} h_i e^{-j\omega i} \tag{4.4}$$

The filter's coefficients, $c_i$, generate the filter's frequency response.

$$\mathcal{H}(\omega) = \sum_{i=-m}^{m} c_i e^{-j\omega i} \tag{4.5}$$

Because the filter coefficients have been truncated by the uniform window, the sum can be extended to $\pm\infty$.

$$\mathcal{H}(\omega) = \sum_{i=-\infty}^{\infty} c_i e^{-j\omega i} \tag{4.6}$$

We will also need the "frequency response" of the window coefficients. Frequency response is in quotes because the window is not a digital filter; it will never have an input nor generate an output. In an effort not to confuse the window and filter, the window's "frequency response" is called the window response and is denoted $\mathcal{W}(\omega)$.

$$\mathcal{W}(\omega) = \sum_{i=-m}^{m} w_i e^{-j\omega i} \tag{4.7}$$

or

$$\mathcal{W}(\omega) = \sum_{i=-\infty}^{\infty} w_i e^{-j\omega i} \tag{4.8}$$

Our study now involves three separate frequency responses: the desired, the window, and the actual filter. The next section develops the relationship among them.

## 4.2   WINDOW RESPONSES AND CONVOLUTION

This section computes $\mathcal{H}(\omega)$ in terms of the desired response and the window response. We will find that $\mathcal{H}(\omega)$ is the periodic convolution (whatever that is) of $\mathcal{W}(\omega)$ and $\mathcal{D}(\omega)$.

We begin the development by computing the filter's frequency response.

$$\mathcal{H}(\omega) = \sum_{i=-\infty}^{\infty} c_i e^{-j\omega i} \tag{4.9}$$

But the filter's coefficients are just the product of the Fourier and window coefficients.

$$\mathcal{H}(\omega) = \sum_{i=-\infty}^{\infty} w_i h_i e^{-j\omega i} \tag{4.10}$$

The next step is to express the sum in terms of the window response and the desired frequency response. This is most directly performed through an unabashed trick. We will resort to this trick by expressing the $h_i$ as sum of all the desired coefficients multiplied by an integral of exponentials.

$$h_i = \frac{1}{2\pi} \sum_{l=-\infty}^{\infty} h_l \int_{-\pi}^{\pi} e^{j(i-l)s}\, ds \tag{4.11}$$

There is no need for panic. This integral is the integral of sines and cosines over an integer number of periods. We have seen this before; it is $2\pi$ if $l$ equals $i$ and is 0 otherwise.

$$\int_{-\pi}^{\pi} e^{j(i-l)s}\, ds = \begin{cases} 2\pi & \text{if } l = i \\ 0 & l \neq i \end{cases} \tag{4.12}$$

All of the $h_l$ coefficients in the sum are multiplied by 0 except for the $i$th coefficient, which is multiplied by $2\pi$. The $2\pi$ is canceled by the $1/2\pi$ term out front, so the equality is true. This does not mean that you have to like it. Remember that this is a trick.

We now exploit the equality by substituting it into the expression for $\mathcal{H}(\omega)$.

$$\mathcal{H}(\omega) = \sum_{i=-\infty}^{\infty} w_i \left[ \frac{1}{2\pi} \sum_{l=-\infty}^{\infty} h_l \int_{-\pi}^{\pi} e^{j(i-l)s}\, ds \right] e^{-j\omega i} \tag{4.13}$$

Rearrange the integral and the sums and factor the exponential.

$$\mathcal{H}(\omega) = \frac{1}{2\pi} \int_{-\pi}^{\pi} \sum_{i=-\infty}^{\infty} w_i e^{-j\omega i} \sum_{l=-\infty}^{\infty} h_l e^{jsi} e^{-jls}\, ds \tag{4.14}$$

The last step is to consolidate the summation over $i$ by moving an exponential and collecting terms.

$$\mathcal{H}(\omega) = \frac{1}{2\pi} \int_{-\pi}^{\pi} \left[ \sum_{i=-\infty}^{\infty} w_i e^{-j(\omega-s)i} \right] \left[ \sum_{l=-\infty}^{\infty} h_l e^{-jls} \right] ds \qquad (4.15)$$

These bracketed terms should look familiar. The first one is the window response evaluated at $\omega - s$, and the second one is the desired frequency response, $\mathcal{D}(\omega)$. The integral and the shifts are the periodic convolution. Therefore, $\mathcal{H}(\omega)$ is the periodic convolution of the window response and the desired frequency response.

$$\mathcal{H}(\omega) = \frac{1}{2\pi} \int_{-\pi}^{\pi} \mathcal{W}(\omega - s) \mathcal{D}(s) \, ds \qquad (4.16)$$

The rippling and transition regions are generated by this convolution. But before we proceed with the filter issues, let's take a short side trip and look at periodic convolution.

**Periodic Convolution**

The periodic convolution (sometimes called *circular convolution*) of two periodic functions is defined as

$$z(\omega) = \frac{1}{L} \int_{\frac{L}{2}}^{\frac{-L}{2}} x(\omega - s) y(s) \, ds. \qquad (4.17)$$

where $x(\ )$ and $y(\ )$ are periodic functions with a period of $L$.

The convolution is the integral of the product of $y(s)$ and $x(s)$ that has been mirror-imaged and shifted by $\omega$. The variable $\omega$ is also the independent variable of the result, so each shift of $x(\ )$ generates another value for the convolution.

The convolution produces a periodic result, with a period of $L$. We prove this by looking at $z(\omega + L)$.

$$z(\omega + L) = \frac{1}{L} \int_{\frac{L}{2}}^{\frac{-L}{2}} x(\omega + L - s) y(s) \, ds \qquad (4.18)$$

But $x(\ )$ has a period of $L$.

$$x(\omega + L - s) = x(\omega - s) \qquad (4.19)$$

Therefore,

$$z(\omega + L) = \frac{1}{L} \int_{\frac{L}{2}}^{\frac{-L}{2}} x(\omega - s) y(s) ds$$
$$= z(\omega) \qquad (4.20)$$

Most people use a sketch of the functions to aid them in the computation of periodic convolution. The sketch gives them insight into the operation of the convolution and also serves as a quick check of the results.

The actual computation of periodic convolution is not conceptually difficult once you get the hang of it. As a matter of fact, the computation tends to be both mechanical and boring. You may find the following seven-step approach to periodic convolution helpful.

1. Decide which one of the functions is the stationary function, $y(s)$, and which will be the shifted function, $x(\ )$. This is a truly arbitrary decision, but once made you better stick to it.

2. Sketch the $y(s)$ and a mirror image of $x(s)$, $x(-s)$. Mirror imaging is just flipping $x(\ )$ around the vertical axis, or equivalently, replacing all $x(s)$ with $x(-s)$.

3. Pick a value of $\omega$ between $-L/2$ and $L/2$. There is no reason for using $\omega$s outside this interval because the result of the convolution is periodic, with a period of $L$. It is best to start with $\omega = 0$ and gradually pick larger $\omega$'s. Use your good judgment here and pick significant $\omega$'s by using the results in steps 4, 5, and 6. Each $\omega$ can require a great deal of work, so use only the necessary $\omega$'s.

4. Shift the mirror image of $x(s)$ $\omega$ units to the right [with respect to $y(s)$, which is stationary]. Move $x(s)$ to the right for positive $\omega$'s and to the left for negative $\omega$'s.

5. Multiply the stationary and shifted functions together. You need the result for only the $-L/2$ to $L/2$ interval, so do not do this for all $\omega$.

6. Compute the integral of the product of the two functions. This is the area under the product from $-L/2$ to $L/2$ and divide it by $L$. This value is the result of the convolution for the particular value of $\omega$ that you selected in step 3.

7. Decide if you have had enough. If you can sketch the result from the work you have done, then quit. If you need some more points, go back to step 3 and thoughtfully pick another $\omega$.

If you follow these seven steps or any other technique that works for you, you can convolve any two functions, at least in principle. The real problem behind convolution is that it is tedious and invites errors because of the sheer mass of computation and bookkeeping. Use your sketches to direct and double check your work, and more important use you head while picking $\omega$'s. Most beginners waste a lot of time needlessly computing results that can be inferred. Generally, it is a waste of time to pick evenly spaced values of $\omega$ (i.e. $\omega = 0, 0.1, 0.2, 0.3, \ldots$).

**Example:** Periodic Convolution

Perform the periodic convolution of the two functions that are sketched in Figure 4.2. Notice that they are periodic in $2\pi$, just like frequency responses.

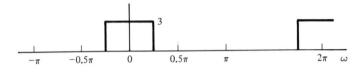

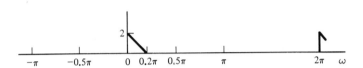

**Figure 4.2** Periodic convolution.

We will select the square function as the stationary function and the triangle function as the shifted. Figure 4.3a shows these functions: the square function and the unshifted ($\omega = 0$) mirror image of the triangle function. Notice that the mirror imaging has flipped the triangles around.

We compute the first result ($\omega = 0$) with the help of Figure 4.3a. Because the square overlaps the triangle, the multiplication yields a single triangle. Therefore, the value of the convolution for $\omega = 0$ is the area of a triangle, $0.6\pi$, divided by $2\pi$ (this is our $L$). This process is repeated for $\omega = 0.1\pi, 0.2\pi, 0.3\pi, 0.4\pi, 0.5\pi$ as illustrated in Figure 4.3b-f. As the triangles are first shifted to the right, the multiplication of the two functions keeps producing a single triangle, and gives the same area. But when it is shifted more than $0.25\pi$ the multiplication begins to truncate the triangle, and thereby decreases the area and the result. Notice that we wasted our time with the $0.1\pi$ and $0.2\pi$ shifts — we should have taken care of those by inspection. The results of the convolution are sketched in Figure 4.3g. Notice that the convolution produces a periodic result.

A final note on periodic convolution. Be careful not to ignore the contributions of the other periods to the convolution. If the functions are wide, as in Figure 4.4, pieces of more than one period may appear in the multiplication and integration. In these cases the result is the sum of the areas of the pieces. Some people erroneously think that only one period can affect the convolution, because we are integrating from $-\pi$ to $\pi$. As illustrated in Figure 4.4, this is clearly not so.

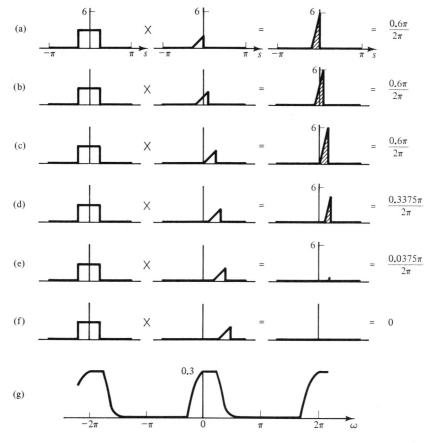

**Figure 4.3** Convolution example: (a) $\omega = 0$; (b) $\omega = 0.1\pi$;
(c) $\omega = 0.2\pi$; (d) $\omega = 0.3\pi$; (e) $\omega = 0.4\pi$
(f) $\omega = 0.5\pi$; (g) result.

## 4.3  WINDOW RESPONSE OF THE UNIFORM WINDOW

We have shown that the frequency response of the actual filter is the periodic convolution of the window response and the desired response. This section develops the window response of the uniform window and shows how this particular window affects the filter's frequency response.

The general definition of the window response is as follows:

$$\mathcal{W}(\omega) = \sum_{i=-m}^{m} w_i e^{-j\omega i} \tag{4.21}$$

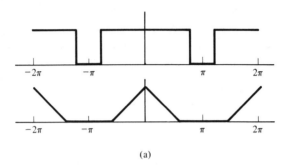

(a)

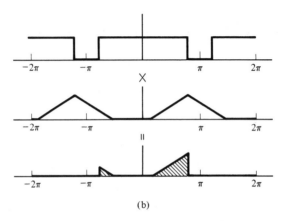

(b)

**Figure 4.4** Example of convolution of wide functions:
(a) two wide functions; (b) overlap when $\omega = 0.8\pi$.

The nonzero coefficients of the uniform window are 1. Therefore, the uniform window response is the sum of $2m + 1$ exponentials.

$$\mathcal{W}_u(\omega) = \sum_{i=-m}^{m} e^{-j\omega i} \tag{4.22}$$

This window response can be expressed as the sum of cosines.

$$\mathcal{W}_u(\omega) = 1 + 2\sum_{i=1}^{m} \cos \omega i \tag{4.23}$$

We can derive a simpler expression for it by noting that $\mathcal{W}_u(\omega)$ is a truncated geometric progression.

$$\mathcal{W}_u(\omega) = \frac{e^{-j\frac{2m+1}{2}\omega} - e^{j\frac{2m+1}{2}\omega}}{e^{-j\frac{\omega}{2}} - e^{j\frac{\omega}{2}}} \tag{4.24}$$

This expression is rich in Euler applications.

$$\mathcal{W}_u(\omega) = \frac{\sin\left(\frac{2m+1}{2}\omega\right)}{\sin\left(\frac{\omega}{2}\right)} \tag{4.25}$$

The uniform window response is the ratio of sines. The numerator changes as $(2m+1)/2$ and the denominator varies more slowly as $1/2$. The window response is shown in general in Figure 4.6a and for $m=5$ and $m=10$ in Figure 4.6b and c.

The window response is dominated by two features. First there is a large hump around $\omega = 0$. This is called the *main lobe* of the response and is that portion that lies between the first two zero crossings. The rest of the window response is called the *side lobes*. The side lobes are defined as the portion of the response for $\omega < -2\pi/(2m+1)$ or $\omega > 2\pi/(2m+1)$. The main lobe and side lobe definitions are illustrated in Figure 4.5.

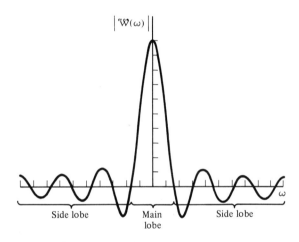

**Figure 4.5** Definition of the main and side lobes.

The side lobes of a uniform window are characterized by oscillations with zero crossings every $2\pi/(2m+1)$ and decreasing amplitude. As the window is made longer (longer filters) the main lobe becomes narrower and higher, and the side lobes become more concentrated around $\omega = 0$. Lengthening the window causes the window response to compress around zero frequency.

Now let's apply this window response to the periodic convolution. This will give the frequency response of the truncated filter. For the purpose of this development the window response will be split into its main and side lobes. This is simply a device to more clearly see the affect of the convolution on the desired response and does not imply that the main and side lobes act independently. We denote the

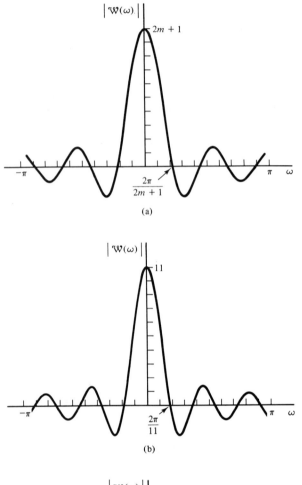

(a)

(b)

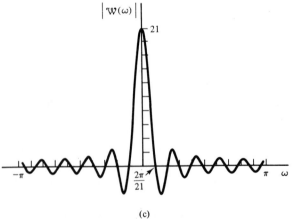

(c)

**Figure 4.6** Window function of the uniform window: (a) general form; (b) 11-point window; (c) 21-point window.

main lobe $M(\omega)$ and the side lobe $S(\omega)$. This separation of the window response is illustrated in Figure 4.7.

$$W(\omega) = M(\omega) + S(\omega) \tag{4.26}$$

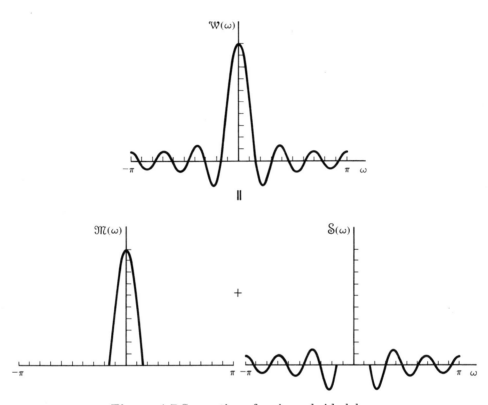

**Figure 4.7** Separation of main and side lobes.

We can also break the periodic convolution into the convolution with the main lobe and the convolution with the side lobe.

$$\mathcal{H}(\omega) = \frac{1}{2\pi} \int_{-\pi}^{\pi} W_u(\omega - s)D(s) \ ds \tag{4.27}$$

or

$$\mathcal{H}(\omega) = \frac{1}{2\pi} \int_{-\pi}^{\pi} M(\omega - s)D(s) \ ds + \frac{1}{2\pi} \int_{-\pi}^{\pi} S(\omega - s)D(s) \ ds \tag{4.28}$$

Through this separation, we are able to investigate the impact of the main and side lobes independently.

As illustrated in Figure 4.8 the main-lobe convolution causes a broadening or "smearing" of the features of the desired response. When the main lobe is totally contained in the passband the convolution is simply the area of the main lobe, a constant. When the main lobe is shifted so that it totally lies in the stopband the convolution results in 0 — the stopband of the filter. When the main lobe interacts with the desired response's transition from passband to stopband, the area computed by the convolution gradually decreases from the area of the main lobe to zero as the mainlobe is shifted completely into the stopband. This transition area is the shifts from $\omega_c - 2\pi/(2m+1)$ through $\omega_c + 2\pi/(2m+1)$. As the main lobe is shifted out of the passband and to the right, the convolution produces smaller results. At a shift of exactly $\omega_c$ the convolution yields a value of half the area of the main lobe.

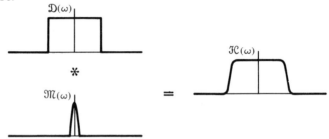

**Figure 4.8** Convolution of the desired response and the main lobe.

We conclude that the convolution with the main lobe causes the broadening of the filter's transition region. The broadening is approximately the width of the main lobe, $4\pi/(2m+1)$. As the filter gets longer, the main lobe becomes narrower and the broadening becomes less noticeable. This supports our earlier observation that longer filters have shorter transition regions.

The convolution of the desired response and the window response's side lobes gives rise to the rippling in the filter. Figure 4.9 shows the convolution of a high-pass filter and the side lobes of the uniform window. When the side lobes are primarily confined to the passband or stopband of the desired response the convolution yields small, constant results. As the side lobes are shifted through the transition, the convolution generates an oscillatory result. The zero crossings of the oscillations are separated by $2\pi/(2m+1)$, and the amplitude of the oscillation is determined by the amplitude of the side lobe that is passing by the transition. The ripples are small as the small side lobes are slid by the transition, but as the ripples grow as the larger side lobes encounter the transition.

We conclude that the convolution of the side lobes causes the rippling in the filter's frequency response. The ripples' zero crossings are separated by $2\pi/(2m+1)$ rad, so longer filters have faster ripples. The amplitude of the ripples is dictated by the amplitude of the side lobes. Large side lobes cause larger ripples. For the uniform window, the amplitude of the side lobes is unaffected by the length of the

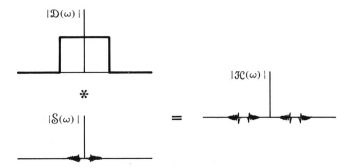

**Figure 4.9** Convolution of the desired response and the side lobe.

window. So lengthening the filter will not reduce the rippling. J. W. Gibbs showed that a finite-length low-pass filter will possess an 8.9% maximum ripple no matter how long the filter is made. As shown in Figure 4.10, this maximum ripple occurs just before and after the transition band.

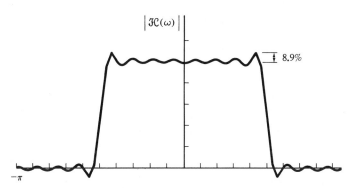

**Figure 4.10** Gibbs phenomenon.

In summary, the application of the uniform window (truncation) causes a broadening of the transition region and rippling around the transition region. The broadening is attributed to the window response's main lobe. The ripples are caused by the side lobes. Lengthening the window will result in faster ripples, but will not reduce the amplitude of the ripples. A finite-length uniform window generates a maximum ripple of about 8.9% of the gain change in the transition. The effect of window length on a high-pass filter is illustrated in Figure 4.11.

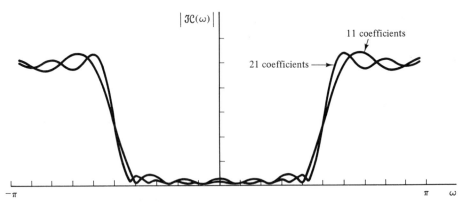

**Figure 4.11** Eleven- and 21-coefficient uniform windows
on a high-pass filter.

## 4.4   WINDOW CHARACTERISTICS

The rippling and transition regions of the filter are caused by windowing. We
have seen that the width of the transition region is directly associated with the
width of the window response's main lobe, and the amplitude of the rippling is
proportional to the amplitude of the side lobes. The ideal window response produces
the narrowest main lobe and the smallest side lobes. Unfortunately, attempts to
generate window coefficients that give rise to such window responses have failed.
For a given length window, smaller-amplitude side lobes generally mean a wider
main lobe, and vice versa. The uniform window has the narrowest main lobe of any
set of window coefficients of the same length. However, this narrow main lobe of
the uniform window is paid for by large side lobes.

We can always reduce the width of the main lobe by making the filter longer
— simply increase $m$. But the side lobes are unaffected by lengthening the filter.
So, when looking for new windows, the amplitude of the side lobes is really the
primary consideration. This is true even though smaller side lobes generally dictate
a wider main lobe. We can always make the window longer to take care of the wider
transition regions.

The search for the ideal window has generated close to 200 variations, but
no clear winners. The problem is that different windows provide features that are
desirable for different applications. If you are forced to squeeze the last drop of
capability out of the window, you will find yourself pouring through the catalogs
of windows looking for the "best." Fortunately, most digital filter designers are
not that picky and are satisfied with only a few windows. We are going to look
at three additional windows: von Hann, Hamming, and Kaiser. We consider the
von Hann because it is the easiest "clever" filter, and it is useful for motivating the
Hamming window. The Hamming window is the most widely used, general-purpose

window. The Kaiser window is more sophisticated and allows the designer to tailor the window to suit the particular application.

**von Hann Window**

A window is fully defined by a set of window coefficients, $w_i$. The selection of the particular coefficients for the von Hann window is motivated by a gradual rather than an abrupt truncation of the Fourier coefficients. If practicality forces you to throw away coefficients, why do it abruptly like the uniform window? Rather than make a hard yea or nay decision (keep the coefficient or toss it), why not gradually taper the Fourier coefficients so that there is no abrupt differentiation between those you keep and those you truncate. The von Hann coefficients smoothly truncate the Fourier coefficients.

The von Hann window is generated by a raised cosine (sometimes it is called the "raised cosine" window).

$$w_i = \begin{cases} \frac{1}{2} + \frac{1}{2}\cos\left(\frac{\pi i}{m+1}\right) & |i| \leq m \\ 0 & \text{otherwise} \end{cases} \tag{4.29}$$

These window coefficients are sketched in Figure 4.12.

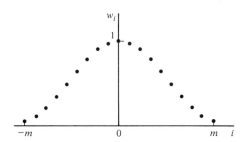

**Figure 4.12** Coefficients of the von Hann window.

The von Hann window multiplies the central Fourier coefficients by approximately unity, so they are left pretty much unaltered. The coefficients toward the ends of the filter are gradually discounted as they are multiplied by smaller window coefficients.

The window response of the von Hann window is computed by evaluating the following sum.

$$\mathcal{W}_{vH}(\omega) = \sum_{i=-m}^{m} \left[\frac{1}{2} + \frac{1}{2}\cos\left(\frac{\pi i}{m+1}\right)\right] e^{j\omega i} \tag{4.30}$$

An involved and tedious set of manipulations leads to the closed form.

$$\mathcal{W}_{vH}(\omega) = \frac{\sin[(m+1)\omega]\cos\frac{\omega}{2}}{2\sin(\frac{\omega}{2})} \left[ \frac{1}{1 - \left(\frac{\sin(\omega/2)}{\sin(\pi/2(m+1))}\right)^2} \right] \qquad (4.31)$$

The exact form of this expression is not as important as an appreciation for its shape. The von Hann window function is sketched in Figure 4.13. The uniform window is also shown for comparison.

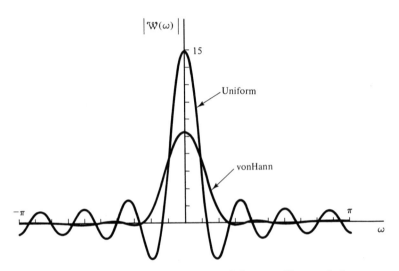

**Figure 4.13** Window response of the von Hann window.

Notice that the first zero crossings are at $\pm 2\pi/(m+1)$, so the main lobe of the von Hann window is about twice as wide as the uniform window's. Also note that the side lobes of the von Hann window are about one-tenth of those of the uniform. Therefore, the use of the von Hann instead of the uniform window results in a doubling of the transition region and much smaller ripples. This difference is illustrated in the 21-point low-pass filter that is shown in Figure 4.14.

We conclude that if your application is sensitive to ripples in the frequency response, it is best to use the von Hann window. The von Hann will double the transition regions of the filter, but that can always be corrected if you can afford to double the length of the filter.

**Hamming Window**

R. W. Hamming looked at the window responses of the uniform and Von Hann windows and noticed that their side lobes generally have opposite signs (von Hann is

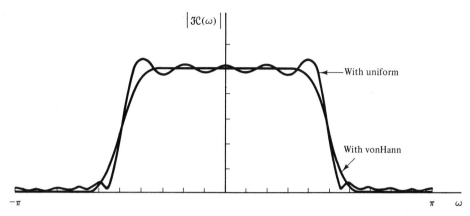

**Figure 4.14** Low-pass filter with a 21-point von Hann window.

positive when uniform is negative, and vice versa). He reasoned that the amplitude of the side lobes could be reduced further if he constructed a window that was a mixture of the uniform and the von Hann windows. He proposed a "generalized von Hann" window that is a function of parameters $a$ and $b$.

$$w_i = \begin{cases} 2a \cos \frac{\pi i}{m} + b & |i| \leq m \\ 0 & \text{otherwise} \end{cases} \tag{4.32}$$

where $2a + b = 1$.

The question is: how do you pick the values of $a$ and $b$? If $a = 0$ and $b = 1$, this generalized window is uniform. If $a$ is increased to $\frac{1}{4}$ and $b$ decreased to $\frac{1}{2}$, the window is almost a von Hann (except that the end coefficients, $w_{-m}$ and $w_m$, are zero). A window that has features that are between the von Hann's and the uniform's would require $a$'s and $b$'s that lie between these limits.

$$0 \leq a \leq 0.25 \qquad\qquad 4.33$$

$$0.5 \leq b \leq 1$$

Hamming went to his trusty computer and began searching for the values and $a$ and $b$, which minimize the amplitude of the maximum side lobe. This is the mini-max criterion, or the Chebyshev criterion. Many operations later he found the optimal values, but they turned out to be functions of the filter length. These values are given in Figure 4.15. Short filters require a Hamming window that looks more like a uniform window; $b$ is large. As the filters become longer, $b$ becomes smaller and $a$ becomes larger; the window looks more like a von Hann window.

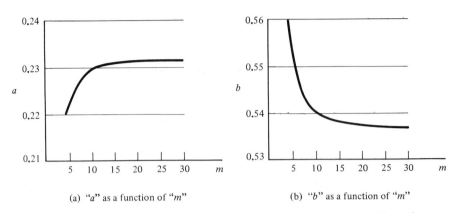

(a) "$a$" as a function of "$m$"          (b) "$b$" as a function of "$m$"

**Figure 4.15** Hamming window parameters as a function of length.

The window response of a Hamming window is plotted in Figure 4.16. Note that it is very close to the response of the von Hann window — it has slightly smaller side lobes. Because the Hamming generates less ringing than the von Hann and it does not widen the transition region, the Hamming window is generally preferred. Do not use the von Hann window when you have a better one at your disposal.

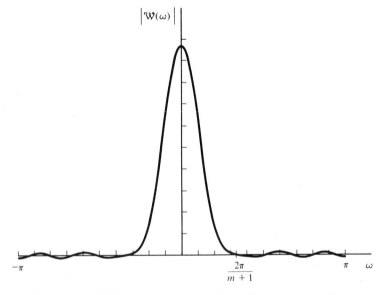

**Figure 4.16** Window response of the Hamming window.

**Example:** Find the Hamming window coefficients for a 19-point ($m = 9$) bandpass filter.

The type of the filter (low-pass, high-pass, band-pass, or what have you) has nothing to do with the window. It is only the filter's length that counts. By consulting Figure 4.15, we find that a 19-point filter requires that $a = 0.227$ and $b = 0.546$. Therefore, the window is defined as follows:

$$w_i = \begin{cases} 0.454 \cos \frac{\pi i}{9} + 0.546 & |i| \le m \\ 0 & \text{otherwise} \end{cases} \tag{4.34}$$

**Kaiser Window**

J. F. Kaiser was also looking at windows, but he had a different approach. He though that it would be useful to find a window function that would be adjustable. That is, the window contains a parameter that explicitly controls the main/side lobe trade-off. He searched for a function that would make a good window and allow for the inclusion of this adjustment. He settled on the prolate spheroidal functions. These functions have the nasty properties that they are not well known and are difficult to compute. But all of this should be overlooked because these functions make great, adjustable windows — narrow main lobes with small-amplitude side lobes. The prolate spheroidal function, $I_o(x)$, is listed in Table 4.1.

Kaiser used this function for a window by making the function's argument depend on the window coefficient, $i$.

$$w_i = \begin{cases} \dfrac{I_o\left[\alpha\sqrt{1-\left(\frac{i}{m}\right)^2}\right]}{I_o(\alpha)} & |i| \le m \\ 0 & \text{otherwise} \end{cases} \tag{4.35}$$

The argument of the numerator (the contents of the brackets) starts at $\alpha$ when $i = 0$ and decreases to 0 as $i$ increases to $m$. The denominator normalizes the window coefficients — it is constant with respect to $i$.

The parameter $\alpha$ simply scales the argument of the spheroidal function. When $\alpha$ is 0, both the numerator and denominator of the window coefficients are 1; the Kaiser window becomes the uniform window. When $\alpha = 5.4414$ the Kaiser window becomes the Hamming window (it is beyond the scope of this presentation to show this). As $\alpha$ becomes larger, the main lobe of the Kaiser window is made wider and the side lobes are made smaller. Therefore, we can adjust the Kaiser window to achieve ripple and/or transition specifications.

These specifications are dictated when the desired response is specified. We should realize now that it is fruitless to specify a filter's response exactly, because the rippling and the transition regions will keep us from meeting precise specifications. So we should begin the design by specifying the filter's response with some explicit uncertainity. As illustrated in Figure 4.17, the design should define acceptable regions for the filter's response.

**Table 4.1** Prolate Spheroidal Function.

| $x$ | $I_o(x)$ | $x$ | $I_o(x)$ |
|-----|----------|-----|----------|
| 0.0 | 1.0000 | 4.0 | 11.302 |
| 0.1 | 1.0025 | 4.2 | 13.443 |
| 0.2 | 1.0100 | 4.4 | 16.010 |
| 0.4 | 1.0404 | 4.6 | 19.093 |
| 0.6 | 1.0921 | 4.8 | 22.794 |
| 0.8 | 1.1665 | 5.0 | 27.240 |
| 1.0 | 1.2661 | 5.2 | 32.584 |
| 1.2 | 1.3938 | 5.4 | 39.010 |
| 1.4 | 1.5534 | 5.6 | 46.738 |
| 1.6 | 1.7500 | 5.8 | 56.039 |
| 1.8 | 1.9696 | 6.0 | 67.235 |
| 2.0 | 2.2796 | 6.2 | 80.717 |
| 2.2 | 2.6292 | 6.4 | 96.963 |
| 2.4 | 3.0492 | 6.6 | 116.54 |
| 2.6 | 3.5532 | 6.8 | 140.14 |
| 2.8 | 4.1574 | 7.0 | 168.59 |
| 3.0 | 4.3306 | 7.2 | 202.92 |
| 3.2 | 5.7472 | 7.4 | 244.34 |
| 3.6 | 8.0278 | 7.6 | 294.33 |
| 3.8 | 9.5169 | 7.8 | 354.68 |

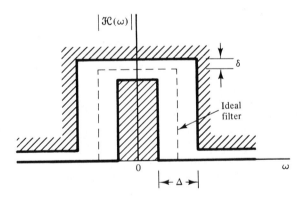

**Figure 4.17** Specification of a low-pass filter.

These regions are determined by three elements:

1. An ideal frequency response, which is shown as the dashed line
2. A ripple restriction of $\delta$ percent of the filter's gain change from pass to stop band
3. A transition width of $\Delta$

The goal is to design a filter with a frequency response that is confined to the unshaded regions of Figure 4.17.

Kaiser developed a design procedure for meeting such design specifications. It begins by computing the Fourier coefficients from the ideal frequency response. Next, the coefficients of the actual filter are computed by multiplying the Fourier coefficients and the Kaiser window coefficients. This means that we must determine values of $\alpha$ and $m$ to meet the design specifications.

The rippling is determined by the amplitude of the side lobes, so the design specification $\delta$ is really a restriction on the side-lobe amplitudes, hence a restriction on the window parameter, $\alpha$. Similarly, the transition region is determined by the width of the main lobe. The window response's main-lobe width is controlled by $\alpha$ and the length of the window. Therefore, for a given $\alpha$, the transition width $\Delta$ is really a restriction on the length of the filter, $m$. Kaiser noted that for a given $\alpha$ the transition width is approximately $D(\alpha)/2m$, where $D(\alpha)$ is the width of the main lobe that has been normalized to the length of the filter. For example, the uniform window has a $D(\alpha)$ of 5.97 rad, and the Hamming window has a $D(\alpha)$ of about 21.68 rad.

Based on these observations, Kaiser developed the following window design.

- Given a $\delta$, find the window's $\alpha$, the shape of the window.
- Given the $\alpha$, find $D(\alpha)$ the normalized main-lobe width of the window.
- Given the normalized main-lobe width, compute the length of the filter by dividing $D(\alpha)$ by twice the transition restriction, $\Delta$, $m = D(\alpha)/2\Delta$. This will more than likely lead to a fractional coefficient, so round $m$ up to the next integer.

Kaiser tabulated the relationships between $\delta$, $\alpha$, and $D(\alpha)$ on a computer. His results are shown in Table 4.2. So, given a particular ripple specification, the window parameters can be read from the corresponding entries in the $\alpha$ and $D(\alpha)$ columns. The $\alpha$ parameter is used directly in the window definition, and $D(\alpha)$ is divided by twice the transition specification to get the length of the window.

**Example:** Kaiser Window

We wish to compute a high-pass filter with ripples less that 0.1% and a transition region less than $0.05\pi$ rad. Find the Kaiser window.

We first go to the design table of Table 4.2 and find the values of $\alpha$ and $D(\alpha)$ for this ripple specification. We find that $\alpha = 5.65$ and $D(\alpha) = 22.77$ rad. We compute the length of the window by dividing the normalized main

**Table 4.2** Kaiser's Design Table

| Ripple | $\alpha$ | $D(\alpha)$rad/sec |
|--------|----------|--------------------|
| $<9\%$ | 0.0 | 5.794 |
| 5% | 1.34 | 7.477 |
| 1% | 3.39 | 14.024 |
| 0.5% | 3.98 | 16.336 |
| 0.1% | 5.65 | 22.777 |
| 0.05% | 6.21 | 25.007 |
| 0.01% | 7.857 | 31.017 |
| 0.001% | 10.061 | 40.275 |

lobe width by twice the transition specification.

$$m = \frac{D(\alpha)}{2\Delta} = \frac{22.78}{2(0.05)\pi}$$

$$= 72.5 \mapsto 73$$

(4.36)

We need a 147-coefficient Kaiser window with an $\alpha$ of 5.653 to meet our design specifications.

We could design a shorter version of the filter by relaxing the design specifications. Suppose that we are willing to tolerate a 1% ripple and a transition region of $0.1\pi$. Table 4.2 shows us that $\alpha = 3.395$ and $D(\alpha) = 14.02$. This design will require a filter that is only 46 coefficients long.

Notice that Kaiser's table does not bother to go above 9% ripple. If your design can tolerate a ripple greater than 9% you should use the uniform window. It has 9% ripples and generates the narrowest transition regions.

## 4.5  SUMMARY

In this chapter we have explored the consequences of truncating potentially infinite-length digital filters. We found that truncation introduced both rippling and broad transition regions; both are undesirable. The concept of windowing was introduced first to study the effects of truncation and then to mitigate these effects. Four windows were introduced: the uniform, von Hann, Hamming, and Kaiser. We found that the uniform window generates the narrowest transition regions, the Hamming is the most widely used window, and the Kaiser is the most versatile. Most serious digital filter designers rely on the Kaiser window to meet their design specs.

## EXERCISES

4-1. Perform the circular convolution of the two functions sketched below. Assume a period of $2\pi$.

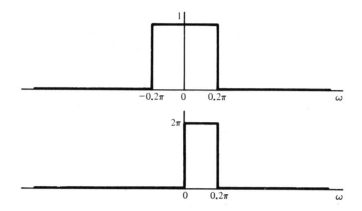

4-2. Perform the cicular convolution of the two *wide* functions sketched below. Assume a period of $2\pi$.

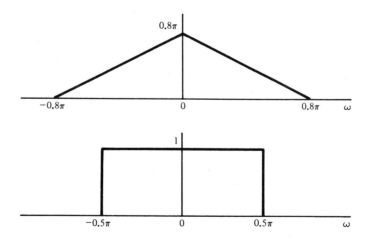

4-3. Perform the circular convolution of a high-pass filter with a pseudo window response.

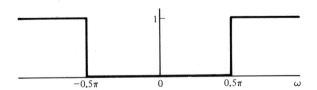

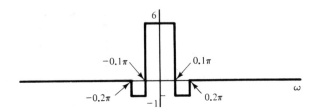

(a) Sketch the result.

(b) How wide is the transition band?

(c) How high are the ripples?

(d) How does the height of the ripples relate to the area of the side lobes?

4-4. Show that the uniform window produces a lower design error (Chapter 3) than that produced by the von Hann window.

4-5. Compute the excess design error (Chapter 3's design error) caused by using the von Hann window instead of the uniform window. The excess design error is the difference between the error resulting from the von Hann window and the error caused by the uniform window.

$$\epsilon_{excess} = \epsilon_{vonHann} - \epsilon_{uniform}$$

4-6. Consider a Bartlett window,

$$w_i = 1 - \frac{|i|}{m+1} \qquad |i| \leq m$$

(a) Express the Bartlett window as the convolution of two uniform windows. What are the lengths and amplitudes of the uniform windows?

(b) Plot the window response of a 21-point Bartlett window.

(c) Compare the window response of the 21-point Bartlett to that of an 11-point uniform window.

4-7. Consider the Lanczos window,

$$w_i = \frac{\sin \frac{\pi i}{m}}{\frac{\pi i}{m}} \qquad |i| \leq m$$

(a) Plot the window response of a 21-point Lanczos window.

(b) Compare the Lanczos window response to a 21-point Hamming window.

4-8. Consider a bogus window: the "every other point" uniform window.

$$w_i = 1 \qquad |i| = 0, 2, 4, \ldots, m$$

(a) Compare the window response of this window to the regular uniform window.

(b) How does this window affect the frequency response of a low-pass filter?

4-9. Consider another bogus window: the von Hann squared window,

$$w_i = \left( \frac{1}{2} + \frac{1}{2} \cos \frac{\pi i}{m+1} \right)^2 \qquad |i| \leq m$$

(a) Plot its 21-point window response.

(b) Compare the squared vonHann's window response with the regular von Hann window.

4-10. Consider a bogus window: the ramp window,

$$w_k = |k| \qquad |k| \leq m$$

(a) Plot the window response of a 15-point ramp window.

(b) Comment on its main and side lobes.

(c) How does this compare with the useful windows?

(d) When would you use the ramp window?

4-11. Compute the first five terms $(w_0, w_1, w_2, w_3, \text{and } w_4)$ of a 21-point Hamming window.

4-12. Consider the three simple windows: uniform, von Hann, and Hamming.

(a) When would you use the uniform window?

(b) When would you use the von Hann window?

(c) When would you use the Hamming window?

4-13. The "ideal" window should have a very narrow main lobe (small transition region) and very low side lobes (small ringing). The impulse is such a function — it has a zero-width main lobe and no side lobes.

$$\delta(\omega) = \begin{cases} \infty & \omega = 0 \\ 0 & \text{otherwise} \end{cases}$$

and

$$\int_{-\infty}^{\infty} \delta(\omega) \, d\omega = 1$$

(a) Compute the coefficients of a window whose window response is $\delta(\omega)$.

(b) How does this window affect the frequency response of the filter?

4-14. We wish to design a notched filter as sketched below. It has a narrow stopband centered at $\pi/2$ with a width of $\Delta$.

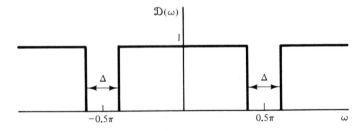

(a) Compute the minimum value of $\Delta$ that will result in a zero gain at $\pi/2$ when we use a 21-point uniform window. You may ignore the side lobes.

(b) Repeat part (a) for an 11-point uniform window.

(c) Repeat part (a) for a 21-point Hamming window.

(d) Repeat part (a) for a 41-point Hamming window.

4-15. Compute the Kaiser parameters ($\alpha$ and $m$) for a low-pass filter with the a cutoff frequency of $\pi/2$, ripples less than 0.5%, and a transition band less than $0.1\pi$.

4-16. Compute the Kaiser parameters ($\alpha$ and $m$) for a low-pass filter with a cutoff frequency of $0.05\pi$, maximum peak-to-peak ripple of 1%, and a transition band of $0.01\pi$. Notice that this filter has a very small passband.

4-17. Compute the Kaiser coefficient, $w_0, w_{10},$ and $w_{30}$ of a Kaiser window for a high-pass filter. The filter has a unity gain, a cutoff frequency of $0.3\pi$, a maximum gain of 1.01, and a transition region of $0.1\pi$.

4-18. Use the Kaiser table (Table 4.2) to compute the maximum transition region and the minimum and maximum passband gains for a unity-gain 21-coefficient low-pass filter using a uniform window.

4-19. Repeat Exercise 4-18 but use a 41-coefficient uniform window. How are the ripples and transition region affected by doubling the filter length?

4-20. Use the Kaiser design table (Table 4.2) to find the maximum ripple and transition band for a 21-point Hamming window.

4-21. Repeat Exercise 4-20 but use a 41-coefficient Hamming window. How are the ripples and transition region affected by doubling the filter length?

4-22. We note that decreasing the ripple or transition region requirement forces us to use longer Kaiser windows. Is the length of the Kaiser window more sensitive to halving the ripple specification or to halving the transition region?

4-23. Design a bandpass digital filter with the following specifications.

Passband $0.4\pi$ to $0.6\pi$

Passband gain: 1.99 to 2.01

Transition region: $0.2\pi$

(a) Compute the impulse response of this filter via the Fourier design method. Give a general expression for $h_k$ before the windowing.

(b) Compute the Kaiser window parameters, $\alpha$ and $m$, for this filter.

(c) Compute the windowed coefficients and list them.

(d) Plot the frequency response of this filter. Overlay the plot with your specifications to show that the filter, indeed, meets your specifications.

# 5

# Recursive Digital Filters and the z-Transform

We have been concentrating on nonrecursive digital filters because they are easier to deal with than their recursive cousins. In this chapter we explore the wonderful world of recursive filters, both their characterization and their design. Unfortunately, most of the tools developed previously are useless for recursive filters, so we will have to forge some new tools.

One might ask: why consider recursive filters if they are so hard to work with and we already know how to design nonrecursive filters? The answer is simple: recursive filters with relatively few coefficients can have frequency responses that vary quickly with $\omega$. The frequency response of a recursive filter is the ratio of two polynomials in $e^{j\omega}$. Neither of these polynomials can vary quickly with $\omega$, but as the denominator approaches zero the ratio can change quite quickly. In this sense, recursive filters are more economical than nonrecursive filters — it takes fewer coefficients to do the same job. Figure 5.1 compares a five-coefficient recursive low-pass filter with some nonrecursive filters. The recursive filter gives a much better response with fewer coefficients.

## 5.1 THE $z$-TRANSFORM

Before we can design or even discuss recursive filters, we must develop the tools to characterize them. Unfortunately, the frequency response that worked so well with the nonrecursive filters is not enough. This section introduces an extension of the frequency response, called the *z-transform*.

Recall the development of the frequency response. We got the frequency re-

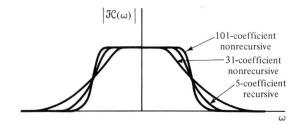

**Figure 5.1** Comparison of recursive and nonrecursive frequency responses.

sponse with an eigenvalue-eigenfunction argument. When the eigenfunctions $e^{j\omega k}$ are applied to the input of a filter, the output is the product of the input and the eigenvalue, $\mathcal{H}(\omega)$. The frequency response is the most useful characterization of recursive and nonrecursive filters, but it gives us information on how the filter behaves with exponential inputs only. The $z$-transform shows how the filter responds to a broader class of inputs. Although the $z$-transform can also be applied to nonrecursive filters, we did not use it before because nonrecursive filters did not demand it.

The $z$-transform is derived through an eigenfunction-eigenvalue argument that is identical to the one used to develop the frequency response. In this case we consider inputs of $x_k = z^k$, where $k$ is the index and $z$ is a complex number. Examples of such functions are given below.

$$z = 1: \qquad \ldots, x_{-2} = 1, x_{-1} = 1, x_0 = 1, x_1 = 1, x_2 = 1, \ldots$$

$$z = 0.5: \qquad \ldots, x_{-2} = 4, x_{-1} = 2, x_0 = 1, x_1 = 0.5, x_2 = 0.25, \ldots$$

$$z = e^{j\frac{\pi}{2}}: \qquad \ldots x_{-2} = -1, x_{-1} = -j, x_0 = 1, x_1 = j, x_2 = -1, \ldots$$

We must first show that $z^k$ is indeed an eigenfunction of a digital filter, by applying $z^k$ to the input. The filter's output is the convolution of the input and the filter's impulse response.

$$y_k = \sum_{i=-\infty}^{\infty} h_i z^{k-i} \qquad \text{when input} = z^k \qquad (5.1)$$

The sum in the exponent is factored into the product of $z^k$ and $z^{-i}$.

$$y_k = \sum_{i=-\infty}^{\infty} h_i z^{-i} z^k \qquad (5.2)$$

But the $z^k$ term is independent of the index of the summation, so it can be factored out.

$$y_k = z_k \left[ \sum_{i=-\infty}^{\infty} h_i z^{-i} \right] \tag{5.3}$$

The output of the filter is the product of the input and the bracketed term. That term is independent of $k$, so $z^k$ is indeed an eigenfunction and the bracketed term is the associated eigenvalue. This eigenvalue is called the $z$-transform of the filter's impulse response, $\mathcal{Z}\{h_i\}$, or simply the $z$-transform of the filter, $\mathcal{H}_z(z)$ .

$$\mathcal{Z}\{h_i\} = \mathcal{H}_z(z) = \sum_{i=-\infty}^{\infty} h_i z^{-i} \tag{5.4}$$

The $z$-transform is the weighted sum of the impulse response. We adopt the notation $\mathcal{H}_z(z)$ to differentiate the $z$-transform from the filter's frequency response $\mathcal{H}(\omega)$.

The complex number $z$ is the independent variable of the $z$-transform , as $\omega$ is the independent variable of the frequency response. Both $z$ and $\mathcal{H}_z(z)$ are complex, so a sketch of the $z$-transform requires four dimensions: a real and an imaginary part for both $z$ and $\mathcal{H}_z(z)$. The plot of a $z$-transform can be reduced to only three dimensions if we are willing to consider only the magnitude of $\mathcal{H}_z(z)$. A plot of the magnitude of a $z$-transform is shown in Figure 5.2. The real and imaginary components of $z$ form a plane (called the $z$-plane, of course), and $|\mathcal{H}_z(z)|$ is sketched on top of the $z$-plane.

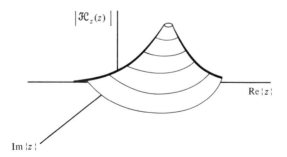

**Figure 5.2** Sketch of the magnitude of the $z$-transform.

Because the $z$-transform is an extension of the frequency response, it does not represent a significant departure from the thinking we have used in the past. As a matter of fact, the frequency response is contained in the $z$-transform — if we have the $z$-transform of a filter, we also have its frequency response. This is shown by restricting $z$ to the complex exponent $e^{j\omega}$.

$$\mathcal{H}_z(z)\,|_{z=e^{j\omega}} = \sum_{i=-\infty}^{\infty} h_i\left(e^{j\omega}\right)^{-i}$$

$$= \sum_{i=-\infty}^{\infty} h_i e^{-j\omega i} \tag{5.5}$$

But the right-hand side is the frequency response of the filter. Therefore,

$$\mathcal{H}(\omega) = \mathcal{H}_z(z)\,|_{z=e^{j\omega}} \tag{5.6}$$

The frequency response is the $z$-transform evaluated along $e^{j\omega}$. Since $e^{j\omega}$ has a magnitude of 1 and an angle of $\omega$, the frequency response is the $z$-transform along a unit radius circle that is centered at the origin. This circle turns out to be pretty important, so we will give it a name — the unit circle. The unit circle and a $z$-transform are depicted in Figure 5.3. The magnitude of the frequency response at $\omega$ is simply the value of $\mathcal{H}_z(z)$ at $z = e^{j\omega}$. Notice that this evaluation is periodic; the circle is completely traversed every $2\pi$ change in $\omega$. This is another manifestation of the periodicity of the frequency response.

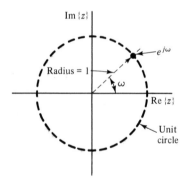

**Figure 5.3** The $z$-plane and the unit circle.

**Example:** $z$-Transform of a Causal, Nonrecursive Filter
Find the $z$-transform of the causal, nonrecursive filter

$$y_k = \sum_{i=0}^{m} c_i x_{k-i} \tag{5.7}$$

We need the impulse response of this filter before we can charge ahead on the $z$-transform computation. Fortunately, we know from earlier work that the impulse response of a nonrecursive filter is just the filter's coefficients. Therefore, this $z$-transform is just a weighted sum of the filter's coefficients.

$$\mathcal{H}_z(z) = \sum_{i=0}^{m} c_i z^{-i} \tag{5.8}$$

**Example:**   $z$-Transform of a Recursive Filter
     Find the $z$-transform of the simple recursive filter

$$y_k = c_0 x_k + d_1 y_{k-1} \tag{5.9}$$

Previous work has shown that this filter has simple geometric progression as an impulse response.

$$h_k = \begin{cases} c_0 \left(d_1\right)^k & k \geq 0 \\ 0 & k < 0 \end{cases} \tag{5.10}$$

The $z$-transform is just a weighted sum of this impulse response.

$$\mathcal{H}_z(z) = \sum_{k=0}^{\infty} c_0 \left(d_1\right)^k z^{-k} \tag{5.11}$$

This looks like a dead end unless you are fortunate enough to remember a handy identity.

$$\sum_{i=0}^{\infty} a^i = \frac{1}{1-a} \qquad \text{if} \quad |a| < 1 \tag{5.12}$$

We can apply this result directly to the $z$-transform after rearranging the exponentiation.

$$\mathcal{H}_z(z) = c_0 \sum_{k=0}^{\infty} \left(d_1 z^{-1}\right)^k = \frac{c_0}{1 - d_1 z^{-1}} \qquad \text{if} \quad \left|d_1 z^{-1}\right| < 1 \tag{5.13}$$

This is a remarkably simple expression for this $z$-transform .

In the preceding example we were forced to compute the filter's impulse response before we could compute its $z$-transform . This is because the $z$-transform was defined in terms of the impulse response. It is much more convenient to express the $z$-transform in terms of the filter's coefficient, so we can go directly from the coefficients to the $z$-transform without the arduous computation of the impulse response.

Let's apply $z^k$ to the input of a filter that is expressed in terms of its coefficients.

$$y_k = \sum_{i=-m}^{m} c_i z^{k-i} + \sum_{i=1}^{n} d_i y_{k-i} \tag{5.14}$$

However, we have shown that $z^k$ is an eigenfunction of the filter, so the output is simply the product of the input and the $z$-transform.

$$y_k = z^k \mathcal{H}_z(z) \tag{5.15}$$

We create an algebraic expression for $\mathcal{H}_z(z)$ by substituting this product into the sums.

$$z^k \mathcal{H}_z(z) = \sum_{i=-m}^{m} c_i z^{k-i} + \sum_{i=1}^{n} d_i z^{k-i} \mathcal{H}_z(z) \tag{5.16}$$

Next, we multiply both sides by $z^{-k}$, collect the $\mathcal{H}_z(z)$ terms, and divide.

$$\mathcal{H}_z(z) = \frac{\sum_{i=-m}^{m} c_i z^{-i}}{1 - \sum_{i=1}^{n} d_i z^{-i}} \tag{5.17}$$

The $z$-transform is the ratio of two polynomials in $z$. The coefficients of the numerator are determined by the nonrecursive coefficients, and the coefficients of the denominator are the recursive coefficients. Notice that the denominator has a minus sign in front of the sum of the $d_i$s. Many people tend to ignore that minus sign — be careful.

A causal filter ($c_i = 0$ for $i < 0$) has a $z$-transform whose order of the numerator is less than or equal to the order of its denominator. We can see this from direct inspection of equation (5.17). If the filter is causal, the numerator's highest power of $z$ possible is $z^0$. But the denominator always has a $z^0$ (1), so there is no way for the numerator to have a higher power than the denominator, if the filter is causal.

**Example:** $z$-Transform of a Simple Filter

Find the $z$-transform of the following simple recursive filter:

$$y_k = c_0 x_k + d_1 y_{k-1} \tag{5.18}$$

We can use our new definition of the $z$-transform and compute it from inspection.

$$\mathcal{H}_z(z) = \frac{c_0}{1 - d_1 z^{-1}} \tag{5.19}$$

Most of us do not like to see polynomials in $z^{-1}$, so we will clear the negative exponents by multiplying top and bottom by $z$.

$$\mathcal{H}_z(z) = \frac{c_0 z}{z - d_1} \tag{5.20}$$

This is identical to the result we obtained from the impulse response method [equation (5.13)], but is a far easier development.

**Example:** $z$-Transform and the Frequency Response

We have shown that the frequency response is the $z$-transform when the z variable is restricted to the unit circle. Let's confirm this by plugging $z = e^{j\omega}$ into the general form of the $z$-transform — note that we indeed get the frequency response.

$$\left. \mathcal{H}_z(z) \right|_{z=e^{j\omega}} = \frac{\sum_{i=-m}^{m} c_i \left(e^{j\omega}\right)^{-i}}{1 - \sum_{i=1}^{n} d_i \left(e^{j\omega}\right)^{-i}} \tag{5.21}$$

But the right-hand side of this equation is just the frequency response of a recursive digital filter. Therefore, the relationship between the $z$-transform and the frequency response checks.

By using the polynomial form of the $z$-transform we can readily go from the coefficients to $\mathcal{H}_z(z)$ and from $\mathcal{H}_z(z)$ back to the filter's coefficients. The $z$-transform and coefficient representations of the filter are equivalent. Going from the coefficients to the $z$-transform is easy; simply plug the $c_i$s and $d_i$s into the definition of $\mathcal{H}_z(z)$. Going the other way — computing the coefficients from the $z$-transform — is a little more involved because $\mathcal{H}_z(z)$ must be manipulated into the form of the definition. Once we get it into that form the coefficients can be picked off by inspection. The definition form requires that the denominator have a $z^0$ ($z^0 = 1$) and negative powers of $z$. We get an arbitrary $\mathcal{H}_z(z)$ into that form by multiplying the denominator and numerator by $a^{-1}z^{-l}$, where $l$ is the largest exponent of $z$ in the denominator and $a$ is the associated coefficient. The multiplication does not alter the $z$-transform but does get the denominator into the form of "1 minus negative powers of $z$." Consider some examples.

**Example:** Designing a Filter from a $z$-Transform

Find the coefficients of the digital filter that has the $z$-transform of equation (5.22).

$$\mathcal{H}_z(z) = \frac{12z}{3z^2 + 6z - 9} \tag{5.22}$$

We begin by getting this $\mathcal{H}_z(z)$ into the proper form. We multiply top and bottom by $\frac{1}{3}z^{-2}$.

$$\mathcal{H}_z(z) = \frac{4z^{-1}}{1 + 2z^{-1} - 3z^{-2}} \tag{5.23}$$

This is the form of the definition, so we get the coefficients from inspection.

$$c_1 = 4 \qquad d_1 = -2 \qquad d_2 = 3 \qquad \text{all others zero} \tag{5.24}$$

Notice that the coefficients of the filter have opposite signs from the denominator's coefficients. This is because of the "$1 - \sum$" in the definition's denominator.

**Example:**  Designing a Filter from a Tricky $z$-Transform

Find the coefficients that are associated with the following $z$-transform .

$$\mathcal{H}_z(z) = \frac{1}{0.5z^{-4} + z^{-2}} \tag{5.25}$$

This $z$-transform is put into its definitional form by multiplying top and bottom by $z^2$ (because $-2$ is greater than $-4$).

$$\mathcal{H}_z(z) = \frac{z^2}{1 + 0.5z^{-2}} \tag{5.26}$$

The filter coefficients are obtained by inspection.

$$c_{-2} = 1 \qquad d_2 = -0.5 \qquad \text{all others zero} \tag{5.27}$$

The moral of this example is, don't be tricked by the order in which the denominator's terms are written.

## 5.2  POLES AND ZEROES

In Section 5.1 we showed that a digital filter can be represented as a set of filter coefficients or as a $z$-transform. This section extends our search for the perfect representation by showing that the $z$-transform can be represented by a gain factor and a set of features called *poles* and *zeros*. This new representation is no more than a clever way of expressing the ratio of polynomials.

The poles of the $z$-transform are those values of $z$ where $\mathcal{H}_z(z)$ is infinity. The $z$-transform can go to infinity because the denominator goes to zero or the numerator goes to infinity. Those poles that cause the denominator to go to zero are called *finite poles*, and those that cause the numerator to go to infinity are called *infinite poles*. The zeros of the $z$-transform are those values of $z$ that cause $\mathcal{H}_z(z) = 0$. This occurs when the numerator goes to 0 (*finite zeros*) or when the denominator goes to $\infty$ (*infinite zeros*).

The $z$-transform is completely specified by its finite poles and zeros and a gain factor. We denote the zeros $\varsigma_i$, the poles $p_i$, and the gain factor $G$. So the $z$-transform can be expressed as the ratio of the zero locations over the pole locations.

$$\mathcal{H}_z(z) = G\frac{(z - \varsigma_1)(z - \varsigma_2)\dots(z - \varsigma_m)}{(z - p_1)(z - p_2)\dots(z - p_n)} \tag{5.28}$$

This is simply an alternative way of expressing the ratio of polynomials. If we perform the multiplications, we will have a ratio of polynomials. It is time for some examples.

**Example:**   Filter Design from Gain, Poles, and Zeros

Design a recursive digital filter with zeros at $-1$ and $0$, and poles at $0.5$, $0.1 + j0.2$, and $0.1 - j0.2$, and a gain of 10. We begin the design by expressing the $z$-transform in terms of its poles, zeros, and gain — a ratio of products.

$$\mathcal{H}_z(z) = 10 \frac{(z+1)(z-0)}{(z-0.5)(z-0.1-j0.2)(z-0.1+j0.2)} \tag{5.29}$$

Multiply to get $\mathcal{H}_z(z)$ as a ratio of polynomials.

$$\mathcal{H}_z(z) = \frac{10z^2 + 10z}{z^3 - 0.5z^2 + 0.1z - 0.025} \tag{5.30}$$

We massage this into the definitional form [equation (5.17)] by multiplying top and bottom by $z^{-3}$.

$$\mathcal{H}_z(z) = \frac{10z^{-1} + 10z^{-2}}{1 - 0.5z^{-1} + 0.1z^{-2} - 0.025z^{-3}} \tag{5.31}$$

The coefficients of the digital filter are obtained by inspection.

$$c_1 = 10 \qquad c_2 = 10 \qquad d_1 = 0.5 \qquad d_2 = -0.1 \qquad d_3 = 0.025 \tag{5.32}$$

Are there any infinite poles or zeros for this filter? We find the infinite features of the filter by letting $z$ go to $\infty$ and looking at $\mathcal{H}_z(z)$ as it does. If $\mathcal{H}_z(z)$ goes to zero, there is at least one zero at infinity, and if it goes to $\infty$ there is at least one pole. If you simply plug $z = \infty$ into the expression for $\mathcal{H}_z(z)$, you will get an indeterminate result. Therefore, we must apply l'Hospital's rule to find the limit. Two applications of the rule to equation (5.30) show us that this filter has a single zero at infinity.

$$\lim_{z \to \infty} \mathcal{H}_z(z) = \lim_{z \to \infty} \frac{20}{6z} = 0 \tag{5.33}$$

A rule of thumb is when the denominator is higher order than the numerator, the $z$-transform has infinite zeros. When the numerator is higher order than the denominator, the $z$-transform has infinite poles.

It is also possible to go from the polynomial representation of $\mathcal{H}_z(z)$ to the gain, poles, and zeros. The finite zeros are the roots of the numerator, the finite poles are the roots of the denominator, and the gain factor is a scaling that makes the whole thing come out right. Unfortunately, finding the roots is difficult because it is equivalent to factoring the polynomial. Unless the polynomial is low order or in a convenient form, you are forced to use a computer to calculate the roots. Most computer centers and even most home computers have utilities to factor polynomials. You supply the computer with the coefficients and it returns the roots. However, first- and second-order polynomials can be easily factored by hand. Consider the following example.

**Example:** Computing the Poles and Zeros of a Digital Filter

Find the gain, poles, and zeros for the following filter.

$$c_0 = 2 \qquad c_1 = \frac{1}{2} \tag{5.34}$$

$$d_1 = 1 \qquad d_2 = \frac{3}{4} \tag{5.35}$$

We begin by computing the $z$-transform.

$$\mathcal{H}_z(z) = \frac{2 + \frac{1}{2}z^{-1}}{1 - 1z^{-1} - \frac{3}{4}z^{-2}} \tag{5.36}$$

or

$$\mathcal{H}_z(z) = \frac{2z^2 + \frac{1}{2}z}{z^2 - z - \frac{3}{4}} \tag{5.37}$$

We can factor the numerator by inspection.

$$2z^2 + 1z = 2z\left(z + \frac{1}{4}\right) \tag{5.38}$$

Therefore, this filter has finite zeros at 0 and $-\frac{1}{4}$.

Factorization of the denominator is not so easy, and we must resort to the quadratic formula. A quadratic formula in the form of $ax^2 + bx + c$ has roots given by

$$\frac{-b \pm \sqrt{b^2 - 4ac}}{2a} \tag{5.39}$$

The roots of the denominator are computed from the quadratic formula with $a = 1$, $b = -1$, and $c = -\frac{3}{4}$.

$$p_{1,2} = \frac{1 \pm \sqrt{1 + 3}}{2} \tag{5.40}$$

$$p_1 = \frac{3}{2} \qquad p_2 = -\frac{1}{2} \tag{5.41}$$

The gain factor was computed in the numerator's factorization. The 2 sitting out in front of the zeros is the gain. Therefore, this filter can be written in terms of its poles and zeros.

$$\mathcal{H}_z(z) = 2\frac{z\left(z + \frac{1}{4}\right)}{\left(z - \frac{3}{2}\right)\left(z + \frac{1}{2}\right)} \tag{5.42}$$

It is always a good idea to check such calculations by computing the coefficients of the digital filter that has these poles and zeros. We should come up with the filter we started with.

We begin the check by expressing $\mathcal{H}_z(z)$ as a ratio of polynomials.

$$\mathcal{H}_z(z) = \frac{2z^2 + \frac{1}{2}z}{z^2 - z - \frac{3}{4}} \tag{5.43}$$

Get this $\mathcal{H}_z(z)$ into the form of the definition by multiplying the previous equation by $z^2$ over $z^2$.

$$\mathcal{H}_z(z) = \frac{2 + \frac{1}{2}z^{-1}}{1 - z^{-1} - \frac{3}{4}z^{-2}} \tag{5.44}$$

The coefficients of the digital filter can now be determined by inspection.

$$c_0 = 2 \qquad c_1 = \frac{1}{2} \qquad d_1 = 1 \quad d_2 = \frac{3}{4} \tag{5.45}$$

Our pole/zero expansion checks — these are the original coefficients.

It is important to realize that we are exploring alternative representations of a digital filter and that all these representations are equivalent. If you are presented with the gain, poles, and zeros, you can compute the polynomial form of $\mathcal{H}_z(z)$ and from that determine the filter's coefficients. Given the filter coefficients, you can go the other way and compute $\mathcal{H}_z(z)$ and then the poles and zeros.

One of the benefits of the pole-and-zero representation is that it allows us to "plot" the $z$-transform in only two dimensions. Except for the filter's gain, all the information is contained in the locations of the poles and zeros in the $z$-plane. If we mark the pole locations with ×s on the $z$-plane and the zero locations with $\bigcirc$s, this two-dimensional plot will give us the $z$-transform within a gain factor.

We can also visualize the general shape of the magnitude of $\mathcal{H}_z(z)$ from the pole-zero plot. The poles mark locations where $\mathcal{H}_z(z) = \infty$ and the zeros mark the places where it is 0. Because the $z$-transform is composed of polynomials, it makes smooth transitions between the poles and zeros. Some people find it helpful to think of the surface of $|\mathcal{H}_z(z)|$ as a sheet of rubber. The sheet is "tacked" down to the $z$-plane by the zeros and is "elevated" by the poles. The stretchiness of the rubber accounts for the smoothness of the polynomials as the $z$-transform is "stretched" over the poles and tacked down by the zeros.

**Example:** Pole-Zero Plot of the Preceding Example

These concepts are illustrated in Figure 5.4 in the case of the preceding example. Visualize "poles" sticking out of the paper at the pole locations, and a piece of rubber draped over these poles. The rubber is tacked to the z-plane at the two zero locations. This picture is completed by finding the height of the "sheet of rubber" at the periphery of the z-plane; what happens to $\mathcal{H}_z(z)$ as $z \to \infty$? Since the denominator and the numerator are the same order, we must compute the limit by repeatedly applying l'Hospital's rule. The first application of l'Hospital's rule to equation (5.43) produces the indeterminate result

$$\mathcal{H}(\infty) = \frac{4z + \frac{1}{2}}{2z - 1} \Big|_{z=\infty} \tag{5.46}$$

The second application provides the answer:

$$\mathcal{H}(\infty) = \frac{4}{2} = 2 \tag{5.47}$$

Therefore, the $|\mathcal{H}_z(z)|$ surface has a height of 2 when the magnitude of $z$ is very large.

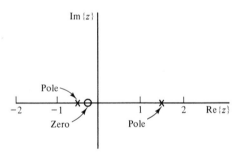

**Figure 5.4** Pole-zero plot.

By stretching the "sheet of rubber" over the poles and pinning it down by the zeros of Figure 5.4, we can visualize the magnitude of $\mathcal{H}_z(z)$ for this particular filter. $\mathcal{H}_z(z)$ becomes very large near $z = 1\frac{1}{2}$ and $z = -\frac{1}{2}$. It is small near $z = 0$ and $z = -\frac{1}{4}$, and it goes to a height of 2 for large $z$. The behavior of $\mathcal{H}_z(z)$ in the other regions of the z-plane is governed by the stretchiness of the rubber sheet. Although in many cases it is hard to visualize, the z-transform makes smooth transitions between the poles and zeroes. For example, $\mathcal{H}_z(z)$ is $\infty$ at $z = 1\frac{1}{2}$ and becomes smaller as $z$ becomes closer to 0. The smoothness of the z-transform is illustrated in Figure 5.5a, a cross section of $\mathcal{H}_z(z)$ along the real axis of $z$. Notice that the z-transform grows very quickly near the poles and varies smoothly near the zeros. Figure 5.5b shows a cross section of the same $z$-transform, but in this case along the imaginary axis. Notice the wild gyrations along the real axis as the $z$-transform encounters the two poles. $\mathcal{H}_z(z)$ changes very rapidly in the vicinity of the poles. The cross section along the imaginary axis is much smoother because $\mathcal{H}_z(z)$ directly encounters only the zero at the origin. So, along the imaginary cross section $\mathcal{H}_z(z)$ smoothly increases from 0 at the origin to a value of 2 at $z = \infty$. Using these insights, it is possible (but not necessarily easy) to visualize the cross section of $\mathcal{H}_z(z)$ along any direction.

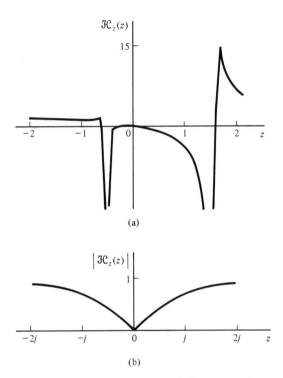

(a)

(b)

**Figure 5.5**  Cross sections of the $z$-transform:
(a) along the real $z$-axis
(b) along the imaginary $z$-axis

You are probably wondering why we should put such an effort into understanding and visualizing the $z$-transform. The reason lies in equation (5.17). Through the $z$-transform it is possible to relate the pole-zero locations and the filter's frequency response (at least its magnitude). Because the frequency response is the $z$-transform evaluated along the unit circle ($z = e^{j\omega}$), if we can visualize the $z$-transform we should be able to get a good feeling of the frequency response. Consider the following example.

**Example:** Frequency Response from a Pole-Zero Plot

The filter of the preceding example has poles at $-0.5$ and $1.5$ and zeros at $-0.25$ and $0$. The pole-zero plot is shown in Figure 5.4 and some of the cross sections are shown in Figure 5.5. We know that the frequency response is the value of the $z$-transform at angle $\omega$ along the unit circle, so we can infer the frequency response from the pole-zero plot. The dc gain of the filter $[\mathcal{H}(0)]$ is the $z$-transform evaluated at $z = e^{j0} = 1$. We find this actual value through Figure 5.5a: $\mathcal{H}_z(1) = -3.33$. To find the frequency response for higher frequencies, we move counterclockwise along the unit circle, evaluating $\mathcal{H}_z(z)$ as we go. We do not have any hard numbers until we hit the positive imaginary axis ($\omega = \pi/2$), but we are moving away from the pole at $z = 1.5$, so we would expect that the $z$-transform will decrease as we move along the unit circle from $e^{j0}$ to $e^{j\pi/2}$. Continuing our journey around the unit circle (from $e^{j\pi/2}$ to $e^{j\pi}$), we would expect that the frequency response would gradually increase as $\mathcal{H}_z(z)$ is raised by the pole at $z = -0.5$. In this manner it is possible to get a rough feeling of the frequency response based solely on the pole-zero plot. The actual frequency response is shown in Figure 5.6. Indeed, the gain is high at dc (because of the pole at $z = 1.5$) and it smoothly decreases as the frequency increases until it begins to increase because of the pole at $z = -0.5$. Such an inspection is a handy way to link the concept of poles and zeros with our old friend the frequency response.

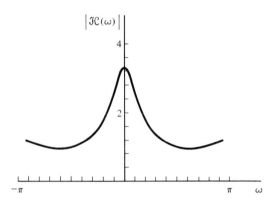

**Figure 5.6** Frequency response corresponding to Figure 5.4.

We can also use the relationship between the poles and zeros and the frequency response to characterize the EKG filters of Chapter 1 (remember those?).

**Example:** Chapter 1's Nonrecursive EKG Filter

Chapter 1 used a seven-coefficient nonrecursive low-pass filter to clean up an electrocardiogram.

$$y_k = -2x_k + 3x_{k-1} + 6x_{k-2} + 7x_{k-3} + 6x_{k-4} + 3x_{k-5} - 2x_{k-6} \qquad (5.48)$$

This filter has a $z$-transform of

$$\mathcal{H}_z(z) = -2z^0 + 3z^{-1} + 6z^{-2} + 7z^{-3} + 6z^{-4} + 3z^{-5} - 2z^{-6} \qquad (5.49)$$

The filter has no poles (it is nonrecursive) and has six zeros, which are found with the help of a trusty computer.

$$\varsigma_1 = 3.00$$
$$\varsigma_2 = 0.3324$$
$$\varsigma_3 = -0.8778 + j0.4791 \quad \text{or} \quad 1\angle 151.37^o$$
$$\varsigma_4 = -0.8778 - j0.4791 \quad \text{or} \quad 1\angle 208.63^o$$
$$\varsigma_5 = -0.0426 + j0.9991 \quad \text{or} \quad 1\angle 92.44^o$$
$$\varsigma_6 = -0.0426 - j0.9991 \quad \text{or} \quad 1\angle 267.56^o$$

The pole-zero and frequency plots are shown in Figure 5.7. In this instance $\mathcal{H}_z(z)$ blows up for large $z$, so the $z$-transform is elevated around the periphery of the $z$-plane and it is pinned down by the zeros. The four zeros on the unit circle generate the stopband of the low-pass filter. The two zeros on the real axis (one is off the plot) give the passband its flat top. Therefore, we can use the relationship between the zeros and the frequency response to explain the operation of a nonrecursive filter.

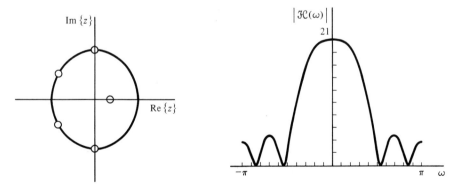

**Figure 5.7** Pole-zero and frequency response of a nonrecursive filter.

**Example:** Chapter 1's Recursive Filter

Chapter 1 also presented a recursive low-pass filter that removed noise from the EKG.

$$y_k = 0.14x_{k-2} + 1.77y_{k-1} - 1.19y_{k-2} + 0.28y_{k-3} \qquad (5.50)$$

This filter has a single zero at the origin and three poles.

$$p_1 = 0.5150$$

$$p_2 = 0.6275 + j0.3872 \quad \text{or} \quad 0.74\angle 31.67^{\circ}$$

$$p_3 = 0.6275 - j0.3872 \quad \text{or} \quad 0.74\angle -31.67^{\circ}$$

Its pole-zero plot and frequency response is shown in Figure 5.8. In this case the order of the denominator is larger than the numerator; this filter's $z$-transform goes to 0 as $z$ gets large. So the three poles elevate $\mathcal{H}_z(z)$ at low frequencies (portions of the unit circle near $z = 1$), and the zero at the origin with the zero at $z = \infty$ forces the stopband at high frequencies.

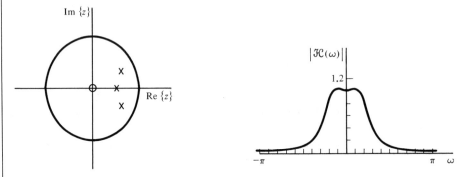

**Figure 5.8** Pole-zero plot and frequency response of a recursive low pass filter.

We finish this section with yet another example. This one shows a mock design of a two-pole, one-zero filter. The $z$-transform and, hence, the frequency response are sculpted by moving the poles and zeros around in the $z$-plane.

**Example:** Pole-Zero Design of a Simple Filter

The following discussion focuses on the diagrams in Figure 5.9. There are five pairs of figures showing the pole-zero diagram and the corresponding frequency response. By watching the evolution of the frequency response as the poles and zeros are moved around in the $z$-plane it is possible to get a better appreciation of the relationship between the poles and zeros and the frequency response.

Our filter has a single zero and two poles. Therefore, the denominator is second order and the numerator is first order; the $z$-transform goes to zero as $z$ gets large. The shape of the frequency response is attributed to the poles elevating the $z$-transform at the proper places and the zeros protecting the stopband.

Our discussion begins with the zero and the origin and the two poles at a radius of $\frac{1}{2}$ and angles of $45^o$ and $-45^o$, as shown in figure 5.9a. With this orientation, we expect that the filter has high gain at low frequencies [because of the poles pushing $\mathcal{H}_z(z)$ up near $z = 1$], and low gain at higher frequencies because of the zero pinning $\mathcal{H}_z(z)$ down at the origin. The frequency response proves these observations out; this is indeed a low-pass filter.

When the poles are moved out to a radius of 0.7 (figure 5.9b), they come closer to the unit circle and thereby increase the $z$-transform in the regions around $e^{j\pi/2}$ and $e^{-j\pi/2}$. Figure 5.9c and d show what happens when the poles are moved out to a radius of 0.9 and 0.95, respectively. Notice that the peaks become more pronounced, and the gain increases as the poles become closer to the unit circle.

This example concludes by moving the zero, which up to now has been fixed at the origin, to a radius of 0.8 on the real axis. Moving the zero closer to $z = 1$ pulls the $z$-transform down around $z = 1$, so we expect a lower dc gain. The plot of the frequency response supports these insights: the dc gain is lower and the peaks at $45^o$ are somewhat lower, but with much more definition.

## 5.3   STABILITY

As shown in Chapter 1, it is possible to design a recursive digital filter whose impulse response increases with time. Such a filter is called *unstable* and should be avoided because it is likely to generate infinitely valued output sequences, which are impossible to represent. This section shows that an unstable filter has at least one of its poles outside the $z$-plane's unit circle. In other words, one of the poles has a magnitude greater than 1. Therefore, all useful recursive filter designs must restrict the poles to the inside of the unit circle.

Before beginning the derivation, we must precisely define the notion of stability. A filter is said to be stable if any sequence of bounded (finite-valued) inputs produces a bounded output sequence. In other words, an unstable filter can produce an arbitrarily large output while given a bounded input (note that all reasonable filters will produce an unbounded output from an unbounded input). The outputs of unstable filters have the nasty habit of "blowing up" when you use them.

A filter must be stable to be generally useful. This is because all digital filters have a maximum representable number. Any attempt to represent a value beyond this maximum results in inaccuracies, at best, and usually disaster. An unstable filter has the potential of generating output values that will exceed the representation capacity of any filter; therefore, an unstable filter will almost always

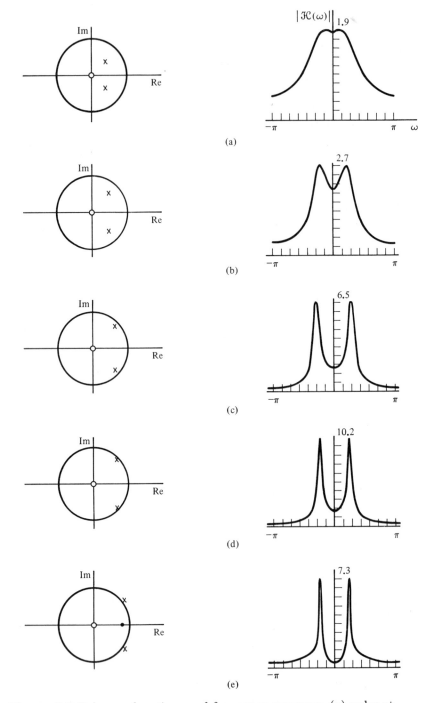

**Figure 5.9** Pole-zero locations and frequency response: (a) poles at radius 0.5; (b) poles at radius 0.7; (c) poles at radius 0.95; (d) poles at radius 0.95; (e) poles at radius 0.95, zero at 0.8

cause system malfunction.

We begin our study of stability by considering the simplest filter with the potential for instability. It is the single-pole filter

$$y_k = ax_{k-1} + by_k \qquad (5.51)$$

This filter has a pole at $b$. For the purpose of this discussion, we will allow a complex-valued pole — $b$ can be a complex number.

We have shown [equation (5.10)] that this filter has an impulse response of

$$h_k = ab^k \qquad (5.52)$$

If the magnitude of $b$ is less than 1, the impulse response decays to zero as $k$ becomes large. If $|b|$ is small, the impulse response decays very rapidly. The decay slows as $|b|$ becomes larger. When the magnitude of $b$ is 1, the magnitude of the impulse response is constant, the response stays at a constant value $a$ if $b$ is real, or oscillates at a constant amplitude if $b$ is complex. But when $|b|$ is increased beyond 1, the magnitude of the impulse response grows with $k$. That is, the filter produces an unbounded output in response to a bounded input (the impulse). Therefore, this filter is unstable. Larger values of $|b|$ cause the response to blow up more quickly. So if the magnitude of $b$ is just a tiny bit larger than unity, the filter's impulse response will increase very slowly, but will ultimately reach infinity — an unstable filter. Some examples of impulse responses from single-pole filters are shown in Figure 5.10.

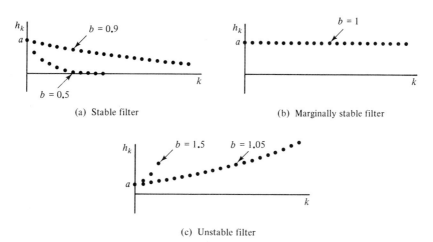

Figure 5.10 Impulse responses of a single-pole filter:
(a) stable filter; (b) marginally stable filter;
(c) unstable filter.

We conclude that a single-pole filter has a growing impulse response when $|b| > 1$, and such a filter violates the definition of stability. Because in this example $b$ is also the location of the filter's pole, we can conclude that a pole with a magnitude greater than 1 produces an unstable single-pole filter. A pole on the unit circle generates a constant-magnitude impulse response, and such a filter is called marginally stable.

Based on the preceding observations, a filter's stablity — or lack thereof — appears to be controlled by the pole location. The impact of zeros on a filter's stability is studied by adding some zeros to our single-pole filter.

$$y_k = \sum_{i=-m}^{m} c_i x_{k-i} + b y_{k-1} \tag{5.53}$$

The nonrecursive coefficients (the zeros) affect the impulse response for indices from $-m$ to $m$, but after $k = m$ the impulse has passed through the nonrecursive portion of the filter and the response's behavior is totally controlled by the pole.

$$h_k = b h_{k-1} \tag{5.54}$$

So the zeros cannot control whether or not the impulse response grows to infinity — they simply affect the response for too short a time. It is the pole that determines the growth or decay of the impulse response, so it is the pole that determines stability.

We are tempted to conclude that the zeros cannot affect stability. That statement is correct, with an exception: a zero can effectively counteract an unstable pole and make an otherwise unstable filter stable. To see this, consider the following example.

**Example:** Pole-Zero Cancellation

Consider the following single-pole filter:

$$y_k = x_{k-1} - 2x_{k-2} + 2y_{k-1} \tag{5.55}$$

This filter has a pole at $z = 2$, which is outside the unit circle, and we therefore expect that it is unstable, but that is not so. Compute the first few terms of the impulse response.

$$h_0 = 0 \quad h_1 = 1 \quad h_2 = 0 \quad h_3 = 0 \tag{5.56}$$

Not only does the impulse response not blow up, but it goes to zero in just one step. This filter is most certainly stable, so what happened?

This filter does not really have a pole at 2, because it has a zero at 2. This pole-zero pair cancel each other. We see this through the $z$-transform.

$$\mathcal{H}_z(z) = \frac{z^{-1}(1 - 2z^{-1})}{1 - 2z^{-1}} = z^{-1} \tag{5.57}$$

This filter is a complicated way of realizing a delay of one unit. In this case, the zero at $z = 2$ turned a seemingly unstable filter into a stable one.

We can extend our stability results to higher-ordered filters in two ways. We could attempt to repeat the single-pole stability argument by computing the impulse response of all higher-order filters and searching for conditions that will guarantee stability. Or we could develop techniques for expressing higher-order filters in terms of single-pole filters and then apply our single-pole stability result. We are going to take the latter approach because it is easier and it provides us with a tool that we will need later in our design techniques.

The question is: Given a particular filter (e.g., its $z$-transform), how do we go about expressing it in terms of lower-order filters? This process is called *decomposition*; the original filter is decomposed into smaller filters. There are really only two ways of decomposing a filter. It can be decomposed into a cascade combination or a parallel combination of lower-order filters.

The $z$-transform of the cascade of filters is simply the product of the individual $z$-transforms.

$$\mathcal{H}_z(z) = \mathcal{H}_{z1}(z)\mathcal{H}_{z2}(z)\ldots\mathcal{H}_{zN}(z) \tag{5.58}$$

We are used to working equation (5.58) from right to left. That is given the $z$-transforms of the cascaded filters, we can compute the transform of the equivalent filter by multiplying the individual transforms together. But for decomposition we wish to work equation (5.58) the other way, from left to right. Given a high-order $z$-transform (the left-hand side) we wish to find $N$ lower-order $z$-transforms [$\mathcal{H}_{zi}(z)$] such that their product is the $z$-transform of the original filter. The original $z$-transform must be factored into the lower-order $z$-transforms. Such a factorization can be performed by inspection when the original filter is presented as poles and zeros. The decomposition process attributes the first pole to $\mathcal{H}_{z1}(z)$, the second pole to $\mathcal{H}_{z2}(z)$, and so on. The zeros can be arbitrarily paired with the poles or can be lumped together in an all-zero filter. This decomposition is illustrated as follows:

$$\mathcal{H}_z(z) = \frac{(z - \varsigma_1)\ldots(z - \varsigma_m)}{(z - p_1)\ldots(z - p_n)}$$

$$= \{(z - \varsigma_1)\ldots(z - \varsigma_m)\}\left\{\frac{1}{z - p_1}\right\}\ldots\left\{\frac{1}{z - p_n}\right\} \tag{5.59}$$

The first filter in the cascade form is an all-zero filter, the second filter has a pole at $p_1$, the third filter has a pole at $p_2$, and so on. This decomposition is not unique, because the poles and zeros can be paired in an arbitrary way. For example, we could have paired the second zero with the first pole and have generated a filter:

$$\mathcal{H}_{z1}(z) = \frac{z - \varsigma_2}{z - p_1} \tag{5.60}$$

An arbitrary filter can be decomposed into the cascade of single-pole filters by simply factoring the original $\mathcal{H}_z(z)$. However, this is not to say that the single-pole filters are realizable. If the original $\mathcal{H}_z(z)$ has complex poles or zeros, the single-pole or single-zero filters will require complex coefficients (remember that real coefficients demand that complex poles or zeros appear in conjugate pairs). If we are performing the cascade decomposition for conceptual reasons and have no intent of actually realizing the filters, we can decompose the original filter into filters with compex, nonconjugate roots. But if we intend to implement the filters, we are forced to identify all pairs of complex, conjugate roots with second-order filters.

A similar argument holds for the pairing of poles and zeros. Conceptually, we could identify a filter with two zeros and one pole. This is a noncausal filter because the order of the numerator exceeds the order of the denominator. If we intend to build the cascaded filters, we must be sure to preserve the causality of the individual filters; the number of zeros in any filter must be less than or equal to the number of poles.

Suppose that we take an $N$th order filter and break it up as a cascade of an all-zero filter and $N$ single-pole filters (we are not worried about implementing them). This process is illustrated in Figure 5.11. Each of the single-pole filters contains one of the poles from the original filter and the cascade has the same $z$-transform as the original. Therefore, the cascade has the same impulse response as the original filter.

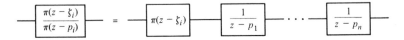

**Figure 5.11** Cascade decomposition.

Now, suppose that the original filter has at least one pole outside the unit circle. This means that at least one of the single-pole filters in Figure 5.11 is unstable, which means that the entire cascade filter is unstable. Therefore, all the poles of the $N$th-order filter must be in the unit circle for the filter to be stable.

The impulse response of the original filter is the convolution of the impulse responses of the cascaded filters. Because of this, it is difficult to visualize the relationship between the individual impulse responses and the response of the original filter. For this reason, we turn to a parallel decomposition and express the original filter as a parallel combination of lower-order filters. Notice that we did not say "single-pole" filters, because the parallel decomposition cannot reduce an arbitrary filter to the parallel combination of single-pole filters.

The $z$-transform of the parallel combination of $N$ filters is simply the sum of the $z$-transforms of the individual filters.

$$\mathcal{H}_z(z) = \mathcal{H}_{z1}(z) + \mathcal{H}_{z2}(z) + \ldots + \mathcal{H}_{zN}(z) \tag{5.61}$$

Again, we are familiar with going from right to left in equation (5.61). We simply put the individual $z$-transforms over a common denominator and add them together.

But the decomposition of a filter into parallel filters (going left to right) is a far more difficult process; it requires a partial-fraction expansion. If all the poles are distinct (there are no repeated poles) and the order of the numerator is less than or equal to the order of the denominator (the filter is causal), the partial-fraction expansion is straightforward. Attribute a single pole from the original filter to each of the parallel filters and solve for the numerator coefficients that make the terms add to the original. If $\mathcal{H}_z(z)$ has no repeated poles and is causal, the partial-fraction expansion has the following form:

$$\mathcal{H}_z(z) = \sum_{i=1}^{n} \frac{A_i}{z - p_i} \tag{5.62}$$

Solve for the $A_i$s that make the numerators match when the right side is put over a common denominator, which just happens to be the denominator of $\mathcal{H}_z(z)$. Consider the following example.

**Example:** Parallel Decompositions

Express the following filter as the parallel combination of first-order filters.

$$\mathcal{H}_z(z) = \frac{(z - \varsigma_1)}{(z - p_1)(z - p_2)} \qquad p_1 \neq p_2 \tag{5.63}$$

Because this filter does not have repeated poles, its partial-fraction expansion is of the form

$$\mathcal{H}_z(z) = \frac{A_1}{z - p_1} + \frac{A_2}{z - p_2} \tag{5.64}$$

We solve for $A_1$ and $A_2$ by putting them over a common denominator and equating the resulting numerator to the numerator of the left-hand side of equation (5.64).

$$A_1(z - p_2) + A_2(z - p_1) = z - \varsigma_1 \tag{5.65}$$

or

$$\begin{aligned} A_1 + A_2 &= 1 \\ A_1 p_2 + A_2 p_1 &= \varsigma_1 \end{aligned} \tag{5.66}$$

We plug in the specific values for the poles and zeros and solve for the $A$'s.

The partial-fraction expansion becomes more complicated when $\mathcal{H}_z(z)$ has repeated poles. A pole that is repeated $l$ times generates $l$ terms in the expansion.

$$\frac{1}{(z - p)^l} = \frac{A_1}{z - p} + \frac{A_2}{(z - p)^2} + \ldots + \frac{A_l}{(z - p)^l} \tag{5.67}$$

Therefore, a distinct pole generates one term in the expansion, a double pole generates two terms, and so on. An $n$th-order filter always has $n$ terms in its partial-fraction expansion.

**Example:** Parallel Decomposition of Repeated Poles.

Consider the filter with the following $z$-transform.

$$\mathcal{H}_z(z) = \frac{1}{(z - p_1)(z - p_2)^2} \tag{5.68}$$

Its partial-fraction expansion takes the form

$$\mathcal{H}_z(z) = \frac{A_1}{z - p_1} + \frac{A_2}{z - p_2} + \frac{A_3}{(z - p_2)^2} \tag{5.69}$$

Put the right-hand side of equation (5.69) over a common denominator and solve for the $A$ coefficients.

$$\mathcal{H}_z(z) = \frac{A_1(z - p_2)^2 + A_2(z - p_1)(z - p_2) + A_3(z - p_1)}{(z - p_1)(z - p_2)^2} \tag{5.70}$$

Suffice it to say that an arbitrary filter can be expressed in terms of the parallel combination of lower-order filters. Each pole of the original filter appears as a single pole in one of the parallel filters. This decomposition is illustrated in Figure 5.12.

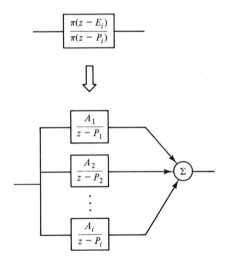

**Figure 5.12** Parallel decomposition.

The impulse response of the parallel combination is the sum of the impulse responses of the individual filters, which equals the impulse response of the original filter. So if the original filter has a pole outside the unit circle, one of the filters in the parallel combination will have this pole; this particular filter will therefore be unstable. The impulse response of the parallel combination will blow up if any of the individual filters is unstable. Therefore, a stable filter must have all its poles within the unit circle.

## 5.4  SUMMARY

The frequency reponse is not enough for the characterization of recursive digital filters. For that reason we introduced a generalization of the frequency response — the $z$-transform. The $z$-transform can be treated as the ratio of two polynomials, or a set of poles and zeros. The pole and zero locations in the $z$-plane can provide the designer a great deal of insight into the filter's performance and its frequency response. We found that recursive filters have the potential for being unstable and a stable filter has all its poles within the unit circle. Finally, recursive digital filters can be crudely designed by placing the poles and zeros in the $z$-plane. The next chapter presents some practical techniques for designing recursive digital filters.

## EXERCISES

5-1.  Are the following signals eigenfunctions of digital filters? Support your answer.

(a) $(z+1)^k$

(b) $z^{2k}$

(c) $z^{-k}$

5-2.  Compute the z-transform of the following filters.

(a) $y_k = 2x_{k-1} + 3x_k + 1y_{k-1}$

(b) $y_{k+1} = x_k + 2y_{k-1}$

5-3.  We know that $\mathcal{H}_z(z)$ is the z-transform of $h_k$. So what is the highest power of $z$ in the z-transform of a causal filter?

5-4.  What is the $z$-transform of the cascade combination of three filters: $\mathcal{H}_{z1}(z)$, $\mathcal{H}_{z2}(z)$, and $\mathcal{H}_{z3}(z)$?

5-5.  Consider a filter with an impulse response of $h_k$ and a z-transform of $\mathcal{H}_z(z)$. Express the impulse responses of the following filters in terms of $h_k$.

(a) $z^n \mathcal{H}_z(z)$

(b) $z^{-n} \mathcal{H}_z(z)$

5-6. Are the following $z$-transforms associated with causal filters?

(a) $\mathcal{H}_z(z) = \frac{z^2+z}{z^3+2z^2}$

(b) $\mathcal{H}_z(z) = \frac{z^3+z}{z^2+1}$

(c) $\mathcal{H}_z(z) = \frac{z^2+z}{z^2}$

5-7. Compute the impulse responses of the filters that have a zero at the origin and a pole at the following locations.

(a) $z = 0.9$

(b) $z = 0.98$

(c) $z = 1$

(d) $z = 1.02$

5-8. Plot the impulse responses of Exercise 5-7.

5-9. Design digital filters (find the $c_i$'s and $d_i$'s) that have the following $z$-transforms.

(a) $\mathcal{H}_z(z) = \frac{2z^2+z}{3z^2}$

(b) $\mathcal{H}_z(z) = \frac{z^3}{z^3-z-2}$

(c) $\mathcal{H}_z(z) = \frac{1}{2z^2+z}$

(d) $\mathcal{H}_z(z) = \frac{z^{-1}}{z^{-2}-0.5z^{-1}}$

5-10. Design digital filters (find the $c_i$'s and $d_i$'s) with the following poles, zeros, and gain.

(a) Zeros at $j$ and $-j$

Poles at $\frac{1}{2}$, $\frac{1}{2}+j\frac{1}{2}$, and $\frac{1}{2}-j\frac{1}{2}$

Gain of 1

(b) Zeros at 0 and 0 (a double zero at the origin)

Poles at $0.5\angle 60^\circ$ and $0.5\angle -60^\circ$

Gain of 2

(c) Zeroes at 0, $1\angle 45^o$, and $1\angle -45^o$

No finite poles

Gain of 10

5-11. Compute the finite poles, zeros, and gain of the following integrators from Chapter 2.

(a) Running sum:
$$y_k = x_k + y_{k-1}$$

(b) Trapezoid rule:
$$y_k = 0.5x_k + 0.5x_{k-1} + y_{k-1}$$

(c) Simpson's rule:
$$y_k = \frac{1}{3}x_k + \frac{4}{3}x_{k-1} + \frac{1}{3}x_{k-2} + y_{k-2}$$

5-12. Compute the poles, zeros, and gains of the following filters. Express the poles and zeros as real-imaginary and magnitude-angle. Plot the poles and zeroes in the $z$-plane.

(a) $c_0 = 1$ , $c_1 = 2$

$d_1 = 0.707$ , $d_2 = -0.25$

(b) $c_3 = 1$

$d_1 = 0$ , $d_2 = -1$

(c) $c_2 = 1$

$d_1 = 0$ , $d_2 = -1$

(d) $c_0 = 1$ , $c_3 = 1$

$d_1 = 2$ , $d_2 = -4$

5-13. Consider the low-pass filter designed in the example in Chapter 3.

(a) Compute and plot the zero locations of an 11-coefficient implementation.

(b) How are the zero locations in the $z$-plane related to the frequencies where this filter's frequency response is zero?

(c) Repeat part (a) for a 19-coefficient implementation.

(d) How are the 11- and 19-coefficient zeros related? What do the extra zeros do to the frequency response?

5-14. A three-pole Butterworth low-pass filter has poles and zeros in the following locations.

Zeros: $-0.5$

Poles: $0.37\angle 0°, 0.6\angle 50°, 0.6\angle -50°$

(a) Plot the poles and zeros in the $z$-plane and the filter's frequency response.

(b) Move the real pole to $0.2\angle 0°$ and replot the pole-zero diagram and the frequency response. What effect did this move have on the frequency response, and why?

(c) Move the real pole back to $0.36\angle 0°$ and move the complex poles to a radius of 0.8 (leave the angle at $50°$ and $-50°$). What does this do to the frequency response, and why?

5-15. Realize the following filters as a cascade combination of realizable and causal first- and second-order filters.

(a) $H_z(z) = \frac{16(z+1)z^2}{(4z^2-2z+1)(4z+3)}$

(b) $H_z(z) = \frac{z^2-4z+3}{z(z+.5)^2}$

(c) $H_z(z) = \frac{z^2-0.25}{(z^2+0.25)(z^2+z+0.5)}$

5-16. Repeat Exercise 5-15, but realize the filters as **parallel** combinations of the simplest first- and second-order filters.

5-17. Consider the following two-pole filter.

$$H_z(z) = \frac{1}{z^2 - z + 0.09}$$

(a) Compute and plot its pole locations.

(b) Realize this filter as a parallel combination of two first-order filters. Don't worry if these filters have complex coefficients.

(c) Compute the impulse responses of the two first-ordered filters, and from those the impulse response of the original second-order filter.

5-18. Compute the impulse response of the parallel combination of two filters. Each filter has a zero at 0 and a single complex pole at the following locations.

(a) $0.8\angle 5^o$ and $0.8\angle -5^o$

(b) $0.9\angle 5^o$ and $0.9\angle -5^o$

(c) $0.99\angle 5^o$ and $0.99\angle -5^o$

(d) How does the angle of the poles affect the impulse response?

(e) How does the magnitude of the poles affect the impulse response?

5-19. Plot the impulse responses in parts (a) through (c) of Exercise 5-18.

5-20. Compute the impulse response of a filter with a pair of zeros at the origin and a pair of poles at:

(a) $0.8\angle 5^o$ and $0.8\angle -5^o$

(b) $0.9\angle 5^o$ and $0.9\angle -5^o$

(c) $0.99\angle 5^o$ and $0.99\angle -5^o$

(d) How does the angle of the pole affect the impulse response?

(e) How does the magnitude of the pole affect the impulse response?

5-21. Plot the impulse responses in Exercise 5-18.

5-22. Suppose that we had defined the $z$-transform as the eigenvalue of $z^{-k}$ rather than $z^k$.

(a) How are the poles and zeros of this new transform related to the poles and zeros of the old?

(b) Which poles are stable for this new transform?

5-23. Design a filter (find the $c_i$'s and $d_i$'s) with the following impulse responses.

(a) $h_k = 10\cos 0.01k$ for $k \geq 0$

(b) $h_k = 0.9^k$ for $k \geq 0$

(c) $h_k = 0.9^k + \cos 0.01k$ for $k \geq 0$

5-24. Design a filter (find the $c_i$'s and $d_i$'s) with the following impulse responses.

  (a) $h_k = 10 \sin 0.01k$ for $k \geq 0$

  (b) $h_k = 0.5^k + 0.1^k$ for $k \geq 0$

  (c) $h_k = 0.9^k + 0.9^k \sin 0.01k$ for $k \geq 0$

5-25. "Design" a four-pole causal digital filter by using the observations gained from Figure 5.9. This filter should have have a passband from $0.3\pi$ to $0.6\pi$.

  (a) Sketch your filter's pole-zero plot.

  (b) Plot your filter's frequency response.

5-26. Suppose that you modify a digital filter by replacing each pole with a pole that has the same angle and a magnitude that is the inverse of the magnitude of the original filter's pole, and do likewise for the zeros. That is, if the original filter has a pole at $m\angle\theta$, then the new filter has a pole at $1/m\angle\theta$. How are the frequency responses of the original and new filter related?

# Design
# of
# Recursive Filters

In Chapter 5 we showed that the frequency response of a recursive filter is completely determined by its pole and zero locations. We have seen that it is possible to crudely "design" a recursive filter by simply visualizing the $z$-plane and arranging the poles and zeros to elevate (poles) or lower (zeros) the $z$-transform at the unit circle. However, pole and zero shuffling is too imprecise for good recursive filter design. This chapter develops a workable methodology for the design of recursive digital filters.

Unfortunately, the design techniques for recursive filters are not as straightforward as those for their nonrecursive cousins. Attempting to apply the Fourier design development leads to a set of unsolvable equations for the recursive $(d_k)$ coefficients. This is because the $d_k$'s are in the frequency response's denominator, and when we differentiate with respect to these coefficients we generate a set of equations without a closed-form solution.

The feedback coefficients (denominator of the frequency response) frustrate the development of any straightforward design technique. But rather than reverting to pole and zero shuffling, we are going to make an "end run" around the insurmountable problems. We do this by exploiting the past successes of analog filter designers. This chapter develops a somewhat convoluted technique, in which we begin the design with a good analog filter and approximate it with a digital filter. This approach is not as comprehensive or as satisfying as the design techniques developed for nonrecursive filters, but it is usable and is the best that can be done without resorting to computer-aided design techniques.

## 6.1 ANALOG FILTERS

A rudimentary understanding of analog filters is necessary to appreciate the design techniques for digital recursive filters. Analog filters are more difficult to design and analyze than are their digital counterparts because the analog filters are based on the operation of differentiation. This section is not a comprehensive treatment of analog filters; there are many good books that do that job. Rather, the intention of this section is to give you enough appreciation of the beasts to understand their role in the design of digital filters.

In the introduction of this book, we found that a filter is, in general, a box of rules that somehow generates an output signal from an input. We divided the filters into analog (those filters processing analog signals) and digital filters. Up until now, we have concentrated on digital filters, but now we must look at analog filters.

A general one-input, one-output analog filter is shown in Figure 6.1. It accepts an analog input, $x(t)$, and produces an analog output, $y(t)$. The variable $t$ is used as the general continuous independent variable, much as $k$ is used as the digital index.

**Figure 6.1** General analog filter.

We will restrict our attention to analog filters that are linear and time invariant (much as we restricted the class of digital filters). These filters are described by a constant-coefficient differential equation — the output of the filter is the weighted sum of derivatives of the input and output signals. The definition of the analog filter is as follows:

$$y(t) = \sum_{k=0}^{N} a_k \frac{d^k x(t)}{dt^k} + \sum_{k=1}^{M} b_k \frac{d^k y(t)}{dt^k} \tag{6.1}$$

For example, the simplest analog filter is a straight wire,

$$y(t) = x(t) \tag{6.2}$$

It is obtained when $a_0 = 1$, and all other coefficients are zero.

A filter that performs differentiation,

$$y(t) = \frac{dx(t)}{dt} \tag{6.3}$$

is a filter with $a_1 = 1$, and all other coefficients equal to zero.

This differential equation should look familiar. It is the definition of a recursive digital filter with the delay operators, $x_{k-i}$, replaced by derivatives, $d^i x(t)/dt^i$. Most sane people prefer to work with delays instead of derivatives, so that is why digital filters are usually considered easier to understand. Because of the similarities between the two, it should not surprise you that analog filters can be analyzed with many of the tools used on digital filters.

**Eigenfunctions and Eigenvalues for Analog Filters**

Eigenfunctions and values played such an important role in the analysis and design of digital filters that it would be foolish not to try the same concepts on analog filters. We found that $e^{j\omega k}$ was an eigenfunction of digital filters, so let's try $e^{st}$ ($s$ is a complex variable) as an eigenfunction for analog filters. First we must make sure that our candidate is an eigenfunction of the differential operator.

$$\frac{d}{dt}\left\{e^{st}\right\} = se^{st} \tag{6.4}$$

It is an eigenfunction and has an eigenvalue of $s$. Our $e^{st}$ is also an eigenfunction of repeated applications of the differential operator and generates an eigenvalue of $s$ raised to the order of the derivative. For example,

$$\begin{aligned}
\frac{d^2}{dt^2}\left\{e^{st}\right\} &= \frac{d}{dt}\left\{\frac{d}{dt}\left\{e^{st}\right\}\right\} \\
&= \frac{d}{dt}\left\{se^{st}\right\} \\
&= s^2 e^{st}
\end{aligned} \tag{6.5}$$

In general,

$$\frac{d^i}{dt^i}\left\{e^{st}\right\} = s^i e^{st} \tag{6.6}$$

Therefore, $e^{st}$ is an eigenfunction of multiordered differentiation. Since it is also an eigenfunction of addition, it must be an eigenfunction for analog filters. Consider the following example.

**Example:** Find $e^{st}$'s eigenvalue for the following analog filter.

$$y(t) = a_0 x(t) + a_1 \frac{dx(t)}{dt} \tag{6.7}$$

We begin by applying $e^{st}$ as an input to the filter, $x(t) + e^{st}$.

$$\begin{aligned}
y(t)\big|_{x(t)=e^{st}} &= a_0 e^{st} + a_1 s e^{st} \\
&= (a_0 + a_1 s)\, e^{st}
\end{aligned} \tag{6.8}$$

Therefore, the eigenfunction is $a_0 + a_1 s$.

The eigenfunction and value play such an important role in the analysis of analog filters that it is given a name. It is called the *transfer function* and is denoted $\mathcal{H}_a(s)$. Do not confuse this eigenvalue with the eigenvalues used for digital filters, $\mathcal{H}_z(z)$ and $\mathcal{H}(\omega)$. They have similar roles in the analysis, but we will see later that they have very different meanings.

We will now compute the transfer function of a general analog filter by using the same trick that we used for digital filters. If we assume that the output of an analog filter is the product of $\mathcal{H}_a(s)$ and $e^{st}$ when $e^{st}$ is applied to the filter, we can solve for the transfer function as the ratio of two polynomials. The numerator of the polynomial is attributed to the derivatives of the input, $d^i x(t)/dt^i$, and the denominator is generated by the derivatives of the output. A few lines of algebra is all that is necessary.

We begin by assuming that the output is the product of the transfer function and the complex exponential.

$$y(t) = \mathcal{H}_a(s)e^{st} \qquad \text{when} \qquad x(t) = e^{st} \tag{6.9}$$

Therefore,

$$\mathcal{H}_a(s)e^{st} = \sum_{i=0}^{N} a_i \frac{d^i}{dt}\left\{e^{st}\right\} + \sum_{i=1}^{M} b_i \frac{d^i}{dt}\left\{\mathcal{H}_a(s)e^{st}\right\} \tag{6.10}$$

$$\mathcal{H}_a(s)e^{st} = \sum_{i=0}^{N} a_i s^i e^{st} + \mathcal{H}_a(s)\sum_{i=1}^{M} b_i s^i e^{st} \tag{6.11}$$

So

$$\mathcal{H}_a(s) = \frac{\sum_{i=0}^{N} a_i s^i}{1 - \sum_{i=1}^{M} b_i s^i} \tag{6.12}$$

The transfer function is to the analog filter what the $z$-transform is to the digital filter. The transfer function is the ratio of polynomials in $s$, and the $z$-transform is a ratio in $z$. But do not let the similarities fool you. The transfer function's coefficients (the $a_i$'s and $b_i$'s) are weightings on derivatives of the inputs and outputs. The $z$-transform's coefficients ($c_i$'s and $b_i$'s) weight the delays of the input and output. Since derivatives and delays are radically different operations, $\mathcal{H}(z)$ and $\mathcal{H}_a(s)$ represent very different filter operations. In other words, do not expect an analog filter and digital filter with identical coefficients to behave the same way. Always keep the differences in mind as we work with the transfer function using the same tools that we used on the $z$-transform.

Because $\mathcal{H}_a(s)$ is a ratio of polynomials, it can be represented by the coefficients of the polynomials ($a_i$s and $b_i$s) or by its poles, zeros, and gain. In this case the finite poles are the values of $s$ that drive the denominator to zero and the finite zeros are those values that force the numerator to zero. The gain is a multiplicative factor that causes the whole thing to come out correctly. Many analog filter designers gain a great deal of insight by showing the locations of the poles and zeros in the $s$-plane (analogous to the $z$-plane). The $s$-plane is shown in Figure 6.2. The real parts of the poles and zeros are plotted along the horizontal axis and the imaginary parts are plotted along the vertical.

**Figure 6.2** The $s$-plane.

**Example:** Find the transfer function and the poles, zeros, and gain of the following filter.

$$y(t) = x(t) + \frac{dx(t)}{dt} - 2\frac{dy(t)}{dt} \tag{6.13}$$

We can compute the transfer function by applying $e^{st}$ to the differential equation or by inspection. Either method will yield a one-pole and one-zero filter.

$$\mathcal{H}_s(s) = \frac{1+s}{1+2s} \tag{6.14}$$

This transfer function has a zero at $s = -1$ and a pole at $s = -\frac{1}{2}$, and a gain factor of $\frac{1}{2}$.

$$\mathcal{H}_s(s) = \frac{1}{2}\frac{s+1}{s+\frac{1}{2}} \tag{6.15}$$

The pole and zero plot of this filter is shown in Figure 6.3.

The concept of frequency response is as important to the analysis and design of analog filters as it is to digital. The frequency response of an analog filter is the filter's eigenvalue when its input is the complex sinusoid, $e^{j\omega t}$. The analog frequency response is denoted $\mathcal{H}_a(j\omega)$.

We can compute the frequency response by applying an input of $e^{j\omega t}$ and assuming an output of $\mathcal{H}_a(j\omega)e^{j\omega t}$, then solving for $\mathcal{H}_a(j\omega)$. This is no more than repeating our previous development for the transfer function. Rather than grind through the same development, we can do it an easier way. Notice that $e^{j\omega t}$ is a special case of $e^{st}$.

$$e^{j\omega t} = e^{st}|_{s=j\omega} \tag{6.16}$$

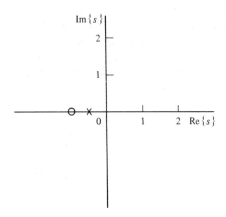

**Figure 6.3** Pole and zero plot of $y(t) = x(t) + \frac{dx(t)}{dt} - 2\frac{dy(t)}{dt}$.

By exploiting this relationship we are able to compute the frequency response by inspection. The frequency response of an analog filter is its transfer function with $s$ replaced by $j\omega$.

$$\mathcal{H}_a(j\omega) = \mathcal{H}_a(s)\,|_{s=j\omega} \tag{6.17a}$$

or

$$\mathcal{H}_a(j\omega) = \frac{\sum_{i=0}^{N} a_i(j\omega)^i}{1 - \sum_{i=1}^{M} b_i(j\omega)^i} \tag{6.17b}$$

The frequency response is simply the transfer function evaluated at $s = j\omega$, along the imaginary axis. The imaginary axis of the $s$-plane is analogous to the unit circle of the $z$-plane.

### Analog Filter Impulse Response

We have characterized analog filters by their differential equations [equation (6.1)], transfer functions [equation (6.12)], or frequency response [equation (6.17)]. It is also useful to describe an analog filter in terms of its outputs when presented with certain inputs. As with digital filters, the most important analog input is the impulse and the most important filter response is the impulse response. An analog impulse is usually denoted $\delta(t)$, which is the Dirac delta function. It is a bizarre function because it is zero for all nonzero $t$ (almost everywhere), it is infinite for $t = 0$, and it has unity area. These characteristics are summarized below.

$$\delta(t) = 0 \quad \text{for} \quad t \neq 0$$
$$\delta(t) = \infty \quad \text{for} \quad t = 0$$
$$\int_{-\epsilon}^{\epsilon} \delta(t) = 1 \quad \text{for all } \epsilon \neq 0 \tag{6.18}$$

Do not let the strangeness of this function bother you. For the purpose of this work you may think of it as a very large spike at $t = 0$, as depicted in Figure 6.4.

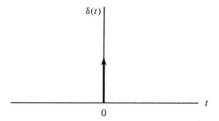

**Figure 6.4** Sketch of an impulse.

The impulse response of an analog filter is its output when it is presented with an impulse. The impulse response is denoted $h(t)$.

$$h(t) = y(t)\,\big|_{x(t)=\delta(t)} \qquad (6.19)$$

In general, the computation of an impulse response is quite tedious. It requires the solution of the filter's differential equation or the evaluation of the inverse Laplace transform of the filter's transfer function. Fortunately, a digital filter designer need not worry about the computation of the impulse response. Rather, we will deal with the impulse response as a concept and use only a few specific responses.

**Stability**

Because the derivatives of the outputs are fed back to form the output, an analog filter can be unstable. An unstable analog filter is not only undesirable in and of itself, but it must also be avoided when using analog filters as a basis for digital filters. Bad analog filters almost always yield bad digital filters, and we have already convinced ourselves that unstable filters are useless.

An analog filter is called **stable** if all bounded inputs (those of finite amplitude) generate bounded outputs. It is called *unstable* if any bounded input causes an infinite output. This bounded-input, bounded-output rule is really a restriction on the filter's impulse response, because a filter is stable if and only if its impulse response goes to zero with increasing time.

$$\text{stability: } h(t) \to 0 \text{ as } t \to \infty$$

If the impulse response increases with time (known as "blowing up"), the filter is unstable.

It might seem that we must compute a filter's impulse response to test its stability. But fortunately this is not the case. It is possible to determine the stability, or lack of, by the filter's pole locations. This argument is similar to the one used for recursive digital filters.

We begin by investigating the stability of the simplest recursive digital filter.

$$y(t) = a_0 x(t) + b_1 \frac{dy(t)}{dt} \tag{6.20}$$

This filter has a transfer function with one pole and no finite zeros.

$$\mathcal{H}_a(s) = \frac{a_0}{1 - b_1 s} \tag{6.21}$$

It has a single pole at $s = 1/b_1$.

We find the impulse response of this filter by computing the homogeneous solution to equation (6.20), or computing the inverse Laplace transform of equation (6.21), or asking an analog filter designer. In any case, the impulse response is an exponential, starting at $t = 0$ and decaying or growing with increasing time.

$$h(t) = \begin{cases} \frac{a_0}{b_1} e^{\frac{1}{b_1} t} & t \geq 0 \\ 0 & t < 0 \end{cases} \tag{6.22}$$

This filter is stable only if the impulse response decays with time, which it does when $1/b_1$ is negative. Since $1/b_1$ is also the pole location, this filter is stable only if the pole is negative — the pole must lie to the left of the imaginary axis. If the pole is positive (lies in the right half of the $s$-plane), the impulse response will steadily increase with time, and this filter is unstable. These results are depicted in Figure 6.5.

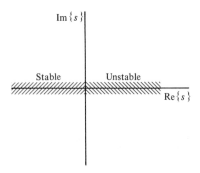

**Figure 6.5** Stable and unstable regions for a single-pole filter.

This result is readily extended to more complicated filters without resorting to computing their impulse responses. We know the stability criterion for a single-pole filter, so let's express an arbitrary filter as a collection of single-pole filters (this should sound familiar). Consider an analog filter with $M$ poles.

$$\mathcal{H}_s(s) = G\frac{(s - z_1)(s - z_2)\dots(s - z_N)}{(s - p_1)(s - p_2)\dots(s - p_M)} \tag{6.23}$$

Assume that the poles are unique; there are no repeated poles. We can express this filter as the parallel combination of $M$ single pole filters by performing a partial-fraction expansion.

$$\mathcal{H}_s(s) = \frac{g_1}{s - p_1} + \frac{g_2}{s - p_2} + \dots + \frac{g_M}{s - p_M} \tag{6.24}$$

In this parallel form, the impulse response of the original filter is the sum of the impulse responses of the single-pole filters. So if the impulse response of any of these filters "blows up," the response of the original filter also grows without bound — it is unstable. In other words, each single-pole filter must be stable if the original filter is stable. Just one unstable single-pole filter means that the original filter was unstable.

From our previous work with single-pole filters, we know that the $i$th single-pole filter of this parallel combination is governed by a first-order differential equation.

$$y_i(t) = g_i x(t) + \frac{1}{p_i}\frac{dy(t)}{dt} \tag{6.25}$$

Therefore, the $i$th filter has an exponential impulse response.

$$h_i(t) = g_i e^{p_i t} \tag{6.26}$$

The $i$th filter is stable when its impulse response goes to zero with time.

This general case is more involved than our simple single-pole filter because $p_i$ can be a complex number. We deal with this complication by expressing $p_i$ as the sum of its real and imaginary components, $p_i = \mathrm{Re}\{p_i\} + j\mathrm{Im}\{p_i\}$. The impulse response is the product of a purely real exponential (corresponding to the real part of $p_i$) and a complex sinusoid (from the imaginary part).

$$\begin{aligned} h_i(t) &= g_i e^{\mathrm{Re}\{p_i\}t} e^{j\mathrm{Im}\{p_i\}t} \\ &= g_i e^{\mathrm{Re}\{p_i\}t}\left[\cos(\mathrm{Im}\{p_i\}t) + j\sin(\mathrm{Im}\{p_i\}t)\right] \end{aligned} \tag{6.27}$$

The decay of the impulse response is completely controlled by the real part of the pole since the imaginary part contributes only a unity-amplitude oscillation. If $\mathrm{Re}\{p_i\}$ is positive, the impulse response grows with time. If the real part of the pole is negative, the impulse response decays with time and the filter is stable. Therefore, a single-pole filter with a complex pole is stable if and only if its pole is to the left of the $s$-plane's imaginary axis. This stable region is called the left-half plane.

Our $M$-pole filter is stable only if each of its single-pole filters is stable, and the single-pole filters are stable only if their poles lie in the left-half plane. Therefore, the $M$-pole filter is stable if and only if all of its poles lie in the left-half plane. If even one of the poles is in the right-half of the $s$-plane, the filter is unstable. The $s$-plane stability regions are shown in Figure 6.6.

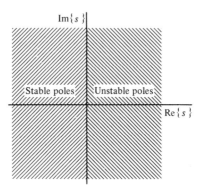

**Figure 6.6** Stability regions of the $s$-plane.

Notice the similarities between the $s$- and $z$-plane stability results. Digital filters are stable when their poles are confined within the unit circle. Analog filters are stable when their poles are in the left-half plane. So the inside of the unit circle is the digital filter's equivalent to the left-half of the $s$-plane.

In summary, this brief exposure to analog filters has introduced the concept of the transfer function, frequency response, and impulse response. There are strong parallels between the characterization of analog and digital filters, but at the same time they are very different. We will postpone further discussion of analog filters until we develop the digital design techniques that are based on analog filters.

## 6.2  IMPULSE INVARIANT TECHNIQUE

Suppose that you design or are given an analog filter and wish to generate a digital filter with similar characteristics. As noted previously, you could begin from scratch and directly design the digital filter or you could apply techniques that approximate the analog filter with a digital one. One approximation is to find a digital filter whose impulse response is as close as possible to the analog filter's. This is called the *impulse invariant technique*.

The impulse invariant technique is intuitively satisfying because the digital and analog filters will have the closest possible impulse responses. Because of the important role the impulse response plays in both analog and digital filtering, we would expect that filters with similar impulse responses would have similar characteristics.

We will develop the impulse invariant technique in two phases. The first phase will present a straightforward way of matching the impulse responses, but unfortunately this method is too computationally difficult to be of much use. The second phase will build on these results and develop a more convoluted approximation technique, which is in fact much more practical.

Suppose that we are presented with the impulse response of an analog filter, which we wish to approximate with a digital filter. Call the analog impulse response $h_a(t)$ and the digital filter's impulse response $h_k$. Furthermore, suppose that the digital filter is running at $T$ seconds per sample. It should be clear that we will never be able to exactly match the analog impulse response because of the basic nature of analog and digital signals — $h_a(t)$ has a value for all $t$, and $h_k$ is defined for only integer $k$'s. But we can approximate the analog impulse response by finding a digital filter whose impulse response is the samples of the analog filter's response.

$$h_k = h_a(kT) \tag{6.28}$$

The digital filter's response exactly matches the analog filter's response at the sampling times — that is as good as we can do.

Although the concepts behind the impulse invariant approximation are easy to understand, the actual design is tough. The reason for this is that few analog filters are given in terms of their impulse responses. Analog filters are generally described by their transfer function or pole-zero locations. Therefore, to determine the impulse response of the digital approximating filter, the designer must first compute the impulse response of the analog filter, which is difficult. The second problem with this method is what to do with the digital impulse response once you have it. If the digital filter is nonrecursive, $h_k$ is the coefficients and the design is easy. But we have better methods of designing nonrecursive digital filters, so the impulse invariant method should be reserved for recursive filters. If the digital filter is recursive, we must transform the impulse response to the $z$-transform before we can compute the filter coefficients. In Chapter 5 we showed that converting a digital impulse response to $\mathcal{H}(z)$ is, in general, difficult. Therefore, a straightforward application of the impulse invariant concept is simply too complex to be used in all but the simplest examples.

**Example:** Approximate an analog integrator with a recursive digital filter.

$$y(t) = \int_0^t x(\tau)d\tau \tag{6.29}$$

The impulse response of this filter is a step function.

$$h_a(t) = \begin{cases} 1 & t \geq 0 \\ 0 & t < 0 \end{cases} \tag{6.30}$$

So let's find a digital filter with a step function impulse response.

$$h_k = \begin{cases} 1 & k \geq 0 \\ 0 & k < 0 \end{cases} \tag{6.31}$$

Fortunately, we are not required to compute the $z$-transform of this impulse response (although it is simple enough to do), because we can guess at this filter. This is no more than the digital integrator.

$$y_k = x_k + y_{k-1} \tag{6.32}$$

We have approximated our first analog filter.

The preceding example was doable because it did not require the computation of the analog filter's impulse response (we did it from inspection), nor did it require the computation of the digital filter's $z$-transform. We will now enter the second phase of our development and present an impulse invariant technique that does not require the computation of the impulse responses. This technique approximates the analog filter without dropping below the pole and zero representation.

As before, denote the digital filter's impulse response $h_k$ and the analog filter's $h_a(t)$. The analog filter's transfer function is $\mathcal{H}_a(s)$, and the digital filter's $z$-transform is $\mathcal{H}(z)$. Our goal is to compute $\mathcal{H}(z)$ directly from $\mathcal{H}_a(s)$, thereby avoiding the complications of the impulse responses.

We begin the derivation by expressing $\mathcal{H}_a(s)$ in its parallel form through a partial-fraction expansion. For now, assume that $\mathcal{H}_a(s)$ has no repeated poles (no two poles are in the same location), so the analog filter's transfer function can be represented as the sum of $M$ single-pole filters.

$$\mathcal{H}_a(s) = \sum_{i=1}^{M} \frac{A_i}{s - p_i} \tag{6.33}$$

This representation is illustrated in Figure 6.7.

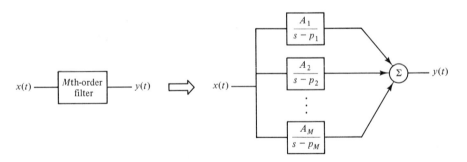

**Figure 6.7** Parallel decomposition of an $M$th-ordered analog filter.

We saw previously that each of these single-pole filters has an exponential impulse response. The impulse response of the $i$th filter is denoted $h_{ai}(t)$.

$$h_{ai}(t) = \begin{cases} A_i e^{p_i t} & t \geq 0 \\ 0 & t < 0 \end{cases} \tag{6.34}$$

Because these single-pole filters all share a common input and their outputs are summed, the impulse response of the original, $M$th-order filter is simply the sum of the individual responses.

$$h_a(t) = \sum_{i=1}^{M} h_{ai}(t) \tag{6.35}$$

Rather than attempting to approximate the original filter's impulse response, let us find $M$ digital filters that approximate the single-pole responses, the $h_{ai}(t)$'s. We would then put the $M$ digital filters in parallel, thereby "building" a digital filter whose impulse response approximates the original analog filter's response. In this manner we are dividing a complex analog filter into $M$ simpler filters and then approximating them. We put the $M$ digital approximations together to create the approximation to the original filter. This is called "divide and conquer" and is attributed to the Romans, but they never designed digital filters.

We approximate the overall impulse response by sampling equation (6.35).

$$h_k = h_a(kT) = \sum_{i=1}^{M} h_{ai}(kT) \tag{6.36}$$

Next, we identify each of the $M$ impulse responses with a digital filter. We will denote the impulse response of the $i$th digital filter $h_{ik}$ (watch the notation; $i$ is the filter's number and $k$ is the digital index).

$$h_{ik} = h_{ai}(kT) \tag{6.37}$$

But we have an exact form for $h_{ai}(t)$ as a function of the $i$th filter's pole location [equation (6.34)].

$$h_{ik} = A_i e^{p_i kT} \qquad k = 0, 1, 2, \ldots \tag{6.38}$$

The final step is to design the $i$th digital filter by computing its $z$-transform, $\mathcal{H}_i(z)$.

$$\begin{aligned}
\mathcal{H}_i(z) &= \sum_{k=0}^{\infty} A_i e^{p_i kT} z^{-k} \\
&= \sum_{k=0}^{\infty} A_i \left( e^{p_i T} z^{-1} \right)^k \\
&= \frac{A_i}{1 - e^{p_i T} z^{-1}} \\
&= \frac{A_i z}{z - e^{p_i T}}
\end{aligned} \tag{6.39}$$

The digital filter that approximates the $i$th single-pole analog filter has a zero at 0, a pole at $e^{-p_i T}$, and a gain of $A_i$.

The $z$-transform of the digital filter that is the impulse invariant approximation to the original analog filter is the sum of the $\mathcal{H}_i(z)$s.

$$
\begin{aligned}
\mathcal{H}(z) &= \sum_{i=1}^{M} \mathcal{H}_i(z) \\
&= \sum_{i=1}^{M} \frac{A_i z}{z - e^{p_i T}}
\end{aligned}
\tag{6.40}
$$

The impulse invariant technique is illustrated in Figure 6.8. The analog filter is decomposed into a parallel combination of single-pole filters. These filters are individually approximated with single-pole digital filters, which are then combined in parallel to create the approximation.

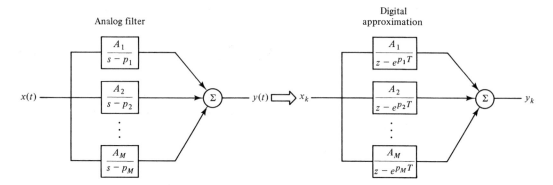

**Figure 6.8** Impulse invariant approximation.

Most users of the impulse invariant technique choose to ignore the zero at 0 in the digital filters. So they use a digital filter with a $z$-transform of

$$
\mathcal{H}(z) = \sum_{i=1}^{M} \frac{A_i}{z - e^{p_i T}}
\tag{6.41}
$$

If we compare equation (6.41) with the second half of equation (6.40), we see that ignoring the zero is equivalent to multiplying the $z$-transform by $z^{-1}$. Since $z^{-1}$ is one unit of delay, these two approximations differ by only one unit of delay. This delay is seldom important, so we will also drop the zero at 0. For the purist, it is possible to again derive the impulse invariant technique so that the zero is never generated. This is done by approximating the analog impulse response with its samples delayed by one sampling period.

$$
h_k = h_a(kT - T)
\tag{6.42}
$$

Try it and convince yourself that the zero naturally disappears in equation (6.39).

Before proceeding to some examples, let's formalize the impulse invariant design technique.

### Impulse Invariant Design

Step 1:  We begin the design by selecting the transfer function (or the poles and zeros) of an analog filter. Call this transfer function $\mathcal{H}_a(s)$.

Step 2:  Select the sampling rate of the digital filter, $T$ seconds per sample. Note that higher sampling rates (small $T$) generally yield better approximations.

Step 3:  Express the analog filter's transfer function as the sum of single-pole filters. This requires a partial fraction expansion.

$$\mathcal{H}_a(s) = \sum_{i=1}^{M} \frac{A_i}{s - p_i} \tag{6.43}$$

Step 4:  Approximate the impulse response of the single-pole analog filters by finding a single-pole digital filter whose impulse response is the samples of the analog response. This is done by mapping the $s$-plane poles to $z$-plane poles.

$$p_i \text{ in } s-\text{plane} => e^{-p_i T} \text{in } z-\text{plane}$$

Each analog filter is approximated by a digital filter whose $z$-transform is

$$\mathcal{H}_i(z) = \frac{A_i}{z - e^{-p_i T}} \tag{6.44}$$

Step 5:  Compute the $z$-transform of the digital filter that approximates the analog filter by summing the individual $z$-transforms.

$$\mathcal{H}(z) = \sum_{i=1}^{M} \frac{A_i}{z - e^{-p_i T}} \tag{6.45}$$

Step 6:  Realize the digital filter by choosing a form (parallel, cascade, or consolidated) and computing the coefficients for the filter(s). The coefficients for the $M$ filters of the parallel realization can be determined by inspection ($a_1 = A_i$ and $b_1 = e^{-p_i T}$). The other realizations require the designer to put equation (6.45) over a common denominator(s).

**Example:** Approximate an analog integrator with a digital filter. Use a sampling rate of 1000 samples per second ($T = 0.001$).

An analog integrator has a single pole at $s = 0$.

$$\mathcal{H}_a(s) = \frac{1}{s} \tag{6.46}$$

The sampling rate is given to us, so we can go directly to step 3. But there is no need to perform the partial-fraction expansion because this is a single-pole filter. So we can go directly to step 4. The approximating digital filter has a single pole at

$$z = e^{(-0)(0.001)} = 1 \tag{6.47}$$

The digital filter has a pole at $z = 1$ and the pole location is independent of the sampling rate.

$$\mathcal{H}(z) = \frac{1}{z - 1} \tag{6.48}$$

In this simple example, step 5 is superfluous, so we go directly to the realization. The digital integrator has the following difference equation.

$$y_k = x_{k-1} + y_{k-1} \tag{6.49}$$

Notice the delay in the input. This is the result of ignoring the zero. The frequency responses of the analog and digital filters are shown in Figure 6.9.

**Example:** Approximate a three-pole low-pass Butterworth filter with a cutoff frequency of 10 rad/sec. Assume a sampling rate of 20 samples/sec.

This three-pole Butterworth filter has poles at radius 10 and angles of 120, 180, and 240 degrees.

$$\begin{aligned} p_1 : & \quad 10\angle 120^o = -5 + j8.66 \\ p_2 : & \quad 10\angle 180^o = -10 \\ p_3 : & \quad 10\angle 240^o = -5 - j8.66 \end{aligned} \tag{6.50}$$

The filter has a three-pole transfer function.

$$\mathcal{H}_a(s) = \frac{1}{[s - (-5 + j8.66)]\ [s - (-10)]\ [s - (-5 - j8.66)]} \tag{6.51}$$

This multipole filter must be expressed in its parallel form before we can map the analog poles. We do so with the partial-fraction expansion.

$$\mathcal{H}_a(s) = \frac{A_1}{s - (-5 + j8.66)} + \frac{A_2}{s - (-10)} + \frac{A_3}{s - (-5 - j8.66)} \tag{6.52}$$

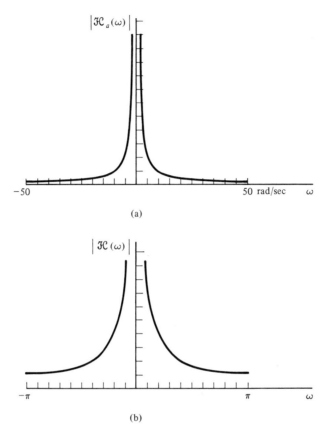

(a)

(b)

**Figure 6.9** Analog and digital responses of an analog integrator
and its digital approximation: (a) Frequency response
of analog integrator; (b) Frequency response of
impulse invariant approximation.

After a great deal of algebra and a few mistakes, we solve for the partial
fraction expansion coefficients.

$$A_1 = 0.00577\angle 210^o$$
$$A_2 = 0.01 \tag{6.52}$$
$$A_3 = 0.00577\angle 150^o$$

Notice that $A_1$ and $A_3$ are complex conjugates. This is always the case when
we encounter complex poles of real filters. Now we go to step 4 and map the
$s$-plane poles to the $z$-plane. The first pole is mapped as follows:

$$e^{(-5+j8.66)(0.05)} = e^{-0.25}e^{j0.433} = 0.7788\angle 24.8^o \tag{6.54}$$

The second pole is easier because it does not have an imaginary part.

$$e^{(-10)(0.05)} = e^{-0.5} = 0.6065 \tag{6.55}$$

The third pole is even easier to map because it is the complex conjugate of the first poles. Convince yourself that complex-conjugate poles in the $s$-plane map to conjugate poles in the $z$-plane.

$$e^{(-5-j8.66)(0.05)} = 0.7788\angle - 24.8^o \tag{6.56}$$

The pole locations of this filter are shown in Figure 6.10. Notice that all poles are within the unit circle (the digital filter is stable) and they are closely clustered around $z = 1$.

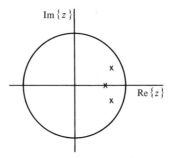

**Figure 6.10** Pole locations of a digital Butterworth filter ($T = 0.05$).

We complete this design by realizing the filter. Its $z$-transform is the sum of the three single-pole filters.

$$\mathcal{H}(z) = \frac{0.00577\angle 210^o}{z - 0.7788\angle 24.8^o} + \frac{0.01}{z - 0.6065} + \frac{0.00577\angle 150^o}{z - 0.7788\angle - 24.8^o} \tag{6.57}$$

The rest of the realization depends on how we want to realize the filter. We have the choice of the parallel combination of a first- and second-order filter (why can't we implement it as the parallel combination of three, single-pole filters?) or a single, three-pole filter.

Let's do it as a single filter by putting equation (6.57) over a common denominator. After a great deal of algebra (this really should be done on a computer), we get the following $z$-transform.

$$\mathcal{H}(z) = \frac{0.0008701z + 0.0006365}{z^3 - 2.020z^2 + 1.464z - 0.3678} \tag{6.58}$$

Therefore, our digital Butterworth filter has the following filter coefficients.

$$c_2 = 0.0008701 \quad c_3 = 0.0006365 \tag{6.59}$$

$$d_1 = 2.020 \quad d_2 = -1.464 \quad d_3 = 0.3678$$

Figure 6.11 shows the frequency response of the analog and digital Butterworth filters. Note the closeness between the analog Butterworth filter and our digital approximation.

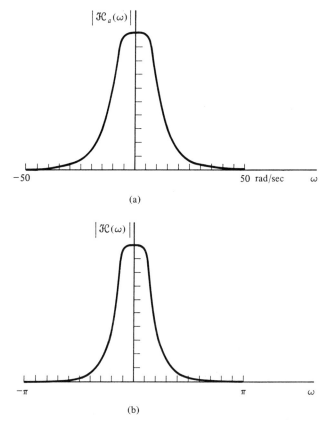

**Figure 6.11** Frequency response of analog and digital Butterworth filters: (a) Analog Butterworth filter; (b) Digital approximation ($T = 0.05$).

Notice that the sampling rate plays an important role in the impulse invariant design. As it becomes larger ($T$ becomes smaller) the analog poles are mapped closer to $z = 1$, because $e^{p_i T}$ goes to 1 as $T$ becomes small. Let's see how the sampling rate affects our example by trying it again with a much lower rate.

**Example:** Approximate a three-pole Butterworth filter with a cutoff frequency of 10 rad/sec. This time, use a sampling rate of 10 samples/sec.

Much of this example is identical to the preceding one, so a lot of it will be skipped. This is the same analog filter, so there is no reason to repeat the partial-fraction expansion. The analog poles are mapped to different locations in the $z$-plane because of the lower sampling rate. The pole mappings are as follows:

$$p_1: \quad e^{(-5+j8.66)\frac{1}{10}} = 0.6060\angle 49.6^o$$

$$p_2: \quad e^{(-10)\frac{1}{10}} = 0.3679\angle 0^o \tag{6.60}$$

$$p_3: \quad e^{(-5-j8.66)\frac{1}{10}} = 0.6060\angle -49.6^o$$

The pole locations are shown in Figure 6.12. Notice that the lower sampling rate caused the poles to move closer to the center of the unit circle (radii are smaller), and the angles of the poles are larger.

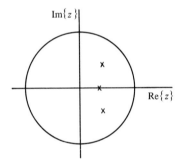

**Figure 6.12** Pole locations of a digital Butterworth filter $(T = 0.1)$.

Compute the $z$-transform by expressing the filter in its parallel form.

$$\mathcal{H}(z) = \frac{0.00577\angle 210^o}{z - 0.6060\angle 49.6^o} + \frac{0.01}{z - 0.36791} + \frac{0.00577\angle 150^o}{z - 0.6060\angle -49.6^o} \tag{6.61}$$

We finish the design by putting the parallel form over a common denominator.

$$\mathcal{H}(z) = \frac{0.002411z + 0.001248}{z^3 - 1.153z^2 + 0.6561z - 0.1351} \tag{6.62}$$

The frequency response of this filter is shown in Figure 6.13. Notice that this is not as good an approximation of the Butterworth filter as our earlier example. The lower sampling rate caused higher gain in the stopband. This is the major drawback of the impulse invariant method, as we will see in the next section.

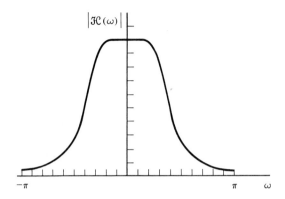

$$|\mathcal{H}(\omega)|$$

$-\pi$                          $\pi$      $\omega$

**Figure 6.13** Frequency response of a digital Butterworth filter $(T = 0.1)$.

We have assumed that the analog filter does not contain repeated poles, but occasionally a designer is confronted with an analog filter with multiordered poles. In these cases the partial fraction expansion of the transfer function generates second- or even higher-order filters, which must be approximated. So let us consider a filter with a twice-repeated pole and find an impulse invariant approximation to it.

$$\mathcal{H}_a(s) = \frac{A}{(s-p)^2} \tag{6.63}$$

This filter has an impulse response that is the inverse Laplace transform of equation (6.63). Here it is (but don't worry how to do it).

$$h_a(t) = Ate^{pt} \quad t \geq 0$$
$$= 0 \qquad t < 0 \tag{6.64}$$

Therefore, this analog filter is approximated with a digital filter having the following impulse response.

$$h_k = AkTe^{pkT} \tag{6.65}$$

It has a $z$-transform of

$$\mathcal{H}(z) = \sum_{k=0}^{\infty} AkTe^{pkT} z^{-k}$$

$$= AT \sum_{k=0}^{\infty} k \left(e^{pT} z^{-1}\right)^k \tag{6.66}$$

Surprisingly, this sum has a closed form. The approximating filter has a second-order pole at $z = e^{pT}$.

$$\mathcal{H}(z) = \frac{ATe^{pT} z^{-1}}{\left(1 - e^{pT} z^{-1}\right)^2} \tag{6.67}$$

So we can approximate analog filters with twice-repeated poles. A similar derivation will generate approximations for higher-ordered poles, but they are seldom encountered in practice.

The impulse invariant design is computationally arduous, so many designers rely on computers to do the bulk of the work. For those of you who must do it by hand, the partial fraction expansion of the transfer function and the realization of the digital filter are the toughest part of the design. Mapping the poles from the $s$- to the $z$-plane is the most conceptually challenging part. The partial fraction expansion and realization are little more than complicated bookkeeping, so there is little to say about them, except be careful. But the pole mapping has a number of interesting features that warrant further discussion.

## 6.3 IMPULSE INVARIANT POLE MAPPING

We saw in the previous examples that the impulse invariant technique yields good approximations when the sampling rate is high, but slower sampling rates degrade the approximation. This section explores this phenomenon by looking at the $s$-plane to $z$-plane mapping performed by the impulse invariant mapping. We will find that slow sampling rates will cause aliasing of the analog filter's frequency response, as approximated by the digital filter.

Consider a single pole somewhere in the $s$-plane, say at location $s = \sigma + j\omega$. The impulse invariant technique maps the pole to a point in the $z$-plane, say $p_z$, via the transformation

$$p_z = e^{(\sigma + j\omega)T}$$
$$= e^{\sigma T} e^{j\omega T} \tag{6.68}$$

The first term in the product, $e^{\sigma T}$, has a magnitude of $e^{\sigma T}$ and an angle of 0 — it is a real number. The second term, $e^{j\omega T}$, has unity magnitude and an angle of $\omega T$. Therefore, our analog pole is mapped to a place in the $z$-plane of magnitude $e^{\sigma T}$ and angle $\omega T$. The real part of the analog pole determines the radius of the $z$-plane pole and the imaginary part of the analog pole dictates the angle of the digital pole. With this in mind, let's explore the impulse invariant pole mapping.

Consider any analog pole with a zero real component, $\sigma = 0$. They lie on the $j\omega$ axis in the $s$-plane. These poles map to the $z$-plane at a radius of $e^{0T} = 1$; they map to the unit circle, with an angle of $j\omega$. This mapping is illustrated in Figure 6.14a. Therefore, the impulse invariant mapping maps poles from the $s$-plane's $j\omega$ axis to the $z$-plane's unit circle.

Now consider stable analog poles, those poles in the left half of the $s$-plane. They map to $z$-plane poles with magnitudes less than 1.

$$e^{\sigma T} < 1 \quad \text{for} \quad \sigma < 0 \tag{6.69}$$

Therefore, all $s$-plane poles with negative real parts map to $z$-plane poles inside the unit circle — stable analog poles are mapped to stable digital poles. The impulse

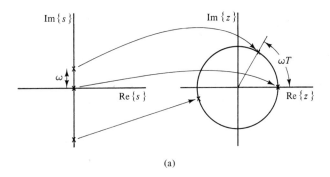

(a)

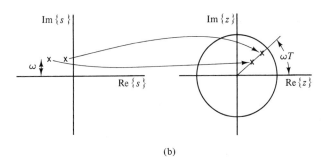

(b)

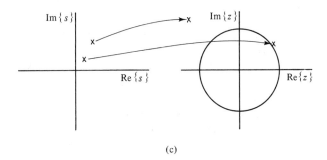

(c)

**Figure 6.14** Impulse invariant pole mappings: (a) $j\omega$ axis maps to the
unit circle; (b) stable poles map inside the unit
circle; (c) unstable poles map outside the unit circle.

invariant mapping preserves the stability of the filter; this is a necessary feature of
a useful design technique. In a similar vein all poles in the right half of the $s$-plane
map to digital poles outside the unit circle.

$$e^{\sigma T} > 1 \quad \text{for} \quad \sigma > 0 \tag{6.70}$$

These mappings are illustrated in Figure 6.14b and c.

We've noticed that the imaginary component of the analog pole, $j\omega$, determines the digital pole's angle in the $z$-plane. So, two analog poles with the same imaginary component (lying on a horizontal line in the $s$-plane) map to the same angle in the $z$-plane. But in actuality, the mapping is more complicated than that because the angle is periodic, with a period of $2\pi$. The easiest way to see this complication is to consider two poles in the $s$-plane with identical real parts, but with imaginary components differing by $2\pi/T$ (you'll see the reason for this choice in a moment).

$$\text{spole}_1 : \qquad \sigma + j\omega$$

$$\text{spole}_2 : \qquad \sigma + j\left(\omega + \frac{2\pi}{T}\right) \tag{6.71}$$

These poles map to $z$-plane poles, $z\text{pole}_1$ and $z\text{pole}_2$, via the impulse invariant mapping.

$$z\text{pole}_1 : \qquad e^{\sigma T} + e^{j\omega T}$$

$$z\text{pole}_2 : \qquad e^{\sigma T} + e^{j\left(\omega T + \frac{2\pi}{T}T\right)} \tag{6.72}$$

These poles map to the same radius in the $z$-plane at apparently different angles. But, not so fast. The angles differ by exactly $2\pi$, which is no difference at all. So these two poles map to the same location in the $z$-plane. There are an infinite number of $s$-plane poles that map to the same location in the $z$-plane. They must have the same real parts and imaginary parts that differ by some integer multiple of $2\pi/T$.

This is the big deficiency of the impulse invariant mapping. It has the potential of generating ambiguities in the pole locations if the $s$-plane poles have imaginary parts greater than $\pi/T$ or less than $-\pi/T$. This ambiguity is another form of the "aliasing" encountered when sampling analog signals. If we sample the analog filter's impulse response too slowly, we get an aliased version of it, which manifests itself in the $z$-plane as aliased poles.

The analog poles will not be aliased by the impulse invariant mapping if they are confined to the $s$-plane's "primary strip" (within $\pi/T$ of the real axis). Any analog pole lying outside this strip will be undifferentiable from an equivalent pole within the strip. This phenomenon is illustrated in Figure 6.15. You prevent pole aliasing by making the primary strip wide enough (small enough $T$) to embrace all the analog poles. In actuality, the primary strip must be much larger than the poles to prevent aliasing in the frequency response. Consider an example.

**Example:** Find the lowest sampling rate that can be used to approximate a three-pole Butterworth filter with a cutoff frequency of 10 rad/sec.

The Butterworth filter has poles at $-5 + j8.66$, $-10$, and $-5 - j8.66$. The primary strip must contain all the poles, so it must be at least $2 \times 8.66$ radians wide. We find the maximum sampling period by "mapping" this pole with a generalized sampling period and solving for the largest period, $T_{\max}$, that will map the pole into the primary strip.

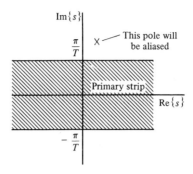

**Figure 6.15** The $s$-plane's primary strip.

$$\frac{\pi}{T_{\max}} = 8.66$$
$$= 0.363 \text{ sec} \tag{6.73}$$

The minimum sampling rate is, therefore, $\frac{1}{T_{\max}} = 2.76$ samples/sec. However, we noticed some distortion of the frequency response in the example where we approximated the Butterworth filter with a sampling rate of 20 samples/sec. So it must be possible to get aliasing, even when all the poles are within the primary strip.

The impulse invariant technique can distort the frequency response by aliasing it even when all analog poles are within the primary strip. We show this by considering the frequency response of a single-pole analog filter and looking at its digital approximation.

$$\mathcal{H}_a(s) = \frac{A}{s - p} \tag{6.74}$$

Its frequency response is its transfer function with $s$ replaced with $j\omega$.

$$\mathcal{H}_a(\omega) = \frac{A}{jw - p} \tag{6.75}$$

The digital approximation has a single pole at $e^{pT}$.

$$\mathcal{H}(z) = \frac{A}{1 - e^{pT}z^{-1}} \tag{6.76}$$

The digital frequency response is $\mathcal{H}(z)$ evaluated at $z = e^{j\omega}$.

$$\mathcal{H}(\omega) = \frac{A}{1 - e^{pT}e^{-j\omega}} \tag{6.77}$$

$$\mathcal{H}(\omega) = \frac{A}{1 - e^{-T\left(j\frac{\omega}{T} - p\right)}} \tag{6.78}$$

The next step is to relate the analog [equation (6.75)] and digital [equation (6.78)] frequency responses. Unfortunately they are in very different forms so we must massage equation (6.78) to look like equation (6.75). This effort takes a great deal of work and much of it is messy. So why not skip it and be satisfied that the digital frequency response can be written as an infinite sum?

$$\mathcal{H}(\omega) = \frac{1}{T} \sum_{k=-\infty}^{\infty} \frac{A}{j\frac{\omega}{T} + j\frac{2\pi}{T}k - p} \tag{6.79}$$

The terms on the right-hand side look a great deal like the analog frequency response. As a matter of fact, these terms are the analog response with $\omega$ replaced with $\omega/T + (2\pi/T)k$. Therefore, the digital frequency response is the sum of frequency-shifted versions of the analog response.

$$\mathcal{H}(\omega) = \frac{1}{T} \sum_{k=-\infty}^{\infty} \mathcal{H}_a\left(\frac{\omega}{T} + \frac{2\pi}{T}k\right) \tag{6.80}$$

The terms on the right-hand side are the analog frequency response, with its frequency scaled by $1/T$ and frequency shifted by $(2\pi/T)k$ radians. So the digital frequency response is the sum of an infinite number of these frequency-scaled and shifted analog responses.

The meaning of equation (6.80) is illustrated in Figure 6.16. The top of the figure is the frequency response of an analog low-pass filter. The next three plots are the first three terms of equation (6.80), the analog response shifted by 0 ($k = 0$), $2\pi/T$ ($k = 1$), and $4\pi/T$ ($k = 2$). The bottom plot shows the frequency response of the digital filter (the sum of the shifted analog responses). Notice that the digital frequency response perfectly reproduces the analog response every $2\pi/T$. This is because none of the shifted versions of the analog frequency response overlapped in frequency. If they had, the digital response would have been distorted by aliasing.

Consider the example in Figure 6.17. In this case the same analog filter is approximated but with a much lower sampling frequency. Because of the larger $T$, the shifted versions have significant overlap, so the digital frequency response is distorted when they are added. This is aliasing, which can be overcome by designing a more bandlimited analog filter (making the analog filter narrower) or increasing the sampling rate. The analog filter of Figure 6.17 would have been fine if the sampling rate had been increased by 50%.

Aliasing can and generally does degrade the filter dramatically. So it must be prevented or kept to a minimum by picking a high enough sampling rate. The sampling period must be small enough that the analog frequency response is negligible above $\pi/T$ rad. To prevent noticeable aliasing,

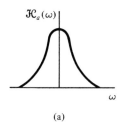

$$\mathcal{H}_a(\omega)$$

(a)

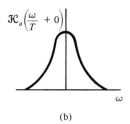

$$\mathcal{H}_a\left(\frac{\omega}{T} + 0\right)$$

(b)

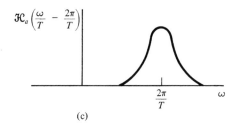

$$\mathcal{H}_a\left(\frac{\omega}{T} - \frac{2\pi}{T}\right)$$

(c)

$$\mathcal{H}_a\left(\frac{\omega}{T} - \frac{4\pi}{T}\right)$$

(d)

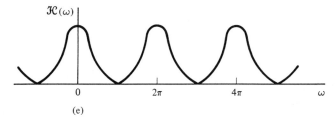

$$\mathcal{H}(\omega)$$

(e)

**Figure 6.16** Analog and digital frequency responses: (a) Analog frequency response; (b) Analog response shifted by 0; (c) Analog response shifted by $2\pi/T$; (d) Analog response shifted by $4\pi/T$; (e) Digital filter's frequency response.

$$\mathcal{H}_a(\omega) \approx 0 \quad \text{for} \quad |\omega| > \frac{\pi}{T}$$

Now that we understand the impulse invariant design method, it is important to realize the role it plays in digital filter design. After the derivation, many people come away with the feeling that it is primarily used for implementing analog filters with digital. That is seldom the case, because a good analog filter should be realized using analog techniques (capacitors, op amps, and all of that stuff). The impulse invariant method uses the analog filter as a "backdoor" into the design of digital filters, because we cannot go through the "front".

You begin the design process by specifying the general characteristics (low-pass, band-pass, etc.) of the digital filter and the critical frequency points (generally cutoff points). Then you design or have someone design an analog filter that will generate the desired digital filter when approximated by the impulse invariant method. For example, if you want a low-pass digital filter, go out and design a Butterworth low-pass filter with the appropriate cutoff frequency. But how do you select the frequency? The answer lies in equation (6.80). The digital and analog frequencies are related through the sampling period, $T$. The digital frequency, $\omega_d$, is the analog frequency, $\omega_a$, scaled by the sampling period, $T$.

$$\omega_d = \omega_a T \tag{6.81}$$

The most expeditious way of handling this frequency scaling is to ignore it by using a $T = 1$ in your design, even though the actual digital filter is running at some other rate. When $T = 1$ the analog and digital frequencies are the same, so you design an analog filter with the same critical frequency points as your desired digital filter. If the impulse invariant approximation does not cause aliasing, the digital filter will have the analog filter's frequency response replicated every $2\pi$ rad/sample.

**Example:** Specify an analog filter that will yield a digital filter with a passband from $\pi/4$ to $3\pi/4$. The digital filter runs at 1 sample every 10 sec, $T = 10$.

Our first approach is to ignore the actual speed of the filter and perform the design using $T = 1$. This requires us to design an analog filter with a passband from $\pi/4$ to $3\pi/4$ rad/sec. Then map this filter to a digital filter with $e^{p1}$ (pretend that $T = 1$).

The second approach is to pigheadedly use the actual sampling period of $T = 10$ sec. This forces us to use equation (6.81) to scale the digital frequency. Therefore, the analog filter must have a passband from $\pi/40$ to $3\pi/40$ in order for the digital frequency to be correct after the impulse invariant design. Then approximate the analog filter is approximated by using the mapping $e^{p10}$. Notice that scaling the analog specification by $1/T$ is canceled by mapping the poles with $e^{pT}$, so we might as well ignore the actual sampling period and use the most convinient sampling period, $T = 1$.

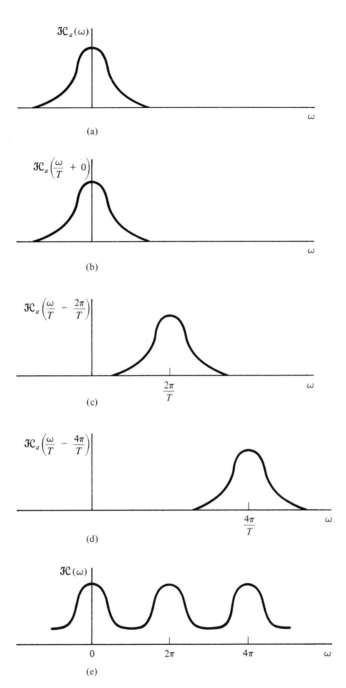

**Figure 6.17** Aliasing of the analog frequency response:
(a) Analog frequency response;
(b) $k = 0$; (c) $k = 1$; (d) $k = 2$;
(e) digital frequency with aliasing.

The moral to this story is to forget about the actual sampling period and use $T = 1$ in your designs.

Many designers shy away from the impulse invariant technique because of the aliasing. These people have been given a good analog filter, but without realizing it have approximated it with a digital filter that was too slow. The resulting aliasing can turn a low-pass filter into a bandpass, or worse yet, an all-pass. Those faint-hearted designers turn to another approximation technique which will not cause aliasing: the bilinear transformation.

## 6.4 BILINEAR TRANSFORMATION

The bilinear transformation provides the designer with an alternative technique of approximating analog filters with digital filters. This method is derived by approximating a first-order differential equation with a difference equation. This different perspective yields an approximation technique which is generally more useful than the impulse invariant method.

All linear time-invariant analog filters are described with an $M$th-ordered differential equation. Rather than trying to approximate a general analog filter, we begin our derivation of the bilinear transform by looking at a simple first-order differential equation.

$$a\frac{dy(t)}{dt} + by(t) = cx(t) \qquad (6.82)$$

Because the following development involves many derivatives, let's use the short-hand notation for the differential operator.

$$y'(t) = \frac{dy(t)}{dt} \qquad (6.83)$$

So

$$ay'(t) + by(t) = cx(t) \qquad (6.84)$$

This equation defines an analog filter with a single pole at $-b/a$ and a gain of $\frac{c}{a}$.

$$\mathcal{H}_a(s) = \frac{c}{as + b} \qquad (6.85)$$

Equation (6.82) involves both $y(t)$ and its derivative. It is easier to work with the equation if we get rid of the $y(t)$ and use only $y'(t)$. We do this by expressing $y(t)$ as the integral of $y'(t)$ plus an initial condition. This step is more of a trick to get the bilinear transformation.

$$y(t) = \int_{t_0}^{t} y'(\tau)\, d\tau + y(t_0) \qquad (6.86)$$

We have expressed the filter as an integral equation because it will be easier to approximate with a digital filter. A digital filter operates on the data at integer multiples of the sampling period, $T$, so let's select $t = kT$ and $t_0 = kT - T$.

$$y(kT) = \int_{kT-T}^{kT} y'(\tau)d\tau + y(kT - T) \tag{6.87}$$

This equation is very close to a difference equation except for the integral operator and the derivatives. We get rid of the integral by approximating it with the trapezoid rule.

$$\int_{kT-T}^{kT} y'(\tau)\,d\tau \approx \frac{T}{2}\left[y'(kT) + y'(kT - T)\right] \tag{6.88}$$

Remember that the trapezoid rule is only an approximation, so from here on we are approximating the differential equation.

$$y(kT) \approx \frac{T}{2}\left[y'(kT) + y'(kT - T)\right] + y(kT - T) \tag{6.89}$$

This approximation is closer to a digital filter, but it still has the derivatives. We get rid of them by solving for $y'(t)$ in equation (6.84),

$$y'(t) = \frac{c}{a}x(t) - \frac{b}{a}y(t) \tag{6.90}$$

then substituting the result into equation (6.89).

$$y(kT) \approx \frac{T}{2}\left[\frac{c}{a}x(kT) - \frac{b}{a}y(kT) + \frac{c}{a}x(kT - T) - \frac{b}{a}y(kT - T)\right] + y(kT - T) \tag{6.91}$$

In other words, the following digital filter approximates our single-pole analog filter.

$$y(kT) = \frac{Tc}{2a + Tb}x(kT) + \frac{Tc}{2a + Tb}x(kT - T) - \frac{Tb - 2a}{2a + Tb}y(kT - T) \tag{6.92}$$

This filter has a $z$-transform of

$$\mathcal{H}(z) = \frac{Tc + Tcz^{-1}}{(2a + Tb) + (Tb - 2a)z^{-1}}. \tag{6.93}$$

We have derived a first-order digital filter that approximates the analog filter, but this is not the design procedure. The final step in the derivation is to relate the $z$-transform of the approximating filter to the transfer function of the analog filter.

We do so by rearranging the $z$-transform so it looks like the transfer function — put $\mathcal{H}(z)$ into the form of

$$\mathcal{H}(z) = \frac{c}{a(\text{function of } z) + b} \tag{6.94}$$

This is done by rearranging equation (6.93),

$$\mathcal{H}(z) = \frac{Tc(1 + z^{-1})}{Tb(1 + z^{-1}) + 2a(1 - z^{-1})} \tag{6.95}$$

then dividing by $T(1 + z^{-1})$.

$$\mathcal{H}(z) = \frac{c}{a\left[\frac{2}{T}\frac{1-z^{-1}}{1+z^{-1}}\right] + b} \tag{6.96}$$

This expression is the analog filter's transfer function with $s$ replaced by the bracketed function of $z$.

$$\mathcal{H}(z) = \mathcal{H}_a(s)\Big|_{s=\frac{2}{T}\frac{1-z^{-1}}{1+z^{-1}}} \tag{6.97}$$

Equation (6.97) shows that the single-pole analog filter can be approximated with a digital filter by simply replacing $s$ with the function of $z$. This relationship between $s$ and $z$ is the bilinear transformation — hence the name of this design technique.

The bilinear transformation technique is extended to higher-order analog filters by expressing the analog filter in its parallel form (partial-fraction expansion again).

$$\mathcal{H}_a(s) = \frac{A_1}{s - p_1} + \frac{A_2}{s - p_2} + \ldots + \frac{A_M}{s - p_M} \tag{6.98}$$

Each of these single-pole filters can be approximated with the bilinear transformation.

$$\mathcal{H}(z) = \frac{A_1}{\{\ \} - p_1} + \frac{A_2}{\{\ \} - p_2} + \ldots + \frac{A_M}{\{\ \} - p_M} \tag{6.99}$$

where

$$\{\ \} = \frac{2}{T}\frac{1 - z^{-1}}{1 + z^{-1}} \tag{6.100}$$

However, if we put this $z$-transform over a common denominator, we would have $\mathcal{H}_a(s)$ with all $s$'s replaced with the bilinear function of $z$. Therefore, there is no need to express the transfer function in its parallel form before performing the bilinear transform. Simply perform the substitution.

$$s = \frac{2}{T}\frac{1 - z^{-1}}{1 + z^{-1}} \tag{6.101}$$

Designs with the bilinear transform are generally much easier to make than are those with the impulse invariant, and as we will see later the bilinear transform does not have the aliasing problem.

Before we go to some examples, let's formalize the bilinear transform design method.

### Bilinear Transform Design Technique

Step 1: Find the transfer function of an analog filter that has the desired characteristics.

Step 2: Select the sampling rate of the digital filter. Call it $T$ seconds per sample.

Step 3: Substitute

$$s = \frac{2}{T} \frac{1 - z^{-1}}{1 + z^{-1}} \tag{6.102}$$

into the transfer function found in step 1.

Step 4: Compute the $z$-transform by multiplying the denominator and numerator by the highest power of $1 + z^{-1}$ and collecting terms.

Step 5: Realize the digital filter from its $z$-transform. Because the bilinear transformation generates an $\mathcal{H}(z)$ which is nonfactored, it is generally easier to implement the approximation as one filter rather than parallel combinations.

**Example:**  Approximate an analog integrator using the bilinear transformation. Assume a sampling rate of 1000 samples/sec.

The analog filter has a single pole at $s = 0$.

$$\mathcal{H}_a(s) = \frac{1}{s} \tag{6.103}$$

We approximate this filter by performing the substitution of step 3.

$$\mathcal{H}(z) = \frac{1}{\frac{2}{0.001} \frac{1 - z^{-1}}{1 + z^{-1}}} \tag{6.104}$$

$$= 0.0005 \frac{1 + z^{-1}}{1 - z^{-1}}$$

This filter has a pole at $z = 1$, a zero at $z = -1$, and a gain of 0.0005.

Compare the results of example with the filter from the impulse invariant method and note that they produce different integrators. They have different gains (no big deal), but the bilinear transformation developed a zero that the impulse invariant did not have. The frequency response of the integrator obtained through the bilinear transformation is shown in Figure 6.18.

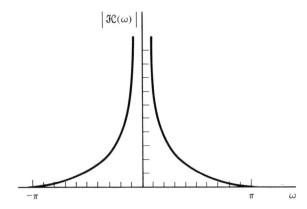

**Figure 6.18** The frequency response of a bilinear integrator.

**Example:** Approximate a three-pole low-pass Butterworth filter with the bilinear transformation. Assume a sampling rate of 100 samples/sec.

This is the filter we used in the earlier examples. It has three poles.

$$
\begin{array}{ll}
p_1: & 10\angle 120^o \\
p_2: & 10\angle 180^o \\
p_3: & 10\angle 240^o
\end{array}
\tag{6.105}
$$

However, our rendition of the bilinear transform technique requires the transfer function. So after a good deal of algebra, we can come up with the Butterworth filter's transfer function.

$$
\mathcal{H}_a(s) = \frac{1}{s^3 + 20s^2 + 200s + 1000}
\tag{6.106}
$$

Now we go directly to step 2 — perform the $s$-to-$z$ substitution.

$$
\mathcal{H}(z) = \frac{1}{\left(\frac{2}{T}\frac{1-z^{-1}}{1+z^{-1}}\right)^3 + 20\left(\frac{2}{T}\frac{1-z^{-1}}{1+z^{-1}}\right)^2 + 200\left(\frac{2}{T}\frac{1-z^{-1}}{1+z^{-1}}\right) + 1000}
\tag{6.107}
$$

Here comes the fun part — we multiply top and bottom by $T^3(1+z^{-1})^3$ and start collecting terms.

$$
\begin{aligned}
\mathcal{H}(z) &= \frac{10^{-6}\left(1 + 3z^{-1} + 3z^{-2} + z^{-3}\right)}{2.221 - 6.177z^{-1} + 5.783z^{-2} - 1.819z^{-3}} \\
&= 10^{-6}\frac{0.4502 + 1.350z^{-1} + 1.350z^{-2} + 0.4502z^{-3}}{1 - 2.781z^{-1} + 2.603z^{-2} - 0.819z^{-3}}
\end{aligned}
\tag{6.108}
$$

The frequency response of this filter is shown in Figure 6.19.

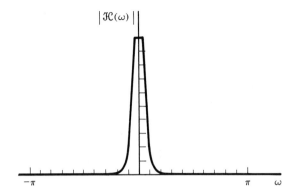

**Figure 6.19** Frequency response of a bilinear Butterworth filter.

The preceding example showed that the bilinear method can become quite involved when the analog filter is given in terms of its poles. We had to first come up with the analog filter's transfer function. There is an alternatve method of performing the bilinear transform, which is especially useful when you are given poles and zeros. Rather than transforming the variable $s$ in the transfer function, this method maps the poles and zeros. Mapping the poles and zeros with the bilinear transformation is equivalent to mapping the variable and generates identical filters.

Consider an analog filter with poles $p_i$ and zeros $\varsigma_i$.

$$\mathcal{H}_a(s) = \frac{(s - \varsigma_1)(s - \varsigma_2)\dots}{(s - p_1)(s - p_2)\dots} \tag{6.109}$$

This filter is approximated by a digital filter.

$$\mathcal{H}(z) = \frac{(\frac{2}{T}\frac{1-z^{-1}}{1+z^{-1}} - \varsigma_1)(\frac{2}{T}\frac{1-z^{-1}}{1+z^{-1}} - \varsigma_2)\dots}{(\frac{2}{T}\frac{1-z^{-1}}{1+z^{-1}} - p_1)(\frac{2}{T}\frac{1-z^{-1}}{1+z^{-1}} - p_2)\dots} \tag{6.110}$$

Solve for the poles of this digital filter by finding the values of $z$ where the denominator goes to 0. In other words, we are looking for the solutions to the following equation.

$$\frac{2}{T}\frac{1 - z^{-1}}{1 + z^{-1}} - p_i = 0 \tag{6.111}$$

Fortunately, the bilinear transformation can be inverted, so the digital filter has poles at

$$z = \frac{2 + p_i T}{2 - p_i T} \tag{6.112}$$

A similar argument holds for the zeros, so the digital filter has zeros at

$$z = \frac{2 + \varsigma_i T}{2 - \varsigma_i T} \tag{6.113}$$

Therefore, steps 3 and 4 of our bilinear design procedure can be replaced by the pole and zero mappings of equations (6.112) and (6.113).

**Example:** Approximate a three-pole Butterworth filter with a cutoff frequency of 10 rad/sec. Use a digital filter running at 100 samples/sec.

This time we will use the pole and zero mapping interpretation of the bilinear transformation. We first map the three poles.

$$p_1 = 10\angle 120^o = -5 + j8.66$$
$$p_2 = 10\angle 180^o = -10 \tag{6.114}$$
$$p_3 = 10\angle 240^o = -5 - j8.66$$

These map to the following $z$-plane poles.

$$p_{z1} = \frac{2 + (-5 + j8.66)T}{2 - (-5 + j8.66)T} = 0.9521\angle 4.95^o$$
$$p_{z2} = \frac{2 + (-10)T}{2 - (-10)T} = 0.9047 \tag{6.115}$$
$$p_{z3} = \frac{2 + (-5 - j8.66)T}{2 - (-5 - j8.66)T} = 0.9521\angle -4.95^o$$

You might be tempted to say that you are done because there are no zeros to map. That's not true. This filter has no finite zeros, but it has three zeros at infinity. These infinite zeros must be mapped as well if we are using the pole and zero mapping interpretation of the bilinear transform. All three zeros map to $z = -1$:

$$\varsigma_{z1} = \varsigma_{z2} = \varsigma_{z3} = \frac{2 + \infty T}{2 - \infty T} \tag{6.116}$$
$$= -1$$

Therefore, the digital approximation to this filter is

$$\mathcal{H}_z(z) = \frac{(z+1)^3}{(z - 0.9521\angle 4.95^o)(z - 0.9047)(z - 0.9521\angle 4.95^o)} \tag{6.117}$$

It is straightforward, but tedious, to compute the filter coefficients from these pole and zero locations.

Many designers feel that the bilinear mapping is far easier to use than the impulse invariant. Not only is it easier to use, but it also prevents the designer's nemesis — aliasing. We will see how in the next section.

## 6.5  BILINEAR TRANSFORMATION POLE MAPPING

We have shown that an analog filter can be approximated with a digital filter by simply mapping the analog poles and zeros to the $z$-plane. This section explores the nature of the mapping and looks at mapping's impact on the frequency response.

Consider an analog pole at $s = \sigma_a + j\omega_a$ (we could just as easily do this derivation with zeros). This pole is mapped to the $z$-plane pole, $p_z$, through the bilinear transform

$$
\begin{aligned}
p_z &= \frac{2 + (\sigma_a + j\omega_a)T}{2 - (\sigma_a + j\omega_a)T} \\
&= \frac{2 + \sigma_a T + j\omega_a T}{2 - \sigma_a T - j\omega_a T}
\end{aligned}
\tag{6.118}
$$

We'll gain more insight into the mapping by expressing the $z$-plane pole location in magnitude and angle.

$$
p_z = \sqrt{\frac{(2 + \sigma_a T)^2 + (\omega_a T)^2}{(2 - \sigma_a T)^2 + (\omega_a T)^2}} \angle \left( \tan^{-1} \frac{\omega_a T}{2 + \sigma_a T} - \tan^{-1} \frac{-\omega_a T}{2 - \sigma_a T} \right)
\tag{6.119}
$$

We will first look at the magnitude of the pole. If $\sigma_a < 0$, it will make the magnitude of the numerator smaller than the denominator; the magnitude of the pole is less than 1. If $\sigma_a = 0$ (the pole is on the $s$-plane $j\omega$ axis), the $z$-plane pole has a magnitude of 1 — it lies on the unit circle. Finally, if the $s$-plane pole lies in the right-hand plane ($\sigma_a > 0$), it is mapped to a $z$-plane pole outside the unit circle (magnitude greater than 1). In other words, stable $s$-plane poles are mapped to stable $z$-plane poles, poles on the $j\omega$ axis are mapped to the unit circle, and unstable analog poles are mapped to unstable digital poles. Therefore, the bilinear transform technique maps stable analog filters to stable digital filters, a necessary property.

The expression for the angle of the $z$-plane pole is too complicated to allow us much insight. But the special case of $\sigma_a = 0$ reduces the angle to a much simpler form.

$$
\angle p_z |_{\sigma_a = 0} = \tan^{-1} \frac{\omega_a T}{2} - \tan^{-1} \frac{-\omega_a T}{2}
\tag{6.120}
$$

But the inverse tangent is an odd function.

$$
\angle p_z \Big|_{\sigma_a = 0} = 2 \tan^{-1} \frac{\omega_a T}{2}
\tag{6.121}
$$

Therefore, an analog pole on the $j\omega$ axis with an imaginary part of $j\omega_a$ maps to a digital pole on the unit circle with an angle of equation (6.121). There is a nonlinear (tangent) relationship between the imaginary component of the $s$-plane and the angle in the $z$-plane, and its effect is illustrated in Figure 6.20. This is the primary difference between the impulse invariant and bilinear transform methods. This phenonenon is called *frequency warping* and will be developed in the next section.

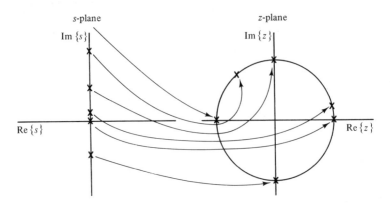

**Figure 6.20** Mapping $j\omega$ poles to the unit circle.

### Frequency Warping

Let's begin with an analog filter with a transfer function of $H_a(s)$ and a frequency response of $H_a(j\omega)$. This filter is approximated by a digital filter with a $z$-transform of $H_z(z)$.

$$H_z(z) = H_a\left(\frac{2}{T} \; \frac{1 - z^{-1}}{1 + z^{-1}}\right) \tag{6.122}$$

The digital filter has a frequency response of $H(\omega)$, which is its $z$-transform with $z$ replaced by $e^{j\omega}$.

$$H(\omega) = H_z(z)|_{z=e^{j\omega}} = H_a\left(\frac{2}{T} \; \frac{1 - e^{-j\omega}}{1 + e^{j\omega}}\right) \tag{6.123}$$

The ratio of the exponentials in Equation (6.123) is just another way of expressing the tangent of $\omega/2$. So the digital and analog frequency responses are related through the equation

$$H(\omega) = H_a\left(j\frac{2}{T} \; \tan\frac{\omega}{2}\right) \tag{6.124}$$

The analog and digital filters have the same frequency response, except that there is a nonlinear relationship between the frequencies. Equation (6.122) tells us that the digital filter's frequency response at $\omega$ is the analog filter's response at $j\frac{2}{T} \tan(\omega/2)$. So the analog and digital frequencies, $\omega_a$ and $\omega_d$, are related through the following:

$$\omega_a = \frac{2}{T} \; \tan\frac{\omega_d}{2} \tag{6.125}$$

and

$$\omega_d = 2 \; \tan^{-1}\frac{\omega_a T}{2} \tag{6.126}$$

   This frequency warping is illustrated in Figure 6.21.  The top part shows the analog frequency as a function of digital frequency [equation (6.123)] and the bottom plot shows the digital as a function of the analog.  Note that the complete range of analog frequencies ($-\infty$ to $\infty$) is mapped to the $-\pi$ to $\pi$ range of digital frequencies.  Therefore, there is no aliasing — a major benefit of the bilinear design method.

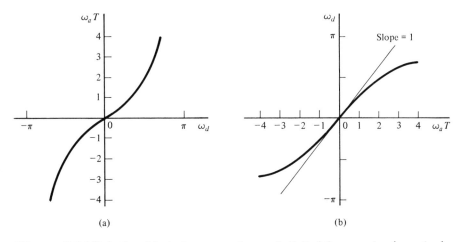

**Figure 6.21** Relationship between analog and digital frequencies (warping).

   However, the frequency warping causes a noticeable distortion of the higher analog frequencies as they are mapped to the digital frequency response.  At low analog frequencies (near the origin of Figure 6.21b), the digital frequency is almost a linear function of the analog; the curve has a slope of $T$.  But as the analog frequency becomes larger, the slope becomes increasingly smaller, so the analog frequency response is increasingly compressed into the digital response.  This high-frequency warping can cause problems, as illustrated in the following example.

**Example:**  Consider a contrived analog filter with a frequency response as shown in Figure 6.22.  Find the frequency response of its bilinear approximation.  Assume a sampling rate of 1 sample/sec.

   This hypothetical analog filter has a constant gain from 0 to $0.3\pi$ rad/sec and a linearly decreasing gain from $0.3\pi$ to $\pi$.  This filter was chosen to vividly show the warping.

   The relationship between the analog and digital frequencies for $T = 1$ is shown in Table 6.1.  Note that there is less than 10% error for analog frequencies under $0.4\pi$, and the error grows rapidly with increasing analog frequency.

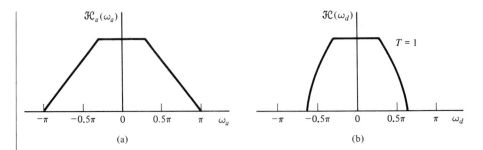

**Figure 6.22** Bilinear frequency warping: (a) Analog frequency warping; (b) Frequency response of bilinear approximation.

**Table 6.1** Digital frequencies for various analog frequencies $(T = 1)$.

| Analog Frequency | | Digital Frequency |
|---|---|---|
| 0 | $\Longrightarrow$ | 0 |
| $0.1\pi$ | $\Longrightarrow$ | $0.0992\pi$ |
| $0.2\pi$ | $\Longrightarrow$ | $0.1938\pi$ |
| $0.3\pi$ | $\Longrightarrow$ | $0.2804\pi$ |
| $0.4\pi$ | $\Longrightarrow$ | $0.3571\pi$ |
| $0.5\pi$ | $\Longrightarrow$ | $0.4238\pi$ |
| $0.6\pi$ | $\Longrightarrow$ | $0.4812\pi$ |
| $0.7\pi$ | $\Longrightarrow$ | $0.5302\pi$ |
| $0.8\pi$ | $\Longrightarrow$ | $0.5702\pi$ |
| $0.9\pi$ | $\Longrightarrow$ | $0.6081\pi$ |
| $\pi$ | $\Longrightarrow$ | $0.6391\pi$ |

The frequency response of the bilinear approximating filter is shown in Figure 6.22b. Notice the differences between the analog filter and its approximation. The breakpoint of the analog filter, $0.3\pi$, is mapped to a digital frequency of $0.2803\pi$. The linearly decreasing portion of the frequency response is distorted into a curve, and the $\pi$ breakpoint is mapped to $0.6391\pi$. The bilinear mapping has moved the breakpoints of the filter and has distorted the higher-frequency slopes.

This nonlinear relationship between the analog and digital frequencies will distort the frequency response. This distortion is especially noticeable at higher frequencies. There is nothing that we can do to prevent the distortion, but we can anticipate it by designing "prewarped" analog filters. These filters are designed with the bilinear distortion in mind, so when they are passed through the distortion, the digital filter still meets its specifications.

Suppose that you wish to design a digital filter with a frequency response of $\mathcal{D}(\omega)$. If you start with a analog filter with a frequency response of $\mathcal{D}(\omega)$, the bilinear transform will distort it, so your digital filter will be incorrect. But suppose that you design an analog filter with a predistorted frequency response.

$$\mathcal{H}_a\left(j\frac{2}{T}\ \tan\frac{\omega}{2}\right) = \mathcal{D}(\omega) \tag{6.127}$$

This is equivalent to distorting the frequency response of the desired filter.

$$\mathcal{H}_a(j\omega) = \mathcal{D}\left(2\ \tan^{-1}\frac{\omega}{2}\right) \tag{6.128}$$

When this prewarped analog filter is applied to the bilinear transform, the prewarping pays off.

$$\mathcal{H}(\omega_d) = \mathcal{H}_a\left(j\frac{2}{T}\ \tan\frac{\omega}{2}\right) = \mathcal{D}(\omega) \tag{6.129}$$

Seldom is a complete analog filter prewarped — that is simply too difficult. Rather, the designer leaves the shape of the analog filter unaltered and merely concentrates on the filter's breakpoints. With this strategy, the slopes of the analog filter are distorted by the bilinear transformation but breakpoints come out correctly. This form of prewarping is achieved by altering all of the desired breakpoints through the tangent to generate the breakpoints for the analog filter,

$$\omega_a = \frac{2}{T}\ \tan\frac{\omega_d}{2} \tag{6.130}$$

then designing the analog filter with those breakpoints. This process essentially stretches the analog filter in frequency, so that when it is compressed by the bilinear transformation, the breakpoints are preserved. This scheme is illustrated in the example.

**Example:**  Design a digital filter with a bandpass from $0.2\pi$ to $0.5\pi$, and a sampling rate of 1 sample every 10 sec ($T = 10$). Use the bilinear transformation with prewarping.

If we do not prewarp the design, the bandpass will lie from $0.1938\pi$ to $0.4238\pi$ (Table 6.1). We prewarp the breakpoints by applying them to equation (6.128).

$$\omega_{a1} = \frac{2}{10}\ \tan\frac{0.2\pi}{2} = 0.0207\pi \tag{6.131}$$

$$\omega_{a2} = \frac{2}{10}\ \tan\frac{0.5\pi}{2} = 0.0637\pi \tag{6.132}$$

Therefore, we will have someone design a filter with a passband from $0.0207\pi$ to $0.0637\pi$ and apply that filter to the bilinear transform with $T = 10$:

$$z = \frac{2 + s10}{2 - s10} \tag{6.133}$$

But there is an easier way of mapping this filter. Again, notice that the scaling of the analog frequency by $1/T$ is counteracted by the $T$ in the bilinear transform. Why not ignore the sampling period by assuming a $T = 1$? In this case we specify an analog filter with breakpoints at

$$\omega_{a1} = 2\tan\frac{0.2\pi}{2} = 0.207\pi \tag{6.134}$$

$$\omega_{a2} = 2\tan\frac{0.5\pi}{2} = 0.637\pi \tag{6.135}$$

and use a bilinear transformation of

$$z = \frac{2 + s}{2 - s} \tag{6.136}$$

As with the case of the impulse invariant mapping, it is easier and much less confusing to artificially use a $T = 1$ for the specification of the analog filter and the transformation.

Most digital approximations are performed through the bilinear transform. It is computationally easier and will not cause aliasing. Prewarping of critical frequency points will mitigate many of the detrimental effects of the frequency warping. Because of the frequency warping, the bilinear transformation should not be used in applications when the high-frequency slopes of the analog filter must be preserved.

## 6.6 SUMMARY

The fact that a recursive filter's frequency response has a denominator frustrates the development of a direct design method. Therefore, we have developed two ways of designing recursive digital filters based on approximations of analog filters. The impulse invariant scheme approximates the impulse response of the analog filter, thereby approximating the frequency response. Designers must be careful when using this technique because it can cause aliasing of the analog response. The bilinear transform method also approximates analog filters with digital, but it is based on the solution of integral equations. The bilinear transform causes a nonlinear frequency warping, which becomes more severe for higher frequencies, but does not alias the response.

Therefore, a digital filter designer has two alternatives when designing recursive filters. The specifics of the situation dictate which one is used, but most designers rely solely on the bilinear transform. In either case, the design begins with the selection of the features of the desired digital filter. The next step is to find an analog filter whose digital approximation will satisfy the design requirements, and the final step is to apply the bilinear or impulse invariant technique.

## EXERCISES

6-1. Show that $e^{st}$ is an eigenfunction for an analog integrator,

$$y(t) = \int_{-\infty}^{t} x(\tau) \, d\tau$$

Find the eigenvalue.

6-2. Compute the $z$-transform of the digital filters that approximate a single-pole analog filter,

$$h_a(t) = Ae^{at}$$

when

(a) The digital filter's impulse response is the analog filter's impulse response delayed and sampled.

$$h_k = h_a(kT - T)$$

(b) The digital filter approximates only the first six terms of the analog filter's impulse response.

$$h_k = \begin{cases} h_a(kT) & 0 \le k \le 5 \\ 0 & \text{otherwise} \end{cases}$$

6-3. Approximate an analog differentiator,

$$y(t) = \frac{d}{dt} x(t)$$

with a digital filter. Mimic the development of the impulse invariant technique and assume that the impulse response of a analog differentiator is a positive impulse followed by a negative impulse. Assume that $T = 1$. Plot the frequency response of your digital differentiator and compare it to the frequency response of the analog differentiator.

6-4. Map the following analog poles to the $z$-plane with the impulse invariant transformation. Assume a sampling rate of 1000 samples/sec. Denote any aliased poles.

(a) Pole at $s = \frac{1}{2}j$

(b) Pole at $s = -100$

(c) Pole at $s = -1 + j100$

(d) Pole at $s = 2000 \angle 100°$

(e) Pole at $s = 3000 + j4000$

6-5. Plot the pole locations in the $z$-plane that result from mapping the following analog poles with impulse invariant transformation. Assume that $T = 1$.

(a) Poles at $s = 0 + j\omega$; $-\pi/2 < \omega < \pi$

(b) Poles at $-1 + j\omega$; $-\pi/2 < \omega < \pi$

(c) Poles at $\sigma + j\pi/4$; $-1 < \sigma < 1$

(d) Poles at $\sigma + j9\pi/4$; $-1 < \sigma < 1$

6-6. Realize the three-pole Butterworth filter [equation (6.57)] as the parallel combination of a first- and a second-order filter.

(a) Compute the coefficients of the first-order filter.

(b) Compute the coefficients of the second-order filter.

6-7. Use the impulse invariant technique to approximate the following analog filter with a digital filter. Assume a sampling rate of 1 sample/sec.

$$\frac{1}{\left(s - \frac{1}{2}\angle 45°\right)\left(s - \frac{1}{2}\angle - 45°\right)}$$

(a) Compute the coefficients of the digital filter.

(b) Plot the digital filter's frequency response and compare it to the analog filter's frequency response.

(c) Are the poles aliased by this sampling frequency?

(d) Are the digital poles stable? If not, why not?

6-8. Consider an analog filter with the following transfer function.

$$\mathcal{H}_a(s) = \frac{1}{(s+1)(s^2 + s + 1)}$$

(a) Use the impulse invariant technique to approximate this filter with first- and second-order digital filters in parallel. Assume a sampling rate of 1 sample/sec. Compute the coefficients.

(b) Approximate the analog filter with a third-order digital filter. Use the impulse invariant technique and a sampling rate of 1.

6-9. Use the impulse invariant technique to design a digital approximation to a five-pole Butterworth low-pass filter (see Appendix C). The digital filter should have a cutoff frequency of $0.3\pi$ rad/sample. Assume a sampling period of 1 sample/sec. Plot the pole-zero diagram and the frequency response.

6-10. Use the impulse invariant technique to approximate the following analog filters with digital filters. Be careful, there are second-order poles lurking. Assume that $T = 1$.

(a) $\mathcal{H}_a(s) = \frac{2}{(s+\frac{1}{2})^2}$

(b) $\mathcal{H}_a(s) = \frac{s-1}{s(s+1)^2}$

6-11. You are asked to design a low-pass digital filter with a cutoff frequency of $0.4\pi$ rad/sample. This filter is running at a rate of 1,000,000 samples/sec. What is the cutoff frequency of the analog prototype for this filter?

6-12. Consider the analog filters with the following pole locations. Find the maximum sampling period, $T_{max}$, so that none of the poles are aliased by the impulse invariant transformation.

(a) Poles at $-1000$, $50\angle 150^o$, and $50\angle -150^o$

(b) Poles at $-125j$ and $125j$

(c) Poles at $0$, $10\angle 135^o$, and $10\angle -135^o$

6-13. An $N$-pole Butterworth filter has a frequency response of

$$|\mathcal{H}_a(\omega)|^2 = \frac{1}{1 + \left|\frac{\omega}{\omega_c}\right|^{2N}}$$

where $\omega_c$ is the filter's cutoff frequency. Suppose that you approximate a three-pole Butterworth filter with a cutoff frequency of 1000 Hz. Find the maximum sampling period, $T_{\max}$, such that the aliasing caused by the impulse invariant technique results in less than a 1% difference between the magnitudes squared of the frequency responses.

6-14. Repeat the derivation of the bilinear transformation but use the following digital approximation to the integral.

$$\int_{kT-T}^{kT} y'(\tau)d\tau \approx Ty'(kT) \qquad \text{[replaces equation (6.88)]}$$

How are the analog poles mapped by this transformation? Where are the stable analog poles mapped in the $z$-plane?

6-15. Approximate an analog differentiator,

$$y(t) = \frac{d}{dt}x(t)$$

with a digital filter. Do this by following the development of the bilinear transformation by approximating

$$\int y(\tau)\,d\tau = x(t)$$

with a digital filter. Compute the coefficients and plot the frequency response of the digital differentiator. Compare the frequency response to the analog differentiator.

6-16. Map the following analog poles to the $z$-plane with the bilinear transform. Assume a sampling rate of 1000 samples/sec.

   (a) Pole at $s = \frac{1}{2}j$

   (b) Pole at $s = -100$

   (c) Pole at $s = -1 + j100$

   (d) Pole at $s = 2000 \angle 100^o$

   (e) Pole at $s = 3000 + j4000$


6-17. Sketch the pole locations in the $z$-plane that result from mapping the
following analog poles with the bilinear transform.

   (a) Poles at $s = 0 + j\omega;\ -\pi/2 < \omega < \pi$

   (b) Poles at $s = -1 + j\omega;\ -\pi/2 < \omega\pi$

   (c) Poles at $s = \sigma + j\pi/4;\ -1 < \sigma < 1$

   (d) Poles at $s = \sigma + j9\pi/4;\ -1 < \sigma < 1$


6-18. Consider an analog filter with the following transfer function.

$$\mathcal{H}_a(s) = \frac{1}{(s+1)(s^2 + s + 1)}$$

Use the bilinear transformation to approximate this filter with a third-
order digital filter. Assume a sampling period of 1 sec/sample.


6-19. Compute the stopband of an analog filter so that when it is approximated
by a digital filter through the bilinear transformation, the digital filter
will have a stopband from $0.1\pi$ to $0.7\pi$. Assume a sampling period of 1
sec/sample.

6-20. Design a digital low-pass filter by approximating a five-pole Butterworth filter (see Appendix C) with the bilinear transformation. The digital filter should have a cutoff frequency of $0.3\pi$ rad/sample (requires some prewarping). Assume a sampling period of $T = 1$.

(a) Compute the coefficients of the fifth-order digital filter.

(b) Plot its pole-zero diagram and its frequency response.

# 7

# Polynomial Modeling of Digital Signals

Up until now we have processed digital signals exclusively with digital filters. But digital filters represent only a small portion of all possible digital signal processing algorithms. Once you get a signal into a computer, the processing algorithms are limited only by your imagination. In this chapter we consider digital signal processing algorithms that are derived by modeling a digital signal with a polynomial.

Before proceeding with the details of the chapter, let us consider the modeling process in general. There are two appropriate definitions of modeling (my dictionary has 11 in all). The first is a model in the sense of a miniature replication: for example, a model of a house, car or, airplane. The real house, car, or airplane is represented by a likeness, or model, that has many features of the real thing but is not an exact replica. We model the real thing because the model is more convenient or useful. For example, what child would want a real airplane hanging from the bedroom ceiling? (Actually, most children would love it.)

The second definition calls modeling a mathematical description of an entity or state of affairs. In this case, the model is not physical but is a mathematical approximation of a situation, which is generally very complicated. For example, the transfer of heat from a warm body (e.g., an oven) to a cold body (the kitchen) is a complicated process. Molecular mechanics, chemistry, and even quantum mechanics are required to describe the heat transfer process accurately. But heat transfer can be accurately described with a simple, one-line equation. This mathematical model of heat transfer — the second law of thermodynamics – was derived long before the actual mechanisms were understood. It has little to do with the actual physics of the situation. Rather, it replaces the oven, kitchen, and molecules with simple mathematical operators. In this case, a very complicated state of affairs has been described by a simple mathematical model.

We are going to do a similar thing with digital signals. We will model them with polynomials, which are far easier to understand and manipulate than digital signals. After computing the polynomial models, we will use the polynomial rather than the digital signal.

The polynomial is the simplest form of digital signal modeling but not the only form. For example, speech signals are routinely replaced by models of the vocal track that produced the speech. The model is used instead of the speech waveform in systems that recognize speech or in those that synthesize speech. These models are also used in efficient speech transmission systems, because the model can be transmitted more conveniently than the speech itself.

This chapter is organized around the various applications of polynomial modeling. We will first look at the polynomial and learn to fit polynomials exactly to digital data points. Once fitted, a polynomial can be used to estimate missing data points, interpolate data, or extrapolate data. The polynomial models are also quite useful for estimating the integral and derivatives of digital signals, which is the next application we will discuss. Finally, we will look at polynomial modeling as a way of smoothing digital data. But before we can get to the uses of polynomial modeling, we must understand the polynomial itself.

## 7.1 POLYNOMIALS

The polynomial is really the simplest class of mathematical functions. The polynomial has an independent variable, call it $t$, and produces a value by forming a weighted sum of the positive powers of $t$. We'll call the value of the polynomial $p(t)$ and the weighting coefficients $p_i$.

$$p(t) = p_0 + p_1 t + p_2 t^2 + \ldots + p_M t^M \tag{7.1}$$

The highest power of $t$ determines the "order" of the polynomial. Equation (7.1) shows an $M$-order polynomial.

Most of us are quite familiar with the graphs of polynomials. Figure 7.1 shows plots of zero-, first-, second-, and third-order polynomials. The zero- and first-order curves are straight lines. The second-order, better known as a quadratic, has some curvature. The third-order, known as a cubic, has even more curve. In general, the higher-order polynomials have more curvature, because they have more degrees of freedom (more coefficients).

Polynomials are especially convenient functions because they are so well behaved under differentiation and integration. The derivative or integral of a polynomial is itself a polynomial. Furthermore, the coefficients of a polynomial and those

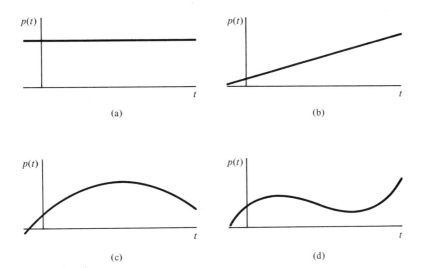

**Figure 7.1** Polynomials: (a) zero order; (b) first order;
(c) second order; (d) third order.

of its derivative or integral are related through simple scaling. For example, the
first derivative of a polynomial with respect to $t$ is a polynomial of one less order.

$$\frac{d}{dt}p(t) = p_1 + 2p_2t + 3p_3t^2 + \ldots + Mp_Mt^{M-1} \qquad (7.2)$$

Notice that $p_0$ disappeared and was replaced with $p_1$. The coefficient for $t$ is now
$2p_2$, which is twice $t^2$'s coefficient for the original polynomial.

Because the derivative of a polynomial is also a polynomial, the second derivative is also easy to compute. Simply apply the derivative to equation (7.2).

$$\frac{d^2}{dt^2}p(t) = 2p_2 + 6p_3t + 12p_4t^2 + \ldots + M(M-1)p_Mt^{M-2} \qquad (7.3)$$

The second derivative is an $(M-2)$-order polynomial and does not involve $p_0$ or
$p_1$.

In summary, polynomials are natural functions for differentiation. So if we are
faced with an application that called for the differentiation of digital data, it might
seem reasonable to model the data with a polynomial and perform the differentiation
on the polynomial rather than the data. More on this later.

Polynomials are also naturals with integration. The integral of an $M$-order
polynomial is as follows:

$$\int p(t)\, dt = p_{-1} + p_0t + \frac{1}{2}p_1t^2 + \frac{1}{3}p_2t^3 + \ldots + \frac{1}{M+1}p_Mt^{M+1} \qquad (7.4)$$

The integral is a polynomial and is one order greater than the original. Notice that the coefficient $p_{-1}$ was included to account for the constant of integration. Since the integral of $p(t)$ is a polynomial, the double integral is also a polynomial of order $M + 2$. Multiple integrals are obtained by repeating the operations used to get equation (7.4). Because polynomials are so easy to integrate, it is reasonable to suspect that they are good models in situations requiring integration of digital signals. Such is the case.

One last nice feature of polynomials is that they are easy to shift. The polynomial of equation (7.1) has its "origin" at $t = 0$. It is possible to move the origin to any particular value of $t$, say $t_0$, by subtracting $t_0$ from each occurrence of $t$. A polynomial with its origin at $t_0$ is

$$p(t) = p_0 + p_1(t - t_0) + p_2(t - t_0)^2 + \ldots + p_M(t - t_0)^M \qquad (7.5)$$

Note that when $t_0$ is positive, the polynomial is shifted to the right. It is shifted to the left when $t_0$ is negative. Also note that the zero coefficient is the value of the polynomial at its origin, $p_0$.

$$p(t_0) = p_0 \qquad (7.6)$$

In later work, we will find it useful to pick certain origins for the polynomials. This will greatly reduce the amount of computation necessary to compute the model.

## 7.2 FITTING POLYNOMIALS TO DIGITAL SIGNALS

Our goal is to model a digital signal, or a portion of a signal, with a polynomial. That is, we wish to find a polynomial that will replace the digital signal while preserving many of the signal's features. Once such a polynomial is found, we will use the polynomial (the model) instead of the digital signal. This section shows how to go about fitting a polynomial to digital data.

Figure 7.2 shows three examples of polynomial approximations of a short digital sequence. The first approximation is clearly unacceptable because the polynomial (shown as the solid line) comes nowhere near the digital signal (the dots). Figure 7.2b shows a "well-fitted" polynomial. This curve goes through each of the digital signal points and behaves smoothly between the points. Therefore, we can actually replace the data, $x_0, x_1, x_2, x_3$ with the polynomial evaluated at $t = 0, 1, 2, 3$, $p(0), p(1), p(2), p(3)$. So, this polynomial is a faithful model of the digital signal. The last figure shows a polynomial that goes through each digital signal point, but behaves peculiarly between the points. This polynomial is an exact model of the digital signal because $p(0) = x_0$, $p(1) = x_1$, $p(2) = x_2$, and $p(3) = x_3$, but its behavior between the points makes it a poor second to the polynomial of Figure 7.2b.

How do we go about finding polynomials that will exactly match a particular digital signal? We demand that the polynomial goes through the data points. This means that the polynomial evaluated at $t = k$ equals $x_k$.

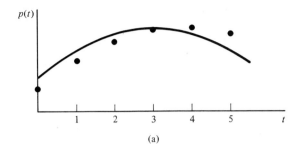

(a)

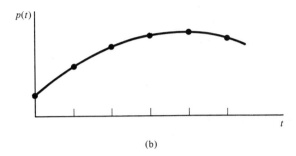

(b)

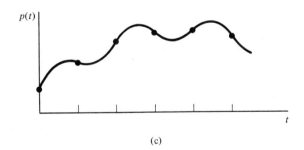

(c)

**Figure 7.2** Polynomial curve fits: (a) too few degrees of
freedom; (b) a good fit; (c) too many degrees
of freedom.

$$p(0) = x_0$$
$$p(1) = x_1$$
$$\vdots$$
$$p(N-1) = x_{N-1}$$

(7.7)

The polynomial is in the form of equation (7.1). So this leads to the following set of simultaneous equations.

$$
\begin{aligned}
p_0 + p_1 0 + p_2 0^2 + \ldots + p_M 0^M &= x_0 \\
p_0 + p_1 1 + p_2 1^2 + \ldots + p_M 1^M &= x_1 \\
p_0 + p_1 2 + p_2 2^2 + \ldots + p_M 2^M &= x_2 \\
&\vdots \\
p_0 + p_1(N-1) + p_2(N-1)^2 + \ldots + p_M(N-1)^M &= x_{N-1}
\end{aligned}
\tag{7.8}
$$

Therefore, the polynomial is fitted to the $N$ data points by solving equation (7.8) for the $M+1$ polynomial coefficients. Now it is time to consider solutions to simultaneous equations.

Equations (7.8) are $N$ equations with $M+1$ unknowns. In general, a set of equations has a solution when the number of unknowns is at least equal to the number of equations, $M+1 \geq N$. The solution is unique when the number of unknowns matches the number of equations $M+1 = N$, and there may not be a solution if there are fewer unknowns than equations, $M < N$. Therefore, we are guaranteed a unique solution for the polynomial coefficients when $M+1 = N$, or when the order of the polynomial is $N-1$. For example, a cubic (order 3) will uniquely match four data points. An order 10 polynomial will match 11 data points. Notice that we must become involved with high-order polynomials when we attempt to match long runs of digital data. For that reason, we will find it useful to break the data into small chunks before modeling it with polynomials.

If the order of the polynomial is greater than the number of data points being matched, the polynomial has too many degrees of freedom and there are many solutions. Such underconstrained situations lead to polynomials that go through the data points but behave peculiarly between the points, as in Figure 7.2c. If the order of the polynomial is less than $N-1$, the system of equations might not have a solution — there is no polynomial of that order that will go through all the data points. In the last section of this chapter, we will look at techniques for fitting low order polynomials to long data sequences. Needless to say, these are not exact fits.

There is always a solution when $M = N-1$; the order of the polynomial is one less than the number of points being modeled. Therefore, the coefficients of the lowest-order polynomial that can match all $N$ data points are found by solving the following equation.

$$
\begin{aligned}
p_0 + p_1 0 + \ldots + p_{N-1} 0^{N-1} &= x_0 \\
p_0 + p_1 1 + \ldots + p_{N-1} 1^{N-1} &= x_1 \\
&\vdots \\
p_0 + p_1(N-1) + \ldots + p_{N-1}(N-1)^{N-1} &= x_{N-1}
\end{aligned}
\tag{7.9}
$$

This is a set of $N$ simultaneous equations with $N$ unknowns, $p_0, p_1, \ldots, p_{N-1}$.

**Example:** Fit a polynomial to three data points of a digital signal, $x_0, x_1, x_2$.

In this case, $N = 3$, so the order of the polynomial is one less, $M = N - 1 = 3 - 1 = 2$. We need at least a quadratic to match these three points. We must solve the following set of equations for $p_0$, $p_1$, and $p_3$.

$$p_0 + p_1 0 + p_2 0 = x_0$$
$$p_0 + p_1 1 + p_2 1^2 = x_1 \qquad (7.10)$$
$$p_0 + p_1 2 + p_2 2^2 = x_2$$

So given the values of $x_0$, $x_1$, and $x_2$, it is possible to grind through the equations and find the polynomial coefficients.

Let's consider the digital signal, $x_0 = 1$, $x_1 = 2$, and $x_2 = 3$. This is a ramp shifted by one. In this case, the equations become as follows:

$$p_0 = 1$$
$$p_0 + p_1 + p_2 = 2 \qquad (7.11)$$
$$p_0 + 2p_1 + 4p_2 = 3$$

Usually, we would have to grind through your favorite technique for solving simultaneous equations to solve for the coefficients. However, in this particular case we can save a good deal of work by realizing that a digital ramp is a first-order polynomial evaluated at $t = 0$, $t = 1$, and $t = 2$. Since it is a first-order polynomial, we know right away that $p_2 = 0$. The first equation of (7.11) demands that $p_0 = 1$, so only $p_1$ remains. We find $p_1$ by plugging $p_0 = 1$ and $p_2 = 0$ into the second equation of (7.11).

$$1 + p_1 + 0 = 2$$
$$p_1 = 1 \qquad (7.12)$$

Therefore, a first-order polynomial matches the three digital data points.

$$p(t) = 1 + t \qquad (7.13)$$

Was it necessary to have the insight that the digital ramp is a first-order polynomial? No, if you blindly solve equations (7.11) you will find the same results. But the insight can make the problem easier and can provide a deeper understanding.

As shown in the example, fitting a polynomial to digital data is little more than solving a set of simultaneous equations. Consider the following continuation of the example.

**Example:** Fit a polynomial to three other data points.

In this example, consider the digital data points, $x_0 = 1$, $x_1 = 2$, and $x_2 = 5$. This is not a digital ramp, so insight will not save us here. We are forced to solve a triplet of equations.

$$p_0 = 1$$
$$p_0 + p_1 1^1 + p_2 1^2 = 2 \qquad (7.14)$$
$$p_0 + p_1 2 + p_2 2^2 = 5$$

Solve this set of equations using Gaussian elimination. The first step reduces the problem to two equations and two unknowns by using the first equation to eliminate $p_0$ from the second and third equations. We do this by subtracting the first equation from the second and third equations of (7.14). This produces equations (7.15).

$$p_0 = 1$$
$$p_1 + p_2 = 1 \qquad (7.15)$$
$$p_1 2 + p_2 4 = 4$$

The next step in the elimination is to remove $p_1$ from the third equation of (7.15). We do this by subtracting two times the second equation from the third. This produces the following set of equations.

$$p_0 = 1$$
$$p_1 + p_2 = 1 \qquad (7.16)$$
$$p_2 2 = 2$$

We complete the solution for the coefficients by solving for the unknowns from the bottom up — this is called *back substitution*. The bottom equation of (7.16) shows that $p_2 = 1$. Applying that to the middle equation shows that $p_1 = 0$. Finally, there is no need for a back substitution for the top equation, because $p_0 = 1$.

This is a two-coefficient polynomial model of the digital signal.

$$p(t) = 1 + t^2 \qquad (7.17)$$

The three-element digital signal can be exactly replaced by the polynomial $1 + t^2$. We will find that in many applications it is more useful to deal with the polynomial model than the data itself.

Up until now we have considered polynomial modeling that starts at the origin, $x_0 \ldots x_{N-1}$. However, it is easy to extend the curve-fitting equation, equation (7.9), to an arbitrary collection of data points. Suppose that we are faced with $N$

contiguous data points beginning at $x_I$. The coefficients of the modeling polynomial are the solutions to the generalization of equation (7.9).

$$
\begin{aligned}
p_0 + \quad p_1 I \qquad\quad + \ldots + \qquad p_{N-1}I^{N-1} \qquad\quad &= \quad x_I \\
p_0 + \quad p_1(I+1) \quad + \ldots + \quad p_{N-1}(I+1)^{N-1} \quad &= \quad x_{I+1} \\
&\ \ \vdots \\
p_0 + p_1(I+N-1) + \ldots + p_{N-1}(I+N-1)^{N-1} \ &= \quad x_{I+N-1}
\end{aligned}
\tag{7.18}
$$

The first equation of equations (7.18) forces the polynomial to match the first data point, $x_I$. The second equation forces a match of the second data point, $x_{I+1}$, and so on.

We can go one step further and consider polynomial fitting to a truly arbitrary collection of data points. The concepts are no more involved than those in the previous work, but the notation becomes somewhat bizarre. Suppose that you are faced with $N$ data points, $x_{I_k}$, where $k = 0, \ldots, N-1$. These are $N$ elements of a digital signal with arbitrary indices. Our only restriction is that no two indices are the same, $I_k \neq I_i$ for $k \neq i$. This restriction prevents two different values of the data for the same index; a polynomial would not have a chance of going through both. A simple example of such a generalized collection of data is the even elements of a digital signal. In this case, $I_k = 2k$ for $k = 0, \ldots, N-1$, and we are modeling the data points, $x_0, x_2, \ldots, x_{2(N-1)}$.

The general form of the curve-fitting equation is shown below. Its solution, the $p_i$s, is a set of coefficients that matches the collection of data points, $x_{I_k}$.

$$
\begin{aligned}
p_0 + \quad p_1 I_0 \quad + \ldots + \quad p_{N-1}(I_0)^{N-1} \quad &= \quad x_{I_0} \\
p_0 + \quad p_1 I_1 \quad + \ldots + \quad p_{N-1}(I_1)^{N-1} \quad &= \quad x_{I_1} \\
&\ \ \vdots \\
p_0 + p_1 I_{N-1} + \ldots + p_{N-1}(I_{N-1})^{N-1} \ &= \quad x_{I_{N-1}}
\end{aligned}
\tag{7.19}
$$

Remember that the only restriction on the data is that no two points can share the same index.

**Example:**  Model the following data points with a polynomial.

$$
x_{-2} = 0.3 \quad x_1 = 1.5 \quad x_4 = 1.7 \quad x_2 = 1.0 \quad x_1 = 1.5
$$

There are five data elements here so we are tempted to use a fourth-order polynomial. But $x_1$ is represented twice, so there are really only four data points. Fortunately, the two occurrences of $x_1$ have the same value, so we can simply ignore the second occurrence of $x_1$. Note that if they had had different values, we would have been stuck because the data are inconsistent.

We plug these values of data into equation (7.19) to generate the following set of equations.

$$
\begin{aligned}
p_0 + p_1(-2) + p_2(-2)^2 + p_3(-2)^3 &= 0.3 \\
p_0 + p_1(1) + p_2(1)^2 + p_3(1)^3 &= 1.5 \\
p_0 + p_1(4) + p_2(4)^2 + p_3(4)^3 &= 1.7 \\
p_0 + p_1(2) + p_2(2)^2 + p_3(2)^3 &= 1
\end{aligned}
\tag{7.20}
$$

Notice that the equations are not ordered by increasing indices. The third equation forces a match on $x_4$ and the last equation matches $x_2$.

As before, we solve this set of equations with Gaussian elimination. We use the first equation to eliminate all occurrences of $p_0$ in the second, third, and fourth equations. This is done by multiplying the first equation by $-1$ and adding it to the other three. This leaves a system of three equations with three unknowns.

$$
\begin{aligned}
p_1(3) + p_2(-3) + p_3(9) &= 1.2 \\
p_1(6) + p_2(12) + p_3(72) &= 1.4 \\
p_1(4) + p_2(0) + p_3(16) &= 0.7
\end{aligned}
\tag{7.21}
$$

We continue the elimination process by multiplying the first equation of (7.21) by -2 and adding it to the second equation. This removes the $p_1$ unknown from the second equation. We then multiply the first equation of (7.21) by $-4/3$ and add it to the third. This removes $p_1$ from the third equation. Now we are left with only two equations with two unknowns.

$$
\begin{aligned}
p_2(18) + p_3(54) &= -1 \\
p_2(4) + p_3(4) &= -0.9
\end{aligned}
\tag{7.22}
$$

We complete the elimination phase of the solution by multiplying the first equation of (7.22) by $-4/18$ and adding it to the second equation.

$$
\begin{aligned}
p_3(-8) &= -0.6777 \\
p_3 &= 0.0846
\end{aligned}
\tag{7.23}
$$

The coefficient of the cubic term is 0.0847. We find the other coefficients by back substituting the results. The squared coefficient is the solution to the first equation of (7.22).

$$
\begin{aligned}
p_2(18) + 0.0847(54) &= -1 \\
p_2 &= -0.3096
\end{aligned}
\tag{7.24}
$$

The linear coefficient, $p_1$, is the solution to the first equation of (7.21).

$$
\begin{aligned}
p_1(3) + (-0.3096)(-3) + 0.0847(9) &= 1.2 \\
p_1 &= -0.1638
\end{aligned}
\tag{7.25}
$$

Finally, the zeroeth coefficient is the solution to the first equation of (7.20).

$$p_0 + (-0.1638)(-2) + (-0.3096)(-2)^2 + 0.0847(-2)^3 = .3$$
$$p_0 = 1.8889 \tag{7.26}$$

Therefore, the four data points are modeled by the following cubic polynomial.

$$p(t) = 1.8889 - 0.1638t - 0.3096t^2 + 0.0847t^3 \tag{7.27}$$

This polynomial and the four data points are shown in Figure 7.3. Notice that the polynomial goes through the data points and smoothly transits between them. Therefore, this polynomial is not only an exact model of the data at -2, 1, 4, and 2; but it also suggests something about the data we do not have: $x_{-1}$, $x_0$, $x_3$, and $x_5$.

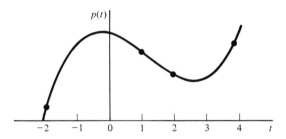

**Figure 7.3** Matching a polynomial to four data points.

There is one last generalization of polynomial modeling that must be considered before going to the applications. This involves using polynomials at arbitrary origins. Previously, we have considered only polynomials that are originated at $t = 0$.

$$p(t) = p_0 + p_1 t + \ldots + p_M t^M \tag{7.28}$$

However, a polynomial can be originated at $t = K$ by simply subtracting $K$ from all occurrences of $t$ in equation (7.28). The shifted polynomial is

$$p_K(t) = p_0 + p_1(t - K) + p_2(t - K)^2 + \ldots + p_M(t - K)^M \tag{7.29}$$

Notice that we have used the notation $p_K(t)$ to denote a polynomial with its origin at $t = K$. So when we drop the subscript and talk about $p(t)$, we are dealing with the polynomial originated at $t = 0$.

We are so interested in $p_K(t)$ because it is often more convenient to model digital data with a polynomial that is centered at an expeditious location. This leads to the most general form of polynomial modeling. Fit a polynomial centered at $t = K$ to an arbitrary collection of data. The polynomial coefficients are found by solving the following set of equations. Notice that these are derived by replacing $p(t)$ with $p_K(t)$ in equation (7.19).

$$
\begin{aligned}
p_0 + p_1(I_0 - K) &+ \ldots + p_{N-1}(I_0 - K)^{N-1} &=& \quad x_{I_0} \\
p_0 + p_1(I_1 - K) &+ \ldots + p_{N-1}(I_1 - K)^{N-1} &=& \quad x_{I_1} \\
&\quad \vdots \\
p_0 + p_1(I_{N-1} - K) &+ \ldots + p_{N-1}(I_{N-1} - K)^{N-1} &=& \quad x_{I_{N-1}}
\end{aligned}
\tag{7.30}
$$

This equation also has the restriction that no two data points can share the same index. The solution to equation (7.30) is comprised of the coefficients of a polynomial that is originated at $t = K$ and passes through the $N$ data points.

In summary, we can exactly model a set of $N$ data points with an $(N-1)$-order polynomial. We do so by plugging the particulars (the origin of the polynomial, the data values, and the indices) into equation (7.30). The coefficients of the polynomial are found by any technique for solving a set of simultaneous equations. The most useful is Gaussian elimination, in which the set of equations is systematically reduced to fewer equations with fewer unknowns until a single equation with one unknown is produced. The other coefficients are found through a back substitution, which produces $p_{N-2}$ from $p_{N-1}$, then $p_{N-3}$ from $p_{N-1}$ and $p_{N-2}$, and so on until $p_0$ is found.

A word of warning is appropriate when such a simple approach to simultaneous equations is proposed. The straightforward application of Gaussian elimination works well in most situations, but it can break down if the data generate an "ill-conditioned" elimination step. For example, consider the following set of equations.

$$
\begin{aligned}
p_{N-3}0 + p_{N-2}1 + p_{N-1}2 &= 3 \\
p_{N-3}1 + p_{N-2}2 + p_{N-1}3 &= 6 \\
p_{N-3}2 + p_{N-2}3 + p_{N-1}4 &= 10
\end{aligned}
\tag{7.31}
$$

The naive application of Gaussian elimination suggests that $p_{N-3}$ is the next coefficient to be eliminated, but this cannot be done. The zero in the first equation cannot be used to eliminate $p_{N-3}$. The way out of this predicament is to switch the first and second equations and use the new first equation to eliminate $p_{N-3}$. This is a primitive application of "pivoting," where the equations are shuffled before performing the next elimination. Gaussian elimination with full pivoting allows you to shuffle the equations and the unknowns to get the largest coefficient into a position to make the next elimination. This works you out of situations like equation (7.31) and dramatically improves the precision of the results. Many numerical analysis books devote several chapters to the solution of simultaneous equations, so a deeper discussion is beyond the scope of our treatment. Suffice it to say, be careful when blindly applying simple procedures to simultaneous equations because your results may be inaccurate. A double check of your polynomial coefficients is always good insurance.

## 7.3 MISSING DATA, INTERPOLATION, AND EXTRAPOLATION

We have considered polynomial modeling of digital signals because of its broad application in digital signal processing. This section presents a major area of application: using a polynomial to estimate data that are not there. This includes missing data, data between data points (interpolation), and data beyond the data points (extrapolation).

### Missing Data

Many experiments demand the acquisition of measurements at regular intervals. However, because of late nights, fooling around, or just plain sloppiness, the experimenter can miss or improperly record one or more measurements. In such situations, the experimenter is faced with the choice of rerunning the experiment or estimating the missing data from the good data that are at hand. Generally, experiments are arduous and expensive, so most people will try to estimate the data rather than rerunning the experiment (after all, you would probably miss some data the second time around). There are many methods for estimating missing data. Most of us would just "eyeball" the data so that the estimates "look right." However, polynomial modeling provides us with a formal, rigorous approach to data estimation.

Missing data are estimated by extracting some pattern from the existing data and extending the pattern to the missing points. In this way, the estimates appear to fit in with the good data. For example, if the data points are alternating 1's and $-1$'s, and we are faced with a missing data point between two $-1$'s, most of us would bet that the missing point is a 1. On the other hand, if the data are completely random with no discernible pattern, estimation of missing data is impossible. Most data have a smooth pattern to successive points. That is, the data gradually change between successive points. If the data are taken in fine enough increments, they appear to fall on a smooth, slowly varying curve. This immediately suggests a polynomial model as a first step in the estimation of missing data.

Suppose that you have data measurements with a missing point at $k = K$, $x_k = ?$. This situation is illustrated in Figure 7.4. The good data suggest a smooth curve pattern to the data. So let's model the existing data with a polynomial and evaluate the polynomial at $t = K$ as an estimate of the missing data point. We assume that the data preceding the missing point, $x_{K-1}, x_{K-2}, \ldots$, have the same pattern as those following. So we will fit the polynomial to the $N$ points preceding $x_K$ and the $N$ points following. Therefore, we will model the $2N$ neighbors of $x_K$ with a $(2N - 1)$-order polynomial.

If we are using only the single points on each side of the missing data, $N = 1$,

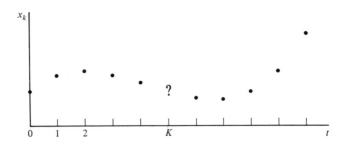

**Figure 7.4** Missing data scenario.

we fit a straight line to the two points. If we are interested in two points on each side, a cubic polynomial must be used.

We must also decide where to originate the polynomial before fitting it to the data. The naive approach is to put the polynomial at $t = 0$ and compute the appropriate coefficients. This will work, but it requires the evaluation of all the polynomial coefficients before the missing data can be estimated with the polynomial.

$$\tilde{x}_K = p(K)$$
$$= p_0 + p_1 K + \ldots + p_{2N-1} K^{2N-1} \tag{7.32}$$

Suppose that we had used our heads and had originated the polynomial at $t = K$. This means that the evaluation of the polynomial requires only $p_0$.

$$\tilde{x}_K = p_K(K)$$
$$= p_0 + p_1(K - K) + \ldots + p_{2N-1}(K - K)^{2N-1} \tag{7.33}$$
$$= p_0$$

We do not need the other coefficients of the polynomial model, which means less computation to compute the missing data point. There is an efficient method for finding just $p_0$ from the system of equations. It is called Cramer's rule and is available at most computer centers.

So our technique for estimating missing data is to fit a $(2N - 1)$-order polynomial to the $2N$ neighbors of the missing data and then evaluate the polynomial at $t = K$. Because we chose the polynomial's origin at $t = K$, we need only the $p_0$ coefficient of the polynomial. The estimate of the missing data point is $p_0$.

The algorithm for missing data takes the following form.

Step 1: Select the number of neighbors to use for the polynomial model. The neighboring points are symmetrically picked on each side of the missing data. Call the number of points $2N$.

Step 2: Solve for $p_0$ from the following system of equations.

$$
\begin{aligned}
p_0 + p_1(-N) + \ldots + p_{2N-1}(-N)^{2N-1} &= x_{K-N} \\
p_0 + p_1(-N+1) + \ldots + p_{2N-1}(-N+1)^{2N-1} &= x_{K-N+1}
\end{aligned}
$$

$$\vdots$$

$$
\begin{aligned}
p_0 + p_1(-1) + \ldots + p_{2N-1}(-1)^{2N-1} &= x_{K-1} \\
p_0 + p_1(1) + \ldots + p_{2N-1}(1)^{2N-1} &= x_{K+1}
\end{aligned}
\tag{7.34}
$$

$$\vdots$$

$$
\begin{aligned}
p_0 + p_1(N-1) + \ldots + p_{2N-1}(N-1)^{2N-1} &= x_{K+N-1} \\
p_0 + p_1(N) + \ldots + p_{2N+1}(N)^{2N-1} &= x_{K+N}
\end{aligned}
$$

Step 3: Estimate the missing data point by evaluating $p_K(t)$ at $t = K$.

$$\tilde{x}_k = p_0 \tag{7.35}$$

This is a fairly straightforward process, so let's try it on the following example.

**Example:** Estimate $x_K$ from $x_{K-1}$ and $x_{K+1}$.

This is a two-point estimator and requires a first-order polynomial to model the data. Plug the specifics into equation (7.34) and solve the following equations.

$$
\begin{aligned}
p_0 + p_1(-1) &= x_{K-1} \\
p_0 + p_1(1) &= x_{K+1}
\end{aligned}
\tag{7.36}
$$

We are interested in only $p_0$, so we eliminate $p_1$ by adding the two equations together.

$$
2p_0 = x_{K+1} + x_{K-1}
$$
$$
p_0 = \frac{x_{K+1} + x_{K-1}}{2}
\tag{7.37}
$$

Therefore, the estimate of the missing data point is just the average of its two nearest neighbors.

$$\tilde{x}_K = \frac{x_{K+1} + x_{K-1}}{2} \tag{7.38}$$

Notice that this example produced a general solution to finding missing data between two existing points. There is no reason to go through the derivation and refit the polynomial when you are confronted with such a problem. Simply put the values of the adjoining data into equation (7.38) to find the estimate of the missing data point.

**Example:**  Estimate $x_K$ from its four neighbors (two on each side).

We substitute $N = 2$ into equations (7.34) to produce the following equations:

$$p_0 + p_1(-2) + p_2(-2)^2 + p_3(-2)^3 = x_{K-2}$$
$$p_0 + p_1(-1) + p_2(-1)^2 + p_3(-1)^3 = x_{K-1}$$
$$p_0 + p_1(1) + p_2(1)^2 + p_3(1)^3 = x_{K+1}$$
$$p_0 + p_1(2) + p_2(2)^2 + p_3(2)^3 = x_{K+2}$$

(7.39)

Because the polynomial is originated at $t = K$, we need only $p_0$ to form the estimate. We eliminate $p_1$, then $p_2$, and finally $p_3$ and are left with a single equation with $p_0$ as the unknown. After a good deal of grinding we come up with the following expression:

$$p_0 = \frac{-x_{K-2} + 4x_{K-1} + 4x_{K+1} - x_{K+2}}{6}$$

(7.40)

So the cubic estimate of a missing data point is a four-coefficient nonrecursive filter.

$$\tilde{x}_K = \frac{x_{K-2} + 4x_{K-1} + 4x_{K+1} - x_{K+2}}{6}$$

(7.41)

This is a general expression and can be used directly when filling in missing data.

The preceding two examples showed the calculations necessary for most missing data applications. The data can be estimated with a linear, cubic, or quintic (fifth-order) polynomial. But these straightforward techniques can be extended to arbitrary situations. For example, suppose that you were unfortunate enough to miss two consecutive data points, $x_K$ and $x_{K+1}$. Both points could be estimated by fitting a polynomial to the $N$ points preceding $x_K$ and the $N$ points following $x_{K+1}$. The resulting polynomial is evaluated at $t = K$ and $t = K + 1$ to produce the estimates of $x_K$ and $x_{K+1}$, respectively. Notice that originating the polynomial at $t = K$ or $t = K + 1$ will not help in this case, because this situation demands two evaluations of the polynomial.

We have been using an equal number of points before and after the missing data element. This is reasonable because the neighbors before and the neighbors after should have the same impact on the missing data. But some situations demand an unequal grouping of points for the model. Consider the following example.

**Example:**  Estimate the missing data point $x_{10}$ when $x_{12}$ is also missing.

There are a number of approaches to this problem. The first is to use only the two available neighbors to estimate $x_{10}$. This is the linear estimate.

$$\tilde{x}_{10} = \frac{x_{11} + x_9}{2} \qquad (7.42)$$

But as shown in Figure 7.5a, this is not a good estimate when the data have a great deal of curvature.

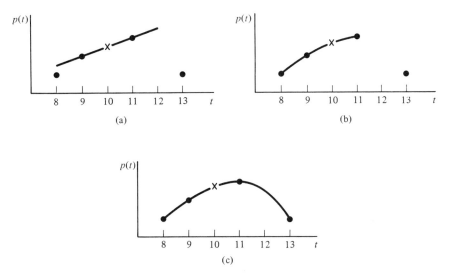

(a)

(b)

(c)

**Figure 7.5** Estimation of missing data: (a) using a first-order polynomial; (b) using a quadratic; (c) using a cubic.

We can go to higher-order estimates by using more neighbors and higher-order polynomials to fit those neighbors. For example, we could model $x_8$, $x_9$, $x_{11}$ with a quadratic centered at $t = 10$. This estimate is shown in Figure 7.5b and is much better than the linear estimate. Or we could fit a cubic to the data points $x_8$, $x_9$, $x_{11}$, and $x_{13}$ and evaluate the cubic at $t = 10$. The cubic estimate is shown in figure 7.5c and is close to the quadratic estimate.

The point of this example is to show the versatility of polynomial modeling as a tool for estimating missing data. Do not feel restricted to the two and four contiguous neighbors. Virtually any situations can be handled with polynomial modeling of the data.

In summary, the polynomial is a useful vehicle for estimating data because the model (polynomial) provides a value for any $t$. We exploit this by evaluating a fitted polynomial at the location(s) of the missing data point(s). Two special cases of missing data will be discussed next. The first is when we wish to estimate data between data points (i.e., $x_{k+\frac{1}{2}}$), and it is called *interpolation*. The second case is when we estimate data beyond the measurement region, which is called *extrapolation*. As you probably suspect, these are simply special cases of missing data. They are individually presented because they are so widely used.

## Interpolation

One of the major shortcomings of digital signals is that they do not tell what is happening between data elements. It is almost a certainty that if you take measurements every hour, your boss will ask for the data in 15-minute increments. Your options are to go back and retake the data at 15-minute increments or to use digital signal processing techniques to estimate the data between your 1-hour measurements. If your data are smoothly varying, you can use polynomial modeling to interpolate the values between the available data.

Suppose that you have the data at points $x_k = x(kT)$, where $k$ is an integer. The interpolation problem is to estimate the data anywhere between existing data points, $x(kT+lT)$, where $0 < l < 1$. This is a special application of the missing-data technique, so we will approach the problem identically. We will fit a polynomial to $N$ data points before and $N$ after the interpolation interval and then evaluate the polynomial to derive the estimate of $x(kT + lT)$.

The question is where to put the polynomial's origin. We could put it at $t = k + l$, so the evaluation of the polynomial at $k + l$ would involve only $p_0$. But this approach causes a great deal of clutter when setting up the equations; all sorts of $k + l$ terms are hanging around. So, sometimes it is better to originate the polynomial at $t = K$, even though the evaluation at $t = k + l$ requires all the coefficients.

If we choose $t = K$ as the origin of a $(2N-1)$-order polynomial, the polynomial is fitted to $2N$ data points by solving the following equations.

$$p_0 + p_1(-N) + \ldots + p_{2N-1}(-N)^{2N-1} \quad = \quad x_{K-N+1}$$

$$\vdots$$

$$p_0 + p_1(0) + \ldots + p_{2N-1}(0)^{2N-1} \quad = \quad x_K \tag{7.43}$$

$$\vdots$$

$$p_0 + p_1(N) + \ldots + p_{2N-1}(N)^{2N-1} \quad = \quad x_{K+N}$$

We interpolate the data by evaluating the polynomial at $t = K + l$.

$$\tilde{x}(kT + lT) = p_0 + p_1 l + \ldots + p_{2N-1} l^{2N-1} \tag{7.44}$$

If we choose the origin of the polynomial to be at $t = K + l$, the equations are a little harder to set up, but we need only $p_0$ to form the estimate.

$$p_0 + p_1(-N-l) + \ldots + p_{2N-1}(-N-l)^{2N-1} \quad = \quad x_{K-N+1}$$

$$\vdots$$

$$p_0 + p_1(-l) + \ldots + p_{2N-1}(-l)^{2N-1} \quad = \quad x_K \qquad (7.45)$$

$$\vdots$$

$$p_0 + p_1(N-l) + \ldots + p_{2N-1}(N-l)^{2N-1} \quad = \quad x_{K+N}$$

Because this polynomial is originated at $t = K + l$, the interpolation is just $p_0$.

$$\tilde{x}(KT + lT) = p_0 \qquad (7.46)$$

We can use either method to interpolate the data between any two points, $x_k$ and $x_{k+1}$, and for any value of $l$. But remember that the accuracy of the interpolation is determined by the appropriateness of the model. If the fitted polynomial is an accurate model of the data, the interpolation will also be accurate. But if the data are wildly fluctuating between the available data points, the polynomial is a poor model and the interpolated values are useless.

**Example:**  Interpolate Temperature Data.

You have risked life and limb to record the temperature of a condor chick in the wild. You have taken the chick's temperature every hour on the hour (you figure out how) and have proudly returned to your office. Unfortunately, you had misread your instructions, which called for readings at 15-minute intervals. Should you scale the 1000-foot cliff again and retake the data, or should you use your head and attempt to interpolate your existing data?

You must first determine if interpolation is appropriate. You plot your data and note that it is slowly and smoothly changing, so a polynomial will make a good model. So you are off interpolating.

Your first problem (although easier than rescaling the cliff) is to select the order of the modeling polynomial. You dismiss a first-order curve fit because it will not follow the curvature of the data. You are also lazy, so you want to fit the fewest points possible. Therefore, you settle on a quadratic model — that fits three data points. You select two points before the interpolation interval, $x_{k-1}$ and $x_k$, and a single point after, $x_{k+1}$.

You decide to originate the polynomial at the beginning of the interpolation interval, so you plug your specifics into equation (7.43).

$$
\begin{aligned}
p_0 + p_1(-1) + p_2(-1)^2 &= x_{k-1} \\
p_0 + p_1(0) + p_2(0) &= x_k \\
p_0 + p_1(1) + p_2(1)^2 &= x_{k+1}
\end{aligned}
\qquad (7.47)
$$

The general solutions (generic data) for the coefficients turned out to be fairly easy because of the sparsity of the middle equation of (7.48).

$$p_0 = x_k$$

$$p_1 = \frac{x_{k+1} - x_{k-1}}{2} \tag{7.48}$$

$$p_2 = \frac{x_{k-1} - 2x_k + x_{k+1}}{2}$$

Therefore, the temperature estimates on the quarter-hour are just the polynomial evaluated at $k + 0.25$ (15 minutes after the hour), $k + 0.5$ (30 minutes after the hour), and $k + 0.75$ (45 minutes).

$$
\begin{aligned}
x(k + 0.25) &= p_k(k + 0.25) \\
&= p_0 + p_1(0.25) + p_2(0.25)^2 \\
&= x_k + \frac{x_{k+1} - x_{k-1}}{8} + \frac{x_{k-1} - 2xk + x_{k+1}}{32} \\
&= \frac{5}{32}x_{k+1} + \frac{30}{32}x_k - \frac{3}{32}x_{k-1}
\end{aligned}
$$

$$
\begin{aligned}
x(k + 0.5) &= p_k(k + 0.5) \\
&= \frac{12}{32}x_{k+1} + \frac{24}{32}x_k - \frac{4}{32}x_{k-1}
\end{aligned}
\tag{7.49}
$$

$$
\begin{aligned}
x(k + 0.75) &= p_k(k + 0.75) \\
&= \frac{21}{32}x_{k+1} + \frac{14}{32}x_k - \frac{3}{32}x_{k-1}
\end{aligned}
$$

So to estimate the temperature at 10:45, use the last equation of (7.49) with the measurements at 9:00, 10:00, and 11:00.

$$\tilde{x}(10 : 45) = \frac{21}{32}x_{11} + \frac{14}{32}x_{10} - \frac{3}{32}x_9 \tag{7.50}$$

Interpolation requires that the user select the order of the polynomial (the number of data points to model minus one) and determine which data points are included in the curve fit. Should the points be symmetrically distributed around the interpolation interval or should more points precede or follow it? The next step is to solve for the polynomial coefficients for general data. Do not use the specific values of the data points at this stage, because that will make your solution too specific. Derive a general form for the interpolation by evaluating the polynomial. Finally, compute the interpolation by supplying specific data values to the expression.

Do not feel restricted by the interpolation schemes developed here. A straightforward extension of these results will handle interpolations in the presence of missing data, or unevenly spaced data. Just remember: set up your problem, fit your polynomial, evaluate the interpolation, and plug in the data. These steps can be applied to many varied situations.

### Extrapolation

The interpolation section shows how to estimate data between measurements, but what happens if you are looking for data before or after the measurements were taken? This calls for extrapolation — to extrapolate the data beyond the measurement range. This is another special case of missing data, and the previously developed concepts can be applied intact.

Suppose that you have taken data readings $x_0, \ldots, x_{N-1}$, but later discovered that you prematurely stopped the experiment. You need the data points $x_N$ and $x_{N+1}$. If the data are smoothly varying, it can be successfully modeled with a polynomial, and we can use polynomial modeling to extend the data. This application can be thought of as a "single-sided missing data" problem.

We begin by modeling the existing data points with a polynomial. Depending on the specifics of the application, we will model only the last few data points or will generate a more global model by matching the polynomial to every tenth or even hundredth data point. Selecting the order of the polynomial and which data points should be matched is the trickiest part of extrapolation. Once we select the points to match, we grind through equation (7.18) to solve for the polynomial coefficients. We extend, or extrapolate, the data sequence by evaluating the polynomial at the desired locations. It is best to originate the polynomial at or near the location to be extrapolated, because one of the extrapolations will require only $p_0$.

**Example:**   Estimate $x_{-1}$ from the data shown in Figure 7.6a.

The data look linear from $x_0$ to $x_5$ and exponential from $x_6$ on. We could fit a polynomial to all of the data, but who wants to solve a tenth-order equation? Rather, we are going to rely on the observation that a linear polynomial is a reasonable model for the data around $x_0$. Notice that this data record could be fooling us and the actual data make some wild departure between $x_0$ and $x_{-1}$. But this is the danger of extrapolation — you are often forced to predict nonexistent data without enough information.

Fit a first-order polynomial to two points of the data and originate it at $t = -1$. I select $x_0$ because it is the closest existing data point and $x_4$ because it is farthest away and still in the linear region. This is a subtle point, but any measurement noise in $x_4$ will have less effect than the same noise in $x_3$, $x_2$, or $x_1$. In this application, we could have just as easily used $x_0$ and $x_1$ for the curve fit.

The polynomial modeling equations for this example are

$$
\begin{aligned}
p_0 + p_1(1) &= x_0 \\
p_0 + p_1(5) &= x_4
\end{aligned}
\tag{7.51}
$$

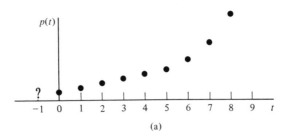

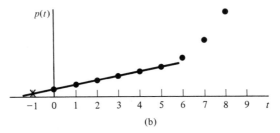

**Figure 7.6** Extrapolation example: (a) data;
(b) curve fit and extrapolation.

Because the polynomial is originated at $t = -1$, the extrapolation is just $p_0$.
We solve for $p_0$ and generate the following estimate.

$$\tilde{x}_{-1} = p_0 = \frac{5x_0 - x_4}{4} \tag{7.52}$$

The polynomial and the extrapolation are shown in Figure 7.6b. This extrapolation appears to be an eminently reasonable extension of the data.

This section on missing data, interpolation, and extrapolation has shown one of the major applications of polynomial modeling in digital signal processing. These three applications all have a common foundation: the available data are used to build a polynomial model of the data, and the model is evaluated to produce estimates of nonexistent data. Remember that the estimate is only as good as the model. This means that if you are using polynomial models, the data points must come from a process that is smoothly changing. Polynomial models are simply unsuitable for rapidly fluctuating data. Furthermore, no model will help if the available data are inherently insufficient to estimate missing data.

## 7.4  DIFFERENTIATION AND INTEGRATION

There are many situations in which the derivative or integral of data is required. If the data are continuous, $x(t)$, the mathematics can be performed directly on them. But digital data present a problem because differentiation and integration are not defined on digital data. Fortunately, we can approximate the calculus operations by using polynomial modeling of the digital data. In this instance, the data are modeled by a polynomial, which produces a continuous representation of the data. Because the polynomial is continuous, it can be differentiated or integrated at will. So in this application we use the polynomial as a bridge between the digital and continuous worlds.

Suppose that we wish to approximate the derivative of a digital signal at $x_k$. A heuristic approach to this problem is to exploit the notion that the derivative is the slope of a function. The slope is just the ratio of the change in the value to the change in the independent variable. This line of reasoning produces the following approximation of the derivative.

$$\frac{d}{dt}x_k = \frac{x_{k+1} - x_k}{k + 1 - k} \tag{7.53}$$

$$= x_{k+1} - x_k$$

This is called the *forward difference* because it uses $x_k$ and $x_{k+1}$. We could just as easily have used the *backward difference* to estimate the slope. Doing so produces the following approximation:

$$\frac{d}{dt}x_k = x_k - x_{k-1} \tag{7.54}$$

These two approximations are widely used, but they are founded in seat-of-the-pants observations. This section explains a formal technique for approximating derivatives as well as integrals. The forward-and backward-difference equations are special cases of polynomially derived derivatives.

Consider a polynomial that is matched to a section of digital data centered at $t = K$. Suppose that the polynomial is originated at the middle of the data section.

$$p_K(t) = p_0 + p_1(t - K) + p_2(t - K)^2 + \ldots \tag{7.55}$$

This polynomial is an exact representation of the data around $x_K$. So if we are interested in the derivative of the digital data at $t = K$, why not compute it from the polynomial model? As shown at the beginning of this chapter, the polynomial is readily differentiated.

$$\frac{d}{dt}p_K(t) = p_1 + 2p_2(t - K) + 3p_3(t - K)^2 + \ldots \tag{7.56}$$

So the polynomial's derivative at the middle of the digital sequence, at $t = K$, is just equation (7.56) evaluated at $t = K$.

$$\frac{d}{dt} p_K(t)\,|_{t=K} = p_1 \tag{7.57}$$

The second derivative of the polynomial is found by differentiating equation (7.56).

$$\frac{d^2}{dt^2} p_K(t) = 2p_2 + 6p_3(t - K) + \ldots \tag{7.58}$$

So the second derivative in the middle of the data sequence is simply $2p_2$.

$$\frac{d^2}{dt^2} p_K(t)\,|_{t=K} = 2p_2 \tag{7.59}$$

In general, the $i$th derivative of a polynomial centered at $t = K$ and evaluated at $t = K$ is the polynomial's $i$th coefficient multiplied by $i!$ ($i$ factorial).

$$\frac{d^i}{dt^i}\,|_{t=K} = i(i - 1)(i - 2) \ldots (1)p_i \tag{7.60}$$

Because the polynomial is such a good model of the digital data around $x_K$, the derivative of the digital data (whatever that means) is approximated by the derivative of the polynomial at $t = K$.

$$x'_K \approx p_1 \tag{7.61}$$

The exact form of equation (7.61) depends on the order of the polynomial and which data points are being matched. Consider the following examples.

**Example:** Use a first-order polynomial to compute the derivative.
The first-order polynomial has only two coefficients.

$$p_K(t) = p_0 + p_1(t - K) \tag{7.62}$$

It will fit two data points. In this example we will consider three collections of points: $x_K$ and $x_{K+1}$, $x_{K-1}$ and $x_K$, and $x_{K-1}$ and $x_{K+1}$.
If we match $x_K$ and $x_{K+1}$ with a polynomial originated at $t = K$, the polynomial coefficients are

$$\begin{aligned} p_0 &= x_K \\ p_1 &= x_{K+1} - x_K \end{aligned} \tag{7.63}$$

Therefore, the estimate of the derivative at $K$ is simply $p_1$. This is the *forward-difference* equation.

$$x'_K \approx x_{K+1} - x_K \tag{7.64}$$

If we select $x_{K-1}$ and $x_k$ as the points to be modeled, the *backward-difference* equation pops out.

$$x'_K \approx x_K - x_{K-1} \qquad (7.65)$$

Finally, if we choose the points on each side of $x_K$, $x_{K-1}$ and $x_{K+1}$, the following polynomial coefficients are generated.

$$p_0 = \frac{x_{K-1} + x_{K+1}}{2}$$
$$p_1 = \frac{x_{K+1} - x_{K-1}}{2} \qquad (7.66)$$

The derivative estimate is $p_1$, and this estimate is called the *central difference* formula.

$$x'_K \approx \frac{x_{K+1} - x_{K-1}}{2} \qquad (7.67)$$

Notice that these three approximations [equations (7.64), (7.65), and (7.67)] will produce slightly different estimates of the derivative. They all have the gratifying property of producing a derivative of zero when the data are constant.

Notice that the derivatives are in their general forms, so there is no need to repeat the curve fit if you are interested in an estimate of the derivative based on a first-order polynomial. Simply pick one of the three equations and apply it to your data.

**Example:** Compute the derivative of the data shown in Figure 7.7a.

Figure 7.7 shows samples of the velocity, $v_k$, of an automobile at 1-second intervals. The problem calls for the derivative of the velocity — the acceleration of the car as a function of time.

The central difference approximation, equation (7.67), is chosen because it equally weights the data before and after the point of interest. Therefore, the acceleration at each second is computed from the velocities through the following equation:

$$a_k = \frac{v_{k+1} - v_{k-1}}{2} \qquad (7.68)$$

We cannot directly compute $a_0$ because $v_{-1}$ is not available. We could linearly interpolate the velocities to estimate $v_{-1}$ or use the forward-difference approximation for this point. Let's assume that $a_0$ is not important for this

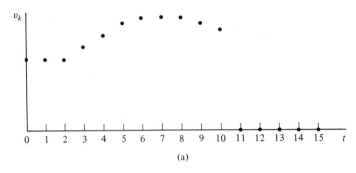

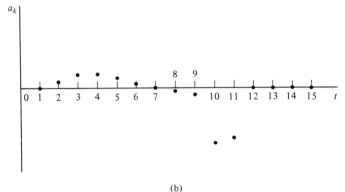

**Figure 7.7** Application of the derivative: (a) velocity data;
(b) estimate of the acceleration.

application and forget it. Therefore, the acceleration estimates begin with $a_1$.

$$a_1 = \frac{v_2 - v_0}{2} = 0$$

$$a_2 = \frac{v_3 - v_1}{2} = 5$$

$$a_3 = \frac{v_4 - v_2}{2} = 10 \qquad (7.69)$$

$$\vdots$$

The acceleration estimates are shown in Figure 7.7b. Notice that the car gradually accelerated and then rapidly decelerated near 10 sec; maybe it hit a wall.

It should be apparent from the preceding examples that the two-point differentiators produce nonrecursive digital filters. We will find that the higher-order polynomials also generate nonrecursive filters as derivative estimators.

**Example:**  Use a quadratic polynomial to estimate the derivative of digital data.

This problem requires the general solution for $p_1$ from the following set of equations.

$$p_0 + p_1(-1) + p_2(-1)^2 = x_{K-1}$$
$$p_0 + p_1(0) + p_2(0)^2 = x_K \qquad (7.70)$$
$$p_0 + p_1(1) + p_2(1)^2 = x_{K+1}$$

Grinding out a few lines of algebra shows that $p_1$ is the same as the first-order polynomial.

$$p_1 = \frac{x_{K+1} - x_{K-1}}{2} \qquad (7.71)$$

So, going to a quadratic does not change the estimate of the derivative.

The quadratic does provide another coefficient, $p_2$, so we can use the quadratic to estimate the second derivative of the digital data. In this case, we solve for $p_2$.

$$p_2 = \frac{x_{K+1} - 2x_K + x_{K-1}}{2} \qquad (7.72)$$

So the second derivative is just this value of $p_2$ applied to equation (7.59).

$$x''_K \approx 2p_2 = x_{K+1} - 2x_K + x_{K-1} \qquad (7.73)$$

The preceding example showed that the first- and second-order polynomials produce the estimates of the derivative. If we pursued this point further, we would find that the third- and fourth-order polynomials also produce identical derivatives, although different from those produced by the first- and second-order curve fits. The same holds for the fifth and sixth. The polynomials are paired in odd and even order. Each pair produces the same estimate of the derivative. We exploit this fact by using the odd-order polynomials, because they generate the same estimate as the next-higher-order polynomial with one fewer equation. Therefore, the cubic is the next polynomial for building derivative estimators.

**Example:**  Use a cubic to estimate the derivative of a digital signal.

In this case, the polynomial is fitted to four points. The question is, which ones? If we fit the polynomial to $x_K$, the remaining three points must be asymmetrically distributed around $x_K$. So let's preserve the symmetric distribution and fit the polynomial to $x_{K-2}$, $x_{K-1}$, $x_{K+1}$, and $x_{K+2}$. This scheme leads to the following equations.

$$p_0 + p_1(-2) + p_2(-2)^2 + p_3(-2)^3 = x_{K-2}$$
$$p_0 + p_1(-1) + p_2(-1)^2 + p_3(-1)^3 = x_{K-1}$$
$$p_0 + p_1(1) + p_2(1)^2 + p_3(1)^3 = x_{K+1} \qquad (7.74)$$
$$p_0 + p_1(2) + p_2(2)^2 + p_3(2)^3 = x_{K+2}$$

This example takes a little more grinding to solve for $p_1$, but after a few tries we get the right answer.

$$p_1 = \frac{-x_{K+2} + 8x_{K+1} - 8x_{K-1} + x_{K-2}}{12} \tag{7.75}$$

So the cubic estimate of the derivative is a four-coefficient digital filter.

$$x'_K \approx \frac{-x_{K+2} + 8x_{K+1} - 8x_{K-1} + x_{K-2}}{12} \tag{7.76}$$

It is always a good idea to check the differentiators against a constant signal, $x_k = 1$, and a ramp, $x_k = k$. The constant signal better produce a zero derivative and the ramp a derivative of 1.

While we are working with a cubic, let's extend the example to estimators of the second and third derivatives. This requires the computation of $p_2$ and $p_3$. The second derivative is twice $p_2$.

$$x''_K \approx \frac{x_{K+2} - x_{K+1} - x_{K-1} + x_{K-2}}{3} \tag{7.77}$$

The estimate of the third derivative is six times $p_3$.

$$x'''_K \approx \frac{x_{K+2} - 2x_{K+1} + 2x_{K-1} - x_{K-2}}{2} \tag{7.78}$$

We cannot directly estimate the fourth derivative because the cubic does not contain a $p_4$ coefficient. Furthermore, seldom is the third derivative needed, and it is even less likely for the fourth derivative ever to be computed.

In summary, polynomial modeling is a natural vehicle for estimating the derivative of digital data. The estimate depends on the order of the polynomial (the number of data points used in the model) and the particular points used for the model. If you are working with an even-order polynomial, an odd number of data points are required for the fit. In this case, it is natural to use $x_k$ and an equal number of neighbors before and after for the fit. An odd-order polynomial complicates the selection of the even-number data points needed for the polynomial fit. If $x_k$ is used, the other points will be unevenly distributed around $k$. Because of this, I prefer to ignore $x_k$ and use an equal number of points before and after $x_k$. Fortunately, it really makes little difference what strategy you use, because the differentiators will be only a little different.

Some of the most popular differentiators are shown below as a handy reference.

First order:

$$x'_k \approx x_k - x_{k-1} \tag{7.79}$$

$$x'_k \approx \frac{x_{k+1} - x_{k-1}}{2} \tag{7.80}$$

Third order:

$$x'_k \approx \frac{-x_{k+2} + 8x_{k+1} - 8x_{k-1} + x_{k-2}}{12} \tag{7.81}$$

Fifth order:

$$x'_k \approx \frac{-x_{k+3} + 9x_{k+2} - 45x_{k+1} + 45x_{k-1} - 9x_{k-2} + x_{k-3}}{30} \tag{7.82}$$

Seventh order:

$$x'_k \approx \frac{1}{280}\Big( -x_{k+4} + 10.666x_{k+3} - 56x_{k+2} + 224x_{k+1} - 224x_{k-1}$$
$$+56x_{k-2} - 10.666x_{k-3} + x_{k-4}\Big) \tag{7.83}$$

Equations (7.79) through (7.83) are the results of computing the first coefficient, $p_1$, of a first-, third-, fifth-, and seventh-order polynomial that fits the data around $x_k$.

We can generate the following approximations to the second derivative by computing the $2p_2$ coefficients of polynomials that match the data around $x_k$. Notice that a first-order approximation is not presented because the first-order polynomial does not have a $p_2$ coefficient.

$$x''_k \approx 2p_2 \tag{7.84}$$

Third order:

$$x''_k \approx \frac{x_{k+2} - x_{k+1} - x_{k-1} + x_{k-2}}{3} \tag{7.85}$$

Fifth order:

$$x''_k \approx \frac{-x_{k+3} + 5.333x_{k+2} - 4.333x_{k+1} - 4.333x_{k-1} + 5.333x_{k-2} - x_{k-3}}{8} \tag{7.86}$$

Seventh order:

$$x_k'' \approx \frac{1}{25.72}\big(x_{k+4} - 7.714x_{k+3} + 24.143x_{k+2} - 17.429x_{k+1}$$
$$-17.429x_{k-1} + 24.143x_{k-2} - 7.714x_{k-3} + x_{k-4}\big) \tag{7.87}$$

It is seldom that you will find an application that is not satisfied by the blind application of one of the foregoing approximations. But if you find yourself in such an unfortunate situation, drop back to the underlying principles of this section. You can always choose the order of the polynomial and which data points are used for the curve fit. Take the derivative of the general polynomial and find the relationship between the desired derivative and the polynomial coefficients. The difficult part is solving for the coefficients with general data, $x_k$. Do not put the specific values of your data into the problem this early. Finally, once you have the general form of the coefficients, plug them into the polynomial's derivative to compute the estimate of the derivative.

This general approach can be extended to any computable function of a polynomial. Since polynomials differentiate well, the derivative is a natural application of polynomial modeling. But polynomials also integrate well, and that leads us to the next application.

### Integration

There are many applications in which we are interested in computing the integral of the data. If the data are continuous, the integral is the area under the curve, and there are a number of schemes for measuring that. But if the data are digital, we must approximate the integral. There are a number of heuristic approaches for estimating the area under a group of data points. This section develops a formal technique for generating integration estimators through polynomials.

Suppose that we are interested in the integral of the digital data in Figure 7.8a.

$$\int_0^{N-1} x_k \, dt \tag{7.88}$$

Notice the strange mix of notation in equation (7.88). This comes from the fact that we are attempting to perform a continuous operation on discrete data. A better way of stating the problem is to integrate a continuous function, of which $x_k$ are the samples.

Integration has this nice property — it can be broken up. Rather than attempting to fit a polynomial to all $n$ data points, let's break the data into bite-size chunks of length $M$.

$$\int_0^{N-1} x_k \, dt = \int_0^M x_k \, dt + \int_M^{2M} x_k \, dt + \ldots + \int_{N-M}^{N-1} x_k \, dt \tag{7.89}$$

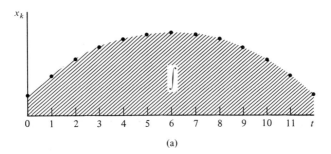

(a)

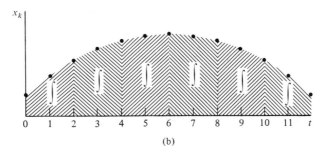

(b)

**Figure 7.8** Integration of digital data: (a) integral of
the data; (b) breaking the integral up.

This process is illustrated in Figure 7.8b.

Now the problem is to approximate each of the subintegrals by using polynomials. Once we have the approximations, we can add them up to compute the integral from 0 to $N-1$. The subintegrals are approximated by fitting a polynomial to the data points in each of the subintegrals. Make this a generalized fit (independent of the data values), so it can be used for any data. Now that we have a model of the data in the subintegral, integrate the polynomial model. So the integral is now in terms of the polynomial coefficients. We express the integral in terms of the data, by substituting the polynomial coefficient calculations. This produces an estimate of the integral in terms of the data points.

For example, the first subintegral in equation (7.89) is approximated by fitting a polynomial to $x_0, \ldots, x_M$. That is, solving for the polynomial coefficients from the following equations:

$$
\begin{aligned}
p_0 + p_1(0) + \ldots + p_M(0)^M &= x_0 \\
p_0 + p_1(1) + \ldots + p_M(1)^M &= x_1 \\
&\vdots \\
p_0 + p_1(M) + \ldots + p_M(M)^M &= x_M
\end{aligned}
\tag{7.90}
$$

The indefinite integral of this polynomial is an $(M+1)$-order polynomial.

$$\int p(t)dt = p_0 t + \frac{1}{2}p_1 t^2 + \frac{1}{3}p_2 t^3 + \ldots + \frac{1}{M+1}p_M t^{M+1} + c \qquad (7.91)$$

The constant of integration, $c$, is usually zero, so it is dropped from the rest of this discussion. If you are faced with a situation in which the contant of integration is necessary, it can be readily added to the following derivation.

The next step is to evaluate the definite integral by plugging the limits of integration into equation (7.91). The first subintegral has limits of 0 and $M$. Zero is a nice limit to apply to equation (7.91), because all the terms fall out. So the approximation becomes equation (7.91) evaluated at $t = M$.

$$\int_0^M p(t)dt = p_0(M) + \frac{1}{2}p_1(M)^2 + \ldots + \frac{1}{M+1}p_M M^{M+1} \qquad (7.92)$$

If the polynomial is a good model of the data points, $x_0 \ldots x_M$, the integral of the data is approximately the integral of the polynomial.

$$\int_0^M x_k dt \approx p_0(M) + \frac{1}{2}(M)^2 + \ldots \frac{1}{M+1}p_M(M)^{M+1} \qquad (7.93)$$

In this way, each of the subintegrals can be approximated with the integral of a fitted polynomial. Without some judicious picking of the origins, we will have difficulty evaluating the other polynomials because they do not include a limit of zero. However, this is really not an issue because we can effectively force all subintegrals to begin at $t = 0$ by moving the origin of the polynomials to the beginning of the subinterval. For example, the subinterval beginning at $K$, $x_K \ldots x_{K+M}$, calls for a polynomial with an origin at $K$.

$$
\begin{array}{rcl}
p_0 + \quad p_1(K-K) \quad + \ldots + \quad p_M(K-K)^M & = & x_K \\
p_0 + p_1(K+1-K) + \ldots + p_M(K+1-K)^M & = & x_{K+1} \\
\vdots & & \\
p_0 + p_1(K+M-K) + \ldots + p_M(K+M-K)^M & = & x_{K+M}
\end{array}
\qquad (7.94)
$$

This is the same set of equations as (7.90) with the data $x_0 \ldots x_M$ replaced with $x_K \ldots x_{K+M}$. Therefore, the polynomial coefficients are identically computed for all subintegral — just use different data.

The indefinite integral takes on a different form for each subintegral, because we are dealing with $p(t-K)$ rather than the $p(t)$ of equation (7.91).

$$\int p(t-K)\,d(t-K) = p_0(t-K) + \frac{1}{2}p_1(t-K)^2 + \ldots + \frac{1}{M+1}p_M(t-K)^{M+1} \quad (7.95)$$

But the differences go away when the definite integral is evaluated. The $K$ limit of the definite integral contributes zero, so the integral depends only on the $K + M$ limit.

$$\int_K^{K+M} = p_0 M + p_1 M^2 + \ldots + \frac{1}{M+1} p_M (M)^{M+1} \tag{7.96}$$

This is identical to the approximation for the 0 to $M$ subintegral. Therefore, all subintegrals can be handled identically. Simply apply the data to the right-hand side of equation (7.90) (replace $x_0 \ldots x_M$ with the data in question) and approximate the integral by evaluating (7.93). Notice that the integral approximations depend only on the polynomial coefficients, which are computed from the data in the subintegral and the length of the subintegral.

Let's firm up these ideas by applying them to some examples.

**Example:**   Approximate the integral of the data in Figure 7.9a by using a first-order polynomial.

$$\int_{-1}^{3} x_k \; dt \tag{7.97}$$

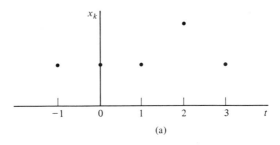

(a)

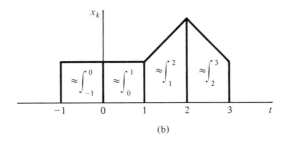

(b)

**Figure 7.9**  Integration: (a) data to be integrated; (b) approximated by trapezoidal rule.

The first-order polynomial will match only two data points, so in this case $M = 1$.

$$\int_{-1}^{3} x_k = \int_{-1}^{0} x_k + \int_{0}^{1} x_k + \int_{1}^{2} x_k + \int_{2}^{3} x_k \tag{7.98}$$

We find the coefficients associated with the subintegral beginning at $x_K$ by solving the following system of equations [application of equation (7.90)]:

$$\begin{aligned} p_0 + p_1(0) &= x_K \\ p_0 + p_1(1) &= x_{K+1} \end{aligned} \tag{7.99}$$

Flip back through this chapter to find the solution, or, if you must, grind through it again.

$$\begin{aligned} p_0 &= x_K \\ p_1 &= x_{K+1} - x_K \end{aligned} \tag{7.100}$$

Plug these results into equation (7.92) and find that the subintegral beginning at $K$ is approximated by the average of $x_K$ and $x_{K+1}$.

$$\int_{K}^{K+1} x_k \approx x_K(1) + \frac{x_{K+1} - x_K}{2}(1) \tag{7.101}$$

$$\approx \frac{x_{K+1} + x_K}{2}$$

This is the famous trapezoidal rule of integration. As shown in Figure 7.9b, each subintegral is approximated by the area of a small trapezoid – equation (7.101).

We complete this example by adding the four subintegrals to get the integral of the data from $-1$ to 3.

$$\int_{-1}^{3} x_k \, dt \approx \sum_{k=-1}^{2} \frac{1}{2} x_{k+1} + \frac{1}{2} x_k \tag{7.102}$$

If you were to repeat the previous example with a zeroth-order polynomial, $p(t) = p_0$, you would find the following approximation to the integral.

$$\int_{-1}^{3} x_k dt \approx \sum_{k=-1}^{2} x_k \tag{7.103}$$

This is the rectangular rule of integration, named so because the subintegrals are approximated by the areas of little rectangles of height $x_k$ and length one.

It should be apparent that the rectangle and trapezoid rules are too-simple approximations when the data has a lot of curvature. As illustrated in Figure 7.10, the trapezoid rule underestimates the area when the curve is convex (between $x_1$ and $x_2$) and overestimates the integral when the curve is concave (between $x_5$ and $x_6$). The reason for this is that a first-order polynomial cannot model a curve. Therefore, we should expect better integrators from higher-order polynomials. The following examples show that such is the case.

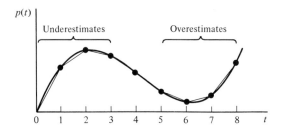

**Figure 7.10** Errors from the trapezoidal rule

**Example:**  Build an integrator by fitting a quadratic to the data.

In this case, $M = 2$, so we are dealing with three data points per fit.

$$\int_0^{N-1} x_k \; dt = \int_0^2 x_k \; dt + \int_2^4 x_k \; dt + \ldots + \int_{N-3}^{N-1} x_k \; dt \qquad (7.104)$$

The polynomial coefficients of the subintegral beginning at $K$ are found by applying $M = 2$ to equation (7.90).

$$\begin{aligned}
p_0 + p_1(0) + p_2(0)^2 &= x_K \\
p_0 + p_1(1) + p_2(1)^2 &= x_{K+1} \\
p_0 + P_1(2) + p_2(2)^2 &= x_{K+2}
\end{aligned} \qquad (7.105)$$

The general solutions of the coefficients are as follows:

$$\begin{aligned}
p_0 &= x_k \\
p_1 &= \frac{-x_{K+2} + 4x_{K+1} - 3x_K}{2} \\
p_2 &= \frac{x_{K+2} - 2x_{K+1} + x_K}{2}
\end{aligned} \qquad (7.106)$$

Therefore, the approximation to the subintegral beginning at $K$ is just equation (7.93) with $M = 2$ and the coefficients of equation (7.106).

$$\begin{aligned}
\int_K^{K+2} x_k \; dt &\approx x_K 2 + \frac{1}{2} \left( \frac{-x_{K+2} + 4x_{K+1} - 3x_k}{2} \right) 2^2 \\
&\quad + \frac{1}{3} \left( \frac{x_{K+2} - 2x_{K+1} + x_K}{2} \right) 2^3 \\
&\approx \frac{x_{K+2} + 4x_{K+1} + x_K}{3}
\end{aligned} \qquad (7.107)$$

Therefore, the complete integral is simply the sum of the subintegrals.

$$\int_0^{N-1} x_k \, dt = \sum_{k=0,2,4,\ldots,N-3} \frac{x_{k+2} + 4x_{k+1} + x_k}{3} \qquad (7.108)$$

The integration approximation produced by the preceding example [equation (7.107)] is called *Simpson's rule of integration*. It is generally preferred to the rectangular or trapezoid approximations because its quadratic curve fit allows it to follow curvature in the data.

If we were to repeat the example for a cubic polynomial, we would find that each subintegral is approximated by fitting a cubic to four data points. Each subinterval is approximated by the following expression.

$$\int_K^{K+3} x_k \, dt \approx \frac{3x_{K+3} + 9x_{K+2} + 9x_{K+1} + 3x_k}{8} \qquad (7.109)$$

This is called the $\frac{3}{8}$'s *rule of integration*. Because this rule is based on a cubic, rather than a quadratic, the $\frac{3}{8}$'s rule produces a more accurate estimate when the data have higher-order curvature. In most applications the $\frac{3}{8}$'s rule and Simpson's rule give nearly identical results.

The equations derived from this integration section are repeated for handy reference. Note that each one is a nonrecursive digital filter and can be applied without being derived again. An understanding of the derivation most certainly improves the likelihood that the integral technique will be applied intelligently.

Rectangular (zeroth-order polynomial):

$$\int_K^{K+1} x_k \, dt \approx x_k \qquad (7.110)$$

Trapezoid (first-order polynomial):

$$\int_K^{K+1} x_k \, dt \approx \frac{x_{K+1} + x_K}{2} \qquad (7.111)$$

Simpson's rule (quadratic polynomial):

$$\int_K^{K+2} x_k \, dt \approx \frac{x_{K+2} + 4x K + 1 + x_K}{3} \qquad (7.112)$$

$\frac{3}{8}$'s rule (cubic polynomial):

$$\int_{K}^{K+3} x_k \, dt \approx 3 \frac{x_{K+3} + 3x_{K+2} + 3x_{K+1} + x_k}{8} \qquad (7.113)$$

These four integration techniques will handle most of your integration needs, but do not feel confined to these. Many different integration approximations can be developed through polynomial curve fitting for special applications. For example, there are a whole class of double integral approximations leading from a second integration of equation (7.91).

$$\int \int p(t) \, dt = \frac{1}{2} p_0 t^2 + \frac{1}{6} p_1 t^3 + \ldots + \frac{1}{(M+1)(M+2)} p_M t^{M+2} \qquad (7.114)$$

The idea is to make a generalized fit of the polynomial to a chunk of data (typically, two to five points) and put the resulting coefficients into equation (7.114).

If you find yourself developing integration approximations, consider writing a short computer program to solve the simultaneous equations and otherwise help out with the bookkeeping of these algorithms. Also, make sure you check your results with a couple of simple cases. For example, put in constant data, $x_k = 1$, and make sure that the approximation produces the length of the subintegral, $M$.

## 7.5  LEAST-SQUARES POLYNOMIAL MODELING

Our previous work on polynomial modeling has assumed that the polynomial exactly matches the data points. An exact match is the result of fitting $N$ data points with an $(N-1)$-order polynomial. There are also applications where it is desirable to fit a lower-order polynomial to the data points. In general, this prevents an exact match, so we must look for polynomials that give the "best" match — in our case the *least-squared-error* match.

Suppose that we have $N$ data points and wish to find the $M$-order polynomial that comes closest to the data. We have previously shown that if $M \geq N$, there will be many polynomials that exactly match the data. If $M = N - 1$, there is only one polynomial that is an exact match. In either case, we find the coefficients of the polynomial by forcing the polynomial to equal (match) the data. If the order of the polynomial is smaller, $M < N - 1$, it is usually impossible to exactly match the data with the polynomial. A low-order polynomial cannot be made to go through all the data points.

The question is: How do we find the "best" polynomial match in such situations? One approach is to exactly match the polynomial to the first data points and ignore the extra ones. This is a terrible solution because we are not uniformly spreading the polynomial over all the data. In such a scheme, the beginning data points will be perfectly matched and the points that were ignored will be unmodeled. A better solution is to evenly spread the matching error among all data points. This is most easily accomplished with the least-squared-error approach.

This should not be a new concept for you, because it was used in Chapter 3 to develop the nonrecursive design technique. The least-squares fitting of polynomials is the same technique, with different notation. Suppose that we have $N$ data points, $x_0, \ldots, x_{N-1}$, and wish to fit an $M$-order polynomial when $M < N-1$. If we applied the techniques of the preceding sections, we would end up with too many equations ($N - 1$ of them) with too few unknowns — no solution guaranteed.

Rather than attempting to force the polynomial through each data point, let's find a polynomial that comes as close as possible to the data. We do this by monitoring the error between the polynomial at $t = k$ and $x_k$.

$$\epsilon_k = x_k - p(k) \tag{7.115}$$

The problem is to find the polynomial coefficients that make the $N$ errors as close to zero as possible. This is a very difficult problem as stated, because it does not have a closed-form solution. This approach calls for a search of all polynomial coefficients to find the best ones.

Rather than deal with the individual errors, let's combine the errors into a single, global error for all $N$ points of the match. This immediately suggests that we add all the $N$ errors together and try to make the sum as close to zero as possible. But this approach has one insurmountable drawback: very large negative errors can cancel equally large positive errors. Hence the individual errors can be arbitrarily large while the sum of the errors is zero. To prevent the cancellation of errors, let us square the individual errors before adding them together. This forces all nonzero errors to increase the sum. The squared error of the polynomial sum is defined as follows:

$$\mathcal{E} = \sum_{k=0}^{N-1} \epsilon_k^2 = \sum_{k=0}^{N-1} [x_k - p(k)]^2 \tag{7.116}$$

Since $\mathcal{E}$ is nonnegative, the problem reduces to finding the polynomial coefficients, $p_0, \ldots, p_M$, that minimize the squared error. In other words, we are searching for the polynomial that produces the least-squared error. In this manner, the curve-fitting problem becomes a minimization problem.

The $p_0$ coefficient that results in the least-squared error is found by differentiating $\mathcal{E}$ with respect to $p_0$ and setting the derivative to zero.

$$\frac{d}{dp_0}\mathcal{E} = \frac{d}{dp_0} \sum_{k=0}^{N-1} [x_k - p(k)]^2 = 0 \tag{7.117}$$

This is the time for the chain rule of differentiation.

$$\sum_{k=0}^{N-1} 2(x_k - p(k))\frac{d}{dp_0}[x_k - p(k)] = 0 \tag{7.118}$$

The data points are independent of $p_0$, so the derivative of $x_k$ with respect to $p_0$ is zero. Furthermore, the other coefficients of the polynomial are independent of $p_0$, so equation (7.118) becomes an algebraic equation.

$$\sum_{k=0}^{N-1} 2\left[x_k - p(k)\right](-1) = 0 \qquad (7.119)$$

or

$$\sum_{k=0}^{N-1} p(k) = \sum_{k=0}^{N-1} x_k \qquad (7.120)$$

This result makes more sense by writing out the polynomial.

$$\sum_{k=0}^{N-1} p_0 + \sum_{k=0}^{N-1} p_1 k + \sum_{k=0}^{N-1} p_2 k^2 + \ldots + \sum_{k=0}^{N-1} p_M k^M = \sum_{k=0}^{N-1} x_k \qquad (7.121)$$

The polynomial coefficients are independent of $k$, so equation (7.121) is really an equation in the coefficients.

$$p_0 \sum_{k=0}^{N-1} 1 + p_1 \sum_{k=0}^{N-1} k + p_2 \sum_{k=0}^{N-1} k^2 + \ldots + p_M \sum_{k=0}^{N-1} k^M = \sum_{k=0}^{N-1} x_k \qquad (7.122)$$

A similar derivation can be done for each of the coefficients; perform the derivative of the error with respect to the particular coefficient, set the results to zero, and collect the terms of the equation. Let's use our experience with $p_0$ to find the least-squares equation for the general coefficient, $p_i$. In general, the derivative is equation (7.118) with $p_0$ replaced with $p_i$.

$$\frac{d}{dp_i} = \sum_{k=0}^{N-1} 2\left[x_k - p(k)\right] \frac{d}{dp_i}\left(x_k - p(k)\right) = 0 \qquad (7.123)$$

The derivative of $x_k$ is still zero, but the derivative of $p(k)$ with respect to $p_i$ is $k^i$. So the $p_i$ that produces the smallest squared error is a solution to the following equation.

$$p_0 \sum_{k=0}^{N-1} k^i + p_1 \sum_{k=0}^{N-1} k^{i+1} + p_2 \sum_{k=0}^{N-1} k^{i+2} + \ldots + p_M \sum_{k=0}^{N-1} k^{i+M} = \sum_{k=0}^{N-1} x_k k^i \quad (7.124)$$

Notice that the derivative in equation (7.123) brings a $k^i$ into both sides of the equation. Compare equation (7.124) with (7.121) to verify that the general expression works for $p_0$.

We are interested in finding the set of polynomial coefficients that minimizes the sum-squared error. We do so by differentiating the error with respect to each coefficient and set the results to zero. This produces a set of $M+1$ equations (one for each coefficient) with $M+1$ unknowns $(p_0, \ldots, p_M)$.

$$
\begin{aligned}
p_0 \sum_{k=0}^{N-1} 1 \;+\; & p_1 \sum_{k=0}^{N-1} k \;+\; \ldots \;+\; p_M \sum_{k=0}^{N-1} k^M &=\; & \sum_{k=0}^{N-1} x_k \\
p_0 \sum_{k=0}^{N-1} k \;+\; & p_1 \sum_{k=0}^{N-1} k^2 \;+\; \ldots \;+\; p_M \sum_{k=0}^{N-1} k^{M+1} &=\; & \sum_{k=0}^{N-1} x_k k \\
p_0 \sum_{k=0}^{N-1} k^2 \;+\; & p_1 \sum_{k=0}^{N-1} k^3 \;+\; \ldots \;+\; p_M \sum_{k=0}^{N-1} k^{M+2} &=\; & \sum_{k=0}^{N-1} x_k k^2 \\
& \qquad\qquad\qquad \vdots & & \\
p_0 \sum_{k=0}^{N-1} k^M \;+\; & p_1 \sum_{k=0}^{N-1} k^{M+1} \;+\; \ldots \;+\; p_M \sum_{k=0}^{N-1} k^{2M} &=\; & \sum_{k=0}^{N-1} x_k k^M
\end{aligned}
$$

$$(7.125)$$

Therefore, least-squares curve fitting is no more than summing up the indices and data [the summations in equation (7.125)] and solving for the coefficients. Let's apply this to the following example.

**Example:** Find the least-squares quadratic for the following data points:

$$
x_0 = 1 \quad x_1 = 2 \quad x_2 = 3 \quad x_3 = 3
$$

The quadratic fit to this set of four points generates the following set of equations.

$$
\begin{aligned}
p_0(1+1+1+1) + p_1(0+1+2+3) + & \quad p_2(0+1+4+9) \\
= & \quad (1+2+3+3) \\
p_0(0+1+2+3) + p_1(0+1+4+9) + & \quad p_2(0+1+8+27) \\
= (1 \cdot 0 + 2 \cdot 1 + & 3 \cdot 2 + 3 \cdot 3) \\
p_0(0+1+4+9) + p_1(0+1+8+27) + & \quad p_2(0+1+16+81) \\
= (1 \cdot 0 + 2 \cdot 1 + & 3 \cdot 4 + 3 \cdot 9)
\end{aligned}
$$

$$(7.126)$$

We find the coefficients for the least-squares polynomial by solving for $p_0$, $p_1$, and $p_2$ using Gaussian elimination.

$$p(t) = 0.95 + 1.45t - 0.25t^2 \qquad (7.127)$$

This polynomial and the four data points are shown in Figure 7.11. Notice that the polynomial attempts to get as close as possible to each point.

This problem can be worked in the general case without substituting the actual values of the data. This is done by evaluating the sums in the left-hand side of equation (7.125) and leaving the right-hand side in terms of the $x_k$s. Because of the intensive bookkeeeping, a computer program is a must for this

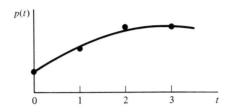

**Figure 7.11** Least-squares curve fitting.

sort of calculation. The general solution for the coefficients of the least-squares quadratic fit of $x_0, x_1, x_2, x_3$ is as follows:

$$p_0 = 0.95x_0 + 0.15x_1 - 0.15x_2 + 0.05x_3$$
$$p_1 = -1.05x_0 + 0.65x_1 + 0.85x_2 - 0.45x_3 \qquad (7.128)$$
$$p_2 = 0.25x_0 - 0.25x_1 - 0.25x_2 + 0.25x_3$$

By using equation (7.128), you can fit a quadratic to four data points by simply plugging the values of the data into the equation. There is no need to set up the simultaneous equations and solve them.

We have developed the least-squares curve fitting technique for $N$ contiguous data points starting at $x_0$. This technique can be readily extended to an arbitrary collection of data by employing the same tricks used earlier. It is just a question of notation and bookkeeping to extend the least squares to arbitary data.

Consider the $N$ data points at $x_{I_k}$. As before, the generalized index, $I_k$, provides the flexibility to consider data at arbitrary indices. For example, if the data are contiguous and begin at $k = 0$, then $I_k = k$. If we are dealing with the even-indexed data starting at $k = 100$, then $I_k = 100 + 2k$. If we are working with arbitrary data, it is convenient to move around the origin of the polynomial. So we are interested in fitting an $M$-order polynomial with an origin at $t = K$ to the data points $x_{I_k}$.

We begin the development by looking at the new sum-squared error. This is the sum of the square differences between the polynomial and the data points.

$$\mathcal{E} = \sum_{k=0}^{N-1} [x_{I_k} - p(I_k - K)]^2 \qquad (7.129)$$

We generate a set of simultaneous equations by differentiating the error with respect to the polynomial coefficients. The $i$th coefficient produces the following equation.

$$p_0 \sum_{k=0}^{N-1} (I_k - K)^i + p_1 \sum_{k=0}^{N-1} (I_k - K)^{i+1} + \ldots + p_M \sum_{k=0}^{N-1} (I_k - K)^{i+M} = \sum_{k=0}^{N-1} x_{I_k} (I_k - K)^i$$

$$(7.130)$$

Notice that this is equation 7.124 with $k$ replaced by $I_k - K$. Therefore, the generalized least-squares polynomial fit requires the solution of the following set of simultaneous equations.

$$p_0 \sum_{k=0}^{N-1} 1 \quad + \quad p_1 \sum_{k=0}^{N-1}(I_k - K) \quad + \dots + \quad p_M \sum_{k=0}^{N-1}(I_k - K)^M$$

$$= \sum_{k=0}^{N-1} x_{I_k}$$

$$p_0 \sum_{k=0}^{N-1}(I_k - K) + p_1 \sum_{k=0}^{N-1}(I_k - K)^2 + \dots + p_M \sum_{k=0}^{N-1}(I_k - K)^{M+1}$$

$$= \sum_{k=0}^{N-1} x_{I_k}(I_k - K)$$

$$\vdots$$

$$p_0 \sum_{k=0}^{N-1}(I_k - K)^M + p_1 \sum_{k=0}^{N-1}(I_k - N)^{M+1} + \dots + p_M \sum_{k=0}^{N-1}(I_k - K)^{2M}$$

$$= \sum_{k=0}^{N-1} x_{I_k}(I_k - K)^M$$

$$(7.131)$$

A generalized least-squares polynomial fit is a five step process.

Step 1: Identify the data points to be fitted. This defines the $I_k$s and the $x_{I_k}$s in equation (7.131).

Step 2: Select the order of the polynomial, $M$, and its origin, $K$. In general, higher-order polynomials produce a better fit that lower order. Never select a polynomial with an order equal to or greater than the number of data points being fitted. If you choose too large an order, equations (7.131) will not have a solution.

Step 3: Evaluate the order of summations over $k$ in equation (7.131). If you want a general solution, do not substitute the specific data values for the $x_{I_k}$ and leave them as variables.

Step 4: Solve the set of simultaneous equations. Note that the number of equations and unknowns equals the order plus one of the polynomial. Usually, this solution requires a computer, especially if you are trying it with general data. The solutions to equation (7.131) are the coefficients of the least-squares polynomial.

Step 5: Use the polynomial model as dictated by the particular application.

Step 5 encompasses many of the applications discussed in the sections on exact polynomial modeling. The least-squares polynomial can be used to interpolate, differentiate, or any other operation a polynomial would be useful for.

There are two primary reasons for using a least-squares polynomial over an exact fit. The least-squares spans more data with a lower order polynomial than does the exact solution. This can be a great computational savings in those applications that tolerate the fitting error of the least-squares technique. The second and more important reason for using least-squares is that they tend to smooth the data as the polynomial is fitted. For example, consider the data in Figure 7.11. The sharp break in the data around $k = 2$ was smoothed out by the quadratic model. This smoothing property of least-squares polynomial modeling naturally removes fast transitions in the data or rapid fluctuations that are caused by high-frequency noise. Consider the following examples.

**Example:**  Fit a quadratic to five data points to smooth out the data.

   A typical piece of the data is shown in Figure 7.12a. The data appear to follow a smooth trajectory but are perturbed by random fluctuations. Such perturbations could be the consequence of high-frequency measurement noise. Let's use the smoothing property of least-squares polynomial modeling to reduce the fluctuations in the data.

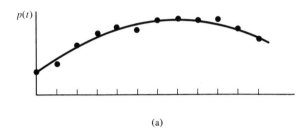

(a)

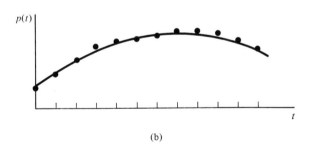

(b)

**Figure 7.12** Five-point smoother: (a) noisy data;
(b) smoothed data.

In this case, we will fit the five data points symmetrically distributed about $x_K$ to smooth the data in that region and use the smooth polynomial to derive a smoothed estimate of $x_k$. This is going to demand an evaluation of the polynomial at $t = K$, so let's save ourselves some time and originate the polynomial at $K$. Plugging these specifics into equation (7.130) produces the following set of simultaneous equations:

$$p_0 \sum_{k=0}^{4} (\underline{K+k-2-K})^i + p_1 \sum_{k=0}^{4} (\underline{K+k-2-K})^{i+1}$$

$$+ p_2 \sum_{k=0}^{4} (\underline{K+k-2-K})^{i+2} \tag{7.132}$$

$$= \sum_{k=0}^{4} x_{K+k-2}(\underline{K+k-2-K})^i$$

Notice that the underlined terms are $I_k$ in this example. This produces the following set of equations. Notice that the index of summation has been changed to $-2$ through $2$ to simplify the notation.

$$
\begin{aligned}
p_0 \sum_{k=-2}^{2} 1 \ + \ p_1 \sum_{k=-2}^{2} k \ + \ p_2 \sum_{k=-2}^{2} k^2 \ &= \ \sum_{k=-2}^{2}(x_{K+k})1 \\
p_0 \sum_{k=-2}^{2} k \ + \ p_1 \sum_{k=-2}^{2} k^2 \ + \ p_2 \sum_{k=-2}^{2} k^3 \ &= \ \sum_{k=-2}^{2}(x_{K+k})k \\
p_0 \sum_{k=-2}^{2} k^2 \ + \ p_1 \sum_{k=-2}^{2} k^3 \ + \ p_2 \sum_{k=-2}^{2} k^4 \ &= \ \sum_{k=-2}^{2}(x_{K+k})k^2
\end{aligned}
\tag{7.133}
$$

We evaluate the summations on the left-hand side to produce a specific set of equations. Notice that any odd power of $k$ produces a zero result because of the symmetric summation. We leave the right-hand side of equation (7.133) in its general form.

$$
\begin{aligned}
p_0 5 \ + \ p_1 0 \ + \ p_2 10 \ &= \ x_{K-2} + x_{K-1} + x_K + x_{K+1} + x_{K+2} \\
p_0 0 \ + \ p_1 10 + \ p_2 0 \ &= \ -2x_{K-2} - 1x_{K-1} + 0x_K + x_{K+1} + 2x_{K+2} \\
p_0 10 + \ p_1 0 \ + \ p_2 18 \ &= \ 4x_{K-2} + 1x_{K-1} + 0x_K + 1x_{K+1} + 4x_{K+2}
\end{aligned}
\tag{7.134}
$$

The general solution for the polynomial coefficients is obtained by typing the foregoing equations into a Gaussian elimination program.

$$
\begin{aligned}
p_0 &= -0.08571x_{K+2} + 0.3429x_{K+1} + 0.4857x_K \\
&\quad + 0.3429x_{K-1} - 0.08571x_{K-2} \\
p_1 &= 0.2x_{K+2} + 0.1x_{K+1} - 0.1x_{K-1} - 0.2x_{K-2} \\
p_2 &= 0.1428x_{K+2} - 0.0714x_{K+1} - 0.1428x_K \\
&\quad - 0.0714x_{K-1} + 0.1428x_{K-2}
\end{aligned}
\tag{7.135}
$$

This example is at step 5 of the least-squares technique. What do we do with the polynomial now that we have it? In this application we exploit the smoothing property of the least-squares fit to reduce the random fluctuations in the data. We do so by fitting the polynomial to each set of five data points, $x_{k-2}, \ldots, x_{k+2}$, and evaluate the polynomial in the middle of the set, $t = k$. This will produce a smoothed estimate of the center point, $x_k$. If we do this for all $k$, we will end up with a smoothed estimate of all our data.

Since we judiciously chose the origin of the polynomial at $t = k$, the evaluation of the polynomial is easy; the smoothed estimate is simply the $p_0$ for that data set. A general expression for $p_0$ is shown in the first equation of (7.135), so the smoothed estimate of $x_k$, call it $\tilde{x}_k$ is a five-coefficient nonrecursive digital filter.

$$\tilde{x}_k = p_0 = -0.08571x_{k+2} + 0.3429x_{k+1} + 0.4857x_k + 0.3429x_{k-1} - 0.08571x_{k-2} \tag{7.136}$$

Figure 7.12b shows the effect of smoothing the data of Figure 7.12a. There is less random fluctuation in the smoothed data; they look "cleaner" than the original. This smoothing filter [as shown in equation (7.136)] discriminates against the rapid fluctuations in the data while preserving the slowly changing components. In actuality, we have designed a low pass filter using least-squares polynomial techniques. The frequency response of the smoothing filter is shown in Figure 7.13.

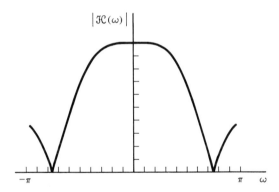

**Figure 7.13**  Frequency response of a five-point smoother.

Suppose that we needed a causal smoother for our particular application (a smoother that uses $x_k$ through $x_{k-4}$). We can produce such a smoother by centering the polynomial at $t = K$ and fitting the data points $x_K, x_{K-1}, x_{K-2}, x_{K-3}, x_{K-4}$. This generates a different expression for $p_0$, one that does not require future $x_k$s.

A whole class of polynomial smoothing filters can be generated by repeating the previous example with different-order polynomials and a different number of points. Some of the more popular filters are shown below.

Quadratic fitted to 5 points:

$$\tilde{x}_k = -\frac{3}{35}x_{k+2} + \frac{12}{35}x_{k+1} + \frac{17}{35}x_k + \frac{12}{35}x_{k-1} - \frac{3}{35}x_{k-2} \qquad (7.137)$$

Quadratic fitted to 7 points:

$$\tilde{x}_k = -\frac{2}{21}x_{k+3} + \frac{3}{21}x_{k+2} + \frac{6}{21}x_{k+1} + \frac{7}{21}x_k + \frac{6}{21}x_{k-1} + \frac{3}{21}x_{k-2} - \frac{2}{21}x_{k-3} \ (7.138)$$

Quadratic fitted to 11 points:

$$\begin{aligned}
\tilde{x}_k = &-\frac{21}{231}x_{k+4} + \frac{14}{231}x_{k+3} + \frac{39}{231}x_{k+2} + \frac{54}{231}x_{k+1} + \frac{59}{231}x_k \\
&+ \frac{54}{231}x_{k-1} + \frac{39}{231}x_{k-2} + \frac{14}{231}x_{k-3} - \frac{21}{231}x_{k-4}
\end{aligned} \qquad (7.139)$$

Fourth-order polynomial fitted to 7 points:

$$\begin{aligned}
\tilde{x}_k = &\frac{5}{231}x_{k+3} - \frac{30}{231}x_{k+2} + \frac{75}{231}x_{k+1} + \frac{131}{231}x_k + \frac{75}{231}x_{k-1} \\
&- \frac{30}{231}x_{k-2} + \frac{5}{231}x_{k-3}
\end{aligned} \qquad (7.140)$$

Fourth-order polynomial fitted to 11 points:

$$\begin{aligned}
\tilde{x}_k = &\frac{15}{429}x_{k+4} - \frac{55}{429}x_{k+3} + \frac{30}{429}x_{k+2} + \frac{135}{429}x_{k+1} + \frac{179}{429}x_k \\
&+ \frac{135}{429}x_{k-1} + \frac{30}{429}x_{k-2} - \frac{55}{429}x_{k-3} + \frac{15}{429}x_{k-4}
\end{aligned} \qquad (7.141)$$

It is also reasonable to fit the second and fourth polynomials to 9, 13, 15, or even larger numbers of data points. Those smoothing filters were left out because the 7- and 11-data point smoothers are usually enough. In most cases, you can use the polynomial smoothers by simply applying equations (7.137) through (7.141). In those special situations in which one of these smoothers cannot be directly applied, a specialized smoother can be derived by following the example.

This example uses least-squares polynomial fitting to derive a differentiator that is less sensitive to the random fluctuations of the data.

**Example:** Construct an estimator for the derivative of a digital signal by fitting a quadratic to five data points.

Fortunately, we have just fitted the quadratic to the center of five data points, so there is no need to repeat that feat. The derivative of the polynomial at $t = K$ is simply $p_1$, so our estimator takes the form of a nonrecursive digital filter.

$$x'_k \approx p_1 = 0.2x_{k+2} + 0.1x_{k+1} - 0.1x_{k-1} - 0.2x_{k-2} \qquad (7.142)$$

This is the estimator of the smoothed derivative of the data. It is handy when the data are smooth but have been corrupted by rapid fluctuations. As shown in Figure 7.14, this differentiator discriminates against the higher-frequency components of the signal, while the conventional differentiator (Figure 7.14a) has more high-frequency gain.

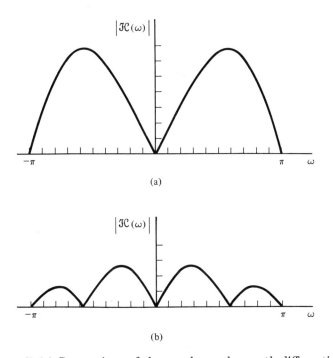

Figure 7.14 Comparison of the regular and smooth differentiators' frequency response: (a) third-order differentiator; (b) smooth differentiator.

In summary, lower-order polynomials can be fitted to data to produce least-squares fits. Because these polynomials do not have enough degrees of freedom (i.e., coefficients), they seldom produce an exact match to the data points. It is always possible to find a polynomial that produces the least-squares error match to the data. This least-squares polynomial generates a smooth model of the data; it does not go through all the data points but it comes as close as "smoothly" possible. These polynomials tend to ignore rapid changes in the data, "glitches," and high-frequency fluctuations. Rather, they model the low-frequency or smooth components of the data. This feature makes the least-squares curve fitting a natural for matching slowly varying data that are corrupted by rapidly varying noise.

## 7.6 Summary

Polynomial modeling of digital data builds a necessary bridge between the digital and analog worlds. With this technique we can replace digital data with continuous models of the data. These polynomial models lend themselves nicely to mathematical operations such as differentiation and integration and can be evaluated at any point to estimate nonexisting data. The primary uses of polynomial modeling are in interpolation, extrapolation, and estimation of mathematical functions on digital data.

We have two options when fitting polynomials to the data points. We can perform an exact fit by choosing a polynomial order of one less than the number of data points being fit. If we use a lower-order polynomial, we can perform a smoothed fit by finding the least-squares polynomial coefficients. The degree of smoothness in a least-squares fit is dictated by the difference between the order of the polynomial and the number of points being fitted. As the polynomial's order is reduced, the model becomes smoother and less like the data points. Therefore, classes of polynomial processing can be developed based on how closely the polynomial matches the data. We can have integrators that are based on exact models of the data or have various degrees of smooth integrators by adjusting the order of the polynomial.

The polynomial methods discussed in this chapter are also appropriate for custom situations. For example, polynomials are used to estimate the trajectory of an object based on discrete measurements of the object's velocity (the first derivative) or acceleration (second derivative). In this case, the first or second derivative of the polynomial is fitted to the data and the polynomial is interpreted as the trajectory. Polynomial modeling is one of the most powerful general-purpose tools in signal processing. When it comes to polynomial curve fitting, the applications are generally limited only by the user's imagination.

Exercises

**253**
## EXERCISES

7-1. Find the lowest-order polynomials that fit the following sets of data.

(a) $x_0$, $x_1$, and $x_2$

(b) $x_0$

(c) $x_0$, $x_{-1}$, $x_{-2}$, and $x_{-1}$

7-2. Find the coefficients of the lowest-order polynomials that match the following sets of data. Originate the polynomials at $t = 0$.

(a) $x_1 = 1$ and $x_2 = 1$

(b) $x_1 = 3$ and $x_2 = 4$

(c) $x_{-1} = 3$, $x_2 = 4$, and $x_5 = 6$

(d) $x_{-1} = 3$, $x_2 = 4$, and $x_5 = 3$

(e) $x_{-1} = 4$, $x.1 = 3$, $x_2 = 4$, and $x_3 = 5$

(f) $x_{-1} = 4$, $x_1 = 3$, $x_2 = 4$, and $x_1 = 3$

7-3. Do Exercise 7-2 but originate the polynomial at the first data point — the data point with the smallest index.

7-4. Polynomials are not the only functions that are useful for modeling. Suppose that we use a cosine function as a model.

$$p(t) = A \cos \omega t$$

In this case, $A$ and $\omega$ are the modeling parameters.

(a) Attempt to fit $A \cos \omega t$ to the data points $x_0$ and $x_1$. Are there any values of data where the cosine will not work?

(b) Attempt to fit $A \cos \omega t$ to the data points $x_1$ and $x_2$.

(c) Attempt to fit $A \cos \omega t$ to the data points $x_{-1}$ and $x_1$. For this attempt, what is the deficiency of the cosine function?

(d) Attempt to fit $A \cos \omega t$ to $x_0$, $x_1$, and $x_2$. What is the deficiency of the cosine function in this situation?

7-5. Do Exercise 7-4 but use $A \sin \omega t$ instead of the cosine.

7-6. Attempt to fit
$$p(t) = p_0 t + p_1 t^3$$
to the following data. For each part remark on the utility of this modeling function.

     (a) $x_0 = 0$, $x_1 = 2$, and $x_2 = 1$

     (b) $x_0 = 1$, $x_1 = 2$, and $x_2 = 1$

     (c) $x_{-1} = -1$, $x_0 = 0$, and $x_1 = 1$

     (d) $x_{-1} = 1$, $x_0 = 0$, and $x_1 = 1$

7-7. Attempt to fit

$$p(t) = p_0 t + p_1 t^2$$

to the following data. Remark on the utility of this polynomial for each part.

     (a) $x_0 = 0$, $x_1 = 2$, and $x_2 = 1$

     (b) $x_0 = 1$, $x_1 = 2$, and $x_2 = 1$

     (c) $x_{-1} = 1$, $x_0 = 0$, and $x_1 = 1$

7-8. Use polynomial curve-fitting techniques to estimate $x_k$ from the following data.

     (a) $x_{k-1}$

     (b) $x_{k+1}$

     (c) $x_{k-1}$ and $x_{k-2}$

     (d) $x_{k-1}$ and $x_{k+2}$

7-9. Use polynomial curve-fitting techniques to estimate $x_k$ from the following data.

     (a) $x_{k-1}$, $x_{k+1}$, and $x_{k+2}$

     (b) $x_{k-2}$, $x_{k-1}$, and $x_{k+1}$

     (c) $x_{k-1}$, $x_k$, and $x_{k+1}$

7-10. Consider polynomial curve fitting to estimate $x_k$ from $x_{k-2}$, $x_{k-1}$, $x_{k+1}$, and $x_{k+2}$.

     (a) What is the lowest-order polynomial for this application?

     (b) Set up the system of equations for a polynomial originated at $t = 0$.

     (c) Set up the system of equations for a polynomial originated at $t = k$.

     (d) Which set of equations [part (b) or (c)] is easier to solve?

7-11. Suppose that $x_{k-2} = 2$, $x_{k-1} = 1$, $x_{k+1} = 2$, and $x_{k+2} = 3$. Estimate $x_k$ by polynomial curve fitting.

7-12. Use polynomial curve fitting to interpolate $x(k+0.5)$ from $x_k$ and $x_{k+1}$.

7-13. Use polynomial curve fitting to interpolate $x(k+0.1)$ from $x_{k-1}$, $x_k$, and $x_{k+1}$. Remember the condor chick example; it just might save you some time.

7-14. Use polynomial curve fitting to interpolate $x(k+0.5)$ from $x_k$, $x_{k+1}$, and $x_{k+2}$.

7-15. Extrapolate $x_{10}$ from $x_9 = 10$ and $x_8 = 8$.

7-16. Extrapolate $x_{10}$ from $x_8 = 8$, $x_7 = 7$, and $x_6 = 5$.

7-17.  Use the central difference formula to estimate the derivative of the following data.

(a) $x_0 = 1$, $x_1 = 3$, $x_2 = 5$, $x_3 = 7$, $x_4 = 8$, and $x_5 = 9$

(b) $x_k = 3 + 0.5k$

What is the accuracy of the central difference formula for this signal? Compare $x_k'$ with the real derivative of these data, 0.5?

(c) $x_k = k^3$

Compare the estimated derivative, $x_k'$, with the actual derivative of these data, $2k$. Why aren't they the same?

7-18.  Suppose that we use polynomial curve fitting to estimate the fourth derivative of digital data.

(a) What is the lowest-order polynomial that will yield such an estimate?

(b) Express the derivative in terms of the polynomial coefficients.

7-19. Use the trapezoidal approximation to estimate the integral of the following data.

$$x_0 = 1 \quad x_1 = 2 \quad x_2 = 4 \quad x_3 = 3 \quad x_4 = 1 \quad x_5 = 1$$

7-20.  Do Exercise 7-19 but use the $\frac{3}{8}$'s rule of integration instead of the trapezoidal rule. Is the $\frac{3}{8}$'s rule more accurate than the trapezoidal?

7-21. What kinds of signals can be integrated with the trapezoidal rule without error?

7-22. Use a first-order polynomial to estimate the double integral of digital data.

7-23. Use a quadratic to estimate the double integral of digital data.

7-24. Compute the coefficients of a first-order polynomial that is the best least-squares fit to the following data. Originate the polynomial at $t = 0$.

    (a) $x_0 = 3$, $x_1 = 5$, and $x_2 = 4$

    (b) $x_0 = 0$ and $x_1 = 3$

    (c) $x_{-1} = 1$, $x_0 = 1$, and $x_2 = 3$

7-25. Compute the coefficients of the quadratic that is the least-squares fit to the following data. Originate the polynomial at $t = 1$.

    (a) $x_0 = 3$, $x_1 = 5$, $x_2 = 4$, and $x_3 = 2$

    (b) $x_0 = 3$, $x_1 = 5$, and $x_2 = 4$

    (c) $x_{-2} = 3$, $x_{-1} = 2$, $x_1 = 2$, and $x_2 = 3$

7-26. Construct an estimator for the second derivative of a digital signal by fitting a quadratic to five data points.

7-27. Construct an estimator for the integral of a digital signal by fitting a first-order polynomial to three data points.

$$\int_k^{k+2} x_k = ?$$

7-28. Construct an estimator for the integral of a digital signal by fitting a quadratic to five data points.

# Discrete and Fast Fourier Transforms

Chapter 2 showed the importance of frequency response in characterizing the behavior of a digital filter. Chapter 3 continued the discussion by developing the relationship between the impulse and the frequency response. We found that sometimes a designer wishes to express a filter in terms of its frequency response, and at other times the impulse response is the best characterization of the filter. In this way the designer can represent the filter, in either the frequency domain (frequency response) or the time domain (impulse response).

This chapter develops a digital technique for going between the time and frequency domains. With this technique, we can use a digital computer to compute the impulse response from a frequency response, or the frequency response from the impulse response. Furthermore, such a tool can be applied to general digital signals, thereby computing the frequency-domain representation of any signal. This technique is the *discrete Fourier transform* (DFT) and its efficient implementation, the *fast Fourier transform* (FFT).

## 8.1 DISCRETE FOURIER TRANSFORM

We begin the development of the DFT by looking for a way to compute the impulse and frequency responses with a computer. Chapters 2 and 3 showed that they are related through integral and summation equations.

$$h_k = \frac{1}{2\pi} \int_{-\pi}^{\pi} \mathcal{H}(\omega)e^{j\omega k} \, d\omega \tag{8.1}$$

**257**

$$\mathcal{H}(\omega) = \sum_{k=-\infty}^{\infty} h_k e^{-j\omega k} \tag{8.2}$$

These two equations are specialized applications of the Fourier series. The first shows how to compute the Fourier coefficients (in this case the $h_k$s) from a periodic function, $\mathcal{H}(\omega)$, and the second equation shows how to express the periodic function in terms of its Fourier coefficients.

Relating the frequency and impulse responses is only one of the many uses of the Fourier expansion. Through this technique it is possible to represent any periodic signal in terms of its spectral or frequency components. This gives an investigator tremendous flexibility, because information that is hidden in a signal might become obvious when the signal's spectrum (Fourier coefficients) is computed. This is simply an extension of our experience with frequency and impulse responses; sometimes one is preferred over the other. Because the Fourier expansion is such an important tool, a convenient method for its computation is highly desirable. This section develops a method for computing Fourier expansions on a digital computer.

It is helpful to start the derivation by asking: Why can't equations (8.1) and (8.2) be evaluated on a computer as they stand? The impediment posed by equation (8.1) is obvious. It requires an integral and computers simply refuse to integrate; summation is the closest a computer can come. Equation (8.2) cannot be evaluated because it involves an infinite summation (requiring infinite computer time) and because $\omega$ is a continuous variable. However, the problems with equation (8.2) appear less formidable than the integral, so let's begin by massaging equation (8.2) into a computable form.

The infinite summation in equation (8.2) is an insurmountable problem. The only way around it is to restrict our attention to FIR filters. While we are simplifying the problem, let's consider only causal FIR filters. The causality restriction is not necessary for the development (as the FIR assumption is), but it is going to simplify notation. The frequency response of an $N$-coefficient, causal filter is shown as follows:

$$\mathcal{H}(\omega) = \sum_{k=0}^{N-1} h_k e^{-j\omega k} \tag{8.3}$$

For any given $\omega$, say $\omega_o$, we can use a computer to evaluate $\mathcal{H}(\omega_0)$.

$$\mathcal{H}(\omega_0) = \sum_{k=0}^{N-1} h_k \cos \omega_0 k - j \sum_{k=0}^{N-1} h_k \sin \omega_0 k \tag{8.4}$$

But we cannot use the computer to evaluate $\mathcal{H}(\omega)$ for all possible $\omega$ because there are too many of them (like an infinite number). The range of $\omega$ is reduced by exploiting the fact that $\mathcal{H}(\omega)$ is periodic in $2\pi$. So it is not necessary to compute the frequency response for all $\omega$; any $2\pi$ interval will do. This still does not make the frequency response computable on a computer, because there are still an infinite number of $\omega$s in any $2\pi$ interval. Hence we must restrict ourselves to a discrete number of $\omega$s in the $2\pi$ interval. In other words, $\omega$ is a continuous independent variable. So, in order to evaluate $\mathcal{H}(\omega)$ on a computer we must sample it. Consider the frequency response at only $M$ evenly spaced intervals from 0 to $2\pi$, $\mathcal{H}(i2\pi/M)$ and $i = 0, 1, \ldots, M-1$. This is called the discretized frequency response and can be evaluated by a computer.

$$\mathcal{H}\left(i\frac{2\pi}{M}\right) = \sum_{k=0}^{N-1} h_k e^{-j\left(\frac{2\pi}{M}i\right)k} \qquad i = 0, 1, \ldots, M-1 \tag{8.5}$$

This is the regular (continuous) frequency response with all occurrences of $\omega$ replaced by $\frac{2\pi}{M}i$.

This frequency response is computed by picking an $i$ (equivalent to picking a frequency) and grinding through the $N$ terms of the summation to generate $\mathcal{H}(i2\pi/M)$. To compute a full period of the discretized frequency, this process is repeated for $i = 0$ through $M-1$.

$$\mathcal{H}(0) = \sum_{k=0}^{N-1} h_k e^{-j\frac{2\pi}{M}0k} = \sum_{k=0}^{N-1} h_k$$

$$\mathcal{H}\left(\frac{2\pi}{M}\right) = \sum_{k=0}^{N-1} h_k e^{-j\frac{2\pi}{M}k} \tag{8.6}$$

$$\vdots$$

$$\mathcal{H}\left((M-1)\frac{2\pi}{M}\right) = \sum_{k=0}^{N-1} h_k e^{-j\frac{2\pi}{M}(M-1)k}$$

The question now is, how does one go about picking the value for $M$? The naive approach is to use the largest value of $M$ possible. The drawback is that larger $M$'s mean more components of equation (8.6) and the frequency response becomes increasingly more expensive to compute. Fortunately, it is not necessary to resort to such a forceful and expensive approach. We will see that selecting $M = N$ is sufficient, and evaluating the frequency response at more points is usually not warranted.

The key to this development is the definition of "sufficient." If we find the dc response of the filter is sufficient, a single term of the frequency response, $\mathcal{H}(0)$, will do. If we declare that nothing short of the complete frequency response is sufficient, we are back to computing $\mathcal{H}(\omega)$ for all $\omega$. Neither of the previous definitions is reasonable — the first provides too little information and the second demands too much. Rather, we are taking a middle track. We say that we have a "sufficient" number of points of the frequency response if it is possible to compute the filter's impulse response from the samples of the frequency response. In other words, we demand sufficient frequency information so that, when some form of equation (8.1) is applied to the samples of the frequency response, a reasonable facsimile of the impulse response results.

Therefore, before proceding with this derivation, we must put equation (8.1) into a form that the computer will accept. The easiest approach is to replace the integral with a summation and see what comes out when $\mathcal{H}(i2\pi/M)$ is applied. It would be unreasonable to assume that such an approximation will produce the filter's impulse response, $h_k$. So we will denote the result of the approximation to equation (8.1) $\tilde{h}_k$ and hope that it will be close to the actual impulse response.

$$\tilde{h}_l = \sum_{}^{M-1} \mathcal{H}\left(i\frac{2\pi}{M}\right) e^{j\frac{2\pi}{M}il} \tag{8.7}$$

the integral is approximated with the summation.

The relationship between $\tilde{h}_k$ and $h_k$ is developed by substituting the expression for $\mathcal{H}(i2\pi/M)$ into equation (8.7).

$$\tilde{h}_l = \sum_{i=0}^{M-1} \left[ \sum_{k=0}^{N-1} h_k e^{-j\frac{2\pi}{M}ki} \right] e^{j\frac{2\pi}{M}il} \tag{8.8}$$

The derivation is continued by combining the exponentials and interchanging the summations.

$$\tilde{h}_l = \sum_{k=0}^{N-1} h_k \sum_{i=0}^{M-1} e^{j\frac{2\pi}{M}i(l-k)} \tag{8.9}$$

The summation over $i$ is a finite sum of a geometric progression. In general, such a sum has a closed form:

$$\sum_{i=0}^{M-1} r^i = \frac{1-r^M}{1-r} \tag{8.10}$$

In this case "$r$" is $e^{j\frac{2\pi}{M}(l-k)}$. So the reconstructed impulse response has the following form.

$$\tilde{h}_l = \sum_{k=0}^{N-1} h_k \frac{1 - e^{j\frac{2\pi}{M}(l-k)M}}{1 - e^{j\frac{2\pi}{M}(l-k)}}$$

$$= \sum_{k=0}^{N-1} h_k \frac{1 - e^{j2\pi(l-k)}}{1 - e^{j\frac{2\pi}{M}(l-k)}} \tag{8.11}$$

The numerator is always zero, because $e^{j2\pi(l-k)}$ is a fancy name for 1 when $k$ and $l$ are integers. But do not jump to the conclusion that the $\tilde{h}_l$s are all zero. When the difference between $l$ and $k$ is an integer multiple of $M$ ($l-k = 0, \pm M, \pm 2M, \ldots$), the denominator is also zero and $\tilde{h}_l$ can take on a nonzero value. A quick application of l'Hospital's rule shows that the terms of equation (8.11) take on the value of $M$ when $l - k$ is an integer times $M$.

$$\frac{1 - e^{j2\pi(l-k)}}{1 - e^{j\frac{2\pi}{M}(l-k)}} = \begin{cases} M & k = l, l \pm M, l \pm 2M, \dots \\ 0 & \text{otherwise} \end{cases} \tag{8.12}$$

We apply this result to equation (8.11) and find that $\tilde{h}_l$ is the sum of all $h_k$ such that $k = l, l - M, l + M, l - 2M, l + 2M, \dots$. In other words,

$$\tilde{h}_l = M \sum_{i=-\infty}^{\infty} h_{l+iM} \tag{8.13}$$

This equation might look hopeless, but it has a nice pictorial interpretation. The reconstructed impulse response, $\tilde{h}_l$, is the sum of an infinite number of elements of the filter's impulse response. For example, $\tilde{h}_0$ is the sum of $h_0$, $h_{-M}$, $h_M$, $h_{-2M}$, $h_{2M}$, and so on. This operation is depicted in Figure 8.1. The top plot shows the filter's unshifted impulse response [corresponding to $i = 0$ in equation (8.13)], the second plot shows the impulse response shifted to the left by $M$ points (corresponding to $i = 1$), the third plot shows the impulse response for $i = -1$, and so on. The reconstructed impulse response is the sum of the filter's impulse response, which is shifted by all possible integer multiples of $M$.

As shown in Figure 8.1, the reconstructed impulse response, $\tilde{h}_l$, is periodic in $M$ and will never strictly equal $h_k$. However, when $M$ is large enough so that the shifted versions of $h_k$ do not overlap (as shown in Figure 8.1), $\tilde{h}_l$ is simply $h_k$ repeated every $M$ indices and scaled by a multiplicative factor of $M$. So, when $M$ is large enough to prevent overlap,

$$\tilde{h}_l = Mh_k \qquad l = 0, 1, 2, \dots, M - 1 \tag{8.14}$$

And the reconstructed impulse response is always periodic.

$$\tilde{h}_l = \tilde{h}_{l+M} \tag{8.15}$$

The question is: How large must $M$ be to prevent overlap? This occurs when $h_k$ and $h_{k+M}$ have no common nonzero terms. The unshifted impulse response, $h_k$, has nonzero terms from $k = 0$ to $N - 1$, and the shifted impulse response, $h_{k+M}$, has nonzero terms from $k = -M$ to $-M + N - 1$. So for them to contain no overlapping nonzero terms, $M$ must be large enough so that the rightmost nonzero term of $h_{k+M}$ (that's $h_{-M+N-1}$) does not overlap the leftmost nonzero term of $h_k$ ($h_0$). This means that

$$M + N - 1 < 0 \tag{8.16}$$

or

$$M \geq N. \tag{8.17}$$

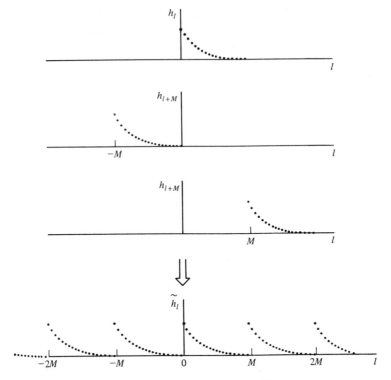

**Figure 8.1** Relationship between $\tilde{h}_k$ and $h_k$.

Studying Figure 8.1 will show that if $M \geq N$, none of the shifted versions of $h_k$ will overlap. Therefore, $N$ samples of the filter's frequency response are sufficient to reconstruct the filter's impulse response. We need only $N$ evaluations of the frequency response. Computing more only increases the period of the reconstructed impulse response, but will not otherwise provide a better reconstruction. In conclusion, we will waste the computer's time (and our money) by calculating more than $N$ points of the frequency response.

In summary, if the frequency response is evaluated at only $N$ frequencies, $i\frac{2\pi}{N}$, the filter's impulse response can be reconstructed from the $N$ values of the frequency response. We compute the discrete values of the frequency response via

$$\mathcal{H}\left(i\frac{2\pi}{N}\right) = \sum_{k=0}^{N-1} h_k e^{-j\frac{2\pi}{N}ki} \qquad i = 0, 1, \ldots, N-1 \qquad (8.18)$$

We reconstruct the impulse response via

$$h_k = \frac{1}{N} \sum_{i=0}^{N-1} \mathcal{H}\left(i\frac{2\pi}{N}\right) e^{j\frac{2\pi}{N}ik} \qquad k = 0, 1, \ldots, N-1 \qquad (8.19)$$

Equation (8.18) is the definition of the discrete Fourier transform, commonly called the DFT, and equation (8.19) is the inverse discrete Fourier transform, commonly called the IDFT. The DFT transforms the filter's impulse response (description of the filter in the time domain) to a frequency response (description in the frequency domain). The IDFT, as its name implies, does the inverse. It transforms the frequency-domain description into the time domain, $\mathcal{H}\left(i2\pi/N\right) \rightarrow h_k$. Remember that the DFT and the IDFT produce periodic results with periods of $N$. So the IDFT does not really reconstruct the filter's impulse response. Rather, it reconstructs a periodic version of the impulse response. Many a DFT user has been mislead by this property of the IDFT — it is important to keep it in mind.

The DFT and the IDFT allow us to represent the filter in either the frequency or time domain without losing information. That is, we can transform the impulse response to the frequency response (DFT), then turn the frequency response back into an impulse response with the IDFT. Later sections will illustrate the utility of moving between the frequency and time domains. But first some examples and further development of the properties of the DFT and the IDFT.

**Example:** Use the DFT to compute the discrete frequency response of a filter with the following impulse response.

$$h_1 = 1 \quad h_2 = 2 \quad h_3 = 3$$

This is a truncated ramp. This impulse response is associated with a nonrecursive filter with three coefficients: $c_1 = 1$, $c_2 = 2$, and $c_3 = 3$. In this case $N = 4$, and the DFT takes on the specific form

$$\mathcal{H}\left(i\frac{2\pi}{4}\right) = \sum_{k=0}^{3} h_k e^{-j\frac{2\pi}{4}ki} \qquad i = 0, 1, 2, 3 \tag{8.20}$$

This DFT is simple enough to compute by hand.

$$\mathcal{H}(0) = \sum_{k=0}^{3} k e^{-j\frac{\pi}{2}k0}$$

$$= 1 + 2 + 3 = 6$$

$$\mathcal{H}\left(\frac{\pi}{2}\right) = \sum_{k=0}^{3} k e^{-j\frac{\pi}{2}k}$$

(8.21a)

$$= e^{-j\frac{\pi}{2}} + 2e^{-j\pi} + 3e^{-j\frac{3\pi}{2}} = -2 + 2j$$

$$\mathcal{H}(\pi) = \sum_{k=0}^{3} k = e^{-j\pi k}$$

$$= e^{-j\pi} + 2e^{-j\pi 2} + 3e^{-j\pi 3} = -2$$

$$\mathcal{H}\left(\frac{3\pi}{2}\right) = \sum_{k=0}^{3} ke^{-j\frac{3\pi}{2}k}$$

$$= e^{-j\frac{3\pi}{2}} + 2e^{-j3\pi} + 3e^{-j\frac{9\pi}{2}} = -2 - 2j$$

(8.21$b$)

The discrete frequency response is shown in Figure 8.2.

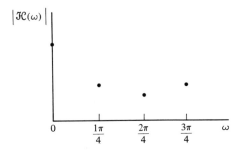

**Figure 8.2** Discrete frequency response.

With these few points the discrete frequency response does not provide much information — we know the filter's gain at only four frequencies. However, this is not really a problem, because such a short filter cannot generate a rapidly changing frequency response. So this filter's frequency response will slowly change between the four points evaluated by the DFT. The complete response for this filter is shown in Figure 8.3. Notice that the four points of the DFT show many of the features of the full frequency response. You might ask: What happens when we deal with longer filters, filters with more rapidly varying frequency responses? Well, the DFT takes care of that because it computes $N$ frequency points, where $N$ is the length of the filter. Longer filters demand more DFT frequency points.

**Example**: Continue the example by showing that the four points of the frequency response are indeed enough to reconstruct the filter's impulse response; they provide sufficient information.

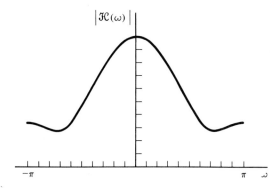

**Figure 8.3** Frequency response of a four-point filter.

This is done by plugging our values of $\mathcal{H}(i2\pi/M)$ into the IDFT equation.

$$h_0 = \frac{1}{4} \sum_{i=0}^{3} \mathcal{H}\left(i\frac{2\pi}{4}\right) e^{j\frac{2\pi}{4}i0}$$

$$= \frac{1}{4}\left[6 + (-2 + 2j) - 2 + (-2 - 2j)\right]$$

$$= 0$$

$$h_1 = \frac{1}{4} \sum_{i=0}^{3} \mathcal{H}\left(i\frac{\pi}{4}\right) e^{j\frac{2\pi}{4}i}$$

$$= \frac{1}{4}\left[6e^{j\frac{\pi}{2}0} + (-2 + 2j)e^{j\frac{\pi}{2}} - 2e^{j\pi} + (-2 - 2j)e^{\frac{j3\pi}{2}}\right]$$

$$= 1$$

(8.22)

In a similar way, $h_2$ and $h_3$ can be computed from the discrete frequency response. Even though we are interested only in $h_0$ through $h_3$ (because the original filter had a short response), the IDFT will provide $h_k$s for any $k$. For instance, we can compute $h_5$ by plugging $i = 5$ into the IDFT, or we can find it by using the feature that the impulse response computed from the IDFT is periodic in $N$; $h_5 = h_1$. Check this by starting the computation of $h_5$.

$$h_5 = \frac{1}{4} \sum_{i=0}^{3} \mathcal{H}\left(i\frac{2\pi}{4}\right) e^{j\frac{2\pi}{4}5k}$$

(8.23)

But note that $e^{j(2\pi/4)5k} = e^{j(2\pi/4 + 2\pi)k} = e^{j(2\pi/4)k}$. So $h_5$ has the same expression as $h_1$. There is no need to complete the computation, and actually there was no reason to start it in the first place. The reconstructed impulse response is periodic in $N$.

The DFT notation developed to date is really too cumbersome to use effectively — we are forced to write out sums and complex exponentials for every DFT. Because the DFT is so widely used and because the rest of this chapter is devoted to discovering it, it is worthwhile to develop some convenient, shorthand notation for the DFT.

First, the discrete frequency response, $\mathcal{H}(i2\pi/N)$ is denoted $\mathcal{H}_i$ — the $2\pi/N$ term is left understood. Second, the DFT and IDFT equations are represented by the $DFT_N\{\ \}$ and $IDFT_N\{\ \}$ operators. These notations are summarized as follows:

$$\mathcal{H}_i = DFT_N\{h_k\} \iff \mathcal{H}\left(i\frac{2\pi}{N}\right) = \sum_{k=0}^{N-1} h_k e^{-j\frac{2\pi}{N}ki} \qquad (8.24)$$

and

$$h_k = IDFT_N\{\mathcal{H}_i\} \iff h_k = \frac{1}{N}\sum_{i=0}^{N-1} \mathcal{H}\left(i\frac{2\pi}{N}\right) e^{j\frac{2\pi}{N}ik}$$

Remember that this compact notation is introduced only to make the discussion more convenient, and nothing of substance has been changed.

The DFT was developed by looking for computer-based techniques for evaluating the frequency response. However, there is no reason to continue to restrict the DFTs to impulse and frequency responses. Mathematically, the DFT can be applied to any finite-length digital signal, say $x_k$, to produce a frequency representation of the signal — call it $X_i$. Of course, the frequency representation, $X_i$, will not be a frequency response unless $x_k$ happens to be an impulse response. But it just might prove to be an informative way of representing $x_k$. This generalization of the frequency response introduces the broad and active field of spectral estimation: where digital signals are transformed from the time domain, $x_k$, to the frequency domain, $X_i$. This transformation is done in an attempt to extract more information out of the signal or to simplify its manipulation. In general, any $N$-point signal can be transformed to its frequency representation via the DFT.

$$X_i = DFT_N\{x_k\} \qquad i = 0, 1, \ldots, N-1 \qquad (8.25)$$

Like all DFTs, this transformation preserves the properties of the $N$-point signal, so the original signal can be reconstructed from the frequency respresentation via the IDFT.

$$x_k = IDFT_N\{X_i\} \qquad k = 0, 1, \ldots, N-1 \qquad (8.26)$$

The remainder of this chapter develops the properties of the DFT as used on impulse responses or general digital signals, and it explores some of the uses of the DFT.

## 8.2    THE DFT AND THE $z$-TRANSFORM

We have developed the DFT as if it were a digital technique for computing frequency responses or a general method for representing digital signals in the frequency domain. Actually, the DFT is just a special case of the $z$-transform. We develop this relationship to show how the DFT is connected to the earlier work.

The $z$-transform of an $N$-point causal filter is the sum of the impulse response weighted by $z^{-k}$.

$$\mathcal{H}_z(z) = \sum_{k=0}^{N-1} h_k z^{-k} \tag{8.27}$$

The DFT of that filter is computed through a similar expression.

$$\mathcal{H}_i = \sum_{k=0}^{N-1} h_k e^{-j \frac{2\pi}{N} ki} \tag{8.28}$$

Equation (8.28) is just a special case of equation (8.27); $z$ has been replaced with $e^{j \frac{2\pi}{N} i}$. Therefore, the $i$th coefficient of the DFT is the $z$-transform evaluated at $z = e^{j \frac{2\pi}{N} i}$.

$$\mathcal{H}_i = \mathcal{H}_z(z) \Big|_{z = e^{j \frac{2\pi}{N} i}} \tag{8.29}$$

This relationship is pictorially shown in Figure 8.4. The DFT coefficients are evaluated around the unit circle. The angle between successive coefficients is $2\pi/N$, so as $N$ increases, the DFT yields a more accurate representation of the $z$-transform around the unit circle.

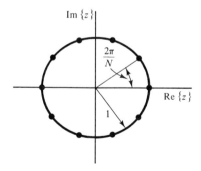

**Figure 8.4** Relationship between DFT and $z$-transform.

This relationship should not be too surprising. The frequency response of the filter is its $z$-transform evaluated around the unit circle, and the DFT is a technique for computing the frequency response. The connection between the DFT and the $z$-transform is mentioned to show the common features of both techniques. Do not misconstrue this and attempt to compute the DFT via the $z$-transform; this is not proposed as a practical computation scheme.

## 8.3  PROPERTIES OF THE DFT

The DFT is so heavily used in digital filter design and digital signal processing that it is worth the effort to review some of the generalized properties of the DFT. In this way the DFT can be used and appreciated without constantly going back to the cumbersome DFT equations.

### The DFT is linear:

The DFT is a linear operator, so we can easily deal with DFTs of sums of signals or scaled signals.

This is shown by resorting to the argument used to show that digital filters are linear. Suppose that an $N$-point digital signal, $x_k$, produces a spectrum, $X_i$, and another $N$-point digital signal, $z_k$, produces the DFT coefficients, $Z_i$. Compute the DFT coefficients produced by the signal $ax_k + bz_k$, where $a$ and $b$ are constants. This problem is fairly straightforward; just plug $ax_k + bz_k$ into the definition of the DFT.

$$DFT_N\{ax_k + bz_k\} = \sum_{k=0}^{N-1} (ax_k + bz_k)e^{-j\frac{2\pi}{N}ki} \qquad (8.30)$$

Now split the sum and move the $a$ and $b$ constants outside the sums.

$$DFT_N\{ax_k + bz_k\} = a\sum_{k=0}^{N-1} x_k e^{-j\frac{2\pi}{N}ki} + b\sum_{k=0}^{N-1} z_k e^{-j\frac{2\pi}{N}ki} \quad (8.31)$$

The right-hand side of equation (8.31) is the sums of the DFTs of $x_k$ and $z_k$, weighted by the constants $a$ and $b$, respectively. Therefore,

$$DFT_N\{ax_k + bz_k\} = aX_i + bZ_i \qquad (8.32)$$

The DFT is a linear operator.

### The IDFT is linear:

The IDFT is a linear operator. That is, if $x_k = IDFT_N\{X_i\}$ and $z_k = IDFT_N\{Z_i\}$, then

$$IDFT_N\{aX_i + bZ_i\} = ax_k + by_k \qquad (8.33)$$

The IDFT is so close to the DFT that it is not necessary to repeat the development. Simply plug $ax_k + bz_k$ into the IDFT equation, which results in an equation that looks like equation (8.30). Then separate the summation to get an equation like (8.31). The development is complete when the summations are recognized as $a$ times the IDFT of $x_k$ and $b$ times the IDFT of $z_k$, similar to equation (8.32).

**The DFT is periodic:**

The frequency components produced by the DFT are periodic with a period of $N$. That is, if $X_i = DFT_N\{x_k\}$, then

$$X_i = X_{i+N} \tag{8.34}$$

This property is shown by going back to the DFT's definition and adding $N$ to the frequency components' subscript.

$$X_{i+N} = \sum_{k=0}^{N-1} x_k e^{-j\frac{2\pi}{N}k(i+N)} \tag{8.35}$$

Now factor the complex exponential.

$$X_{i+N} = \sum_{k=0}^{N-1} x_k e^{-j\frac{2\pi}{N}ki} e^{-j\frac{2\pi}{N}kN} \tag{8.36}$$

The second exponential is just a fancy way of expressing 1, because $k$ is an integer. Therefore,

$$X_{i+N} = \sum_{k=0}^{N-1} x_k e^{-j\frac{2\pi}{N}ki} = X_i \tag{8.37}$$

The frequency components are periodic with a period of $N$.

**The IDFT is periodic:**

The digital signal produced by an $N$-point IDFT is periodic, with a period of $N$. If $x_k = IDFT_N\{X_i\}$ then

$$x_k = x_{k+N} \tag{8.38}$$

This development is a parallel of the previous work. Simply compute the inverse DFT of $x_{k+N}$ [mimic equation (8.35)], factor the $N$ term out of the exponential, then recognize the factored part of the exponent as 1.

**The DFT of real signals is conjugate symmetric:**

If $X_i = DFT_N\{x_k\}$ and $x_k$ is purely real (no imaginary component), then

$$X_i = X_{-i}^* \tag{8.39}$$

Start with the definition of the DFT and replace $X_i$ with $X_{-i}$ and take the conjugate of both sides.

$$(X_{-i})^* = \left[\sum_{k=0}^{N-1} x_k e^{-j\frac{2\pi}{N}k(-i)}\right]^* \tag{8.40}$$

The signal, $x_k$, is unaffected by the conjugate operation, because $x_k$ is purely real. So the sole affect of the conjugation is to change the sign of $j$ in the exponential. Therefore,

$$X_{-i}^* = \sum_{k=0}^{N-1} x_k e^{-j\frac{2\pi}{N}ki} = X_i \tag{8.41}$$

This is the desired result, the DFT coefficients from real signals are conjugate symmetric.

We could go on and develop another couple of dozen properties for the DFT and the IDFT, but they would not be useful for an introductory treatment. So rather than compile an appendium of DFT properties, let's look at the consequences of the properties already developed.

The periodic properties of the DFT mean that any $N$-point period of the DFT coefficients is sufficient. The most obvious period is $X_0$ through $X_{N-1}$, which span the frequencies from 0 to $2\pi\frac{N-1}{N}$ rad/sample. However, most DFT users prefer coefficients that are evenly centered around 0. These are the coefficients $X_{-N/2}, \ldots, X_0, \ldots, X_{N/2-1}$ and correspond to normalized frequencies between $-\pi$ and $\pi - 2\pi/N$ radians per sample. The fact that there are two popular conventions for the DFT coefficients causes some confusion. Sometimes the negative frequencies ($-\pi$ through 0) are explicitly represented by the negative indexed coefficients ($X_{-N/2}$ through $X_0$) and other times they are represented by the DFT coefficients with indices greater than $N/2$. Always keep in mind the periodic nature of the DFT coefficients, so that you can unravel the relationship between $X_{-N/2} \ldots X_{-1}$ and $X_{N/2} \ldots X_{N-1}$.

$$
\begin{aligned}
X_{-\frac{N}{2}} &= X_{\frac{N}{2}} \\
X_{-\frac{N}{2}+1} &= X_{\frac{N}{2}+1} \\
&\vdots \\
X_{-1} &= X_{N-1}
\end{aligned} \tag{8.42}
$$

The IDFT also generates periodic results, with a period of $N$. This too has been known to cause some confusion. This comes from a possible misinterpretation of what the DFT coefficients represent. Some unfortunate users feel that the coefficients represent $N$ points of a digital signal with the rest of the signal zero. That's not the case, because the DFT coefficients assume that the signal is periodic with a period of $N$. This property is illustrated in Figure 8.5, which shows that even though the original signal may have been aperiodic, the reconstructed signal (what the DFT coefficients represent) is periodic.

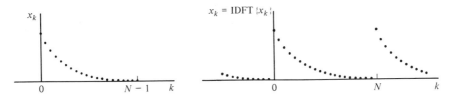

**Figure 8.5** DFT represents periodic functions.

The fact that the spectrum of a real valued signal is conjugate symmetric means that only half of the coefficients need be computed, stored, or plotted for such signals. If the DFT coefficients $X_0$ through $X_{N/2}$ are known then the $X_{N/2+1}$ through $X_N$ or the $X_{-N/2}$ through $X_{-1}$ coefficients can be inferred, because they are the complex conjugates. A similar property holds for signals that are purely imaginary, and they can be fully represented with only $N/2$ coefficients.

## 8.4  DFT OF GENERAL SIGNALS

We noted that any $N$-point digital signal could be applied to the DFT and produce a set of $N$ DFT coefficients. When the original digital signal is a filter's impulse response, the DFT coefficients are samples of its frequency response. But what is the meaning of the coefficients when the digital signal is just a general signal? In the general case, the DFT coefficients represent the spectrum of the digital signal. They are the signal's attributes in the frequency domain and the digital signal is the time-domain representation. Signals are transformed to the frequency domain via the DFT because in some way the spectral representation provides the user with more useful information — analogous to the choice of impulse or frequency response representation of a digital filter.

It is important to realize that the choice of a frequency- or time-domain representation of a signal is simply one of convenience. Both representations hold the same amount of information, and we can go back and forth between the two domains with the DFT and the IDFT. It is a lot like choosing polar or rectangular representations of two dimensional data — it is a question of application, taste, and utility.

The first step in getting some feeling for the frequency domain is to look at the spectrum of our old friend $e^{j\omega k}$. This is a complex signal with a frequency of $\omega$

rad/sample. We will apply $N$ contiguous samples of $e^{j\omega k}$ to the DFT and look at the resulting coefficients. The general form of the DFT is

$$X_i = \sum_{k=0}^{N-1} x_k e^{-j\frac{2\pi}{N}ki} \tag{8.43}$$

So the DFT of the complex exponential is

$$
\begin{aligned}
X_i &= \sum_{k=0}^{N-1} e^{j\omega k} e^{-j\frac{2\pi}{N}ki} \\
&= \sum_{k=0}^{N-1} e^{j(\omega - \frac{2\pi}{N}i)k}
\end{aligned} \tag{8.44}
$$

A straightforward computation of this expression would require a computation for each of the $N$ DFT coefficients, $X_0 \ldots X_{N-1}$. However, we can save a good deal of time while gaining some valuable insight by noting that the $i$th DFT coefficient depends only on the frequency difference, $\omega - \frac{2\pi}{N}i$. This is a frequency difference because $\omega$ is the frequency of the input to the DFT and $\frac{2\pi}{N}i$ is the frequency of the $i$th DFT coefficient. This observation allows us to treat all frequency coefficients identically rather than computing each one individually.

Denote the frequency difference $\Delta\omega$ and call the right-hand side of equation (8.44) the DFT response.

$$\Delta\omega = \omega - \frac{2\pi}{N}i \tag{8.45}$$

So

$$\mathcal{X}(\Delta\omega) = \sum_{k=0}^{N-1} e^{j\Delta\omega k} \tag{8.46}$$

This is a finite sum of a geometric series and has a closed form.

$$\mathcal{X}(\Delta\omega) = \frac{1 - e^{j\Delta\omega N}}{1 - e^{j\Delta\omega}} \tag{8.47}$$

It is important to realize that this is not the value of the DFT coefficients. Rather, the DFT response is used to compute the value of any coefficient when the input to the DFT is a complex exponential. This is done by computing $\Delta\omega$ for the particular coefficient and evaluating equation (8.46).

For example, suppose that the input signal's frequency is $\frac{2\pi}{N}i$. This means that the value of the $i$th coefficient is found by evaluating equation (8.46) with a $\Delta\omega = 0$. In such an instance, the denominator and numerator are both zero and the value of the $i$th coefficient is determined through l'Hospital's rule, $X_i = \mathcal{X}(0) = N$.

Further inspection of equation (8.46) shows that the DFT response is 0 for every nonzero integer multiple of $2\pi/N$. Therefore, $X(l2\pi/N) = 0$ for $l \neq 0$. This means that if the input frequency is precisely an integer multiple of $2\pi/N$ rad/sample, the DFT coefficient that is associated with the input frequency has the value $N$ and all other coefficients are zero. In this case, the DFT coefficients will indicate the frequency of the input, because only the $i$th coefficient will be nonzero.

But this is a very special case of the DFT. Seldom will an input signal have a frequency that is exactly a multiple of $2\pi/N$. When the input signal has an arbitrary frequency, the difference frequency, $\Delta\omega$, can assume any value from $-\pi$ to $\pi$. We can get some insight into the DFT response by returning to equation (8.47). Notice that the magnitude of the denominator increases as $\Delta\omega$ moves away from zero. This implies that the coefficients that are associated with frequencies that are far away from the input frequency (large $|\Delta\omega|$) will have small values. Those coefficients associated with frequencies near the input frequency will generally be larger. So even when the input is not nicely related to the DFT coefficients' frequency, the DFT still indicates the input signal's frequency.

These observations lead to the realization that the DFT is a frequency sorting process. Each of the $N$ DFT coefficients is sensitive to a particular input frequency; $X_i$ is associated with the frequency $i2\pi/N$ rad/sample. The closer the input frequency is to a particular coefficient, the larger is the coefficient. This is a useful way of looking at the DFT, and it suggests one of the major uses of the transform: representing a signal in terms of the frequencies that comprise it.

Figure 8.6 shows the DFT responses for lengths from 10 to 320 points. Notice that all the functions exhibit similar features: the magnitude assumes a maximum of $N$ when $\Delta\omega = 0$ and it decreases in an oscillatory fashion as $\Delta\omega$ moves away from 0. The width of the center peak is $4\pi/N$, so as the DFT becomes longer the peak becomes higher and narrower. For example, doubling the length of the DFT will halve the width of the peak and and double the height. As the DFTs become very long the peak becomes more like a spike and begins to tower over the rest of the response. This suggests that longer DFTs are more sensitive to frequency and, therefore, make better frequency sorters. For example, a $0.1\pi$ change in the input frequency of a 10-point DFT (Figure 8.6a) results in only a 50% reduction in the largest coefficient (around $\Delta\omega = 0$). But the same frequency change in a 320-point DFT causes a 97% reduction. Clearly, the 320-point transform should be used in applications requiring good frequency discrimination.

In practice, few applications can tolerate anything short of a 32-point DFT. Most DFTs are in the 32- to 4096-point region (the section on the FFT will explain this seemingly strange choice of lengths). Occasionally, very long DFTs are used in applications that require very high frequency resolution. For example, a one million-point DFT has a center peak of only $12.56 \times 10^{-6}$ rad/sample wide. So frequency changes as little as $10^{-4}$ rad/sample can reduce a coefficient by 99%; that is fine resolution.

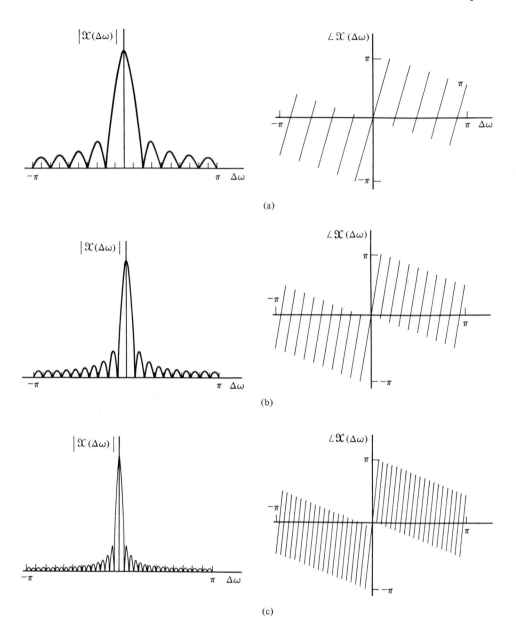

**Figure 8.6** DFT responses: (a) 10-point DFT magnitude and phase;
(b) 20-point DFT magnitude and phase; (c) 40-point
magnitude and phase.

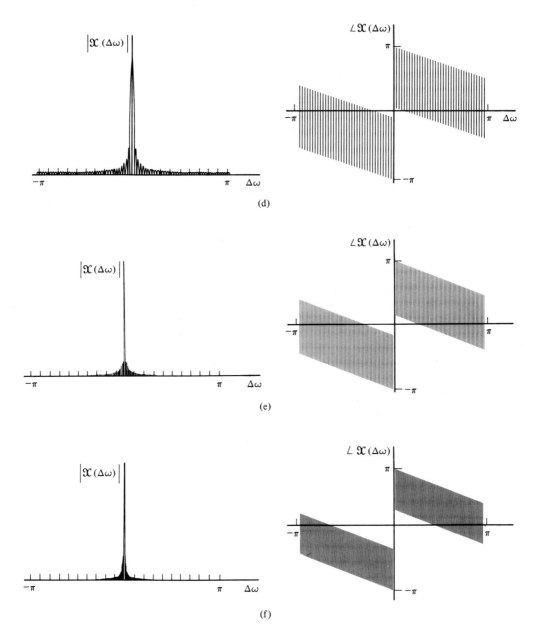

**Figure 8.6** DFT Responses (continued): (d) 80-point DFT magnitude
and phase; (e) 160-point DFT magnitude and phase;
(f) 320-point DFT magnitude and phase.

It is very important to realize that the DFT responses are not plots of the DFT coefficients as a function of input frequency. Rather, the DFT response is a tool to compute a particular DFT coefficient, given the difference between its frequency $(i2\pi/N)$ and the input signal's frequency, $\omega$. Through this tool it is possible to compute all the DFT coefficients by computing the $\Delta\omega$ for each coefficient and determining its magnitude and phase from the appropriate plot in Figure 8.6.

**Example:** Suppose that we apply 40 samples of $x_k = e^{j\frac{2\pi}{10}k}$ to a DFT. What are the resulting coefficients?

We determine the coefficients by going to Figure 8.6c — the 40-point DFT response. The problem is to compute $X_0, X_1, \ldots, X_{39}$, which correspond to frequencies of $0, \frac{2\pi}{40}, \ldots, \frac{2\pi}{40}39$ rad/sample.

Evaluate $X_0$ by first computing its $\Delta\omega$. Because the input frequency is $2\pi/10$ and $X_0$ corresponds to a frequency of 0, $\Delta\omega = 2\pi/10 - 0 = 2\pi/10$. We go to Figure 8.6c and find that $2\pi/10$ is exactly at the fourth null. Therefore, $X_0 = 0$.

We next compute $\Delta\omega$ for $X_1$ as preparation for looking it up on the plot. In this case $\Delta\omega = 2\pi/10 - 2\pi/40 = 6\pi/40$. This is exactly the third null in Figure 8.6c. So $X_1 = 0$ also.

One can doggedly go through all the coefficients, but it should be apparent now that this input signal will generate only one nonzero coefficient and 39 zero coefficients. The nonzero coefficient is the one with a $\Delta\omega$ of 0 and its value lies on the peak of the plot. The fourth coefficient, $X_4$, is associated with a frequency of $\frac{2\pi}{40}4 = \frac{2\pi}{10}$ rad/sample, and thereby has a $\Delta\omega$ of 0. So $X_4$ has a value of 40 and all other coefficients have values of 0. Therefore the DFT coefficients that result for applying $x_k = e^{j\frac{2\pi}{40}k}$ to a DFT are

$$X_i = \begin{cases} 40 & \text{if } i = 4 \\ 0 & \text{otherwise} \end{cases} \qquad (8.48)$$

These DFT coefficients are plotted in Figure 8.7.

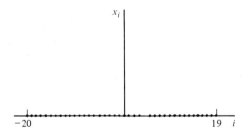

**Figure 8.7** DFT coefficients produced by $e^{j\frac{2\pi}{10}k}$.

Why not repeat this example for an 80-point DFT? Do you really have to grind through all the work or can you use the property that $80 = 2 \times 40$?

Do not let the results of this example fool you. Seldom do the DFT coefficients provide such an unambiguous frequency determination. The example was blessed with the fact that the input frequency was an integer multiple of $2\pi/N$. A different input frequency might generate multiple nonzero coefficients. Many novice users attempt to extend the results of the preceding example to arbitary frequencies and end up misinterpreting the meaning of the DFT coefficients. It is tempting to ignore all the rippling in the DFT response and imagine it looking something like Figure 8.8. Such a DFT response is desired because it generates only one nonzero DFT coefficient for any input frequency; however, it does not accurately represent the operation of the DFT. Given that a real DFT response has rippling, what happens when an arbitrary frequency is applied to the DFT?

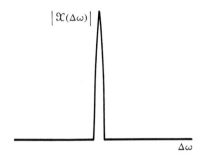

**Figure 8.8** Idealized DFT response.

**Example:** Suppose we make a slight change to the frequency of the input in the preceding example. Now we are interested in the DFT of 40 points of $x_k = e^{j\frac{2.1\pi}{10}k}$.

As before, the DFT will generate DFT coefficients $X_0, X_1, \ldots, X_{39}$, corresponding to frequencies of $0, \frac{2\pi}{40}, \ldots, \frac{2\pi}{40}39$. It is easier to work through the algebra by expressing the input frequency as a multiple of the DFT frequencies — the input has a frequency of $\frac{2\pi}{40}4.2$ rad/sample. Therefore, the input frequency lies two-tenths of the way between $\frac{2\pi}{40}4$ and $\frac{2\pi}{40}5$. This is between $X_4$ and $X_5$.

Compute $X_4$ by calculating its $\Delta\omega$; $\Delta\omega = \frac{2\pi}{40}4.2 - \frac{2\pi}{40}4 = 0.2\frac{2\pi}{40}$. This is two-tenths of the way between the peak and the first null of the 40-point DFT response (Figure 8.6c). Therefore, $|X_4| \approx 36$. The difference frequency for $X_5$ is $-0.8\frac{2\pi}{40}$, which is close to the first null to the left of the peak in Figure 8.6c. Therefore, $|X_5| \approx 10$.

There are many more nonzero coefficients because the input frequency is not an integer multiple of the DFT frequencies. As a matter of fact, all the DFT coefficients are nonzero, because none of the $\Delta\omega$'s were at the nulls in Figure 8.6c. The 40 DFT coefficients are plotted in Figure 8.9 (these were calculated on a computer, not using the techniques of this example). Notice that the spectrum peaks around $2\pi/40$ and the relatively large $X_4$ coefficient indicates that the input frequency was a little larger than $2\pi/40$ rad/sample.

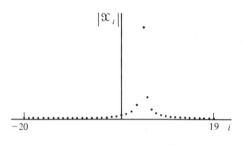

**Figure 8.9** DFT of $e^{\frac{2.1\pi}{10}k}$.

This phenomenon of a single complex sinusoid causing multiple nonzero coefficients is called *spectral leakage*. It got that name because the signal seems to "leak" from its frequency into adjacent frequencies. Leakage is caused by the rippling in the DFT response and is always there. The only way to reduce leakage is to increase the length of the DFT or to modify the DFT by applying windows to the signal before performing the DFT. This windowing technique exploits the same properties as those presented in Chapter 4, and it will be discussed in a later section.

Up until now we have been considering the DFT's response to complex sinusoids, which are seldom found in real applications. But equation (8.26) shows that any periodic signal, $x_k$, can be represented as a weighted sum of complex sinusoids (the weighting coefficients happen to be $X_i$). We can use this fact to help interpret the DFT operation on an arbitrary input signal. For example, consider a cosine.

**Example**: Suppose that we apply 40 samples of $\cos\left(\frac{2.1\pi}{40}k\right)$ to a DFT. What are the DFT coefficients?

We first note that the cosine is the sum of two complex sinusoids, one at $2.1\pi/10$ rad/sample and the other at $-2.1\pi/10$. Because the DFT is linear, we can directly use the results of the preceding example; there is no reason to grind this one out. The positive DFT coefficients should be identical to those of the preceding example, and the negative-frequency component should produce a similar shape around $X_{-4}$. The 40 coefficients are shown in Figure 8.10 and are consistent with our expectations.

In summary, the DFT is a technique for displaying a digital signal as a function of frequency rather than the conventional representation as a function of time. The DFT response is a useful tool for predicting the response of the DFT to complex sinusoids. Fortunately, any periodic digital signal is a weighted sum of sinusoids, so the DFT response can be used to help understand the DFT's coefficients for an arbitrary input. The next section illustrates the power of the DFT by presenting some applications.

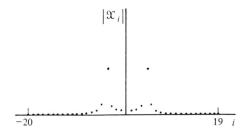

**Figure 8.10** DFT of $\cos \frac{2.1\pi}{10} k$.

## 8.5 MOTIVATION AND APPLICATION

The previous sections introduced the possibility of performing DFTs on general digital signals, $x_0, \ldots, x_{N-1}$. The coefficients produced by the DFT, $X_0, \ldots, X_{N-1}$, are the frequency-domain representation of the signal. Because the frequency and time domains are related through the DFT and IDFT, it is possible to go back and forth between these two domains without losing information. This section will give some reasons for using the frequency-domain representations of digital signals. Because the DFT is a relatively expensive operation (many multiplications and additions), a signal's frequency-domain presentation must be more valuable than its time domain before a user will bear the expense of the transform. This section presents a few applications of the DFT as a way of illustrating its utility.

### DFT and Filtering

In this first application, the DFT is used as an analysis tool for digital filters. Through it we can predict how a filter will affect a specific class of input signals.

Remember that a digital filter produces an output, which is the convolution of the filter's input and its impulse response.

$$y_k = \sum_{i=-\infty}^{\infty} h_i x_{k-i} \tag{8.49}$$

The past experience has shown that the filter's frequency response is an equivalent, but generally more useful, portrait of the filter's operation. So, is it possible to relate the filter's input and output through the frequency response? The answer is yes, but not directly.

Consider a finite-duration input sequence, say $x_0, \ldots, x_{N-1}$, as the input to a digital filter with an impulse response of $h_k$ and a frequency response of $\mathcal{H}(\omega)$. Because of the DFT it is possible to represent $x_k$ in either the time or frequency domain. If we chose the time domain, the convolution operator relates the input and output. But what happens if you use the frequency-domain representation of the filter's input? This produces a characterization of the digital filter in the frequency domain — the input and output are related through the filter's frequency response.

The input signal has DFT coefficients, $X_0 \ldots X_{N-1}$, where

$$X_i = \sum_{k=0}^{N-1} x_k e^{-j\frac{2\pi}{N}ki} \tag{8.50}$$

These coefficients represent a periodic version of the input signal. Call it $\tilde{x}_k$, and it is the result of the IDFT operating on the DFT coefficients.

$$\tilde{x}_k = \frac{1}{N} \sum_{i=0}^{N-1} X_i e^{j\frac{2\pi}{N}ik} \tag{8.51}$$

Remember that $\tilde{x}_k = x_k$ for $k = 0, \ldots, N-1$ and is periodic in $N$. Because the DFT is a representation of a periodic version of the input signal, the rest of this development implicitly assumes periodic input signals.

Equation (8.51) shows that the periodic version of the input to the filter can be expressed as a sum of complex sinusoids. This is quite convenient when working with digital filters because the complex sinusoids are eigenfunctions. So if only one term of equation (8.51) is applied to the digital filter, the output of the filter is just the input scaled by the filter's frequency response at that particular frequency.

$$y_k = \mathcal{H}\left(\frac{2\pi}{N}i\right) X_i e^{j\frac{2\pi}{N}ik} \qquad \text{when} \qquad x_k = X_i e^{j\frac{2\pi}{N}ik} \tag{8.52}$$

When all the components of $\tilde{x}_k$ are applied to the digital filter, its output is just the sum of the outputs that would have been caused by each individual component — an application of the superposition principle.

$$y_k = \frac{1}{N} \sum_{i=0}^{N-1} \underline{\mathcal{H}\left(\frac{2\pi}{N}i\right) X_i e^{j\frac{2\pi}{N}ik}} \qquad \text{when} \qquad \text{input} = x_k \tag{8.53}$$

Equation (8.53) should look awfully familiar. If the underlined term, $\mathcal{H}\left(\frac{2\pi}{N}i\right)X_i$, is treated as a unit, the equation can be interpreted as the IDFT for the filter's output, $y_k$. By definition,

$$y_k = \frac{1}{N} \sum_{i=0}^{N-1} Y_i e^{j\frac{2\pi}{N}ik} \tag{8.54}$$

So, relating equations (8.53) and (8.54) shows that the DFT coefficients of a filter's output is the product of the input's DFT coefficients and the filter's frequency response.

$$Y_i = \mathcal{H}\left(\frac{2\pi}{N}i\right) X_i \tag{8.55}$$

This result gives us a quick and convenient method for investigating a filter's performance in the frequency domain. It is far easier to compute a filter's output in the frequency domain than in the time domain, because it is easier to multiply than convolve. The drawback to this approach is that the interpretation of the results is more challenging. It is easy to see what $y_k$ means, but it is more difficult to give meaning to the DFT coefficients. Consider the following example.

**Example:** Pass the signal of Figure 8.11a through a low-pass digital filter.

Suppose that we have an input signal as shown in Figure 8.11a. This is a composite plot of the time-domain representation of the input signal. The light dots show the samples of the signal, and the heavy dots show the measurement of the signal that is corrupted by a high-frequency sinusoid. The DFT coefficients of the signal plus noise are shown in Figure 8.11b. Notice that the low frequency signal is about $0.25\pi$ rad/sample and the high-frequency noise is about $0.9\pi$.

Suppose that the signal is passed through a low-pass filter with a frequency response shown in Figure 8.11c. The filter's output has DFT coefficients, which are the product, $\mathcal{H}(\frac{2\pi}{N}i)X_i$, and are shown in Figure 8.11d. Notice that the low-pass filter attenuated the higher-frequency components in the input signal. Thus the filter reduced the noise content of the signal. The time-domain representation of the filter's output is shown in Figure 8.11e — the filter removed most of the high-frequency noise while preserving most of the signal (notice that there is some attenuation of the fourth DFT coefficient).

There is nothing magic about this particular choice of filter. In this simple application the noise would have been attenuated by any low-pass filter with a breakpoint between $\pi/3$ and $3\pi/4$. Once you get used to the frequency representations, this approach to filtering provides more insights than the time-domain techniques.

It is very important to remember that the frequency-domain approach to filtering presupposes a periodic input signal, which produces a periodic output signal. This can, and generally does, lead you astray when you misuse the technique to compute a filter's output for nonperiodic signals. It is always possible to represent nonperiodic signals with very long DFTs. This still produces a periodic representation of the signal, but the period can be made to be so long that the periods are isolated by long strings of zeros. For example, Figure 8.12 shows three representations of a 20-point signal. Figure 8.12a shows the representation resulting from a 20-point DFT (the shortest possible in this case), Figure 8.12b shows a 40-point representation, and Figure 8.12c shows an 80-point representation. The longer DFTs have longer periods and the periodic signal looks more and more like the original. If you take this to the limit, it is possible to represent an aperiodic signal, but the DFT sum becomes an integral and is called the Fourier transform.

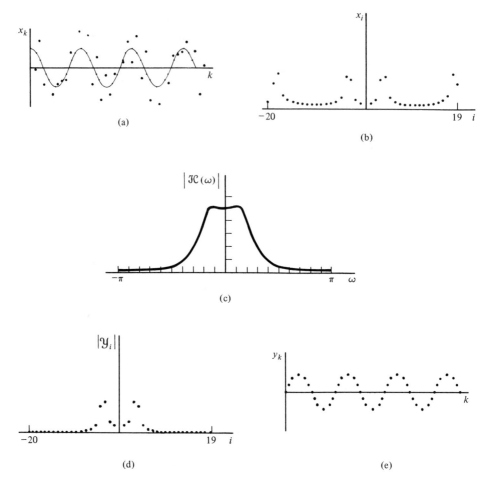

**Figure 8.11** Frequency-domain interpretation of filtering:
(a) input samples (light dots signal, heavy dots
signal plus noise); (b) input's 40-point DFT
coefficients; (c) filter's frequency response;
(d) output's 40-point DFT coefficients;
(e) output samples.

**Example:** Use the frequency representation of the input signal to help specify the
desired frequency response of a filter.

Suppose an application where a measurement, say $x_k$, consists of a signal, $s_k$, plus some additive noise, $n_k$. Furthermore, suppose that the signal
has DFT coefficients that are shown in Figure 8.13a and the noise's DFT coefficients are shown in Figure 8.13b. Specify a filter's frequency response that
will remove the noise without affecting the signal.

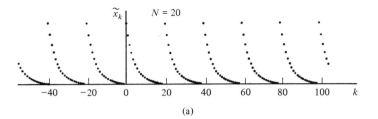

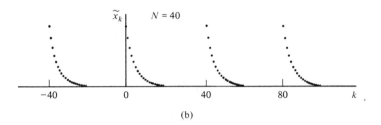

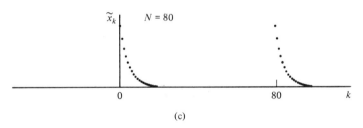

**Figure 8.12** Periodic representations of signals:
(a) from a 20-point DFT; (b) from a 40-point
DFT; (c) from a 80-point DFT.

We want a filter that will multiply [equation (8.55)] the signal's coefficients by 1 and the noise's coefficients by 0. Unfortunately, the signal's and noise's frequency representations overlap, so it is impossible to remove all the noise without removing some of the signal. Therefore, we desire a frequency response that is 1 for all frequencies where the signal is nonzero, and is zero at frequencies where the signal is zero and the noise is nonzero. Two such filters are shown in Figures 8.13d and e. The first filter passes only the signal frequencies and the second filter passes the signal and some of the frequencies where there is no noise. You should convince yourself that these two filters will produce the same outputs, because we do not care what the frequency response is at those frequencies without signal or noise.

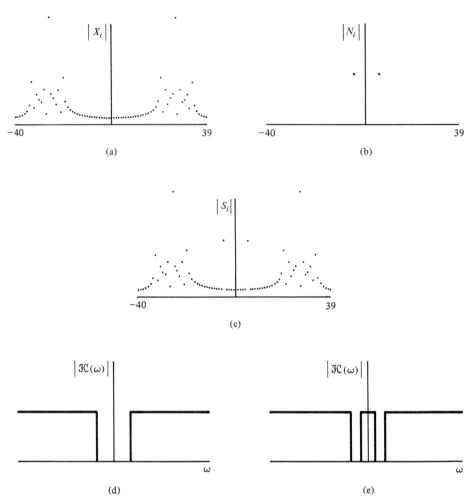

**Figure 8.13** DFT interpretation of filtering: (a) signal's
DFT coefficients; (b) noise's DFT coefficients;
(c) signal plus noise DFT coefficients;
(d) filter that passes signal only;
(e) filter that passes more than signal.

## DFT and Convolution

This second application of the DFT is really a variant of the use of the DFT in filtering. But the DFT is used so widely as a method of performing convolution that it deserves its own section. The preceding section showed that the DFT can be used to circumvent convolution if we are willing to express the signals in the frequency domain. In some applications it is more efficient to compute the DFT coefficients of the signals being convolved, multiply the coefficients, and perform the IDFT, rather than performing the straightforward convolution. In these cases the convolution operation is performed by DFT, multiplication, and IDFT. This approach becomes even more attractive if the signals are already expressed in terms of their DFT coefficients and/or the convolution results are desired in the frequency domain. Because this approach uses the DFT representations of the signals, it produces a periodic, or circular, convolution.

We begin the development by looking at the output of an $(M-1)$-point FIR filter with an input with a period of $N$.

$$y_k = \sum_{i=0}^{M-1} h_i x_{k-i} \quad \text{and} \quad x_k = x_{k+N} \tag{8.56}$$

The notation has been altered somewhat. In this case the length of the filter is denoted $M$ and the length of the data sequence (actually the period) is denoted $N$. The preceding section showed that the result of the convolution (the filter's output in this case) has DFT coefficients,

$$Y_i = \mathcal{H}\left(\frac{2\pi}{N}i\right) X_i \tag{8.57}$$

The $X_i$ are the DFT coefficients of the input signal and $\mathcal{H}(\frac{2\pi}{N}i)$ are the samples of the filter's frequency response. The question is: How do we compute the filter's frequency response with the DFT, and more important how do we handle convolution of general digital signals?

A straightforward extension of the earlier work suggests an $N$-point DFT of $h_i$ to obtain the samples of the frequency response. But this will effectively truncate the impulse response if $M$ happens to be larger than $N$. If the filter length and the signal's period are the same, an $N$-point DFT of the filter's impulse response will generate the samples, $\mathcal{H}(\frac{2\pi}{N}i)$. If the impulse response is shorter than $N$, $M \leq N$, it can be extended by adding $N - M$ zeros to obtain an $N$-point impulse response, which then can be applied to an $N$-point DFT. If the impulse response is longer, the $N$-point transform will no longer suffice. But an $M$-point transform might not result in the frequency points demanded by equation (8.57) — the $M$-point DFT produces $\mathcal{H}(\frac{2\pi}{M}i)$, and the convolution requires $\mathcal{H}(\frac{2\pi}{N}i)$. The DFT will compute the necessary frequency response coefficients only if its length is an integer multiple of $N$ ($N, 2N, 3N, \ldots$). So to use a DFT to compute the coefficients for the convolution, we must extend the filter's impulse response with zeros until the extended impulse response is an integer multiple of $N$, then take the DFT of the extended impulse response. Note that we could extend the impulse response to any multiple of $N$, but efficiency dictates that we extend to only the smallest multiple.

This discussion leads to the following implementation of circular (because $x_k$ and $h_k$ are periodically extended by the DFT) convolution via DFT. We can compute the convolution of the signals $h_i$ and $x_i$,

$$y_k = \sum_{i=0}^{M-1} h_i x_{k-i} \tag{8.58}$$

via DFTs by following a four-step process.

    Step 1: Compute the $N$ DFT coefficients of $x_k$; call them $X_i$, $i = 0, \ldots, N-1$. Remember that $x_k$ is periodic, with a period of $N$.

    Step 2: Compute the $LN$ DFT coefficients of $h_k$, where $L$ is the smallest integer such that $LN \geq M$. Call these coefficients $H_i$. Because we are representing $h_k$ with $LN$ DFT coefficients, $h_k$ has a period of $LN$.

    Step 3: Compute the $N$ coefficients of $y_k$ by multiplying $x_k$s and $h_k$s coefficients.

$$Y_i = H_{Li} X_i \qquad i = 0, \ldots, N-1 \tag{8.59}$$

    Notice the factor of $L$ in the subscript of $H$. This is because $H_{Li} = \mathcal{H}(\frac{2\pi}{N}i)$.

    Step 4: Compute one period of the convolution result by performing an $N$-point IDFT on the $Y_i$ coefficients.

$$y_k = \text{IDFT}_N\{Y_i\} \qquad k = 0, \ldots, N-1 \tag{8.60}$$

The convolution result, $y_k$, is periodic with a period of $N$.

    This four-step process might appear too convoluted (pun) to be useful. It appears that we are replacing the straightforward operator of convolution with a procedure that requires two transforms and one inverse transform. But this method of computing convolution is widely used because one or both of the input sequences are already presented as DFT coefficients (so one or both DFTs are unnecessary), and/or the results of the convolution can be left as DFT coefficients (saving the IDFT). This technique is used even in cases where all three transforms are necessary. It can be more computationally efficient than the straightforward computation of the convolution, because there are some very fast algorithms for computing the transforms and inverse transforms (these are called fast Fourier transforms and are discussed at the end of the chapter). Therefore, the computation of circular convolution through the DFTs is faster than the the straightforward calculation. For example, a 1000-point convolution ($M = 1000$) of a signal with a period of 2000 ($N = 2000$) requires 2,000,000 ($M \times N$) additions and multiplications. An efficient 2000-point DFT or IDFT requires only 90,000 additions and multiplications (it is actually 22,528 complex multiplications and additions). Therefore, the DFT implementation of convolution will take 180,000 operations to compute the DFT coefficients (steps 1 and 2), 2000 complex multiplications (that is 8000 real multiplies and 4000 additions) for step 3, and 90,000 operations for step 4. The DFT approach requires "only" 274,000 adds and 278,000 multiplies rather than 2,000,000 adds and multiplies for the regular convolution. The DFT takes about 10 times fewer operations — well worth the trouble of a more involved algorithm.

Remember that the DFT technique computes circular convolutions and care must be taken when interpreting the results. For example, Figure 14a shows two sequences and their noncircular convolution. Figure 14b shows the same two sequences, which have been periodicaly extended through the DFT, IDFT. Notice that the circular convolution bears no resemblance to its noncircular ancestor. We can mitigate the effects of circular convolution by increasing the period of the periodic signals. The period of the two signals has been doubled in Figure 14c by filling both sequences with zeros. The convolution is still periodic, but the period is long enough to isolate the noncircular result (compare Figure 8.14c with 8.14a). Doubling the length of both sequences will always give an $N$-point noncircular convolution even though circular convolution was used in the computation.

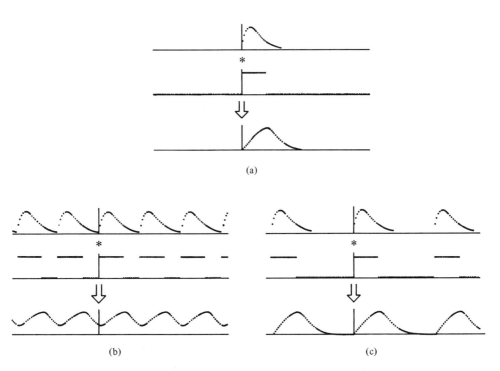

**Figure 8.14** DFT implements circular convolution:
(a) noncircular convolution; (b) 32-point
circular extension of the convolution;
(c) 64-point circular extension of the convolution.

## DFTs and Frequency

There are many applications in which information is carried by the frequency of a signal. Most of us experience such use of frequency every day when we hear the tones generated by a touch-tone telephone. In this case each button (1-9 and the three special buttons) generates a mixture of tones. These tones are passed over the telephone lines and are decoded at the main office. The frequencies used for the touch-tone system are shown in Table 8.1. The telephone company must have systems that "listen" to these tones to determine the frequencies, which indicate which buttons were pushed.

**Table 8.1**    Frequencies Used for Touch-Tone (tm AT&T) Phones

| Button | Low Tone | High Tone |
|--------|----------|-----------|
| 1 | 697 | 1209 |
| 2 | 697 | 1336 |
| 3 | 696 | 1477 |
| 4 | 770 | 1209 |
| 5 | 770 | 1336 |
| 6 | 770 | 1477 |
| 7 | 852 | 1209 |
| 8 | 852 | 1336 |
| 9 | 852 | 1477 |
| * | 941 | 1209 |
| O | 941 | 1336 |
| # | 941 | 1477 |

A DFT is a useful tool for dividing a signal into its frequency components. For this application, $N$ samples of the signal are applied to the DFT. The DFT coefficients indicate which frequencies are present and how strong they are. The DFT coefficients that are associated with frequency components in the signals are large and the other coefficients (those associated with nonexistent frequency components) are small. Remember that spectral leakage will cause some of the signal to leak to adjacent coefficients, so this is not a perfect frequency sorting of the signal. The DFTs are widely used to break a signal into its frequency components or to sort a signal based on frequency. Consider the following examples.

**Example:** Use a DFT to implement a touch-tone decoder. This is a very expensive implementation of a decoder but is proposed to illustrate the frequency sorting ability of the DFT.

The first problem is to select a reasonable sampling rate for the tones. The highest tone generated by a touch-tone phone is 1477Hz, so the sampling rate must be at least twice that — 2954 samples/sec. Let's sample the signal at 3,000 samples/sec.

The next step is to determine the length of the DFT. The length, $N$, is dictated by the desired frequency resolution — more resolution demands longer DFTs. The tones are separated by 73 to 141Hz, so the DFT must be able to resolve signals spaced only 73Hz apart. This corresponds to normalized frequencies of 73/3000 cycles/sample or $\frac{73}{3000}2\pi = .0486\pi$ rad/sample. The DFT coefficients are separated by $\frac{2\pi}{N}$ rad/sample, so the DFT must be long enough so that the frequency separation between adjacent coefficients is less than $0.0486\pi$ rad/sample. Therefore,

$$\frac{2\pi}{N} < .0486$$
$$N > \frac{2\pi}{.0486\pi} = 41.15 \tag{8.61}$$

Actually, a 42-point DFT would be too short because the spectral leakage will blur the results. The DFT should be at least twice that, 84 points, and we will select a length that can quickly be computed with the fast Fourier transform — 128 points.

The results are shown in Figure 8.15. The plots of Figure 8.15a and b show the DFT coefficients when 64 and 128 samples of the "operator" button are transformed. Notice that the coefficients peak near 941 and 1336Hz, the tones of the button. The plots in Figure 8.15c and d show the DFT coefficients from the "7" button — peaks near 852 and 1209Hz. Clearly, this 128-point DFT provides sufficient frequency resolution to decode touch tones. The touch-tone application was proposed to illustrate the utility of the frequency-sorting property of the DFT. The telephone company does a much better job of touch-tone detection.

The DFT is also used to detect coherent signals (sinusoids) in highly non-coherent noise, commonly called "white" noise. This application is based on the fact that the noise power is randomly spread among all DFT coefficients but the signal's power is concentrated in only a few (ideally, the signal is represented by only two coefficients, one for the positive frequency and one for the negative, but spectral leakage smears it to adjacent coefficients). If the DFT is long enough, the coefficients associated with the noise will be much smaller than those of the signal. Therefore, the signal is detected by inspecting the coefficients and looking for the large ones.

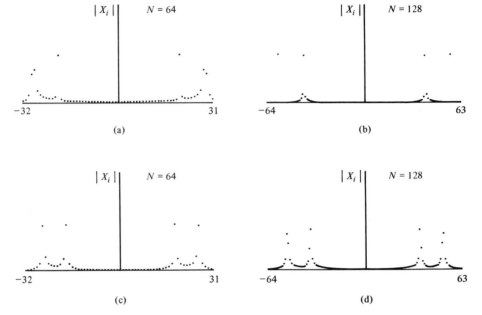

**Figure 8.15** DFT coefficients of touch tones:
(a) 64-point DFT of the "operator" button;
(b) 128-point DFT of the "operator" button;
(c) 64-point DFT of the "7" button;
(d) 128-point DFT of the "7" button.

    This application is illustrated in Figure 8.16. The top plot shows the time-domain representation of a $0.25\pi$ rad/second sinusoid. Figure 8.16b shows the samples of the sinusoid with additive white noise. In this case, the noise power was 10 times the signal's and the noise virtually obliterates the signal. Figure 8.16c shows the DFT coefficients produced by a 32-point DFT of this signal plus noise. The ±eighth coefficient is at the signal's frequency. Notice that the ±fourth coefficients are larger than the signal's. Therefore, this DFT is too short to detect the signal in this much noise. Figure 8.16d shows the results of a 64-point DFT. In this case, the signal's coefficients are ±sixteenth coefficients, and they are larger than the coefficients driven by the noise. Figure 8.16e shows a 128-point DFT of the same signal plus noise. The ±thirty-second coefficients are far above the others, so this DFT does a good job of detecting the signal.

    The noise coefficients depend on the particular sample of noise transformed. Because the noise is random, different samples of the signal plus noise will yield differing DFT coefficients. It is possible, but unlikely, that a different sample of the noise will cause a noise coefficient to be larger than the signal's in the 128-point DFT. In that case, the 128-point DFT could not detect the sinusoid.

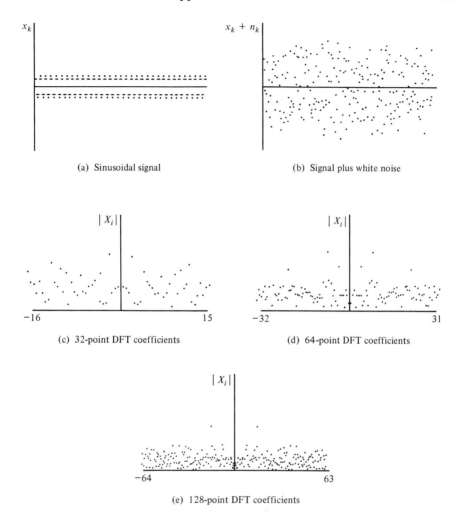

**Figure 8.16** DFT-based sinusoid detector: (a) sinusoidal
signal; (b) signal plus white noise;
(c) 32-point DFT coefficients; (d) 64-point
DFT coefficients; (e) 128-point DFT coefficients.

We can exploit the randomness of the noise coefficients to improve the detection by averaging DFT coefficients. Suppose that we take 128 samples of the signal plus noise and break them up into four groups of 32 samples each. The first 32 samples are applied to a 32-point DFT, the second group of 32 points is applied to a 32-point DFT, and so on. This will generate four sets of DFT coefficients. We compute an average set of coefficients by adding the four coefficients for each frequency and dividing by 4. Denote the DFT coefficients of the first 32 samples,

$X_{1i}$, the coefficients of the second 32 samples, $X_{2i}$, and the coefficients of the third and fourth set of samples, $X_{3i}$ and $X_{4i}$. The average coefficients are simply the arithmetic average of the four sets:

$$\overline{X}_i = \frac{1}{4}\left(X_{1i} + X_{2i} + X_{3i} + X_{4i}\right)$$

where
$$X_{1i} = \mathrm{DFT}_{32}\{x_0 \ldots x_{31}\} \qquad X_{2i} = \mathrm{DFT}_{32}\{x_{32} \ldots x_{63}\}$$
$$X_{3i} = \mathrm{DFT}_{32}\{x_{64} \ldots x_{95}\} \qquad X_{3i} = \mathrm{DFT}_{32}\{x_{95} \ldots x_{127}\} \tag{8.62}$$

Figure 8.17 shows the results of averaging 4 (Figure 8.17a) and 10 (Figure 8.17b) 32-point DFTs. Compare these results to the 32-point results in Figure 8.16c and you should see the improvement that averaging gives.

Care must be taken when averaging the DFT coefficients, because they are complex numbers. The average is called *coherent* when the DFT coefficients are averaged by averaging the imaginary parts of the coefficients to compute the imaginary part of the average and averaging the real parts to get the real part of the average. A coherent average is appropriate when the phase of the sinusoid is the same for all DFTs. If the different groupings of the signal have different phases, coherent averaging will tend to cancel out the signal's DFT coefficients. In such cases, it is necessary to resort to magnitude averaging — average the magnitudes of the coefficients instead of averaging the real and imaginary parts separately.

If the signal was to become smaller or the noise larger, longer DFTs would be required to get the signal's coefficients above the noise's. Furthermore, if the signal's frequency is not an integer multiple of $2\pi/N$, the spectral leakage will spread the signal among adjacent coefficients and the signal's coefficients will not be as pronounced.

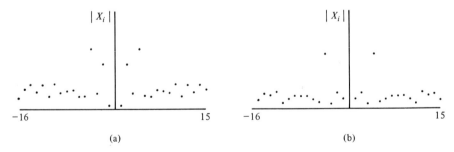

**Figure 8.17** Averaging multiple DFTs: (a) coherent average of four 32-point DFTs; (b) coherent average of ten 32-point DFTs.

These are just a few of the many uses of the DFT. Suffice it to say that the DFT has many applications in science and engineering, and it has even worked its way into medicine and economics. Whatever the use, the DFT's function is to transform a time-domain representation of a signal into its frequency domain.

## 8.6  WINDOWS AND THE DFT

Ideally, we want a DFT response like that depicted in Figure 8.8. The response has a narrow main lobe and no rippling, hence no spectral leakage. This is an identical problem to the one faced at the end of Chapter 3. In that case, we had filters with ripples in the frequency response. In this case, we have a DFT with rippling in the DFT response. Windows helped earlier, and they will help again.

Suppose that we window the signal before applying it to the DFT. That is, we compute the DFT of $w_k x_k$ instead of $x_k$. The terms $w_k$ are the coefficients of the window and the $x_k$s are the samples of the signal. In this way we can think of our earlier work with the DFT as using a uniform window, $w_k = 1$.

The windowed DFT is the old version with $x_k$ replaced by $w_k x_k$.

$$X_i^w = \sum_{k=0}^{N-1} w_k x_k e^{-j\frac{2\pi}{N}ki} \tag{8.63}$$

Compute the DFT response of the windowed DFT by proceeding as before; apply $e^{j\omega k}$ to the DFT and express the results in terms of the difference frequency, $\Delta\omega$.

$$\mathcal{X}^w(\Delta\omega) = \sum_{k=0}^{N-1} w_k e^{j\Delta\omega k} \tag{8.64}$$

This looks a great deal like the definition of the window responses in Chapter 4 [equation (4.21)]. In this case $\omega$ is replaced by $-\Delta\omega$ and the summation is over an asymmetric interval, $k = 0$ to $N-1$, rather than $-m$ to $m$. Using $-\Delta\omega$ instead of $\omega$ is simply changing the dummy variable and is of little consequence. Using the asymmetric interval simply causes a phase shift of the response and does not affect its magnitude. Therefore, the DFT and window responses are different applications of the same mathematics and principles. We can use the windowing concepts, and even the windows, developed in Chapter 4 to reduce the spectral leakage of the DFT.

As a double check, compare the window response of the uniform window, Figure 4.5, with the uniformly windowed DFT responses in Figure 8.6. These functions have the same magnitudes, so the DFT response and the window response appear to be the same things.

How do we go about picking good DFT windows for data? The issues are identical to those in Chapter 4. In this case, we desire the narrowest main lobe for good spectral resolution and no side lobes, which prevent spectral leakage. Unfortunately, there is a trade-off between the width of the main lobe and the height of the side lobes. Small side lobes dictate wider main lobes, and the narrowest main lobe produces the largest side lobes. The use of windows in DFT analysis is further complicated because the "goodness" of a DFT response is not as well defined as the quality of a filter's frequency response. So most DFT windows are selected on the basis of qualitative rather than quantitative measures.

The following windows are widely used to shape the DFT frequency response.

Uniform:

$$w_k = 1 \tag{8.65}$$

This is the easiest window to apply — just perform the transform on the data directly. It produces the narrowest main lobe at the expense of the largest side lobes.

Tapered:

$$w_k = \begin{cases} \frac{1}{2} & \text{if } k = 0 \\ 1 & \text{if } k = 1 \ldots N - 2 \\ \frac{1}{2} & \text{if } k = N - 1 \end{cases} \tag{8.66}$$

This is especially useful when dealing with short DFTs. There are a whole family of tapered windows and they all have the feature of gradually tapering the data near $k = 0$ and $k = N - 1$. This results in a narrow main lobe (the more tapering, the wider the main lobe) with some reduction in the size of the side lobes. The example used here is the tapered window with the least tapering. The tapering can be increased by linearly decreasing the window coefficeints near $k = 0$ or $N - 1$, or using any other monotonic function to gradually decrease the window near the end points.

Bartlett:

$$w_k = 1 - \frac{|2k - N + 1|}{N + 2} \tag{8.67}$$

This is a special case of the tapered window, where the data are continuously tapered. It has a wide main lobe with much smaller side lobes.

Hamming:

$$w_k = 2a \cos\left(\pi \frac{2k - N + 1}{N}\right) + b \tag{8.68}$$

where $a \approx 0.23$ and $b \approx 0.54$.

The Hamming window is especially useful in those applications that can tolerate very little leakage. The Hamming window generates very small side lobes, but results in a main lobe that is twice as wide as the uniform window's. Therefore, the Hamming window causes a great deal of local spectral leakage but very little distant leakage.

These four windows and their DFT responses are shown in Figure 8.18.

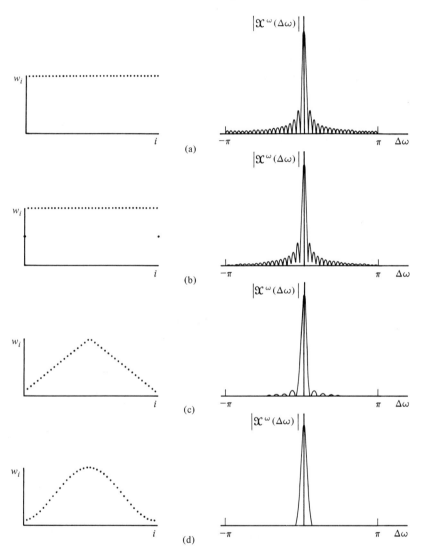

**Figure 8.18** Four popular DFT windows: (a) uniform;
(b) tapered; (c) Bartlett; (d) Hamming.

**Example:** Use the DFT to compute the spectrum of a digital signal. We demand
that the spectral leakage be less than 10% for coefficients that represent frequencies
that are more than $0.1\pi$ away from the signal's frequency, $|\Delta\omega| > 0.1\pi$.

We can achieve this design specification in one of two ways. We could use a uniform window and make the DFT long enough to meet the 10% requirement. This approach requires us to revisit the DFT responses in Figure 8.6. Notice that a 40-point DFT has a 20% side lobe at $0.07\pi$ and a 13% side lobe at $0.12\pi$. The large side lobe at $0.12\pi$ violates the design specification, so a longer DFT is demanded. The 80-point DFT has a 7% side lobe near $0.11\pi$. This is below the 10% specification, so the 80-point DFT will satisfy this application.

A second approach is to use a better window, which might require a shorter DFT to meet the same specification. The side lobes of a Hamming window are obviously less than 10%, so the design specification is met by using a long enough Hamming window so that the main lobe is confined between $\pm 0.1\pi$. This design is actually conservative because a small amount of the main lobe could extend beyond $0.1\pi$ and still meet the 10% requirement. The main lobe of a Hamming window spans between $-4\pi/N$ and $4\pi/N$. So the length of the Hamming window is determined as follows.

$$\frac{4\pi}{N} = 0.1\pi$$

$$N \approx 40 \tag{8.69}$$

Thus a 40-point DFT with a Hamming window will cause very little leakage (on the order of 1%) for frequency differences greater than $0.1\pi$.

Be very careful not to overuse DFT windows, because different windows will result in different DFT coefficients and, thereby, demand different interpretations. For example, Figure 8.19 shows the output of two 80-point DFTs. The top DFT used a uniform window and the lower used the Hamming window. Both DFTs had a common input; a sinusoid at $8\pi/80$ (corresponding to the $\pm 4$ coefficients) and a sinusoid at $21\pi/80$ (halfway between the tenth and eleventh coefficients).

Notice that the uniformly windowed DFT generated spikes only at $X_{-4}$ and $X_4$ for the $8\pi/80$ cosine. The other coefficients are zero because they correspond to $\Delta\omega$'s that are integer multiples of $2\pi/80$. However, the Hamming window generated three nonzero coefficients around $X_{\pm 4}$. This is because the main lobe of the Hamming windowed DFT is $4\pi/80$ rad/sample wide. Therefore, $X_{-3}, X_{-4},$ and $X_{-5}$ and $X_3, X_4,$ and $X_5$ are nonzero. Like the uniformly windowed DFT, the other coefficients around $i = \pm 4$ are zero because they fall on integer multiples of $2\pi/80$ $\Delta\omega$'s.

The situation is more complicated for the coefficients generated by the $21\pi/80$ cosine; not because 21 is much bigger than 8 , but because of the spectral leakage caused by the $\frac{21\pi}{80}$ sinusoid. The Hamming window generated four nonzero coefficients around $X_{\pm 10}$. The rest of the coefficients are nonzero, but because of the very small Hamming side lobes, they are insignificant. The uniformly windowed DFT also produced large coefficients near $X_{\pm 10}$ and $X_{\pm 11}$ and smaller, nonzero coefficients around these points. These leakage coefficients are the result of the side

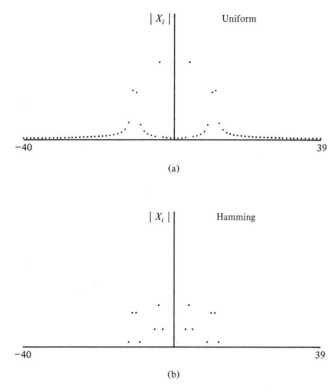

**Figure 8.19** Examples of uniform and Hamming windows:
(a) 80-point DFT with a uniform window;
(b) 80-point DFT with a Hamming window.

lobes in the uniformly windowed DFT response. In conclusion, the uniform window gives a more pronounced peak than the Hamming, but at the expense of a wider range of spectral leakage.

The purpose of this example is to illustrate the effects of windows and how the windows must be factored into the interpretations of the DFT coefficients. For example, it would be foolish to attribute the $X_9, X_{10}, X_{11},$ and $X_{12}$ coefficients generated by the Hamming windowed DFT to four different sinusoids. Rather, an experienced user would know that the Hamming has a wide main lobe and that these coefficients are more than likely the result of a single sinusoid that has been "leaked" into the adjacent coefficients. A really experienced coefficient interpreter would guess that the sinusoid had a frequency that was halfway between $10\frac{2\pi}{80}$ ($X_{10}$) and $11\frac{2\pi}{80}$ ($X_{11}$), because of the symmetry of the coefficients.

But suppose that you were mistakenly given the Hamming DFT results as the output of a uniformly windowed DFT. This interpretation of the coefficients would be far more difficult and, in fact, wrong. In this case, the ninth through twelfth coefficients must be attributed to more than one sinusoid, because a single sinusoid cannot generate that pattern of coefficients from a uniformly windowed DFT. But even this interpretation is unlikely, because the response of Figure 8.19b does not contain the leakage that one would expect from a uniformly windowed DFT. So the windows indeed have a strong effect on the coefficients and they must be factored into the interpretation.

In summary, the DFT responses can be shaped by leaving the DFT algorithm unchanged and windowing the data. Each new window will generate a different DFT response and allow the user to trade off main-lobe width and side-lobe height. Different windows will generate different sets of DFT coefficients, which, if you choose the window correctly, are more meaningful than the unwindowed (uniform) coefficients. Because the window choice is so closely linked to the interpretation of the DFT coefficients, many people approach it as a black art. True, it requires a good deal of experience to pick the appropriate window for a particular application. But once the window is selected, it is a straightforward proposition to apply the window to the DFT.

## 8.7  THE FAST FOURIER TRANSFORM

The DFT is a very useful tool for digital filtering and digital signal processing. There are many computer cycles devoted to computing DFTs and there are even special-purpose DFT machines — as small as a single integrated circuit ranging up to a room-size machine. The DFT is very expensive to implement in its most basic form. This is not because the DFT requires exotic operators; it needs only additions and multiplications. It is because the DFT requires $N$ complex additions and multiplications for each coefficient computed. Since there are $N$ coefficients, a complete DFT requires $N^2$ complex operations.

A single complex multiplication requires four real multiplies and two real additions, and a complex addition involves two real additions (one for the real part, the other for the imaginary). A high-performance, general-purpose computer can perform about 100,000 real multiplications or additions per second. Therefore, such a machine could handle 15,000 complex multiplications per second, 50,000 complex additions, or a complex multiply and addition every 80 $\mu$sec ($8 \times 10^{-5}$ sec). This computation rate sounds awfully fast, but even such a fast machine is easily consumed by the $N^2$ operations appetite of the DFT. A 100-point DFT requires 10,000 complex adds and multiplies and will run in 0.8 sec on a high-performance computer. That length of time might sound reasonable, but consider a 1000-point DFT (typical fare for many DFT computers). This requries $10^6$ complex operations and will consume 80 sec of computer time. Notice that a 10-fold increase in the DFT length resulted in a 100-fold increase in computation time. This is what a factor like $N^2$ does to you.

The DFT is so computationally intensive (expensive to compute) that people began searching for more efficient methods of computing it. Two researchers, J. W. Cooley and J. W. Tukey, found an efficient implementation of the DFT. This became known as the fast Fourier transform (FFT) although it should have been called the fast discrete Fourier transform. It is important to realize that the FFT is just a fast way of computing the DFT. If we ignore the finite precision of computer arithmetic, the FFT and the DFT generate exactly the same results.

Let's start with a four-point DFT and find a more efficient way of computing it. This DFT generates the coefficients, $X_0, X_1, X_2,$ and $X_3$ from the data $x_0, x_1, x_2,$ and $x_3$. The DFT equations are written out below to show explicitly how the coefficients are computed.

$$
\begin{aligned}
X_0 &= x_0 e^{-j\frac{2\pi}{4}0} + x_1 e^{-j\frac{2\pi}{4}0} + x_2 e^{-j\frac{2\pi}{4}0} + x_3 e^{-j\frac{2\pi}{4}0} \\
X_1 &= x_0 e^{-j\frac{2\pi}{4}0} + x_1 e^{-j\frac{2\pi}{4}1} + x_2 e^{-j\frac{2\pi}{4}2} + x_3 e^{-j\frac{2\pi}{4}3} \\
X_2 &= x_0 e^{-j\frac{2\pi}{4}0} + x_1 e^{-j\frac{2\pi}{4}2} + x_2 e^{-j\frac{2\pi}{4}4} + x_3 e^{-j\frac{2\pi}{4}6} \\
X_3 &= x_0 e^{-j\frac{2\pi}{4}0} + x_1 e^{-j\frac{2\pi}{4}3} + x_2 e^{-j\frac{2\pi}{4}6} + x_3 e^{-j\frac{2\pi}{4}9}
\end{aligned}
\tag{8.70}
$$

We said previously that a four-point DFT requires 16 adds and multiplies. But in actuality, this computation requires only 12 complex additions and nine multiplies ($e^{-j\frac{2\pi}{4}0} = 1$ and does not require a multiply).

Note that $e^{-j\frac{2\pi}{4}k}$ is periodic with a period of 4. So the last two terms of $X_2$ and $X_3$ can be written with smaller arguments.

$$
\begin{aligned}
X_2 &= x_0 e^{-j\frac{2\pi}{4}0} + x_1 e^{-j\frac{2\pi}{4}2} + x_2 e^{-j\frac{2\pi}{4}0} + x_3 e^{-j\frac{2\pi}{4}2} \\
X_3 &= x_0 e^{-j\frac{2\pi}{4}0} + x_1 e^{-j\frac{2\pi}{4}3} + x_2 e^{-j\frac{2\pi}{4}2} + x_3 e^{-j\frac{2\pi}{4}1}
\end{aligned}
\tag{8.71}
$$

A thoughtful and somewhat tricky inspection of equations (8.70) and (8.71) shows that the data appear to be processed in pairs: $(x_0, x_2)$ and $(x_1, x_3)$. The following equations are the results of rearranging the DFT to exploit the paired operations:

$$
\begin{aligned}
X_0 &= (x_0 + x_2) + (x_1 + x_3) \\
X_1 &= \left(x_0 + x_2 e^{-j\frac{2\pi}{4}2}\right) + \left(x_1 + x_3 e^{-j\frac{2\pi}{4}2}\right) e^{-j\frac{2\pi}{4}} \\
X_2 &= (x_0 + x_2) + (x_1 + x_3) e^{-j\frac{2\pi}{4}2} \\
X_3 &= \left(x_0 + x_2 e^{-j\frac{2\pi}{4}2}\right) + \left(x_1 + x_3 e^{-j\frac{2\pi}{4}2}\right) e^{-j\frac{2\pi}{4}3}
\end{aligned}
\tag{8.72}
$$

You should convince yourself that this is indeed the four-point DFT.

Notice that this new organization will compute exactly the same coefficients as the DFT of equation (8.70), but it requires only 12 complex additions and five complex multiplies. This is almost a factor-of-2 reduction in the multiplies. So this new organization will cost about half as much as the straightforward DFT computation.

It turns out that similar reorganizations are possible for any DFT with a power of 2 (2, 4, 8, 16, 32, 64, ...) length. This faster organization of the DFT is called the radix 2 fast Fourier transform — the radix 2 FFT. Since almost all FFTs are radix 2 algorithms, the "radix 2" term is generally dropped, and the algorithm is simply called the FFT. The question now is: How do we find the FFT organization for an FFT with any power of 2 length? Fortunately, the development of a general radix 2 FFT algorithm does not require the detailed shuffling and inspection that we suffered through with the four-point FFT. Imagine the bookkeeping required for deriving a 4096-point FFT by inspection; it would be way too much. There is a general method for expressing a power of 2 lengthed DFT as an FFT, and this technique is suggested by revisiting equation (8.72). Equation (8.72) shows that the even samples of the input data appear in the terms $x_0 + x_2$ and $x_0 + x_2 e^{-j2\pi/2}$. These are the DFT coefficients of a two-point signal comprising the even terms of the input. Similarly, the odd input samples appear in the terms $x_1 + x_3$ and $x_1 + x_3 e^{-j2\pi/2}$, which are the DFT coefficients of the two-point odd data sequenece. Therefore, the four-point FFT begins with the computation of two two-point DFTs, one for the even samples and the other for the odd. Then the results of the DFTs are combined as in equation (8.72). This decomposition of the four-point DFT is pictorially shown in Figure 8.20.

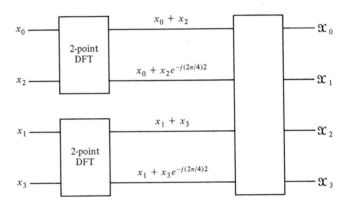

**Figure 8.20** Decomposition of a four-point DFT into two
two-point DFTs — a four-point FFT.

     The notation used in Figure 8.20 is too cumbersome for general use. Instead, a more convenient, shorthand notation is used to represent the processing of digital signals, called data flow graphs. The four-point FFT is represented as a data flow graph in Figure 8.21. The four data points are applied to the left side of the graph, and they move to the right along the data paths (shown as lines). As they move they encounter multiplication and/or addition operators and thereby experience the appropriate arithmetic operations. For example, $x_0$ and $x_2$ are added together by the top left-hand adder. So the adder's output is $x_0 + x_2$. The flow graph shows that $x_2$ is also multiplied by $e^{-j2\pi/2}$ and then added to $x_0$. In this manner, it is possible to pictorially represent the signal processing operations. We can go from the flow graph to the equations or from the equations to the graph. Figure 8.21 is an exact representation of equation (8.72). Notice that the left half of the figure depicts two two-point DFTs, and the right half shows the combinations of the two DFTs to generate the four DFT coefficients. The entire flow graph shows a four-point FFT.

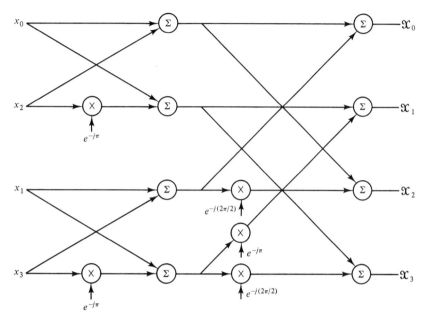

**Figure 8.21** Flow graph representation of four-point FFT.

This interpretation of the four-point FFT suggests that the FFT organization was obtained by dividing the four-point DFT into two two-point DFTs and combining their coefficients. This implies that an eight-point FFT organization might be obtained by dividing the eight-point transform into two four-point DFTs, then combining the two sets of coefficients. Let's try it.

An eight-point DFT is as follows:

$$X_i = \sum_{k=0}^{7} x_k e^{-j\frac{2\pi}{8}ki} \tag{8.73}$$

Break the sum into two parts — one for the even data points of $x_k$ and the other sum for the odd data points.

$$X_i = \sum_{k=0,2,4,6} x_k e^{-j\frac{2\pi}{8}ki} + \sum_{k=1,3,5,7} x_k i e^{-j\frac{2\pi}{8}ki} \tag{8.74}$$

These two summations look a great deal like four-point DFTs. We can get them into DFT form by defining two new data sequences. The even data points are in the sequence $x_{ek}$ and the odd points are in $x_{ok}$.

$$x_{ek} = x_{2k} \qquad k = 0, 1, 2, 3$$
$$x_{ok} = x_{2k+1} \tag{8.75}$$

Now we change the dummy index in equation (8.74) so that both summations are from 0 to 3. This requires some arithmetic in the subscripts of $x_{(\ )}$ and in the exponent.

$$X_i = \sum_{k=0,1,2,3} x_{2k} e^{-j\frac{2\pi}{8} 2ki} + \sum_{k=0,1,2,3} x_{2k+1} e^{-j\frac{2\pi}{8}(2k+1)i} \tag{8.76}$$

The first sum is over the even data sequence and the second sum is over the odd. So we can replace the arithmetic in the subscripts with the two new data sequences. The exponential of the first sum is $e^{-j\frac{2\pi}{4}ki}$, the exponent of a four-point DFT. The exponential of the second sum is a little more difficult to reduce because it is the product of two exponentials, $e^{-j\frac{2\pi}{8}2ki} e^{-j\frac{2\pi}{8}i}$. But the $e^{-j\frac{2\pi}{8}i}$ term is independent of $k$, so it can be factored outside the summation. Therefore, the second sum is also a four-point DFT, and we have shown that the eight-point DFT is the combination of two four-point transforms.

$$X_i = \sum_{k=0}^{3} x_{ek} e^{-j\frac{2\pi}{4}ki} + e^{-j\frac{2\pi}{8}i} \sum_{k=0}^{3} x_{ok} e^{-j\frac{2\pi}{4}ki} \tag{8.77}$$

The actual structure of this decomposition is better illustrated by defining two sets of coefficients, one for the four-point DFT of the even data, $X_{ei}$, and the coefficients of the odd samples, $X_{oi}$. The first term of equation (8.77) is $X_{ei}$ and the second term is $e^{-j\frac{2\pi}{8}i}X_{oi}$. Therefore, the eight-point DFT is the combination of the two sets of four-point results.

$$X_i = X_{ei} + e^{-j\frac{2\pi}{8}i}X_{oi} \qquad i = 0, \dots, 7 \tag{8.78}$$

At first glance, there appears to be a problem with equation (8.78). The coefficients of the eight-point DFT demand that the index, $i$, range from 0 to 7, but the four-point DFTs compute only four distinct coefficients. It is tempting to say that there are no $X_{e4}$ through $X_{e7}$, and equation (8.78) does not make sense. But remember that the DFT coefficients are periodic. Although we compute only $N$ coefficients for an $N$-point transform, the periodicity of the coefficients means that they are defined for any $i$. Therefore, equation (8.78) makes perfect sense — the eight-point

DFT is computed on the basis of two periods of the four-point transforms.

$$X_0 = X_{e0} + X_{o0}$$

$$X_1 = X_{e1} + e^{-j\frac{2\pi}{8}1}X_{o1}$$

$$X_2 = X_{e2} + e^{-j\frac{2\pi}{8}2}X_{o2}$$

$$X_3 = X_{e3} + e^{-j\frac{2\pi}{8}3}X_{o3}$$

$$X_4 = X_{e4} + e^{-j\frac{2\pi}{8}4}X_{o4}$$

$$= X_{e0} + e^{-j\frac{2\pi}{8}4}X_{o0}$$

$$X_5 = X_{e5} + e^{-j\frac{2\pi}{8}5}X_{o5} \qquad (8.79)$$

$$= X_{e1} + e^{-j\frac{2\pi}{8}5}X_{o1}$$

$$X_6 = X_{e6} + e^{-j\frac{2\pi}{8}6}X_{o6}$$

$$= X_{e2} + e^{-j\frac{2\pi}{8}6}X_{o2}$$

$$X_7 = X_{e7} + e^{-j\frac{2\pi}{8}7}X_{o7}$$

$$= X_{e3} + e^{-j\frac{2\pi}{8}7}X_{o3}$$

The data flow representation of the eight-point FFT is shown in Figure 8.22. Notice that this picture is far more busy than that of the four-point transform. To reduce the clutter, the multipliers have been replaced by arrows with the value of the multiplicand shown near the arrow. This organization requires eight complex multiplications and additions to collect the outputs of the four-point DFTs into the eight-point results. Each four-point FFT requires eight multiplies and adds and there are two of them. So, the complete eight-point FFT consumes $2 \times 8 + 8 = 24$ ($8 \log_2 8$) multiplications and additions. The straightforward implementation of the eight-point DFT requires $8^2 = 64$ multiplications and additions, so the FFT is about three times faster than the straightforward implementation of the DFT.

We could continue this development and show that a 16-point DFT can be divided into two eight-point transforms, and so on. But rather than continue in a brute-force manner, we will show that any even-length DFT can be expressed as two DFTs of half the length. This is simply a generalization of the work performed on the eight-point transform.

Consider an $N$-point DFT where $N$ is an even number.

$$X_i = \sum_{k=0}^{N-1} x_k e^{-j\frac{2\pi}{N}ki} \qquad (8.80)$$

It can be split into two sums, one for the even data and one for the odd.

$$X_i = \sum_{k \ even} x_k e^{-j\frac{2\pi}{N}ki} + \sum_{k \ odd} x_k e^{-j\frac{2\pi}{N}ki} \qquad (8.81)$$

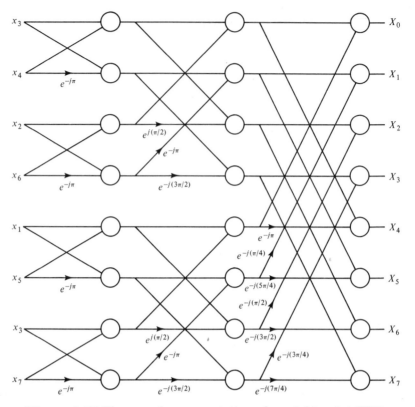

**Figure 8.22** Flow graph representation of an eight-point FFT.

As in the previous development, this equation can be written as the sum of two half-length transforms by defining even and odd data sequences.

$$x_{ek} = x_{2k}$$
$$x_{ok} = x_{2k+1} \qquad (8.82)$$

Next, we change the summation index to range from 0 to $\frac{N}{2} - 1$.

$$X_i = \sum_{k=0}^{\frac{N}{2}-1} x_{2k} e^{-j\frac{2\pi}{N}2ki} + \sum_{k=0}^{\frac{N}{2}-1} x_{2k+1} e^{-j\frac{2\pi}{N}(2k+1)i} \qquad (8.83)$$

These sums are really coefficients of the $\frac{N}{2}$-point transforms of the even and the odd data.

$$X_i = \sum_{k=0}^{\frac{N}{2}-1} x_{ek} e^{-j\frac{2\pi}{(\frac{N}{2})}ki} + e^{-j\frac{2\pi}{N}i} \sum_{k=0}^{\frac{N}{2}-1} x_{ok} e^{-j\frac{2\pi}{(\frac{N}{2})}ki} \qquad (8.84)$$

Simplify the equations by expressing the DFTs in terms of their coefficients. Denote the $\frac{N}{2}$ coefficients of the transform of the even data $X_{ei}$ and the coefficients of the odd transform $X_{oi}$. Using this notation allows us to express the $N$-point coefficients in terms of the two sets of $\frac{N}{2}$ coefficients.

$$X_i = X_{ei} + e^{-j\frac{2\pi}{N}i}X_{oi} \tag{8.85}$$

This computation requires $N$ complex multiplications and additions to produce the $N$ coefficients from two $\frac{N}{2}$-point transforms. Therefore, any even-length DFT can be divided into two smaller DFTs.

The FFT is based on the repeated division of a DFT. If $N$ is a power of 2, the DFTs can be repeatedly halved until we are left with $N/2$, two-point transforms. We execute the FFT by first computing the $N/2$, two-point DFTs, then we combine the coefficients of those DFTs to generate the coefficients of $N/4$, four-point DFTs. We combine those coefficients to make the coefficients of $N/8$, eight-point DFTs, and so on. In this manner we build successively larger DFTs until we get the $N$ coefficients of the required $N$-point DFT.

So, the FFT can be thought of as a series of stages. The first stage is the computation of the two-point DFTs. Each two-point DFT requires two multiplies and additions (complex of course), so the first stage involves $N$ complex operations. The second stage builds the four-point coefficients from the two-point. Each four-point transform requires four multiplications and additions and there are $N/4$ such transforms in the second stage. Therefore, the second stage also demands $N$ complex operations. The third stage builds $N/8$ eight-point DFTs, and it, too, involves $N$ multiplications and additions ($\frac{N}{8} \times 8$). Each successive stage requires $N$ multiplications because the lengths of the DFTs are doubled at each stage but there are only half as many. The final stage, where the $N$-point coefficients are finally assembled, requires $N$ additions and multiplications. An $N$-point FFT ($N = 2^{\text{integer}}$) has $\log_2 N$ such stages, and since each stage requires $N$ multiplies and additions, the $N$-point FFT requires $N\log_2 N$ complex operations. This should be compared with the $N^2$ operations demanded by the straightforward implementation of the DFT. As shown in Table 8.2, as $N$ becomes large, the FFT becomes increasingly more efficient. A relatively small FFT of 64 data points will run about 10 times faster than a 64-point DFT and will produce the same results. A one million-point (actually 1,048,576-point) FFT will run about 50,000 times faster than its DFT counterpart. Therefore, it is generally worth the effort to use the FFT algorithm.

**Example:** Organize a 32-point DFT as an FFT by dividing it into five stages ($5 = \log_2 32$).

The first stage consists of two-point DFTs, and these results are combined to form four-point DFTs in stage two. The third stage combines the four-point coefficients to produce the coefficients of an eight-point DFT. The fourth stage produces two sets of 16-point coefficients, and the last stage combines the 16-point results into the 32-point coefficients. The resulting 32-point FFT is shown in Figure 8.23.

**Table 8.2** Comparison of DFT and FFT Execution Times

| Length $N$ | DFT $N^2$ | FFT $N\log_2 N$ | FFT/DFT $\frac{N\log_2 N}{N^2}$ |
|---|---|---|---|
| 32 | 1024 | 160 | 15% |
| 64 | 4160 | 384 | 9% |
| 128 | 16,384 | 896 | 5% |
| 256 | 65,536 | 2048 | 3% |
| 512 | 262,144 | 4,608 | 1.7% |
| 1024 | 1,049,600 | 10,240 | 1% |

The first step is to divide the 32-point DFT into a combination of two 16-point DFTs. The even DFT uses the data $x_0, x_2, x_4, x_6, \ldots, x_{30}$ and the odd DFT uses the data $x_1, x_3, x_5, x_7, \ldots, x_{31}$. The two sets of DFT coefficients are combined to form the 32-point FFT as shown in equation (8.85).

The next step is to divide the 16-point DFTs into four eight-point transforms; two eight-point transforms are required for each 16-point. The even data sequence is divided into an even-even sequence, $x_0, x_4, x_8, \ldots, x_{28}$ and an even-odd sequence, $x_2, x_6, x_{10}, \ldots, x_{30}$. Each of these sequences is applied to an eight-point DFT and the results are combined to generate the 16-point DFT of $x_0, x_2, x_4, \ldots, x_{30}$. In a similar way, the 16-point odd sequence is divided into two eight-point sequences and these are applied to two eight-point DFTs. The coefficients of the two eight-point DFTs are collected to form the 16-point odd FFT.

The next step is to reduce the eight-point DFTs to four-point DFTs. This will result in a stage with eight four-point DFTs, and requires a further subdivision of the data into eight four-point sequences. The first sequence is the even-even-even sequence of $x_0, x_8, x_{16}$, and $x_{24}$. The second sequence is the even-even-odd sequence of $x_4, x_{12}, x_{20}$, and $x_{28}$. The coefficients of the DFTs of these sequences are combined to form the eight-point DFT of $x_0, x_4, x_8, \ldots, x_{28}$. In a similar way, the other six four-point DFTs are pairwise combined to produce the three other eight-point DFTs.

The final step (whew) of this decomposition is to express each of the eight four-point transforms as the combination of two two-point transforms. This is done by dividing the four-point data sequences into 16 two-point data sequences. The first data sequence is $x_0$ and $x_{16}$, and its DFT coefficients are combined with those from $x_8$ and $x_{24}$ to produce the DFT of the four-point sequence $x_0, x_8, x_{16}$, and $x_{24}$. So the first stage of this FFT requires 16 two-point DFTs. The coefficients of these DFTs are pairwise combined

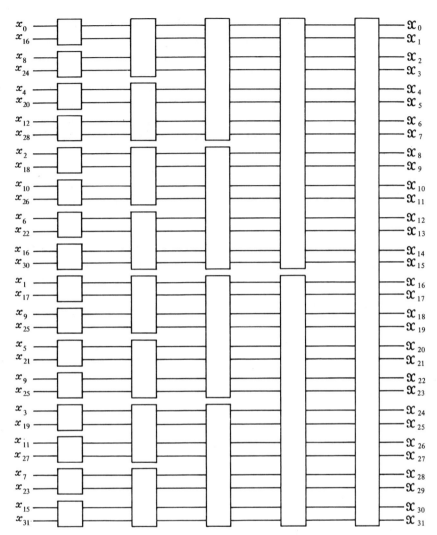

$x_0$
$x_{16}$
$x_8$
$x_{24}$
$x_4$
$x_{20}$
$x_{12}$
$x_{28}$
$x_2$
$x_{18}$
$x_{10}$
$x_{26}$
$x_6$
$x_{22}$
$x_{16}$
$x_{30}$
$x_1$
$x_{17}$
$x_9$
$x_{25}$
$x_5$
$x_{21}$
$x_9$
$x_{25}$
$x_3$
$x_{19}$
$x_{11}$
$x_{27}$
$x_7$
$x_{23}$
$x_{15}$
$x_{31}$

$X_0$
$X_1$
$X_2$
$X_3$
$X_4$
$X_5$
$X_6$
$X_7$
$X_8$
$X_9$
$X_{10}$
$X_{11}$
$X_{12}$
$X_{13}$
$X_{14}$
$X_{15}$
$X_{16}$
$X_{17}$
$X_{18}$
$X_{19}$
$X_{20}$
$X_{21}$
$X_{22}$
$X_{23}$
$X_{24}$
$X_{25}$
$X_{26}$
$X_{27}$
$X_{28}$
$X_{29}$
$X_{30}$
$X_{31}$

**Figure 8.23** Block diagram of a 32-point FFT.

to produce the coefficients of eight four-point DFTs. These coefficients are combined in pairs to produce the coefficients for four eight-point DFTs, which are combined to produce the 16-point DFTs. The final stage produces the 32-point coefficients by combining the two sets of 16-point coefficients.

The radix 2 FFT requires data sequences with lengths of powers of 2. This is so that the DFT can be halved down to two-point DFTs. But the FFT can also be applied to data sequences that do not have lengths that are powers of 2. There are four different approaches to nonpower-of-2 length sequences. The crudest approach is to compute it as a straightforward DFT. This is inefficient, especially for long data sequences, but it is very easy to program. The second approach is to successively divide the DFT in half until you run up against a DFT with an odd length. Perform the odd-length DFTs as a straightforward computation of the DFT and then begin combining the coefficients until the desired coefficients are obtained. For example, a 28-point DFT can be divided twice into four seven-point DFTs. These seven-point transforms can be implemented as straight DFTs and their coefficients can be pairwise combined to get two 14-point DFTs and finally a 28-point DFT. This method is more efficient than the straight DFT computation, but not as fast as the FFT. In the 28-point DFT example, each of the seven-point DFTs would require 49 multiplies and each of the two combining stages would require 28 multiplies and adds. So this hybrid DFT/FFT computes the coefficients with 252 operations ($2 \times 28 + 4 \times 49$). This is a big savings over the $28^2 = 784$ operations required by the straight DFT computation.

The third option is to force the data to a power-of-2 length by adding zeros to the end of the data sequence. Simply extend the sequence with zeros until the length of the augmented sequence is a power of 2. This is called zero filling and does not affect the general shape of the DFT coefficients — the zero data do not contribute to the DFT summation. For example, the 28-point data sequence can be applied to a radix 2 FFT after four zeros are added to the end.

$$x_0, x_1, x_2, \ldots, x_{27}, 0, 0, 0, 0 \tag{8.86}$$

This zero filling does not affect the sum in the DFT.

$$
\begin{aligned}
X_i &= \sum_{k=0}^{31} = x_k e^{-j \frac{2\pi}{32} ki} \\
&= \sum_{k=0}^{27} x_k e^{-j \frac{2\pi}{32} ki}
\end{aligned}
\tag{8.87}
$$

But zero filling will change which DFT coefficients are computed. In this example, a straight DFT of the 28 data points will yield the coefficients $X\left(\frac{2\pi}{28} i\right)$, but the zero-filled FFT produces the coefficients $X\left(\frac{2\pi}{32} i\right)$. Zero filling may, at first, look like a waste of computation, because we are computing extra coefficients. But the efficiencies of the FFT usually outweigh the extra coefficients. For example, a 32-point FFT is computed in only $5 \times 32 = 160$ operations, which is less than the DFT or FFT/DFT hybrid schemes that were proposed earlier.

The final option is to develop an alternate radix FFT to handle the specific problem. Remember that the power-of-2 restriction came from the halving of the DFTs to produce shorter DFTs. Suppose that we had divided the DFTs in thirds rather than halves. If we had, we would have developed a radix 3 FFT, which naturally handles data sequences whose lengths are powers of 3 ($3, 9, 27, 81, 243, \ldots$).

It is possible to develop an FFT based on any prime number, which will efficiently compute the DFT of the lengths of the power of the prime number. It is also possible to divide a DFT into mixed radixes, so as to efficiently compute the DFT for an arbitrary-length data sequence. The 28-point example is a primitive case of this, because we divided the data into radix 2 and radix 7 DFTs. Prime radix and mixed prime radix FFTs are generally reserved for special applications and are seldom used by general users. These techniques may be interesting, but it is beyond the scope of our introductory treatment.

In summary, the FFT algorithm is an efficient scheme for computing the DFTs. It is important to remember that the FFT and the DFT compute exactly the same coefficients, but the FFT does it faster. The major restriction of the radix 2 FFT (almost all FFT algorithms are of this type) is that the data sequence must have a power-of-2 length. But this seldom causes real problems because many applications allow the user to select the length of the transform, or the user can use zero filling to lengthen a given data sequence to a power of 2.

The FFT is a complicated algorithm to program on a computer. There is a great deal of bookkeeping involved in breaking the DFT into smaller and smaller DFTs and then combining the results. Fortunately, few FFT users resort to writing their own FFT algorithms. Most computer centers and even many home computers have prepackaged FFT algorithms. These are usually presented as procedures (subroutines) that are called with an array of data and produce an array of DFT coefficients — after a good deal of number crunching. Each FFT algorithm has its own conventions and these must be followed if the results are to be properly interpreted. For example, some return the DFT coefficients, $X_0, X_1, \ldots, X_{N-1}$, while others return the negative frequencies explicitly, $X_{-\frac{N}{2}}, X_{-\frac{N}{2}+1}, \ldots, X_{\frac{N}{2}-1}$. Some of the FFTs assume that the input data are purely real, so they deal with a real input array and produce only half of the DFT coefficients. (Why can they get away with only half when the input data are real?) Some FFT algorithms require an ancillary working array that is set to the complex exponentials, $e^{-j\frac{2\pi}{N}i}$, at the beginning of the transform. The point is to understand the use of the particular FFT algorithm before you attempt to get meaningful data from it.

## 8.8 SUMMARY

The discrete Fourier transform (DFT) is widely used for transforming data from the time domain to the frequency domain. The inverse discrete Fourier transform (IDFT) performs the inverse transform and allows us to compute time domain representations from the frequency domain. With the DFT and the IDFT, a designer can choose the most convenient domain (time or frequency) to perform the work. It is possible to compute a filter's frequency response automatically from its impulse response or go the other way. Furthermore, it is possible to apply the DFT to arbitrary digital signals to produce their frequency-domain representations. We have discovered that the frequency-domain representation of a signal is sometimes much more useful than the time domain. The primary reason for this is that we are often interested in the frequency components of the signal, and the DFT coefficients give us that information directly.

We have also noticed that the DFT is not a perfect frequency sorter. The finite length of the DFT causes spectral leakage, which means that the input signal leaks into adjacent DFT coefficients. Spectral leakage can be controlled by the adroit use of windows. There are over 100 popularly used DFT windows, and each one has its own trade-off between the spectral leakage and the frequency resolutions.

In practice, the DFT is too costly to implement. It requires $N^2$ multiplies and adds to transform $N$ samples of a signal into its $N$ DFT coefficients. The fast Fourier transform (FFT) performs the same arithmetic as the DFT, but it organizes the operations in a more efficient manner. The FFT makes heavy use of intermediate results, by dividing the transform into a series of smaller transforms. An $N$-point FFT requires $N\log_2 N$ multiplications and additions, which is a big savings over the $N^2$ operations demanded by the DFT. One of the major drawbacks of the radix 2 FFT is that it demands a power-of-2 number of points. However, this is seldom a problem because it is usually possible to append zeros to the end of a data sequence to lengthen it to a power of 2.

## EXERCISES

8-1. Show that the IDFT computes the impulse response from the DFT coefficients by substituting equation (8.18) into equation (8.19). Be sure to change the dummy variable ($k$) in equation (8.18) to something other than $k$ or $i$ before the substitution.

8-2. Compute the discrete frequency response for the following filter:

$$h_0 = 1, \ h_1 = 1, \ h_2 = 1, \ h_3 = 1 \qquad \text{others} = 0$$

Compare these results to the filter's frequency response.

8-3. Compute the discrete frequency response for the following filter:

$$h_0 = 1, \ h_1 = -1, \ h_2 = 1, \ h_3 = -1 \qquad \text{others} = 0$$

Compare these results to the filter's frequency response.

8-4. Consider the following variation on the IDFT definition:

$$h_k = \sum_{i=0}^{2N-1} \mathcal{H}\left(i\frac{2\pi}{N}\right) e^{j\frac{2\pi}{N}ik}$$

This form uses twice as many ($2N$) DFT coefficients as the regular IDFT. How is the impulse response computed by this variation related to that computed by the normal IDFT [equation (8.19)]?

8-5. Consider the following variation on the IDFT:

$$h_k = \sum_{i=0}^{2N-1} \mathcal{H}\left(i\frac{2\pi}{N}\right) e^{j\frac{2\pi}{2N}ik}$$

It uses twice as many DFT coefficients and lower-frequency complex exponentials. How is the impulse response computed by this variation related to that of the normal DFT [equation (8.19)]?

8-6. Under what minimal set of conditions will an $N$-point impulse response produce DFT coefficients that are periodic in $N/2$?

8-7. Consider the following two digital signals:

$$x_k : \qquad k = 0, \ldots, N-1$$

$$z_k : \qquad k = 0, \ldots, 2N-1$$

Suppose that they have DFT coefficients $X_i$ and $Z_i$.

$$X_i = DFT_N\{x_k\}$$

$$Z_i = DFT_{2N}\{z_k\}$$

(a) Compute the DFT coefficients of $2x_k$. Express your results in terms of $X_i$.

(b) Suppose that $x_k$ is extended to a $2N$-point digital signal by appending $N$ zero elements to the end of $x_k$. Call this extended signal $y_k$.

$$y_k = \begin{cases} x_k & \text{if } k < N \\ 0 & \text{if } k \geq N \end{cases}$$

Compute the even DFT coefficients of $y_k$. Express your results in terms of $X_i$s.

(c) Compute the odd DFT coefficients of $y_k$. Can you express them solely in terms of the $X_i$s?

(d) Compute the even DFT coefficients of

$$DFT_{2N}\{y_k + z_k\}$$

Express your results in terms of $X_i$ and $Z_i$.

8-8. Consider an $N$-element digital signal, $x_k$, with DFT coefficients $X_i$.

$$X_i = DFT_N\{x_k\}$$

Periodically extend $x_k$ into a $2N$ sequence, $z_k$.

$$z_k = \begin{cases} x_k & \text{if } k = 0, \ldots, N-1 \\ x_{k-N} & \text{if } k = N, \ldots, 2N-1 \end{cases}$$

Compute the $2N$ coefficients of $z_k$.

$$Z_i = DFT_{2N}\{z_k\} \qquad i = 0, \ldots, 2N-1$$

Express your results in terms of $X_i$.

8-9. Show that the DFT of a purely imaginary signal, $x_k$, is conjugate anti-symmetric.

$$X_i = -X^*_{-i}$$

8-10. Suppose that the DFT coefficients, $X_i$, are produced by purely real signals. How are $X_1$ and $X_{N-1}$ related? (*Hint*: Use the DFT relationship and exploit the periodicity of $e^{j\omega}$.)

8-11. You have just completed a 16-point DFT and expected

$$X_{-8} \ldots X_7$$

Rather, the DFT results are presented as $X_0 \ldots X_{15}$. Relate these coefficients to those that you expected.

8-12. You've just completed a 16-point DFT and expected the frequency response at

$$-\frac{2\pi}{16}8, -\frac{\pi}{16}7, \ldots, \frac{2\pi}{16}7$$

Rather, you are presented the DFT coefficients, $X_0, \ldots, X_{15}$. Relate the DFT coefficients to the frequencies that you were expecting.

8-13. Suppose that we apply $x_k = e^{j0.2\pi k}$ to an eight-point DFT and produce the coefficients, $X_{-4} \ldots X_3$.

(a) Compute the frequencies associated with each of the eight coefficients.

(b) Compute the $\Delta\omega$s associated with each of the eight coefficients.

(c) Which coefficients will have the largest magnitude?

8-14. Suppose that we apply $x_k = 1$ to a 30-point DFT. Which coefficient(s) will have the largest value(s)?

8-15. Suppose that we apply $x_k = e^{j\frac{\pi}{2}k}$ to a 40-point DFT.

(a) Which coefficient(s) will have the largest value(s)?

(b) What are the values of the other coefficients?

8-16. Suppose that we apply a sinusoid at $\frac{25}{40}\pi$ rad/sample to a 40-point DFT.

(a) What are the coefficients that assume the largest magnitudes?

(b) What are the magnitudes of $X_{10}$ and $X_{11}$? (*Hint:* Use figure 8.6.)

8-17. Repeat Exercise 8-16 for an 80-point DFT.

8-18. Show that $x_k = \cos\frac{2\pi}{N}k$ and $z_k = \sin\frac{2\pi}{N}k$ produce DFT coefficients with the same magnitudes, $|X_i| = |Z_i|$.

8-19. Suppose that we sample a 60-Hz sinusoid ($\sin 2\pi 60t$) at 1000 samples/sec and apply the samples to a 40-point DFT.

(a) Compute the magnitudes of the six largest coefficients (don't forget about the negative frequencies).

(b) Find the sampling rate that is closest to 1000 samples/sec that will result in no spectral leakage when applied to a 40-point DFT.

8-20. Suppose we have a measurement that is a signal plus some additive noise. We perform a DFT on the measurement and get the following coefficients:

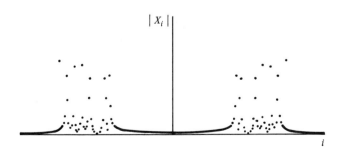

We turn off the signal and perform a DFT on the noise only. This produces the following coefficients:

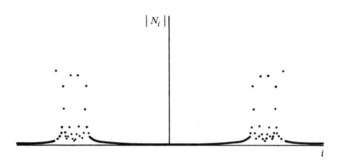

(a) Specify the frequency response of a digital filter that will remove the noise from the signal.

(b) Will this filter alter the signal? Why or why not?

8-21. We have a signal that is the combination of a voice signal from 100 to 1000 Hz and sinusoidal noise at 60 and 1800 Hz. This measurement is sampled at 3000 samples/sec.

(a) Sketch the coefficients produced by an 80-point DFT of the samples of this measurement.

(b) Specify a filter that will remove the sinusoidal noise and preserve the voice.

8-22. Consider the DFT implementation of the following periodic convolution:

$$y_k = \sum_{i=0}^{99} h_i x_{k-i} \qquad \text{where} \quad x_k = x_{k+50}$$

(a) How many DFT coefficients are computed for $\mathcal{H}_i$?

(b) How many $X_i$ coefficients are computed?

(c) What is the period of the output, $y_k$?

(d) Express the DFT coefficients of the output, $Y_i$'s, in terms of the $\mathcal{H}_i$'s and the $X_i$'s.

8-23. Compute the shortest-length, unwindowed DFT to resolve frequencies that are only 0.1 rad/sample apart. Support your answer.

8-24. Suppose that an $N_0$-point DFT will resolve frequencies $\omega_0$ rad/sample apart. What is the shortest DFT that resolves $\omega_0/2$ rad/sample?

8-25. What input signal, $x_k$, produced the following DFT coefficients? You may assume a uniform window.

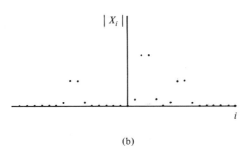

(a)

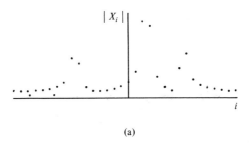

(b)

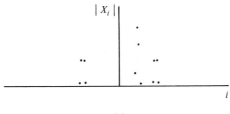

(c)

8-26. What input signal, $x_k$, produced the following DFT coefficients? You may assume a Hamming window.

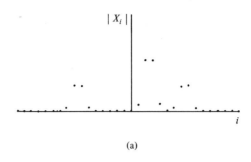

(a)

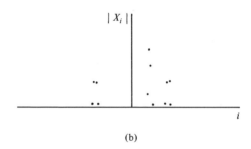

(b)

8-27. What is the shortest DFT that will prevent leakage greater than 5% for coefficients greater than $\pi/20$ away from the input frequency?

    (a) Using a uniform window

    (b) Using a Hamming window

    (c) Using a Bartlett window

8-28. Show that equation (8.70) can be evaluated with only eight multiplies [see equation (8.71) for $X_2$ and $X_3$].

8-29. Write the equations for the following flow graphs. That is, $z_k = ?$.

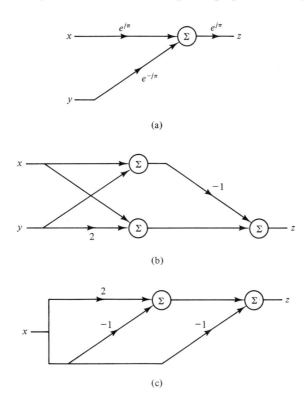

(a)

(b)

(c)

8-30. A 16-point DFT can be expressed as the combination of four four-point DFTs. Write the four-point data sequences that are applied to each four-point DFT so as to build the 16-point transform.

8-31. Suppose that we are faced with a 1025-point data sequence, one element greater than a 1024-point FFT. Suppose that we zero-fill the data to the smallest radix 2 FFT that will handle the data.

(a) What is the length of the smallest FFT that will handle 1025 points?

(b) How many multiplications and additions are required for this FFT?

(c) How many adds and multiplies are required for a 1025-point conventionally computed DFT?

(d) What are the savings, and are they worth it?

8-32. Consider a 1024-point FFT.

    (a) How many stages does it have?

    (b) How many multiplies are required in each stage?

    (c) How many multiplies are required for the entire FFT?

8-33. Perform a radix 3 decomposition of a nine-point DFT by writing it as the combination of three three-point DFTs.

    (a) Find the three data sequences that are applied to the three-point DFTs.

    (b) Derive the equation to show how the three-point DFT results are combined to form the nine-point coefficients.

    (c) Draw a data flow diagram of your nine-point radix 3 FFT.

# Appendix A

# Useful Formulas and Identities

**Trigonometric Identities**

$$\sin(-\theta) = -\sin\theta$$
$$\cos(-\theta) = \cos\theta$$
$$\cos^2\theta = \tfrac{1}{2}\left(1 + \cos 2\theta\right)$$
$$\cos^3\theta = \tfrac{1}{4}\left(3\cos\theta + \cos 3\theta\right)$$
$$\sin^2\theta = \tfrac{1}{2}\left(1 - \cos 2\theta\right)$$
$$\sin^3\theta = \tfrac{1}{4}\left(3\sin\theta - \sin 3\theta\right)$$
$$\sin(\alpha + \beta) = \sin\alpha\cos\beta + \cos\alpha\sin\beta$$
$$\sin(\alpha - \beta) = \sin\alpha\cos\beta - \cos\alpha\sin\beta$$
$$\cos(\alpha + \beta) = \cos\alpha\cos\beta - \sin\alpha\sin\beta$$
$$\cos(\alpha - \beta) = \cos\alpha\cos\beta + \sin\alpha\sin\beta$$
$$\sin\alpha\sin\beta = \tfrac{1}{2}\left[\cos(\alpha - \beta) - \cos(\alpha + \beta)\right]$$
$$\cos\alpha\cos\beta = \tfrac{1}{2}\left[\cos(\alpha - \beta) + \cos(\alpha + \beta)\right]$$
$$\sin\alpha\cos\beta = \tfrac{1}{2}\left[\sin(\alpha - \beta) + \sin(\alpha + \beta)\right]$$

## Complex Exponentials

$$e^{j\theta} = \cos\theta + j\sin\theta$$
$$e^{-j\theta} = \cos\theta - j\sin\theta$$
$$\cos\theta = \tfrac{1}{2}\left(e^{j\theta} + e^{-j\theta}\right)$$
$$\sin\theta = \tfrac{1}{2j}\left(e^{j\theta} - e^{-j\theta}\right)$$
$$= \tfrac{-j}{2}\left(e^{j\theta} - e^{-j\theta}\right)$$

## Differentiation

$$\tfrac{d}{dt}\sin u = \cos u\,\tfrac{du}{dt}$$

$$\tfrac{d}{dt}\cos u = -\sin u\,\tfrac{du}{dt}$$

$$\tfrac{d}{dt}e^{u} = e^{u}\,\tfrac{du}{dt}$$

Chain rule: $\tfrac{d}{dt}f(u) = \tfrac{d}{dt}f(u)\tfrac{du}{dt}$

## Integration

$$\int_a^b \cos u\ du = \sin u \ \Big|_a^b$$

$$\int_a^b \sin u\ du = -\cos u \ \Big|_a^b$$

$$\int_a^b e^{u}\ du = e^{u} \ \Big|_a^b$$

$$\int_a^b \sin^2 u\ du = \tfrac{1}{2}u - \tfrac{1}{4}\sin 2u \ \Big|_a^b$$

$$\int_a^b \cos^2 u\ du = \tfrac{1}{2}u + \tfrac{1}{4}\sin 2u \ \Big|_a^b$$

$$\int_a^b u\sin au\ du = \tfrac{1}{a^2}\sin au - \tfrac{u}{a}\cos au \ \Big|_a^b$$

$$\int_a^b u\cos au\ du = \tfrac{1}{a^2}\cos au + \tfrac{u}{a}\sin au \ \Big|_a^b$$

Integration by parts: $\int_a^b u\ dv = uv \ \Big|_a^b - \int_a^b v\ du$

# Appendix B

# Introduction
# to Complex Variables

This Appendix was contributed by Philip DesJardin, who as a teaching assistant for the undergraduate digital filtering course at Stanford University, became tired of answering questions on complex variables.

## B.1 WHAT ARE COMPLEX NUMBERS?

This is a fundamental and not easily answered question. Undoubtedly, many of you while learning algebra have faced an equation that contained square roots of negative numbers. You might have been tempted to abandon the equation as unsolvable. However, you discovered that there is a solution for this type of equation, but the solution is beyond the realm of real numbers — these are the imaginary numbers.

The term "imaginary" is misleading; imaginary numbers exist, have meaning, and pervade nearly all aspects of engineering and science. Understanding imaginary and complex numbers is essential for understanding digital filters and signal analysis. This brief appendix will give you enough understanding of imaginary numbers and complex variables to manipulate the beasties.

## B.2  IMAGINARY NUMBERS

Since childhood, we have learned the significance of the unit "1" through activities such as counting and measuring. Unlike the real unit "1," the imaginary unit $j$ (we use $j$ rather than the more conventional $i$ as the imaginary unit, because electrical engineers use $i$ for current) is difficult to visualize. So instead of trying to visualize $j$, it is more fruitful to understand its mathematical properties. The symbol $j$ is best understood as a mathematical abstraction that satisfies the equation $j^2 = -1$, rather than as a physical entity.

Multiplying $j$ by any real number, say $c$, yields an imaginary number $jc$ with magnitude $|c|$. For example, $-j3$ is a square root of -9, because

$$(-j3)(-j3) = (-3)(-3)(j^2) = (9)(-1) = -9$$

Adding or subtracting two imaginary numbers forms a third imaginary number:

$$ja + jb = j(a + b)$$
$$ja - jb = j(a - b)$$

(B.1)

## B.3  COMPLEX NUMBERS

Complex numbers have both real and imaginary components. The complex number $z = x + jy$ ($x$ and $y$ being real numbers) has a real component $x$ and an imaginary component $y$, often written as $\text{Re}\{z\}$ and $\text{Im}\{z\}$, respectively. Pure real and pure imaginary numbers are subsets of complex numbers. A real number is a complex number with no imaginary component, and an imaginary number is a complex number with no real component.

Two complex numbers are added or subtracted by adding or subtracting their respective real and imaginary components:

$$z_1 + z_2 = (x_1 + jy_1) + (x_2 + jy_2)$$
$$= (x_1 + x_2) + j(y_1 + y_2)$$

(B.2)

and

$$z_1 - z_2 = (x_1 + jy_1) - (x_2 + jy_2)$$
$$= (x_1 - x_2) + j(y_1 - y_2)$$

(B.3)

Multiplication appears to be difficult, but distributing multiplication across the real and imaginary components simplifies the operation. If $c$ is any real number, then

$$cz = c(\text{Re}\{z\} + j\text{Im}\{z\})$$
$$= c(x + jy)$$
$$= cx + jcy$$

(B.4)

Similarly, scaling a complex number $z$ by an imaginary number $jd$ yields another complex number:

$$
\begin{aligned}
jdz &= jd(x + jy) \\
&= jdx + j^2 dy \\
&= jdx + (-1)dy \\
&= d(-y + jx)
\end{aligned}
\tag{B.5}
$$

Notice that the real component of the result is negative because $j^2 = -1$. Multiplying two complex numbers is an extension of the foregoing two cases.

$$
\begin{aligned}
z_1 z_2 &= (x_1 + jy_1)(x_2 + jy_2) \\
&= x_1 x_2 + jx_1 y_2 + jy_1 x_2 + j^2 y_1 y_2 \\
&= (x_1 x_2 - y_1 y_2) + j(x_1 y_2 + x_2 y_1)
\end{aligned}
\tag{B.6}
$$

Complex division is trickier, and it will be discussed after the next section lays a more solid foundation for understanding complex numbers.

**Examples:** Adding and multiplying complex numbers.

Addition:
$$
\begin{aligned}
(3 + j4) \ + \ (2 - j7) &= (2 + 5) + j(4 - 7) \\
&= 5 - j3
\end{aligned}
\tag{B.7}
$$

$$
\begin{aligned}
(16 - j2) \ + \ (-8 + j2) &= (16 - 8) + j(2 - 2) \\
&= 8
\end{aligned}
\tag{B.8}
$$

$$
(2 + j4) \ - \ 2 = j4
\tag{B.9}
$$

Multiplication:

$$
\begin{aligned}
(1 + j2) \cdot (4 + j9) &= (1 \cdot 4 - 2 \cdot 9) + j(1 \cdot 9 + 2 \cdot 4) \\
&= -14 + j17
\end{aligned}
\tag{B.10}
$$

$$
\begin{aligned}
(3 + j6)(j) &= j3 - 6 \\
&= -6 + j3
\end{aligned}
\tag{B.11}
$$

$$
(3 + j6)(-j) = 6 - j3
\tag{B.12}
$$

$$
\begin{aligned}
(j)(-j) &= (0 + j)(0 - j) \\
&= -(j^2) + j0 = 1
\end{aligned}
\tag{B.13}
$$

## B.4  CARTESIAN AND POLAR REPRESENTATIONS

The preceding section has shown that complex numbers are composed of real and imaginary components. Assigning each component to one of two orthogonal axes yields a graphical domain for complex numbers called the complex plane. This is akin to the number line for real numbers. Any single point on this plane represents a single complex number.

Figure B.1 illustrates the conventional form of the complex plane: the horizontal and vertical axes represents the plane's real and imaginary axes. Point $z$ represents the complex number $1 - j$.

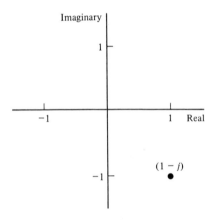

**Figure B.1** The complex plane.

Complex numbers can also be represented in polar form: any complex number $z$ has a magnitude (also called a modulus) $|z|$ and an angle (also called an argument or a phase) $\theta$. Angles are measured in the counterclockwise direction; the real axis is at zero phase. The point $z$ in Figure B.1 is written in polar form as $z = \sqrt{1^2 + (-1)^2} \angle \tan^{-1}(-1/1)$, or $\sqrt{2} \angle -\pi/2$.

A complex number can be readily switched between Cartesian and polar representations by using the following formulas:

$$
\begin{aligned}
z &= x + jy \\
&= r\left(\cos\theta + j\sin\theta\right) \\
&= r\cos\theta + jr\sin\theta
\end{aligned}
\tag{B.14}
$$

where

$$r^2 = x^2 + y^2$$
$$\theta = \tan^{-1} \frac{y}{x} \qquad -\pi \le \theta < \pi$$
$$x = r \cos \theta$$
$$y = r \sin \theta$$

$$(B.15)$$

It turns out that multiplication is a great deal easier when the complex numbers are expressed in polar notation. We can see this by replacing the Cartesian components (the real and imaginary parts) with their polar representations.

$$z_1 = r_1 \cos \theta_1 + j r_1 \sin \theta_1 \tag{B.16}$$

and

$$z_2 = r_2 \cos \theta_2 + j r_2 \sin \theta_2 \tag{B.17}$$

The product of $z_1$ and $z_2$ is expressed in terms of the real and imaginary parts:

$$
\begin{aligned}
z_1 z_2 &= r_1 r_2 \left( \cos \theta_1 \cos \theta_2 - \sin \theta_1 \sin \theta_2 \right) \\
&\quad + j r_1 r_2 \left( \cos \theta_1 \sin \theta_2 + \cos \theta_2 \sin \theta_1 \right) \\
&= r_1 r_2 \left[ \cos(\theta_1 + \theta_2) + j \sin(\theta_1 + \theta_2) \right]
\end{aligned}
\tag{B.18}
$$

Equation (B.18) means that the magnitude of the product equals the product of the multiplicands' magnitudes, and the phase of the product equals the sum of the multiplicands' phases. This important result simplifies complex multiplication, particularly because complex variables are commonly expressed in polar coordinates.

Multiplication of a complex number by $j$ rotates the number's phase by $\pi/2$. For example, multiplying $j$ by itself rotates its phase from $\pi/2$ to $\pi$, resulting in the product $-1$.

## B.5  COMPLEX CONJUGATES

We form the complex conjugate, $z^*$, of a complex number $z = x + jy$ simply by negating the imaginary component.

$$z^* = x - jy \tag{B.19}$$

Similarly, we form the complex conjugate in polar representation by negating the phase:

$$z^* = r \angle - \theta \tag{B.20}$$

Because $\cos(-\theta) = \cos \theta$ and $\sin(-\theta) = -\sin \theta$, $z$ has the same magnitude as its conjugate.

$$|z| = |z^*| \tag{B.21}$$

Furthermore, the conjugate cancels itself. That is, the conjugate of the conjugate is the original number.

$$(z^*)^* = z \qquad\qquad (B.22)$$

The complex conjugate is a useful function. Adding the complex conjugate to a complex number cancels its imaginary component; similarly, subtracting the complex conjugate from a complex number cancels the real component.

$$z + z^* = 2x = 2r \cos\theta \qquad\qquad (B.23)$$

and

$$z - z^* = j2y = j2r \sin\theta \qquad\qquad (B.24)$$

Multiplying a complex number by its conjugate yields its squared magnitude. This is demonstrated in both Cartesian and polar coordinates.

$$
\begin{aligned}
zz^* &= (x + jy)(x - jy) \\
&= (x^2 + y^2) + j(xy - yx) \\
&= x^2 + y^2 \\
&= |z|^2
\end{aligned}
\qquad (B.26)
$$

and

$$
\begin{aligned}
zz^* &= (r\angle\theta)(r\angle - \theta) \\
&= r^2 \angle(\theta - \theta) = r^2 \angle 0 = r^2 \\
&= |z|^2
\end{aligned}
\qquad (B.27)
$$

**Examples:** Complex conjugates

$$
\begin{aligned}
(2 - j6)^* &= 2 + j6 \\
((2 - j6)^*)^* &= 2 - j6 \\
(2\angle\tfrac{\pi}{6})^* &= 2\angle - \tfrac{pi}{6}
\end{aligned}
\qquad (B.28)
$$

$$
\begin{aligned}
|2 - j6|^2 &= (2 - j6)(2 - j6)^* \\
&= (2 - j6)(2 + j6) \\
&= (4 + 36) \\
&= 40
\end{aligned}
\qquad (B.29)
$$

$$
\begin{aligned}
(2 - j6) - (2 - j6)^* &= (2 - j6) - (2 + j6) \\
&= -j12
\end{aligned}
\qquad (B.30)
$$

## B.6  INVERSE OF COMPLEX NUMBERS AND DIVISION

Much like the inverse of a real number, the inverse, $1/z$, of a complex number z satisfies the equation

$$z\frac{1}{z} = 1 \tag{B.31}$$

To satisfy equation (B.31), $|1/z|$ must equal $1/|z|$, and the phase of $1/z$ must oppose $z$'s phase. Thus, if $z$ has a magnitude of $r$ and an angle of $\theta$, $\frac{1}{z}$ must have a magnitude of $\frac{1}{r}$ and a phase of $-\theta$.

$$
\begin{aligned}
\frac{1}{z} &= \frac{1}{r}\angle - \theta \\
&= \frac{z^*}{|z|^2} \\
&= \frac{x - jy}{x^2 + y^2}
\end{aligned} \tag{B.32}
$$

Armed with this understanding, we can easily divide two complex numbers, because division is the same as multiplication by an inverse. Division is accomplished by computing the ratio the magnitudes and subtracting the angles.

$$\frac{z_1}{z_2} = \frac{r_1}{r_2}\angle(\theta_1 - \theta_2) \tag{B.33}$$

We can also perform division in Cartesian coordinates.

$$\frac{z_1}{z_2} = \frac{(x_1 + jy_1)(x_2 - jy_2)}{(x_2)^2 + (y_2)^2} \tag{B.34}$$

You should see that division is much easier in polar coordinates than in Cartesian coordinates.

## B.7  EXPONENTIAL FORM OF COMPLEX NUMBERS

Although polar notation clarifies multiplication and division, using two terms (with $\sin\theta$ and $\cos\theta$) to represent a complex number is cumbersome, and using the symbol "$\angle$" in mathematical operations is awkward. Fortunately, there is a simple, single-term representation for complex numbers, based on the complex exponential.

The complex exponential, $e^{j\theta}$, combines both real and imaginary components into a single term. The following Euler equation, derived by entering $z = j\theta$ into the series expansion for $e^z$, illustrates this combination.

$$e^{j\theta} = \cos\theta + j\sin\theta \tag{B.35}$$

The complex exponential, $e^{j\theta}$ lies on the unit circle at an angle of $\theta$ radians; similarly, $e^{-j\theta}$ lies on the unit circle at an angle of $-\theta$ radians ($\theta$ radians in the clockwise direction). Multiplying $e^{j\theta}$ by a real constant $r$ scales both real and imaginary components, resulting in a complex number with magnitude $r$ and phase $\theta$.

$$re^{j\theta} = r\left(\cos\theta + j\sin\theta\right)$$
$$= r\cos\theta + jr\sin\theta \tag{B.36}$$

This simple representation of a complex number; the complex exponential $re^{j\theta}$, can represent any complex number $z = x + jy$ by appropriately choosing $r$ and $\theta$.

$$r = |z| = \sqrt{x^2 + y^2} \tag{B.37}$$

and

$$\theta = arg(z) = \tan^{-1}\frac{y}{x} \tag{B.38}$$

**Example:** The complex exponential

$$e^{j\pi} = -1$$
$$e^{j\frac{\pi}{2}} = j$$
$$2e^{j\frac{\pi}{4}} = 2\left(\cos\frac{\pi}{4} + j\sin\frac{\pi}{4}\right) \tag{B.39}$$
$$= 1.4 + j1.4$$

Complex exponentials simplify many basic arithmetic operations. For instance, negating the phase conjugates a complex number:

$$\left(re^{j\theta}\right)^* = re^{-j\theta} \tag{B.40}$$

Inverting the magnitude and negating the phase creates a complex inverse:

$$\frac{1}{re^{j\theta}} = \frac{1}{r}e^{-j\theta} \tag{B.41}$$

Because exponents add under multiplication, we gain new insight into why the phase of a product equals the sum of the multiplicands' phases.

Exponential notation compacts complex multiplication, because the magnitude and phase are explicitly shown in the exponential notation of a complex number.

$$r_1e^{j\theta_1}r_2e^{j\theta_2} = r_1r_2e^{j(\theta_1+\theta_2)} \tag{B.42}$$

Similarly, division is no longer troublesome.

$$\frac{z_1}{z_2} = \frac{r_1}{r_2}e^{j(\theta_1-\theta_2)} \tag{B.43}$$

The complex exponential is a valuable tool and the designer who manipulates it well will keenly understand digital signal processing as well as other areas that make extensive use of complex variables.

## B.8  COMPLEX FUNCTIONS

We now turn our attention to complex functions. A complex function $f(z)$ takes a complex argument $z$ and delivers a complex result $f(z)$. Just as with complex numbers, a complex function can be written in Cartesian notation, for it generates a real component $x(z)$ and an imaginary component $y(z)$ for any value of $z$ applied to the function.

$$f(z) = \mathrm{Re}\{f(z)\} + j\,\mathrm{Im}\{f(z)\} \qquad (B.44)$$

Alternatively, $f(z)$ can be written in complex exponential notation, for it produces a magnitude $R(z)$ and a phase $\theta(z)$.

$$f(z) = R(z)e^{j\theta(z)} \qquad (B.45)$$

Multiplication by a complex constant $z_1 = r_1 e^{j\theta_1}$ is a simple function – $z \times z_1$ scales the magnitude of $z$ by $z_1$ and rotates its phase by $\theta_1$. Division involves a division of $|z|$ by $z_1$ and a back-rotation (rotation in a clockwise direction) of $z$'s phase by $\theta_1$. This is a simple example of a complex function, but many complex functions are collections of complex scaling and addition, and those are functions we now can handle.

**Example:**  Evaluate a complex function

$$f(z) = \frac{z^2 + 2z + 2}{z + 2} \qquad (B.46)$$

in both Cartesian and complex exponential notation.

With Cartesian components, $z = x + jy$ is directly plugged into the equation, which produces the following mess.

$$
\begin{aligned}
f(z) &= \frac{(x + jy)^2 + 2(x + jy) + 2}{2 + x + jy} \\
     &= \frac{x^2 + j2xy - y^2 + 2x + j2y + 2}{2 + x + jy} \\
     &= \frac{(x^2 - y^2 + 2x + 2) + j(2xy + 2y)}{2 + x + jy}
\end{aligned} \qquad (B.47)
$$

So now the complex function can be evaluated for any given $z$. For example, when $z = 1 + 2j$, $f(z)$ has the following value.

$$f(1 + 2j) = \frac{1 + j8}{3 + 2j}$$

$$= \frac{19 + j22}{13} \tag{B.48}$$

$$= \sqrt{5}\angle \tan^{-1} \frac{22}{19}$$

A *phasor* is a common function based on the complex exponential. It is usually a function of time and written $e^{j\omega t + \theta}$. The phasor has a magnitude of 1 and an angle of $\omega t + \theta$, so as $t$ increases, the phasor inscribes an arc on the unit circle at the rate $\omega t$ rad/sec, starting at the angle $\theta$. The term $\omega$ is called the *angular frequency*. Increasing $\omega$ increases the rate of rotation, and when $\omega = 0$ the phasor does not change with increasing $t$. Digital filtering, by using sampled signals, uses the sampled phasor, $e^{j\omega k}$. As $k$ increases, this phasor places points on the complex plane at angular intervals of $\omega$. Figure B.2 illustrates the motion of a digital phasor as $k$ increases. Notice that in this example, $\omega$ is negative, so the phasor traverses the unit circle clockwise.

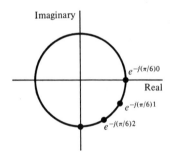

**Figure B.2** The digital phasor, $e^{j\frac{\pi}{10}k}$.

# Appendix C

# Introduction to Analog Filters

The only reason for considering analog filters in a digital filtering book is that we can simplify our digital designs if we start with good designs of analog filters. As analog filter design is about 50 years older than digital design, it should not be surprising that there are many more analog results. This section presents three analog filters with some "nice" properties. They are presented as low-pass filters, but can be transformed into high-pass, bandpass, or stopband filters if your application demands. These filters are called the Butterworth, Chebyshev, and elliptic filters. They were selected because they cover 90% of the analog filter designs, and because they trade off rippling and transition regions in an optimal way.

Before we look at the three filters, let us review some of the theory behind analog filters. This will give you the notation and a "flavor" of analog filters; however, the subject is so rich that a brief discussion cannot do it justice. If this is your first exposure to analog filtering, you will more than likely come away with an incomplete view of the subject.

An analog filter accepts an analog signal, say $x(t)$, and produces an analog output $y(t)$. Both signals are analog functions. That is, they are functions of a continuous variable, $t$, and they can take an infinite number of values. We will consider analog filters that produce $y(t)$ from the derivatives of $x(t)$ and $y(t)$. The input and output relationship of our analog filters is as follows:

$$y(t) = \sum_{i=0}^{N} a_i \frac{d^i x(t)}{dt^i} + \sum_{i=1}^{M} b_i \frac{d^i y(t)}{dt^i} \tag{C.1}$$

Notice that the filter's operation is completely dictated by the coefficients $a_i$ and $b_i$. These coefficients are analogous to the feedforward and feedback coefficients of a digital filter.

As shown in Chapter 6, the complex exponential, $e^{st}$, is an eigenfunction of an analog filter. When this signal is applied to an analog filter, the output becomes, $\mathcal{H}(s)e^{st}$. $\mathcal{H}(s)$ is the filter's eigenvalue, and it plays such an important role in analog filter theory that it has its own name, the filter transfer function. The transfer function of the filter in equation (C.1) is shown below. Like its digital cousin, the analog filter's transfer function is a ratio of polynomials — the numerator is controlled by the feedforward coefficients (in the analog case, the $a_i$s) and the denominator is the result of the feedback coefficients, $b_i$s.

$$\mathcal{H}(s) = \frac{\sum_{i=0}^{N} a_i s^i}{1 - \sum_{i=1}^{M} b_i s^i} \tag{C.2}$$

The analog filter's frequency response is the filter's eigenvalue when $e^{j\omega t}$ is applied to the filter. Notice that this signal is a special case of $e^{jst}$, so the frequency response is simply the filter's transfer function evaluated at $s = j\omega$.

$$\mathcal{H}(j\omega) = \mathcal{H}(s)|_{s=j\omega} \tag{C.3}$$

Therefore, an analog filter can be specified by its coefficients in the differential equation, its transfer function, or equivalently, the poles and zeros of its transfer function. Most analog filters are designed to meet a specification in the frequency response. Now that we have this modicum of information, let's look at the three analog filters.

## C.1   BUTTERWORTH FILTER

The Butterworth filter is so popular because its passband and stopband are without ripples. The Butterworth is called the *maximally flat filter* because of this lack of rippling. However, the Butterworth filter achieves its flatness at the expense of a relatively wide transition region. The Butterworth has the widest transition band of the three analog filters.

The Butterworth filter has only two design parameters: the order of the filter (the order of the denominator of the transfer function) and the filter's cutoff frequency, $\omega_c$. The order of the filter is also the number of poles for the filter and it determines the complexity of the filter. The Butterworth filter is defined by the following squared transfer function. The term $M$ is the order of the filter, and $\omega_c$ is the filter's cutoff frequency.

$$|\mathcal{H}_B(s)|^2 = \mathcal{H}_B(s)\mathcal{H}^*(s)$$

$$= \frac{1}{1 + (s/j\omega_c)^{2M}} \tag{C.4}$$

Equation (C.4) seems to imply that we are considering a Butterworth filter with $2M$ poles. This is not the case, because equation (C.4) is the square of the filter's transfer function, and squaring the transfer function doubles the poles. The actual Butterworth filter, $|\mathcal{H}_B(s)|$, has only $M$ poles.

The magnitude-squared of the Butterworth's frequency response is its squared transfer function [equation (C.4)] with $s$ replaced by $j\omega$.

$$|\mathcal{H}_B(j\omega)|^2 = \frac{1}{1 + \left(\frac{\omega}{\omega_c}\right)^{2M}} \tag{C.5}$$

The frequency responses of third- and eighth-order Butterworth filters are plotted in Figure C.1. Notice that the frequency response is ripple-free and the half point of the frequency response is at $\omega = \omega_c$. Higher-order filters generate flatter stopbands and passbands and shorter transition regions.

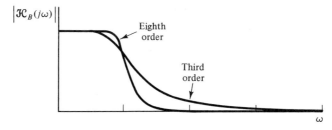

**Figure C.1** Frequency response of a third- and an eighth-order Butterworth filter.

The poles of the squared transfer function of the Butterworth filter are those values of $s$ that cause the denominator to go to zero. Therefore, the poles are found by setting the denominator of equation (C.4) to zero.

$$\left(\frac{s}{j\omega_c}\right)^{2M} = -1 \tag{C.6}$$

The poles are found by taking the $2M$th root of the equation and multiplying both sides by $j\omega_c$.

$$s = (-1)^{1/2M} j\omega_c \tag{C.7}$$

We complete the solution by expressing $-1$ and $j$ in terms of complex exponentials.

$$-1 = e^{j(2k+1)\pi} \qquad \text{where} \quad k = \text{integer} \tag{C.8}$$

and

$$j = e^{j\frac{\pi}{2}} \tag{C.9}$$

Therefore, the poles of the square of the Butterworth filter are as follows:

$$\begin{aligned} s &= e^{j\frac{(2k+1)\pi}{2M}} e^{j\frac{\pi}{2}} \omega_c \\ &= e^{j\frac{(2k+M+1)\pi}{2M}} \omega_c \end{aligned} \tag{C.10}$$

The poles of the square of the transfer function of a Butterworth filter have angles of $\frac{2k+M+1}{2M}\pi$ and magnitudes of $\omega_c$. They are equally distributed around a circle of radius $\omega_c$ and centered at the origin. Many designers remember the Butterworth filter by its pole locations rather than by the form of its transfer function or frequency response.

**Example:** Find the pole locations of the squared transfer function of a third-order Butterworth filter.

We know that the poles lie on a circle with radius $\omega_c$ (the cutoff frequency in rad/sec). Therefore, the poles are completely determined by finding their angles. We begin the computation by computing the zeroth pole location — setting $k = 0$ in equation (C.10).

$$\begin{aligned} p_0 &= e^{j\frac{(2 \cdot 0 + 3 + 1)\pi}{2 \cdot 3}} \omega_c \\ &= \omega_c \angle 120^o \end{aligned} \tag{C.11}$$

The zeroth pole ($k = 0$) is at an angle of $120^o$ from the real axis.

The next pole is computed by plugging $k = 1$ into equation (C.10). This produces a pole with a magnitude of $\omega_c$ and an angle of $180^o$ (this pole lies on the negative real axis).

The other four poles (remember that the squared transfer function of a third-order filter has six poles) can be found by substituting $k = 2$, $k = 3$, $k = 4$, and $k = 5$ into equation (C.10). A more insightful and efficient method would exploit the fact that the poles are equally spaced around the circle. We have a total of six poles consuming $360^o$ of circle, so the poles are separated by $360^o/6 = 60^o$. Therefore, the second pole is at $\omega_c \angle 180^o + 60^o$, the third pole has an angle of $300^o$, the fourth an angle of $360^o$ or $0^o$, and the last pole has an angle of $60^o$. The pole locations of the squared transfer function of the third-order Butterworth are shown in Figure C.2.

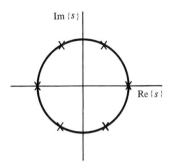

**Figure C.2** Pole locations of $\mathcal{H}^2(s)$ for a
third-order Butterworth filter.

Notice that our technique computes $2M$ poles for an $M$th order Butterworth filter, because we use the square of the filter's transfer function. To design the filter we must find the $M$ poles of the Butterworth filter's transfer function. Fortunately, this process is quite easy, because the poles that we want are in the left half of the $s$-plane. Those poles in the right half are the artifacts of squaring the transfer function. One might ask, why didn't we select the $M$ poles in the right half plane rather than the left half? If we had done that, we would get the Butterworth frequency response, but the filter would be unstable (remember that analog poles in the right half plane are unstable).

**Example:**   Find the poles of a third-order Butterworth filter.

This is a continuation of the preceding example. The prior work computed the six poles of the square of the transfer function, so the design is completed by selecting the three stable poles. A third-order, low-pass Butterworth filter has the following three poles.

$$\omega_c \angle 120^o \quad \omega_c \angle 180^o \quad \omega_c \angle 240^o$$

Therefore, the third-order Butterworth has the following transfer function and frequency response.

$$\mathcal{H}_B(s) = \frac{1}{(s - \omega_c \angle 120^o)\,(s - \omega_c \angle 180^o)\,(s - \omega_c \angle 240^o)}$$

$$\mathcal{H}_B(j\omega) = \frac{1}{(j\omega - \omega_c \angle 120^o)\,(j\omega - \omega_c \angle 180^o)\,(j\omega - \omega_c \angle 240^o)}$$

$$(\text{C.12})$$

The design of a low-pass Butterworth filter reduces to a three-step process. First, select the order, $M$, and the cutoff frequency, $\omega_c$, of the Butterworth filter. Second, plug those values into equation (C.10) to compute the $2M$ poles. You will save a great deal of computation if you compute only one of the poles from equation (C.10) and get the others by successively adding $360°/2M$ to the pole angle. The final step is to select the $M$ stable poles (those in the left half of the $s$-plane) and use those as the poles of your filter.

Remember that the Butterworth filter is appropriate for applications that cannot tolerate rippling in the stopband or passband. It provides a smooth frequency response at the expense of a wide transition region. If you are faced with an application that can tolerate rippling, consider the Chebyshev filter, because the Chebyshev filter has a much shorter transition band than a same-order Butterworth filter.

## C.2  CHEBYSHEV FILTER

The Chebyshev filter has a smaller transition region than the same-order Butterworth filter but it has ripples in either its stopband or passband. This filter gets its name because the Chebyshev filter minimizes the height of the maximum ripple — this is the Chebyshev criterion.

There are two flavors of the Chebyshev transfer function, which differ by whether they allow rippling in the passband or stopband. In this discussion we will consider the Chebyshev filter that has ripples in the passband and a smooth stopband. The square transfer function of the passband rippling Chebyshev filter is shown below. Notice that it is similar to the Butterworth transfer function, except that $s/\omega_c$ has been replaced with the Chebyshev polynomial.

$$|\mathcal{H}_C(s)|^2 = \frac{1}{1 + \epsilon^2 \left[ T_M \left( \frac{s}{j\omega_c} \right) \right] \left[ T_M \left( \frac{s}{j\omega_c} \right) \right]^*} \qquad (C.13)$$

This function $T_N(\ )$ is the $M$th order Chebyshev polynomial. Neither the derivation nor the meaning of this function is central to this development, so we can ignore its intricacies and simply use it as a tool. The first six Chebyshev polynomials are listed in Table C.1.

The parameter $\epsilon$ controls the height of the ripples. The maximum ripple has a peak-to-peak height of $\frac{\epsilon^2}{1+\epsilon^2}$, so small values of $\epsilon$ generate filters with small ripples. Be careful with this line of reasoning, because it suggests that the ripples can be reduced to zero by simply setting $\epsilon = 0$. This is indeed true, but at the expense of making our precious low-pass filter into an all-pass filter [envision equation (C.13) with $\epsilon = 0$].

The frequency response of the Chebyshev filter is computed by restricting $s$ to $j\omega$, which is equivalent to evaluating the transfer function along the $j\omega$ axis.

$$|\mathcal{H}_C(j\omega)|^2 = \frac{1}{1 + \epsilon^2 \left[ T_M \left( \frac{\omega}{\omega_c} \right) \right]^2} \qquad (C.14)$$

**Table C.1** Chebyshev Polynomials.

| Order | Polynomial |
|:---:|:---:|
| 0 | $1$ |
| 1 | $x$ |
| 2 | $2x^2 - 1$ |
| 3 | $4x^3 - 3x$ |
| 4 | $8x^4 - 8x^2 + 1$ |
| 5 | $16x^5 - 20x^3 + 5x$ |

The magnitude squared of the frequency responses of third- and fifth-order Chebyshev filters are shown in Figure C.3. Notice that the higher-order filter has more ripples and a shorter transition region. Also note that $\omega_c$ is no longer the half-power point. In the Chebyshev filter $\omega_c$ is the frequency where the response begins to decrease — at the start of the transition region.

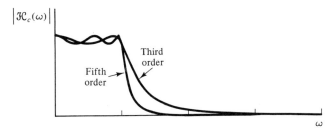

**Figure C.3** Frequency response of third- and fifth-order Chebyshev filters, $\epsilon = 0.5$

**Example:**    Compute the square frequency response of a third-order Chebyshev filter with a cutoff frequency of 1 rad/sec. Assume a maximum ripple height of 10%.

We begin this design by solving for $\epsilon^2$.

$$\frac{\epsilon^2}{1 + \epsilon^2} = 0.1 \tag{C.15}$$

Therefore,

$$\epsilon^2 = 0.11 \tag{C.16}$$

Next, we look into Table C.1 and find the third-order Chebyshev polynomial.

$$|\mathcal{H}_C(\omega)|^2 = \frac{1}{1 + 0.11 \left[ 4\left(\omega/1\right)^3 - 3\left(\omega/1\right) \right]^2} \tag{C.17}$$

The design is completed by plowing through the arithmetic to generate the following frequency response.

$$|\mathcal{H}_C(\omega)|^2 = \frac{1}{1 + 0.99\omega^2 - 2.64\omega^4 + 1.76\omega^6} \tag{C.18}$$

The squared transfer function is plotted in Figure C.4.

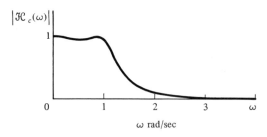

**Figure C.4** Frequency response of a third-order Chebyshev filter
with a cutoff frequency of 1 rad/sec.

It is beyond the scope of this work to press further into the Chebyshev filter. A good book on analog filter design will explain other forms of the Chebyshev filter as well as the design to move the ripples from the passband to the stopband. For our needs in digital filtering, we should be satisfied knowing that the Chebyshev filter exists and is represented as a ratio of polynomials. An $M$-order Chebyshev filter can be represented by the $M$ poles of the filter's transfer function.

## C.3  ELLIPTIC FILTERS

We noted that the Chebyshev filter had a shorter transition region than a Butterworth filter of the same order. The Chebyshev filter achieved this shorter transition region because it allows rippling in the passband or stopband. You may ask: Is it possible to get even shorter transition bands if we allow rippling in both the stopband and passband? The answer is yes, and the elliptic filter has a shorter transition region because it allows ripples in both bands.

The elliptic filter has the shortest transition region of any filter with the same order and ripple heights. Therefore, the elliptic filter is ideal for those applications where ripples can be tolerated and short transition regions are demanded.

The frequency response of an $M$-order elliptic filter looks a good deal like a Chebyshev filter. The difference between the Chebyshev and elliptic filter is that the elliptic uses an $M$-order Chebyshev rational function, $R_M(\ )$, rather than the plain old Chebyshev function, $T_M(\ )$. The magnitude squared transfer function of the elliptic filter is as follows:

$$|\mathcal{H}_E(s)|^2 = \frac{1}{1 + \epsilon^2 \left[R_M\left(\omega/\omega_c, L\right)\right]^2} \tag{C.19}$$

The parameters $\epsilon$ and $\omega_c$ have the same affects as in the Chebyshev filter — $\epsilon$ controls the passband rippling and $\omega_c$ controls the frequency breakpoint. The parameter $L$ controls the width of the transition region, the ripple height in the stopband, and interacts with $\omega_c$ to affect the breakpoint.

It is far beyond the scope of this introductory treatment of analog filters to delve into the intricacies of this function. Rather, we will base our understanding of the elliptical filters on a few observations of the Chebyshev rational function. The Chebyshev rational function oscillates between 0 and 1 for $|\omega| < \omega_c$. When $|\omega|$ is larger, the function oscillates between $L^2$ and $\infty$. Therefore, when applied to an elliptic filter as in equation (C.19), this function causes the passband ($|\omega| < \omega_c$) to oscillate between 1 and $1/(1 + \epsilon^2)$. The Chebyshev rational function causes the stopband of the elliptic filter ($|\omega| > \omega_c$) to oscillate between 0 (when the function becomes infinite) and $1/(1 + \epsilon^2 L^2)$. Most designs of elliptic filters result in large values of $L$, so as to make the stopband oscillate between 0 and approximately $1/\epsilon^2$. In this way, the elliptic filter has equal rippling in the stopband and passband.

The design of elliptic filters is much more involved than the Butterworth and Chebyshev filters. This is because the designer must select the order of the filter, the cutoff frequency, and the parameter $L$. The design is further complicated because $\omega_c$ and $L$ interact in determining the filter's breakpoint. For this reason, elliptic filters are designed via design tables, and that level of design sophistication is beyond the purpose of this treatment.

The elliptic filter is generally considered to be an advanced analog filter, so we are not going to go any deeper into its design. The purpose of this discussion is to present the elliptic filter as a generalization of the Chebyshev. The elliptic filter allows the designer to trade off the length of the transition and the rippling in both the stopband and passband. It is nice to know that such an analog filter exists, but very few digital filter designers are ever really faced with designing one of the beasts.

In summary, we have only skimmed the surface of analog filter design and have found that many "nice" filter features exist in the Butterworth, Chebyshev, and elliptic filters. These analog filters allow the designer to trade off rippling and transition widths to produce filters that are the best in their class. Seldom will a digital filter designer have to go beyond the three analog filters presented here.

The features of the three filters are summarized below:

Butterworth has no ripples but does have a wide transition region. The Butterworth filter is sometimes called the *maximally smooth filter.*

Chebyshev has ripples in either the stopband or the passband, but not both. The peak-to-peak height of the largest ripple is minimized by this design. The Chebyshev filter has a smaller transition band than a Butterworth filter with the same order.

Elliptic has equal ripples in the passband and stopband, and it has the narrowest transition region of any filter with the same order and ripple specification.

# Appendix D

# References

**General**

Antoniou, A., *Digital Filters: Analysis and Design.* New York: McGraw-Hill Book Company, 1976.

Hamming, R. W., *Digital Filters.* Englewood Cliffs, N.J.: Prentice-Hall, Inc., 1983.

Oppenheimer, A. V., and R. W. Schafer, *Digital Signal Processing.* Englewood Cliffs, N.J.: Prentice-Hall, Inc., 1975.

Peled, A., and B. Liu, *Digital Signal Processing: Theory, Design, and Implementation.* New York: John Wiley, 1976

Rabiner, L. R., and B. Gold, *Theory and Application of Digital Signal Processing.* Englewood Cliffs, N.J.: Prentice-Hall, Inc., 1975.

Sterns, S. D., *Digital Signal Processing.* Englewood Cliffs, N.J.: Prentice-Hall, Inc., 1975.

Taylor, F. J., *Digital Filter Design Handbook.* New York: Marcel Dekker, Inc., 1983.

**Complex Variables** — Chapter 2

Churchill, R. V., *Complex Variables and Applications.* New York: McGraw-Hill Book Company, 1960.

**Fourier Transform** — Chapter 3

Bracewell, R. N., *The Fourier Transform and Its Application.* New York: McGraw-Hill Book Company, 1978.

**Windows** — Chapter 4

Kaiser, J. F., "Design Methods for Sampled Data Filters," in *System Analysis by Digital Computer*, edited by F.F. Kuo and J.F. Kaiser. New York: John Wiley & Sons, Inc., 1966.

Kaiser, J. F., "Nonrecursive Digital Filter Design Using the $I_o$-sinh Window Function," *Proc. 1974 IEEE Int. Symp. on Circuits and Syst.*, San Francisco, April 1974, pp. 20-23.

**Nonrecursive Filter Design** — Chapters 3 and 4

McClellan, J. H. and T.W. Parks, "A Unified Approach to the Design of Optimum FIR Linear Filters with Linear Phase," *IEEE Trans. Circuit Theory*, Vol. CT-20, 1973, pp. 697-701.

McClellan, J. H., T.W. Parks, and L.R. Rabiner, "A Computer Program for Designing Optimum FIR Digital Filters," *IEEE Trans. Audio Electroacoust.*, Vol. AU-21, 1973, pp. 506-526.

*z*-**Transform** — Chapter 5

Jury, E. I., *Theory and Application of the z-Transform Method*, New York: John Wiley & Sons, Inc., 1964.

Ragazzini, J. R. and G. F. Franklin, *Sampled-Data Control Systems.* New York: McGraw-Hill Book Company, 1958.

**Analog Filters** – Chapter 6 and Appendix C

Van Valkenburg, M. E., *Introduction to Modern Network Synthesis*. New York: John Wiley & Sons, Inc., 1967.

Van Valkenburg, M. E., *Network Analysis*. Englewood Cliffs, N.J.: Prentice-Hall, Inc., 1974.

Van Valkenburg, M. E., *Analog Filter Design*. New York: Holt, Rinehart, and Winston, 1982.


**DFT and FFT** — Chapter 8

Agarwal, R. C., and J.W. Cooley, "New Algorithms for Digital Convolution," *IEEE Trans. Acoust. Speech Signal Process.*, Voll. ASSP-25, 1977, pp. 392-410.

Bergland, G. D.,"A Guided Tour of the Fast Fourier Transform," *IEEE Spectrum*, Vol. 6, July 1969, pp. 41-52.

Blackman, R. B., and J.W. Tukey, *The Measurement of Power Spectra*, New York: Dover Publications, Inc., 1958.

Brigham, E. O., *The Fast Fourier Transform*. Englewood Cliffs, N.J.: Prentice Hall, Inc., 1974.

Cooley, J. W., and J.W. Tukey, "An Algorithm for the Machine Computation of Complex Fourier Series," *Math. Comp.*, Vol. 19, April 1965, pp. 297-301.

Cooley, J. W., P. A. Lewis, and P. D. Welch, "Historical Notes on the Fast Fourier Transform," *IEEE Trans. Audio Electroacoust.*, Vol. AV-15, June 1967, pp. 76-79.

Elliott, D. F., and K. R. Rao, *Fast Transformations: Algorithms, Analysis, Applications*. New York: Academic Press, Inc., 1982.

Morris, R. L., "A Comparative Study of Time Efficient FFT and WFTA Programs for General Purpose Computers," *IEEE Trans. Acoust. Speech Signal Process.*, Vol. ASSP-26, 1978, pp. 141-150.

Rader, C., "Discrete Fourier Transforms When the Number of Data Samples Is Prime," *Proc. IEEE*, Vol. 56, 1968, pp. 1107-1108.

Singleton, R. C., "An Algorithm for Computing the Mixed Radix Fast Fourier Transform," *IEEE Trans. Audio Electroacoust.*, Vol. AV-17, June 1969, pp. 93-103.

## Other Applications of Digital Processing

Franklin, G. F., and J. D. Powell, *Digital Control of Dynamic Systems.* Reading, Mass: Addison-Wesley Publishing Company, Inc., 1981.

Phillips, C. L., and H. T. Nagle, Jr., *Digital Control Systems Analysis and Design.* Englewood Cliffs, N.J.: Prentice Hall, Inc., 1984.

Rabiner, L. R., and R.W. Schafer, *Digital Processing of Speech.* Englewood Cliffs, N.J.: Prentice-Hall, Inc., 1978.

# Index